MASS COMMUNICATION IN CANADA

SECOND EDITION

Rowland Lorimer & Jean McNulty

M&S

Canadian Cataloguing in Publication Data
Lorimer, Rowland, 1944-
    Mass communication in Canada
    2nd ed.

Includes bibliographical references and index.
ISBN 0-7710-5349-5

1. Mass Media – Canada.   I. McNulty, Jean, 1942–
II. Title.

P92.03L67 1991   302.23′0971   C90-095841-3

DESIGN: Brant Cowie/ArtPlus Limited
PAGE MAKE UP: Valerie Phillips/ArtPlus Limited
Printed and bound in Canada by John Deyell Company

McClelland & Stewart Inc.
The Canadian Publishers
481 University Avenue
Toronto, Ontario
M5G 2E9

Contents

4

CHAPTER 10:
The Global Geopolitics of Information   277

CHAPTER 11:
The Domestic Geopolitics of Information   299

Preface

NOT ALL second editions are created equal. Some are attempts to control second-hand sales. Others lack author commitment. On the first count we are lucky. It would appear that the vast majority of students who have used our first edition are hanging on to their copies. So second-hand sales have not been a pressing issue. As for author commitment, we declare our willingness, even our enthusiasm.

The adoption of our first edition in nearly every Canadian province and at least one territory has blessed us with a responsibility – to ensure that Canadian students who use our book have current examples to which they may refer in their learning about mass communication. We have done our best to fulfil that responsibility. To that end, we have sought to address any ambiguities and infelicities in the first edition and have updated examples to provide easy references for students to contemporary phenomena. As well, we have added new analysis and reorganized other sections for the purposes of clarification.

The following are the specific major changes in this second edition. First, we have moved a major section of Chapter 1 on Canadian communications into Chapter 2 and elsewise reorganized Chapter 2. In Chapter 3, sections have been shifted to clarify the interaction of mass media, politics, and government. Besides updating, in Chapter 4 we have provided short summaries of analytical frameworks additional to semiotics and content analysis and have replaced the former example of semiotic analysis with one using materials from a Black Label ad campaign. Chapter 5 contains updating and general improvements.

Chapters 6, 7, 8, and 11 have been reordered. The section begins with policy (now Chapter 6, previously Chapter 8) as the overarching framework within which ownership (now Chapter 7, previously Chapter 6), journalism (now Chapter 8, previously Chapter 7), and technology (now Chapter 9, previously Chapter 11) are considered. Chapter 6 has been updated significantly to reflect policy changes. Chapters 7 and 8 have undergone general updating and improvements. Chapter 9 has been recast in more current and thorough theoretical terms: what remained relevant from the previous chapter on technology has been toned down and makes up about half the chapter; the other half is devoted to the implications of new technological/industrial developments.

Chapters 10 and 11 (the old 9 and 10), on domestic and global geopolitics, are the least changed of all. They contain only updating and minor changes. Chapter 12, on the other hand, has been recast significantly. It is a much more ambitious effort than in the first edition, encompassing the ideas of the first edition's Chapter 12 but within a larger framework. Essentially, this concluding chapter reviews the preceding chapters and takes advantage of the students' knowledge of those chapters to extend the discussion.

As we noted in the last edition, through Simon Fraser University and the Knowledge Network we have produced a set of half-hour videos that complement the content of the various chapters. We have expanded that series with one new video, a portrait of Harbour Publishing, called *Books and Water.* Harbour Publishing is a book publishing company that has developed a list of cultural titles aided by federal and provincial cultural policy. We now have funds in place to produce a seventh program, titled *Information, Technology, and Democracy.* Thus the programs now complement Chapters 1, 4, 5, 6, 7, 9, and 12. When teaching, we tend to use a CBC video, *Telling Your Story,* for Chapter 2; the NFB's *The Press and the Prime Minister* for Chapter 3; the CBC's *Inside TV News* for Chapter 8; and the NFB's *Magic in the Sky* for Chapters 10 and 11.

As with the first edition, a variety of people have contributed immensely to this publication. Ian Chunn helped to integrate current examples into the material and gave a thorough reading and assessment to both old and new material. Nancy Duxbury and Eric Spalding also assisted with the development of the manuscript while Jo-Anne Ray acted as general co-ordinator, Freda Colbourne provided necessary assistance on the Black Label ads, and Margaret Gibbs created a thorough index. Our reviewers, through Michael Harrison of McClelland & Stewart, provided useful assessments that helped our rewriting. Our editor, Richard Tallman, refined both our writing and our conceptions. To each we express heartfelt gratitude.

Rowland Lorimer
Coquitlam, B.C.

Jean McNulty
Toronto, Ont.

CHAPTER

1

Communication and Society

INTRODUCTION

TWO RENOWNED Canadian scholars, Marshall McLuhan, professor of literature, and Harold Innis, professor of economics, have contributed to the world's understanding of communication. Specifically, they advanced the notion that the rules and patterns of communication in society are a major determining factor of our social, economic, political, and cultural fabric. A consideration of the role of communication on several recent events illustrates the claim of McLuhan and Innis.

The opening of China in the 1980s to visitors, trade, and technology, for example, has been transforming that country. Previously highly centralized and controlled, China's new openness has encouraged contacts between the Chinese and Western people, their culture, economic thought, business, and institutions. Part of this Western business orientation requires the development of modern electronic communication linkages – telephone, facsimile, satellites, and so on. This openness has led to an exposure of the Chinese to the values and orientation of

Western people and their societies. Contacts with the Western world, together with the desire of the Chinese to change their way of life, caused revolutionary fomentation that burst into Western view in June, 1989.

In the presence of the Western media, students and others in Beijing mounted a stirring demonstration of dissent, occupying Tiananmen Square – a vast concrete commons at the entrance to the old Imperial Palace, now called the Forbidden City – until army troops dispersed the crowd, killing many. The most dramatic television footage surrounding the event and the days that followed showed a lone man in Tiananmen Square standing in front of the column of tanks refusing to let them advance without running him over. As they attempted to manoeuvre around him, his few steps sideways again blocked their path. The symbolism of the image was multi-layered: the courage of a single person; the enormous power of the state over that of the individual; the inability of that massive power to manoeuvre; the ability of a single person to disrupt the exercise of state power; and the contradiction of a "people's army" suppressing the will of the people – would they in the end act no differently than others? – all were visible in that momentary confrontation.

Western access to the events and images of the uprising were soon curtailed. Reporters were forced to leave the country and the government reinforced its control over broadcasting and the press. However, using the very technologies that had been put in place to modernize the nation and open it for trade, the Chinese people maintained a flow of unofficial information to the Western world about the events and their aftermath that could not be stopped by the Chinese government. The enabling technology? Telephone and data lines carrying voice, electronic mail, and facsimile messages (faxes).

Canada: In the spring of 1990 a group of Mohawks blocked a road going through the Kanesatake reserve leading to the town of Oka in protest over the proposed extension of a golf course onto land they claim as theirs. On July 11, the Quebec provincial police, the Sureté du Québec, mounted an assault on the Kanesatake barricade on the request of the mayor of Oka. In the mêlée a police corporal was killed. The same day a second group of Mohawks blocked one end of the Mercier bridge, a major bridge leading out of Montreal and through the Kahnawake reserve to the Montreal suburb of Châteauguay.

The Quebec and federal governments attempted to open negotiations to remove the barricades. In mid-August as negotiations remained stalled, they were declared ended by both the federal and provincial governments. The province called in the army. The army made a show of strength in equipment and mobilization, including low-level helicopter flights bathing the Mohawk encampment in light at night and making regular phone calls to demand surrender. At the same time the military showed obvious restraint in not mounting an all-out assault. Their actions were typical of a peacekeeping force dealing with civilians, and they were also careful to keep the media posted on what they were doing and why.

The media waded in – daily. Anxious to exploit all angles, the media produced plenty of pictures of and stories about the army, the barricades, and masked and unmasked Mohawks. They obtained stories from elected Mohawk officials, traditional leaders, the unelected Mohawk Warrior Society, the provincial government, various federal ministers, the Sureté, the army, non-native people whose lives were disrupted, and each other. On one occasion, "dramatic" television footage was obtained of non-natives hurling insults and rocks at passing

One man – the People's Army. *AP wire photo by Jeff Widener.*

carloads of Mohawk families trying to leave the Kahnawake reserve.

Media reports emerged about the poor relations between the Sureté and the Mohawks. The Sureté responded by accusing the English media of mounting a campaign against them. The media dug into Indian grievances across the country and over the years as actions of native solidarity spread across the country. In a post-colonial world that rises to defend racial minorities and small nations, both the federal and provincial governments determinedly rejected the notion that native people have any rights other than those of any citizen of Canada. This was in spite of (a) a ruling of the Supreme Court accepting the notion of special rights in the form of native land claims, and (b) ongoing negotiations of land claims by both the federal and Quebec governments after generations of stalling. This denial of special rights for natives contrasted strikingly with the stance of the Prime Minister on the special place of Quebec in the constitution, taken with much posturing earlier in the summer.

As the removal of the barricades at Kahn-awake was negotiated in early September, tension increased at Kanesatake. In face of considerable army fire power, a masked Mohawk in full cam-ouflage clothing but apparently without a gun strode directly up within a foot of a young sol-dier, stared him in the eye, and said to the soldier and the surrounding media: "I want to look him in the eye before I kill him." A photograph, used nation-wide in newspapers that evening, showed the young soldier with set jaw and no visible emotion looking back at the taller Indian.

A mediated confrontation. *Canapress Photo Service.*

Defeat (?) at Oka. *Canapress Photo Service.*

With the attention of the media refocused on the Kanesatake reserve the army eventually moved to tear down the barricades again at a measured pace. A group of Mohawks retreated to a drug and alcohol treatment centre, inviting certain journalists who had been favourable to their side of the story to join them. Slowly the siege was strengthened with mounting threats and restrictions on supplies and communications, which eventually included blocking the transmissions of journalists on their cellular phones.

Finally, September 26, the Mohawks surrendered. But instead of emerging in single file and walking toward the army, as agreed, they staged a marvelously disordered scene and headed for the cameras. The army, with fixed bayonets, attempted to regain control. The media responded almost universally with coverage of a woman on the ground with her mouth wide open (yelling?), holding a small child "after being stopped" by soldiers. Meanwhile, one of the main negotiators on the Mohawk side walked down the road and disappeared. Not a single life was lost.

First Level of Analysis: The Role of the Media. Without the presence of the media we would know little or nothing of these events. The confrontation between the masked Mohawk and the young soldier likely would never have happened – it was a performance for the cameras. The events would have unfolded differently.

Second Level of Analysis: The Role of Communication. In the Chinese example, McLuhan and Innis would have claimed that the impact of information flows brought about by the recently introduced modern communication technologies associated with the new economic thrust had already been established in the social, economic, and cultural fabric of Chinese society. June, 1989, brought into confrontation the political values inherent in modern economies and communications with the reluctance of the government of the day to recognize the political values inherent in the very system they had fostered.

In the Canadian example McLuhan might have claimed that the Mohawks were representing our espoused values to us in our own backyard. The summer of 1990 not only revisited centuries-old miscommunications between an oral and a literate society, but also reenacted the power relations of natives and non-natives.

Overview. The aftermath of the Chinese confrontation was itself a surprising demonstration of the uncontrollable and unpredictable influence of modern communications technologies. Increased power did not accrue simply to the state, even though, at the time, the state was in firm control of broadcasting and the press in China. Both sides were able to use modern communications for their own ends. On the one hand, the state put radio, television, and the press to work for it. To the consternation of the Western news media they captured Western-produced images of key players and used them to launch a hunt for these "counter-revolutionaries." On the other hand, the Chinese people used the telecommunications infrastructure to send an unceasing, albeit clandestine, barrage of phone calls, electronic mail, and fax messages to the outside world.

The aftermath of the Canadian confrontation revealed the roles not just of the government, the general population, and the native groups. It also revealed, in a number of different ways, a direct and influential role of the media. To take one of the strongest examples, sympathetic reporters joining the Kanesatake Mohawks in the drug treatment centre changed the dynamic of the struggle by acting as self-imposed hostages – perhaps all to the good. But good or bad is not the point. The point is that they intervened as actors and in so doing stretched the boundaries of their legitimate role as journalists. Thereby, they joined the other actors, i.e., the federal government, the Quebec government, the non-native residents of Oka and Châteauguay, the army, the Mohawks, and the Warrior Society as subjects of media coverage.

The above two examples are political. But they are also examples of the role communication plays in human affairs. First, the **news media** plainly influenced the outcome of events. Second, as McLuhan and Innis would have claimed, the nature of the ideas and the **patterns of communication** observed are part and parcel of modern economies and their associated technologies of communication.

CHAPTER OVERVIEW

The task of this chapter is to elaborate on the role of communication in society. We will do this by exploring two axes of communication. One we will refer to as the *range*, the other as the *domain* of communication. Included in the range are:

- the social dimension
- the political dimension
- the economic dimension
- the educational dimension
- the cultural dimension
- the technological dimension
- the familial dimension
- the individual dimension.

Our discussion of the domain of communication is focused on the means by which communication can have the structuring influence on society that McLuhan and Innis claim for it. We examine the logic and processes of oral, literate, and electronic communication and the associated social interaction they tend to produce.

These foundations provide a basis for a discussion of the slightly narrower focus of this book – mass communication, the mass media, and the manner in which these activities interact with society.

THE RANGE OF COMMUNICATION

Like politics, communication permeates virtually every aspect of our lives. A report commissioned by UNESCO, the United Nations Educational, Scientific and Cultural Organization, often called the MacBride Report after the commission chairman, discusses how communication impinges on our lives in six spheres of activity (UNESCO, 1980).

The Social Dimension

(1) Communication fills a **social need**. It provides an information base around which society can coalesce. How could Canadians see themselves as part of a single nation without a national communications system? While it could be argued

that Sir John A. Macdonald had the CPR built primarily for the flow of goods, with the flow of goods came the flow of information – the mail, of course, but also the bits of information, built into every product, about the society in which the goods were produced. Knowing that they were ordering from Eaton's in Toronto gave Prairie catalogue users a very real connection to Toronto society. Ordering a pump organ from Berlin or Clinton, Ontario, or a wood stove from Elmira, Ontario, or Sackville, New Brunswick, gave westerners an economic link with these places and, in addition, a knowledge of life and a social connection to the styles of manufacturing in the East. This they would superimpose on letters from relatives living in other parts of the country and newspapers and books that told of life in those parts.

The Political Dimension

(2) Communication is a **political instrument**. Probably the most famous English-Canadian example of how communication was used as a political instrument is William Lyon Mackenzie's *Colonial Advocate*. Mackenzie used his newspaper to politicize Upper Canadians and eventually lead them into rebellion. Pierre Bédard used *Le Canadien* in much the same way. As the leader of the Parti Canadien (later the Parti Patriote) Bédard used *Le Canadien* as a nationalist party organ opposing the "Chateau Clique." He was arrested in 1810.

But communication is not connected to politics only in attempts at reform. Governments also use the press to advance their own interests. Nearly every day the federal government announces one or another initiative for the benefit of one or another group and, of course, claims the credit for making any positive change. In making such announcements, the government hands over to journalists, mainly

A government ad: selling the GST to the business community.

the parliamentary press gallery, the task of explaining and commenting on their programs.

When they become dissatisfied with that process governments attempt to go around journalistic commentary by creating media events, orchestrating the release of information, or releasing information to outlets that reproduce it rather than rewrite it or present it within a critical context (e.g., television press conferences, end-of-year interviews, or community newspapers). If that fails they can always fall back on advertising, a means of communication all Canadian federal and provincial governments use extensively.

Another side to communication as a political instrument is usually referred to as **freedom of information**. Governments collect vast amounts of information, by surveys, census-taking, satellites, clandestine activities, and mandatory reporting mechanisms such as income-tax reporting. Concern about freedom of information usually arises over what information the government has about any one individual and whether, by virtue of that information, his or

Another government ad, this one from British Columbia. Note the lack of news value, hence the need to advertise the programs of government.

her interests might be damaged by inaccuracies or the access of others to that information. This issue involves also the principle of the right to privacy. How much right does the state have to collect information about individuals? Certainly there has been abuse. The RCMP has had access to tax records of individuals as well as to health records. However, a more general question beyond the political realm is involved as well.

There is considerable value in all the information the government collects, whether on business, politics, the weather, or birth patterns. The government, in keeping information to itself, protects itself against political scandal or accusations of ineptitude; yet, in doing so, it also jeopardizes the ability of its citizens to use this information to advantage, whether that advantage is accumulation of wealth, political reform, or cultural development.

In summary, communication can be a political instrument working in the interests of reform or in the interests of suppression of individuals and information. It can work for the state and the individual at the same time or it can work for one to the detriment of the other.

The Economic Dimension

(3) Communication is an **economic force**. As described above, the information a government collects has potential economic benefit for groups and individuals. The collection of information about markets or weather conditions, for example, can be used to advantage by agricultural producers. Similarly, information that allows the prediction of population trends, migration patterns, or birth rates is important in planning product development and marketing as well as social services.

The economic force of communication does not derive just from information the government collects. Because of the enhanced availability of information, nations and companies producing for export can have knowledge of market trends as sophisticated as that of domestic producers. Exporters are no longer confined to basic products whose characteristics change very slowly and for which there is a steady predictable demand. They can now participate in markets where yearly fashions determine which products will sell for a premium price and which will be down-market items. Shoes and ski clothing are examples of such participation by foreign producers in volatile Canadian markets. In fact, as demonstrated by the electronics industry, such foreign producers as Sony can lead the industry in the introduction of new products and new styles of products. The near collapse of North American car production in the 1970s and 1980s is another example not only of how a foreign producer (Japan) can participate in a market determined by style or even set the style but also how such a producer can use information to better advantage than can the local, traditional

producer. The Japanese seized the small-car industry of North America by sound market analysis and good-quality products. In the same way a number of entrepreneurs from Britain's former colonies such as Canadians Roy Thomson and, more recently, Conrad Black, as well as Australian Rupert Murdoch, have seized control of British money-losing newspapers and turned them into cash cows. Knowing the size and stability of the market and knowing the necessary costs of production, they have been able to purchase the papers and turn red ink to black mainly by firing sometimes more than half the labour force. Automation helped, but more important was knowledge of market and production costs and a willingness to confront featherbedding unions. From a communications perspective the information a foreign producer can have matches what any local producer has, as long as the producer can pay for the information.

The economic force of communications depends not only on the availability of information but also on the ability to analyse it, which is so important that a section of the MacBride Report recommends that each nation achieve an informatics capability to take available information and analyse it from its own national or industrial perspective. The point is that to rely on the information and analysis generated by others for their own purposes will necessarily subordinate the independent efforts of any nation to the priorities of other more analytic, powerful nations.

The Educational Dimension

(4) Communication has an **educational potential**. New communications technologies or facilities are customarily announced in the context of the humanitarian benefits they can provide. These benefits are of two types, medical and educational. In countries such as

Canada new developments in communications are described in terms of enhanced opportunities for people in outlying regions. For example, satellites currently facilitate both medical diagnosis and the delivery of university-level courses. In countries with high rates of illiteracy the educational potential of communications is even more powerful. To a degree this potential circumvents the need for high levels of literacy by extensive broadcast coverage. However, to assume that such a circumvention is possible emphasizes the circulation or spread of information and ignores the very significant analytical capabilities that develop alongside the acquisition of literacy skills. Still, the power of electronic communication to inform should not be underrated, especially when the communications system is designed with education in mind rather than entertainment or political suppression.

A further interesting aspect of the educational potential of communication is that the professions – engineering, medicine, law – are really groups of individuals who have access to a body of information not readily accessible to others and permission to use that information in certain crucial settings, e.g., hospitals or the courts. The power of computers to store the information required by a profession and retrieve it in a selective and flexible manner could open that knowledge to a much larger group of individuals (see Lorimer and Webber, 1987).

Telemedicine is an example of how doctors themselves are spreading their expertise within the profession, while other projects are developing diagnostic services through the use of the computer. Given the vigour of free enterprise there is no reason to believe that medical diagnostic packages will not be developed and sold to interested buyers. The possibility for enhancement of medicine in the Third World is considerable. Yet, with these packages will come the medical, institutional, and economic assumptions of developed-nation medicine. Who benefits when a Bolivian peasant learns that she needs an expensive operation and six months' convalescence in a high-tech, intensive care unit?

The Cultural Dimension

(5) Communication is both **an impulse and a threat to culture**. The preceding example of the Bolivian peasant is appropriate to the cultural implications of communication. Imagine the state of mind of the Bolivian woman as she is given the diagnosis just mentioned. In the first instance she might marvel at the advantages of living in a developed country both for its medicine and for its ability to develop computerized diagnostics and even telemedicine. In turning to her own situation she might easily, as a result of telemedicine or computer diagnostics, become despondent and resentful.

As the MacBride Report phrases it, communications has the ability to distribute information or items of quality widely. Thereby, it can be an impulse to culture. At the same time it has the potential to threaten or eclipse local culture. Medical information is not usually thought of as a "cultural" item. But just as entertainment and educational programs can provide the basis for invidious comparisons of the quality of life, so medical information can do the same. In the case of cultural materials such as those used in entertainment and education, a person can easily see how a cultural impulse could be generated by the spread of items of artistic merit. The myth and the reality of rural children in Canada striving from early childhood to become as accomplished as someone heard or seen on radio or television, whether an entertainer or any other person, are powerful. So, too, is the general rejection of local culture. Movie critic and cultural commentator Martin Knelman reports that movies were something he, as a child growing up in Winnipeg, saw as an escape from a backwater, not as any kind of inspiration to make movies in and about Winnipeg (Knelman, 1977).

The Technological Dimension

(6) Communication also represents a **technological dilemma**. Many people imagine that technological advance is rapid and independent of society. The usual kind of statement made about technology and society is that the latter has a difficult time keeping up with the former. However, as we point out in later chapters, technological advance does not occur as a happy side effect of the pursuance of scientific knowledge. The nuclear bomb was not developed as an "unhappy" side effect of the pursuance of research about Einstein's theory of relativity. In the case of the bomb a team of scientists was set to work with the sole purpose of developing a nuclear device. Similarly, communications technology, from radios to videotex to satellites, is not a spin-off of the pursuit of science; rather, these developments are intentionally pursued because they are technologically feasible and because some person believes there is a market for or a value in such devices.

A good example of a technological dilemma in Canadian communications is pay television. For a number of years before CRTC (Canadian Radio-television and Telecommunications Commission, Canada's communications regulatory agency) approval, pay television was technologically feasible. The CRTC finally gave its approval when two conditions emerged. One was the development of alternative technologies, specifically videocassette recorders (VCRs) and direct broadcast satellites. VCRs meant that the distribution of programming, specifically the movie portion of programming, fell into the hands of unregulated video rental and sales shops. Satellites made it possible for anyone with a satellite receiving dish to have access to every sort of foreign program. Such a situation represented a direct challenge to the possibility of government control over the structure of the communication services available through other means. The second condition to emerge was that those who wished to have pay television licences were willing, as a condition of their licence, to invest a certain proportion of their profits in the development of Canadian programming.

While pay television represented a cultural threat, because of the inevitability of its distributing more foreign programming to Canadians, satellite dishes and video outlets represented a greater threat. The former provided some possibility for the development of Canadian expression, the latter none. Ironically, pay television has been so limited in its penetration of the market, partly because of the success of satellites and VCRs, that it is doubtful whether this will ever have any beneficial effect on Canadian program production. However, as long as pay television does not collapse, the Canadian government will have maintained its ability to affect the structure of what most Canadians watch on television. It can regulate the cable companies that distribute pay TV and other satellite services.

The MacBride Report does not discuss two other spheres of activity, perhaps because the commissioners believed these to be sub-categories of the six already reviewed. We will treat them separately.

The Familial or Primary Social Group Dimension

(7) Communication influences **family or primary social group dynamics**. The penetration of

communications into the family living room in developed countries and into the communities and villages of lesser developed countries changes the dynamics of the group. Children are exposed to a much wider range of information than were their parents at a comparable age. Children are also exposed to potential role models who may behave in ways quite contradictory to what the parents or community sees as desirable. Third, programs designed explicitly for children can contrast with the ability of the family or immediate community to respond to the child's desires. Just as societies must cope with communications, so must small social groups and families. The difference in the amount and the perspective of the information children and their elders have contributes to a lack of understanding between generations.

The Individual Dimension

(8) Communication constrains the development of **individual identity**. The notion that each person is psychologically distinct and should strive to use his or her special passions and talents was concurrent with the development of literacy. Written and now electronic communication open a pantheon of characters beyond our personal experience who can serve as role models. It might even be hypothesized that the diversity of role models has postponed adolescence, so much so that some people feel they have only achieved adulthood at age forty. Whatever communication has to do with developing maturity, we cannot help but see ourselves within a world introduced to us in direct social interaction, through written materials, and by electronic means. The individual as much as the culture is a product of this information environment, both its content and its process.

THE DOMAIN OF COMMUNICATION: SOCIETIES AND COMMUNICATION THROUGH THE AGES

Because communication penetrates so much of our lives it is not difficult to imagine how some theorists might see cultures as having their foundations in communicational processes.

The theorists who postulate a fundamental role for communication are two Canadians, Harold Innis (1950) and Marshall McLuhan (1962). They, in conjunction with others, some of whom worked out of Toronto, have developed a conception of communication that distinguishes among oral, literate, and electronic societies. Collectively they are known as the **Toronto School**.

In what would be regarded as a fairly radical analysis, one of McLuhan's followers and translators, Derrick de Kerckhove, wrote in *The Globe and Mail* of a three-part division in today's world based not on the domination of Russia, China, and the U.S. but on the domination of computers, the book, and the radio: North America, Europe, and Japan are part of Computerland; China, the Soviet Union, and Africa are in the Bookworld; and Radio City is composed of South America, the Middle East, and India. As de Kerckhove claims:

> The phonetic alphabet created the Greek and Roman Empires and print led to the French Revolution and the violence of the Napoleonic Wars. But the telegraph turned the British Empire into the Commonwealth, changing the image of controlling to that of sharing.
>
> Radio, on the other hand, wreaked havoc among literate identities, reaching back to the tribal hordes of Germany and breaking all the national boundaries. Radio has killed more

people in a shorter time than any other means of communication medium ever invented by man. In its encounter with established patterns of literacy, it has proved to be the most violent and aggressive medium of all. Today, the voice of the Ayatollah (Khomeini) is sending 14-year-olds to death, the voices of Ian Paisley and others are sending terrorists into Irish streets, the voices of South American strongmen are blowing up shanties. Television and computers, however, are off-setting the potential violence of radio . . . television pacifies our digestive system and our bowel movements, while computers exteriorize our nervous systems. Computers turn the most deadly weapons into toys, whereas books could turn mental play such as e=mc^2 into deadly weapons.

De Kerckhove follows this analysis with an interesting speculation.

> . . . the nuclear bomb is both the crowning glory of the Industrial Age and the foundation stone of the Information Age. . . . The bomb, which is pure and total destruction, has already become pure and total information. It is the most powerful communication medium invented yet. . . . Respecting the bomb is probably the first step toward a responsible political attitude.

De Kerckhove's statement illustrates the central dilemma in understanding the Toronto School. Claiming that the nuclear bomb is the foundation of a new age rather than Armageddon seems to so underplay its potential destructiveness that such a claim almost appears to be a cruel joke. Two points about the value and validity of this perspective will lead us into what Innis and McLuhan themselves have to say about oral, literate, and electronic cultures.

If literate-industrial traditions and values are strong enough then there will be a rejection of the informational nature of the bomb. Not to mince words, someone or some country will decide a nuclear war is winnable. If, on the other hand, we move toward accepting an informational perspective, a perspective made possible by advances in electronic information-processing technology, then we will develop "responsible political attitudes" that will always prevent nuclear war. Who wants to test the validity of the information we have about the inevitability of total annihilation by starting a nuclear war? Presuming the acceptance of informational values, we may find ourselves a few years down the road understanding more completely what de Kerckhove meant. Indeed, it may even turn out that the statement was only part of the truth. To anticipate the future a bit and to explain a little as well, McLuhan once claimed that the electric light bulb was pure information. Its function was to expose things to our eyes. What makes the bomb a totality of information is that it contains the power to allow our continued existence or to end it.

Contemplation of de Kerckhove's statement can lead to an interesting shift in the meaning of the word "information." Such a shift is to be expected. It is paralleled, for example, by the shift in meaning that must have occurred in the concept of "matter" as science shifted its theoretical underpinnings from Newtonian to Einsteinian physics.

Oral Society

Harold Innis claimed that the means of communication set basic parameters to the functioning of society. More specifically, he analysed how oral and literate societies functioned completely differently because of their predominant means of communication. For example, we as a literate people are governed by what is written in law and by the principles and statements of our constitution. In oral societies people were governed by the knowledge vested in the community and specifically preserved by certain speakers. These speakers or minstrels developed and maintained their knowledge by means of epic poems and what Innis called epic technique. Epic technique involved creating poems in hexameters with certain rigidities and elasticities. The rigidities allowed for memorization, while the elasticities permitted adaptation to local or vernacular speech. Forms, words, stock expressions, and phrases acted as aids while the local language and situation provided the basis for ornamental gloss. The development of such techniques meant epic poetry was in the hands of persons with excellent memories and poetic and linguistic abilities. Because such abilities are not innate, the epic techniques were often passed on within families of professional storytellers and minstrels. According to Innis, such families probably built up a system of memory aids that were privately owned and carefully guarded.

In ancient Greece mastery of words or recitation came to mean intellectual sovereignty. The epics permitted constant adaptation, as required by the oral tradition, and also allowed for the emergence of completely new content to describe conditions of social change. What was socially relevant was remembered, what was not was forgotten. Changing perspectives permitted the incorporation of sacred myths from earlier civilizations. These myths could be transformed and humanized as they were turned into content of the epic poem. The Greeks could thereby foster the development of an inclusive ideology as they expanded their empire, and this ideology could serve colonizing efforts extremely well.

The dynamics of the oral tradition in a more modern context (rural Yugoslavia from 1937 to 1959) are described by Lord (1964) in his *The Singer of Tales*. One of his many telling observations is that, for the oral bard, the recording of the words of a song is a totally foreign experience. Nor, when the recording is finally accomplished, has the bard any use for it. It exists in a dead form, a particular performance at a particular time in a particular setting; not, as we would have it, the correct or best version, which is approximated by subsequent performances. The point is that the oral poet lives in an entirely different world and operates with entirely different cognitive processes than do we. They are the polar opposite to Glenn Gould's perspective (Payzant, 1984). He believed a perfect performance (especially of a composer such as Bach) could be created in the recording studio through the splicing of bits from many different performances. The concert stage merely interfered with musical perfection.

The oral tradition and its ability to preserve the past, to transform that past as necessary, to base law in custom, and to explain all events within a natural cosmology point to the stability of oral societies and their tendency to preserve, extend, and adapt culture. Rather than being concerned with the continued existence of formal structures and institutions, oral societies are most successful at extending the dynamics of interaction. With change comes a type of adaptation that preserves ways of acting, but in new circumstances. The ancient Greeks, for example, perpetuated a stable, continuous, but adapting culture.

Modern Oral Cultures

Today, the influence of oral processes has not entirely passed. In non-literate African cultures there has been considerable opportunity to examine the effects of oral versus literate processes. On the literate side, in the 1900s when early British administrators attempted to record histories of certain tribes to facilitate the administration of British justice, the origin myths of certain groups were carefully recorded. One myth told of the founding of the country by a particular figure who then divided the country among his sons, who became tribal chiefs of the various subsections of the country. As is readily apparent, this myth describes rather well a federation of related tribes in the midst of other "unrelated" tribes.

What amazed researchers in their return to such areas and tribes, for instance the Gonja in northern Ghana (Goody, 1975, p. 35), was the transformation of the origin myths. When asked to recount these myths in face of the further subdivision of the country, tribal narrators told the same story but with the number of sons increased. Confronted by the literate mind and the written records of yesteryear, these oral peoples professed lack of understanding of the earlier "evidence."

The point to be taken is not that members of oral societies are foolish, forgetful, naive, or even inconsistent, but that the ways in which oral societies preserve knowledge and cultural integrity are fundamentally different from those of literate society. Where literate cultures emphasize the "letter of the law," as it were, oral cultures emphasize its meaning. According to the logic of an oral society, if there now exists a federated country of so many parts, given the nature of the mythical form it must have developed from a founder followed by so many sons. The myth serves and justifies present-day reality. The same is true of the myths of literate cultures, but the relation between the present day and the past often involves a much more labyrinthine series of connections. In literate cultures, out of a massive recorded history of figures and events can be drawn the heroes of the day, depending on the needs of the day.

It is not only "anthropological" societies that evidence oral processes. In the days when Bob Dylan was the spiritual leader of the youth of America and some section of the youth of the Western world, his lyrics demonstrated exactly the kind of oral process that we have been discussing in African and Greek societies. Dylan took figures and events out of American history and institutions and gave them identities within a new mythology reflecting the ideas of the youth of the day. Whether the figures were from literature, from the newspaper, or from American popular culture, all were grist for the mill.

Perceived as a set of epic poems, Dylan's early work as a whole can be seen as typical rather than unique. Indeed, it is interesting to see what musical forms arise from time to time and how they communicate the central concerns of the young adults of the time through oral/aural discourse.

The response of societies to new musical forms is also worth noting. It is a tribute to the powerful role of new musical forms and to their autonomy from central societal institutions that popular music is continually subjected to censorship. That censorship existed in Eastern European countries when they were ruled by Communists. The governments of such countries were especially frightened of jazz. In Western countries the absolute bans of the Eastern bloc are replaced with strictures on the medium through which the work can be communicated. For example, AM rock stations and television broadcast channels do not play certain songs and videos respectively, although these may be available through record and video stores.

Literate Society

Greece, for Innis, represented an oral society, whereas Rome represented a literate society. It was not that Greece was unaffected by writing. On the contrary, a number of authors, notably Havelock (1976), claim that the basis of the enormous contribution Greek civilization made to modern civilization is to be found in writing, in their invention of the phonetic alphabet. Innis cites contemporary statements from the time of the emergence of writing that indicate a realization of the significance of the change from oral to written forms. For example, in Plato's *Phaedrus* Socrates reports a conversation between the Egyptian god Thoth, the inventor of letters, and the god Amon. Amon says:

> This discovery of yours will create forgetfulness in the learners' souls, because they will not use their memories; they will trust to the external written characters and not remember of themselves. The specific you have discovered is an aid not to memory, but to reminiscence, and you give your disciples not truth but only the semblance of truth; they will be bearers of many things and will have learned nothing; they will appear to be omniscient and will generally know nothing; they will be tiresome company, having the show of wisdom without the reality.

Socrates continues:

> I cannot help feeling, Phaedrus, that writing is unfortunately like painting; for the creations of the painter have the attitude of life, and yet if you ask them a question, they preserve a solemn silence, and the same may be said of speeches. You would imagine that they had intelligence, but if you want to know anything and put a question to one of them, the speaker always gives one unvarying answer.

Such statements sound like someone discussing the evils of television, and so they should, for the transformation from an oral to a literate society is as major a change as from a literate to an electronic society.

Rome and the Roman Empire represent literate society because the operating concepts and processes of Rome were derived from the written rather than the spoken word: possession of a piece of land or object became subject to an abstract notion of legal property, heretofore never conceived; in other legal proceedings the influence of writing could be seen in the fact that trained lawyers were responsible for defining the exact nature of a dispute within written laws (a literate function), and only then was the case handed to laymen to determine a settlement among the claimants (an oral community function, to gauge the significance of the crime to the community). But perhaps it was in the development of contract law where the Romans shone in their ability to invent an institution to supplant practices founded on the oral process. A contract changes an oral pact into a legal obligation. It is a precise written record of an obligation of one person to another or to others.

Such inventions allowed for both an orderly and a vast expansion of the Roman Empire. The conception of forming abstract laws to apply in all situations and recording these laws by writing them down on a portable medium such as parchment so they could be examined in numerous locations was key to the exercise of the administrative power of the Roman Empire. Greek-inspired teachers of rhetoric and philosophy, for example, were expelled in 168 BC and several years later (154 BC) the first school of grammar was founded. These developments reflected an attempt to rid society of the power of poetic language and to replace it with clear, ordered, unambiguous, logical prose. Less than 100 years later Julius Caesar, in 59 BC, instituted the publication of proceedings of the Senate. He also called for an attempt to summarize and condense written law. The written tradition was already beginning to demonstrate its excessive permanence and lack of a built-in homeostatic factor.

The writing of Cicero (106-43 BC) and other Stoic philosophers brought forward the ideas of the world state, natural justice, and universal citizenship in an ethical sense. The concept of natural law brought enlightened criticism to bear on custom (Innis, 1950, p. 98). Libraries were not only scattered throughout the empire but also became signs of conspicuous consumption. All these were characteristics of literate society. Without writing, without the ability to pursue the static representation of ideas, where by a mere eye movement two ideas could be juxtaposed and compared, they could never have existed.

Most other writings about literate societies focus on modern societies. While they discuss the nature of the influence of writing they do so within a context of an evolved technology and developed institutions (see, for example, McLuhan, 1962; Goody, 1977; Olson, 1980). The basic claim of these writers, and others who have also contributed to the tradition, is that writing has provided the means for the development of logical, linear, and sequential thinking. Literate thought is (or should be) logical because it must be presented in such a way that anyone can understand the meaning of a written passage without benefit of knowing the context within which the passage was written and without the possibility of further reference to the author. It can stand by itself as a statement that is consistent both internally and with reference to other common knowledge. Literate thought is also linear and sequential because only one idea can be presented at a time, followed by another and then another. This contrasts with what can be done on television, where a picture can be providing context

while a text can provide other aspects of meaning. It also contrasts with what is available to a speaker, who can with facial or bodily gesture communicate certain aspects of a message while communicating other aspects in words. The speaker in most situations also has the benefit of monitoring his or her audience during the communication, a direct form of feedback not available with print or with electronic communication.

Electronic Society

Few scholars have given serious consideration to the transformation in our society that has resulted from a growing reliance on electronic communications. Perhaps because we depend so heavily on what we associate with writing, that is, the ability to write clearly and think logically and conceptually, we cannot imagine how electronic information processes are going to replace writing. The diversionary aspect of McLuhan's work, among other things, is that his examples are from entertainment rather than information-processing media. In concentrating on broadcast television and radio he enters a domain foreign to most scholars, a domain from which they get little information of value to their scholarship. They are thus inclined to see it as a system serving needs other than their own professional needs and are therefore reluctant to consider the dynamics of electronic information-processing thoughtfully.

However, as information-processing by electronic means becomes more prevalent, that is, as computers become more pervasive in everything from cars to cameras, it is easier to see the importance of McLuhan's ideas. As scholars begin to take advantage of computers and communication technology in their own writing, information-gathering, information-monitoring, and personal and professional communications, they begin to understand new patterns of information production and consumption, which lead to new biases in the creation and dissemination of knowledge.

McLuhan himself made much of the notion of a **global village**. By that he did not mean that we would soon become members of one big happy family but that we would have the information-gathering capacity to be intimately, perhaps too intimately, aware of the goings on of all people in every kind of situation around the world. Think of the capability the world now has with its global news organizations. It is not difficult for us to find out about nearly every country and its current situation. Nightly we find out about many countries in which "newsworthy" events have recently happened, yet most of us know that our nightly news services rarely avail themselves of news available from parts of the world that for one reason or another are not considered to be of primary interest to Canadians. In Australia in the early 1980s, for example, an hour-long news program on that country's Special Broadcasting Service was designed to bring news from areas not covered by other stations and especially from countries that have supplied many recent immigrants to Australia. The service provided a different image of the world and quite a different image of the news-gathering and presentation process than what we encounter on Canadian and U.S. television.

Our linkage with this always incomplete but steadily more inclusive global village transforms our environment, extending our realm of knowledge but also transforming our attitude to our own local environment. Various studies indicate that people who rely on television for information have a vision of the world that over-estimates the violence and disorder in the world, a view apparently derived from news and other programming that concentrates on violence (see Gerbner, 1978). At times people seem to ignore their own quiet surroundings for the more dynamic impact of the world as presented on television.

Television demands the enactment of a small drama with visual interest for the creation of a news story. Information is not collected and later transformed into a form presentable through television; rather, the event is staged and then "clips" of it are used for television. The television crew must get everyone to act in a way that will make good television; people must be stage-managed so the material can be sifted through to produce what is perceived to be "good" television. Or the newsmakers can stage the event themselves. For television there is not so much a transformation by analysis as a selection. Those who can create good television are those who become newsworthy. Notice that there is a shift in newsworthiness away from what a newspaper might consider an important event to something that is visually interesting, such as a prime minister meeting some workers on an ocean-based oil-drilling rig. What is visually interesting depends on what is currently visually novel.

Numerous other examples of substantial changes to the structure and use of information echo McLuhan's concerns. In late 1984, after moving itself to plush surroundings, the Toronto Stock Exchange decided it was losing too much business to Montreal to forgo any longer the electrification of stock trading. Such electrification reduced confirmation on stock orders from two or three minutes to seconds. As one commentator, Dian Cohen, pointed out, this emphasis on speed does nothing to enhance, for example, the stabilizing value of pension-fund investment. It emphasizes quick stock market play as opposed to long-term stable investments. In another area, Martin Eslin (1980) has argued that our pattern of exposure to ways of presenting ideas has changed in electronic culture. With the advent of television

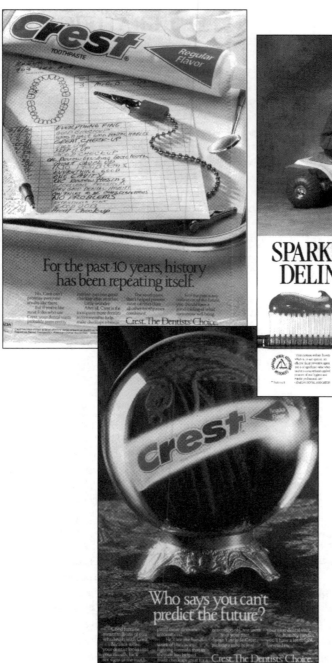

This group of ads illustrates the use of both logical argument (the history of check-ups) and images and lifestyles (the kids and the crystal ball). Having established the "performance" of Crest over the years, Procter & Gamble apparently now wants to attract those who choose a toothpaste brand for other than logical reasons, i.e., to enhance their self-image.
Courtesy Procter & Gamble Inc.

A combination of logic and image. First health, then beauty. *Courtesy Campbell Soup Company Ltd.*

the predominant form of argumentation or presentation of facts has come to be dramatization. Theatricality has replaced the kind of reasoned analysis one finds in a newspaper.

Vivid examples of information presentation that reflect both literate and electronic information processes can be found in the world of advertising. Products that we are meant to purchase because they are of value to our health often reflect literate values. Ads such as those for Crest toothpaste or Anacin make reference to surveys of either results-of-use or consumer preference. They mimic logical argumentation to convince us to choose their product. The term "mimic" is used here because there is no attempt in such ads to ensure exact understanding of actuality; instead, the ad creators make claims that, though logically constructed, tell only part of the story. The audience is led to believe it is receiving the whole story

Products that we are meant to purchase for our own enjoyment or for the enhancement of our self-image rarely reflect literate values. More often they reflect the image-oriented values of electronic society. Lifestyle ads, such as those used to sell beer, present an image of the beer drinker, thus targeting the beer in its market (Grady, 1983). The actual taste of the beer is such that it is indistinguishable from other beers. Bruce McCuaig, marketing vice-president for Labatt's, explains that the difference in taste of any one brand is so elusive that the customer has to keep consuming to remember that difference. The point is that the *image of the consumer is what is being sold and consumed.*

An ad series that is a lovely combination of implied literate reasoning and image-based electronic values is that created for Campbell's soup. The yarn coloured and shaped like a Campbell's soup can, stuck through with knitting needles and accompanied by the caption "Better than a sweater," has the immediate draw of the powerful image accompanied by the subtlety of the logical reasoning behind why one would consume soup in cold weather. The complete ad series plays on the same theme.

SUMMARY AND BOOK OVERVIEW

The purpose of this chapter has been to convey the importance of communication in the affairs of society. We have done so, first, by examining the range of communication, outlining how communication is intrinsic to eight dimensions of human activity. They are:

1. the social dimension
2. the political dimension
3. the economic dimension
4. the educational dimension
5. the cultural dimension
6. the technological dimension
7. the familial dimension
8. the individual dimension.

We then examined the domain of communication, outlining how modes of communication – oral, literate, and electronic – have been fundamental structuring variables in all societies throughout history and pre-history.

The importance of communication in society cannot be over-estimated. Like McLuhan and Innis, we would contend that communication is a structuring force in society. Human affairs cannot be divorced from the communication system used to represent or discuss them. The design of our communication systems impinges on every element of our present and future lives. The purpose of this book as a whole is to explore the nature of communication in general and mass communication in particular. We do so by taking up five areas of discussion.

(1) The first area is meant to orient the reader to **the major elements of the field of mass communication**. The general nature of communication and its interaction with society have been introduced in Chapter 1. This discussion provides a context for exploration of the main focus of the book, mass communication. Chapter 2 outlines mass communication and the mass media and then summarizes the character of the Canadian mass media (i.e., broadcasting, cultural industries, and the press). Having presented the mass media as nationally organized communication systems integrated into the fabric of industrial and post-industrial societies, in Chapter 3 we turn to the interaction of the media with Canada's political system.

(2) The second area, explored in Chapters 4 and 5, is **the production and consumption of mass communication**. Who produces content,

under what conditions, for what purpose, with what resources, and to what effect? Included in this exploration of content is an introduction to models that analysts use to understand the subtle aspects of content. We also explore the role of the audience. To what extent is the audience a homogeneous aggregate of passive consumers? To what extent is it a differentiated set of smaller groupings that have a direct impact on content by means of patterns of social behaviour and media consumption?

(3) An analysis of **the loci of control over mass communication** is the third area of discussion. The analysis encompasses the roles of:

- the state (public policy, in Chapter 6)
- industry (private owners, in Chapter 7)
- content producers (professionals in Chapter 8)
- technology (in Chapter 9).

(4) A fourth area, covered in Chapters 10 and 11, deals with the manner in which these forces or loci of control play themselves out domestically and internationally, hence, **the impact of domestic and global mass communication systems**. What kinds of systems exist, and with what biases, in Canada and in other nations around the world?

(5) The twelfth and final chapter is an examination of **the nature of mass communication in Canada and around the world** and of where that form of communication is taking us. In looking into the future we also identify where issues are developing and what tensions will probably result from these issues.

The book as a whole introduces a range of topics and concerns focused on mass communication and its interaction with society. In using familiar and topical examples, we seek to stimulate a desire for involvement with the mass media. The increasing importance of mass communication in our lives demands the involvement of the most well-meaning and talented people to ensure that the system we create serves us, individually and collectively, as well as possible.

REFERENCES

Audley, P. *Canada's Cultural Industries.* Toronto: James Lorimer, 1983.

Babe, R. "Emergence and development of Canadian communications: technology, industry and government," in R. Lorimer and D.C. Wilson, eds., *Communication Canada.* Toronto: Kagan and Woo, 1988.

Beale, A. "The question of space," in Lorimer and Wilson, eds., *Communication Canada.*

Canada, Department of Communication. *The Challenge of Communication,* videotape.

Crean, S.M. *Who's Afraid of Canadian Culture?* Don Mills, Ontario: General Publishing, 1976.

Goody, J.R. *The Domestication of the Savage Mind.* Cambridge: Cambridge University Press, 1977.

Goody, J.R., ed. *Changing Social Structure in Ghana.* London: International African Institute, 1975.

Grady, Wayne. "The Budweiser Gamble," *Saturday Night* (February, 1983), pp. 28-30.

Havelock, Eric. *Origins of Western Literacy.* Toronto: OISE Press, 1976.

Innis, Harold. *Empire and Communications.* Toronto: Oxford University Press, 1950.

de Kerckhove, Derrick. "McLuhan versus Orwell in 1984," *The Globe and Mail,* 1984.

Knelman, Martin. *This is Where We Came In.* Toronto: McClelland and Stewart, 1977.

Kroker, A. *Technology and the Canadian Mind.* Montreal: New World Perspectives, 1984.

Lord, A.B. *The Singer of Tales.* Cambridge: Harvard University Press, 1964.

Lorimer, R., and L. Webber. "New Technologies and Access to Legal Information," Monograph #1 in *The Economics of Legal Information.* Ottawa: Canadian Law Information Council, 1987.

McLuhan, Marshall. *The Gutenberg Galaxy.* Toronto: University of Toronto Press, 1962.

Olson, David R., ed. *The Social Foundations of Language and Thought.* New York: Norton, 1980.

Payzant, G. *Glenn Gould: Music and Mind.* Toronto: Key Porter, 1984.

UNESCO, International Commission on Communications Problems (MacBride Commission). *Many Voices, One World.* Paris: Unipub, 1980.

STUDY QUESTIONS

1. The section on the range of communication deals with the breadth of influence of communication on society. Is communication all-encompassing?
2. How would you describe the structural influence of communication on society?
3. It is often said that the mass media have made the world seem smaller and we now all live in the "global village." What do you think is meant by this term? Is this where we live?

CHAPTER

2

Mass Communication, the Mass Media, and Canadian Society

INTRODUCTION: DEFINITION

CHAPTER 1 provided an analysis of the inter-action of communication with society on two different axes. The first was a cross section of human affairs, a perspective we labelled the range of communication. The second was, in a sense, an evolutionary viewpoint beginning with the human (oral) and proceeding through two different technological configurations: one based in print, the other on electronic information processing. It also introduced the areas of discussion that will be explored in this book.

This chapter focuses on the second area, mass communication and the mass media. **Mass communication** encompasses part but not all of **communication**. In turn, the **mass media** encompass part but not all of **mass communication**. Our discussion of mass communication introduces both historical examples and contemporary global phenomena. Our exploration of the mass media is definitional in nature. First we outline the general case, then the characteristics of the Canadian media.

MASS COMMUNICATION

In *Key Concepts in Communication* (O'Sullivan *et al.*, 1983) the authors provide a short empirical orientation to **mass communication**: "Usually understood as newspapers, magazines, cinema, television, radio and advertising; sometimes including book publishing (especially popular fiction) and music (the pop industry)." The authors go on to note that mass communication should probably be thought of as a proper noun, a term that denotes something but is not descriptive of it. The reason? The word **mass** encourages us to think of the audience as a vast undifferentiated agglomeration of individuals lacking social bonds and alienated from society by unskilled, meaningless work, subject to the vagaries of markets and the willingness of capitalists to pay a living wage. The word **communication** tends to mask the social and industrial nature of the media and promotes a tendency to think of them as analogous to interpersonal communication. With these and other caveats introduced (including that they know of no successful definition), the authors aim for a more formal definition:

> Mass communication is the practice and product of providing leisure entertainment and information to an unknown audience by means of corporately financed, industrially produced, state regulated, high technology, privately consumed commodities in the modern print, screen, audio and broadcast media.

In spite of its relatively recent formulation, the conception of mass communication put forward by O'Sullivan *et al.* is already becoming dated and problematic. Most importantly, it only partially distinguishes between the mass media and mass communication. Such a differentiation can provide a new foundation for understanding the interaction between communicatior and society.

An Historical Example

In another useful book, *Culture, Society and the Media,* Curran makes the point that every medium of communication to large numbers of people should not be considered part of the mass media. He explains:

> a variety of signifying forms apart from face-to-face interaction – buildings, pictures, statues, coins, banners, stained glass, songs, medallions, rituals of all kinds – were deployed in pre-industrial societies to express sometimes highly complex ideas. At times, these signifying forms reached vast audiences. For instance, the proportion of the adult population in Europe regularly attending mass during the middle ages was almost certainly higher than the proportion of adults in contemporary Europe regularly reading a newspaper. Since the rituals of religious worship were laid down in liturgies, the papal curia exercised a much more centralized control over the symbolic content mediated through public worship in the central middle ages than even the controllers of the highly centralized and monopolistic press of contemporary Europe.

When we speak of the mass media, then, we are speaking of the modern electronic and print-based mass media. At the same time, the insights that can be gained from the study of these media can provide some valuable understandings of other "media" used to communicate to large audiences.

But mass communication is another matter. We can see no reason for not regarding the communication function performed by the church, architecture, education systems, paintings, sculpture, coins, rituals, and the like as mass communication. Indeed, including them may enhance our understanding of mass communication and the mass media.

A Contemporary Example

Another example may contribute to that enhancement of understanding and elucidate the differences between the mass media and mass communication. The example is adapted, with the author's permission, from an essay by Umberto Eco called "The Multiplication of the Media" (1986, pp. 148-50).

1. A firm produces polo shirts with an alligator on them and it advertises them.

2. A generation begins to wear polo shirts.

3. Each consumer of the polo shirt advertises, via the alligator on his or her chest, this brand of polo shirt (just as every owner of a Toyota is an advertiser, unpaid and paying, of the Toyota line and the model he drives).

4. A TV broadcast (program), to be faithful to reality, shows some young people wearing the alligator polo shirt.

5. The young (and the old) see the TV broadcast and buy more alligator polo shirts because they have "the young look."

Which is the mass medium? The ad? The broadcast? The shirt?

Who is sending the message? The manufacturer? The wearer? The TV director? The analyst of this phenomenon?

Who is the producer of ideology? Again, the manufacturer? The wearer (including the celebrity who may wear it in public for a fee)? The TV director who portrays the generation?

Where does the plan come from? This is not to imply that there is no plan but rather that it does not emanate from one central source.

Eco concludes:

Once upon a time there were the mass media, and they were wicked, of course, and there was a guilty party. Then there were the virtuous voices that accused the criminals. And Art (ah, what luck!) offered alternatives, for those who were not prisoners of the mass media.

Well, it's all over. We have to start again from the beginning, asking one another what's going on.

Since this passage was written there has been an advance in the way many people think about the media, brought about in part by questioning along the lines Eco has indicated. For example, CBC radio host Arthur Black produced a short commentary on the occasion of the announcement that the Rolling Stones were planning to endorse a line of clothes. He underlined the transformation of the blue-jeaned and T-shirted rock group into a marketing vehicle for a line of clothes.

The Rolling Stones are not mass media as we would formally define them, although we should not make the mistake of believing that they are not industrially organized media properties. The Rolling Stones are, by virtue of having gained access to the mass media, elements of a mass communication system. Like coins, architecture, company logos, the mass media as a whole, alligator shirts, Wayne Gretzky and Ben Johnson, the Olympics, political leaders, and the World Bank, they are elements of mass communication. Their presence on the world stage, made possible by the mass media, transforms them into media themselves. They gain the ability to be vehicles for messages (and/or products) that are extensions of the identities that brought them onto the world stage in the first place.

A second area properly labelled mass communication is modern telecommunications. Formally defined, telecommunication includes "any transmission, emission or reception of signs, signals, writing, images or sounds or intelligence of any nature by wire, radio, visual or other electromagnetic system" (Radiocommunication Act, RSC 1985, c.R-2, s.2). Strictly speaking this includes broadcasting. But because broadcasting itself is such a large area of concern, telecommunications systems normally refer to what is included in the definition when broadcasting is removed.

Traditionally, the term telecommunications has included the telephone and telegraph industries. With the advent of communications satellites and computers, the area expanded to cover satellite transmissions and data links. In recent years, thanks to inventive communications engineers, a vast array of services have emerged that integrate the capacities of computers, satellites, glass fibres, and light-based as well as electromagnetic-based transmissions. We now have in the consumer and business markets alone, e-mail, electronic bulletin boards, databases, videotex, fax, cellular radio (phones), pocket range phones, packet radio, and vastly expanded satellite capacity, to say nothing of the traditional services such as telex and cable television.

These are properly regarded as mass communication because they are designed to be, and are on their way to being, universally available. As the International Telecommunications Union notes, its goal is to have a telephone within access of every individual in the world. As the access of individuals to personal computers and data and voice lines increases along with affordable transmission capacity and electronically accessible information (databases), these services are indeed becoming part of our system of mass communication. As such services ensconce themselves in our day-to-day life, they are changing the nature of our communities, bringing to them geographically neutral and therefore global referents.

Given this expansion, to conform to the definition of mass communication proffered by O'Sullivan et al. we need to remove the implied notion that mass communication is solely the surround of the mass media and replace it with the understanding that mass communication includes the provision of the capacity for affordable storage and transmission, and widespread retrieval of a vast array of information. To revise their definition:

> Mass communication is the practice and product of providing information and leisure entertainment to large and often unknown audiences. When undertaken by means of modern technologies, this process involves institutionally financed and organized, state regulated, high-technology organizations that provide commodities and associated free services in print, on the screen, electronically, and by electromagnetic broadcast. When undertaken by more traditional means, mass communication includes any means of providing information, images, and/or leisure entertainment to large numbers of people from all social strata and demographic groups but who are homogeneous in their behaviour of choosing to attend to an information source.

THE MASS MEDIA

The mass media are a subset of mass communication and can be said to be, following McQuail (1983):

1. *a distinct set of activities* (creating media content)
2. *involving particular technological configurations* (television, radio, videotex, newspapers, books)
3. associated with *formally constituted institutions* or media outlets (systems, stations, publications, and so on)
4. acting according to *certain laws, rules, and understandings* (professional codes and practices, audience and societal expectations and habits)

5. carried out by *persons occupying certain roles* (owners, regulators, producers, distributors, advertisers, audience members)
6. which, together, convey *information, entertainment, images, and symbols*
7. to the *mass audience.*

1. A Distinct Set of Activities

The mass media can be considered to be a distinct set of activities in their communicative function as well as in their form. The common-sense image of the nature of communication is that of a conduit. Some piece of information that exists at point "A" or time "A" or in the mind of person "A" is transposed, largely unaffected by its mode of transmission, to point "B," time "B," and/or into the mind of person "B." A predominant emphasis in socially oriented (as opposed to technically oriented) communication theory is on the *transposing* function, which is really seen as a *transforming* function.

To use the words of two different kinds of theorists to describe this transforming function, the media "construct" (see Berger and Luckmann, 1966) or "signify" (see any introduction to semiotics) reality. Their primary function as symbol- or meaning-producing agents is to put together or assist us in defining key and subordinate characteristics of reality. Thereby they are distinguished from other non-communicative activities. (See Chapter 3 for a further elaboration of this function.)

Modern communication theory also posits that this function is not a secondary or derivative activity. As Bennett (in Gurevitch *et al.,* 1982, p. 187) argues, the ideas that long held sway insisted that:

the media can reflect only what is there. . . . the world of signs is granted only a shadowy, twilight existence; it 'hovers' above 'reality' as

an ethereal appendage to it, deriving such substance as it has merely from what is reflected in it.

More recent developments in the theory of language have pulled in a direction directly contrary to this, stressing not only the independent materiality of the signifier – the fleshiness of the sign – but also the activity and effectivity of signification as a process which actively constructs cognitive worlds rather than simply passively reflecting a pre-existing reality. . . . Sign orders world.

In summary the mass media are a distinct set of activities because they have a primary and non-derivative signifying or reality-constructing function. To some degree they are the organizers of our perceptions. But our perceptions are organized as well by the prevailing dynamics of our communities, our acquired ideas, and even our personalities.

2. Particular Technological Configurations

Considerations of the role of technology in the modern mass media are not exhausted simply by identifying them as modern as opposed to ancient. In examining the context out of which these modern technologies have developed, together with their particular properties, we gain a sense of the role of technology itself in the functioning of the various mass media.

Raymond Williams, in *Television: Technology and Cultural Form* (1974), provides a thorough account of the relationship between technology and society using television as an example. In brief, he points out that technologies do not arise from the brain of a genius working in isolation from any social context; they arise from and are incorporated into society on the basis of the structure and functioning of society. For example, television did not so much arise as an inevitable offshoot of the search for scientific knowledge but rather from the interests and conceptions of technical investigators and industrial entrepreneurs who, on the basis of their cultural background and their technical expertise, were able to imagine an electronic medium of sound and visual communication. Nor do we need to use television technology in the manner that we now do. The domination of the medium by advertisers and by certain types of programming is not necessary but the result of the interests of the persons and institutions that control content.

Television is but one example of a modern mass medium. As we know, there are many more and each decade brings several brand new ones. One company, Sony, has been particularly active in bringing forward new technological configurations and is beginning to advertise that fact. Two of their great successes (they have had failures) were the Walkman and the compact disc. In the case of the Walkman, Sony took existing cassette playback technology, improved a battery-operated version of it, miniaturized it, and made it resistant to shakes and joggling, thereby creating a vast market for the pocket-sized cassette recorders. In the case of the compact disc, Sony took a new technology (videodiscs) invented by a competitor, Phillips, which was hailed for the amount of information it could carry and for the fidelity and flexibility of retrieval of that information. Sony reduced the disc to a manageable size, capable of holding slightly more information than that contained on a long-playing (LP) record. In the cases of both the Walkman and the compact disc, success was built on an analysis of the social use to which the technology could be put.

As with television, in both these cases particular technological configurations have been chosen and marketed. To emphasize the point with another example, audio tape recordings never really were accepted by consumers until they were downsized, put in little plastic boxes, and called cassettes. At that point, when a person did not have to fiddle with two reels and winding the tape onto a take-up reel to make it play, cassette tapes took off as a consumer item. With compact discs or CDs physical size was probably not engendering consumer resistance. But informational capacity was: it was too great. Once that aspect was dealt with, again, consumer acceptance followed. With the CD it is also interesting that Sony and others decided there would be market acceptance for a non-rewriteable disc. Already, discs that can be erased and rewritten on are sitting in the wings. Their market fate is yet to be determined.

Stepping back in our analysis somewhat, we see that we have in the modern mass media a set of technological configurations that bring us information in a variety of forms. In print we have broadsheet and tabloid newspapers, magazines, journals, and books. Each could be subcategorized. For example, books can be subdivided into a variety of types including mass paperbacks, quality paperbacks, hardbound, textbooks, schoolbooks, limited editions, coffee table, talking books, large-print books, children's literature, and so forth. In the electronic media we have public, community, educational, and commercial television and radio delivered by broadcast, cable, and satellite. We also have feature film as well as non-theatrical film. Finally, there are sound recordings now available in vinyl disc (LP), audio cassette, and CD, as well as, in their promotional version, on video cassette. Inventing the right technology and even boasting of that fact is marketable in itself, as the following set of ads demonstrates.

Together the above technologies make up the mass media, a set of industries that contribute significantly to economic and cultural activity within the country. Table 2.1 provides a summary of the extent of their economic contribution.

Various companies battle it out for the high-tech ground in digital disk technology.

TABLE 2.1

Media Outlets and Industry Size (1980)[1]

Outlet		Output	Ad Revenue[2]
Newspapers[3]	No.	Circulation ('000)	Net Ad Rev. ($000)
Dailies	117	32,445	892,000
Weekend Sup.	3	4,024	17,100
Weekly, semi- tri-weekly	1,187	12,591	210,000
Periodicals		Circulation[4]	
Gen. Mags	644	36,596	152,000
Business	507	8,622	97,800
Farm	112	2,378	15,000
Directories	52	4,311	236,000
Relig., scholarly, other	48	908	11,500
Broadcast	No. of Stns.	Total Rev.	
Radio (1979)[5]			
Private	493	562,036	
CBC	65		
Total	558		391,965
Television			
Private	80	397,194	
CBC	31		
Total	111		610,334
Priv. Broad.	573	959,230	
CBC	96	647,004	
Cable		352,172	
Other Print			
Catalogue, Direct Mail		774,679	
Outdoor			
Billboards, car cards, signs		236,000	
Books	Titles	Sales ($000)[6]	
Domestic	3,502	256,700	
Foreign		675,000	
Total		931,700	
Records and Tapes[7]		Rev. R&T alone ($000)	Total Rev. ($000)
6 largest		181,700	271,000
Total Industry		235,100	339,000
Movie Theatres[8]		Pd. Admissions ('000)	Receipts ($000)
Total		101,000	311,400

1. Unless otherwise indicated, as of 1980.
2. SOURCE: Maclean Hunter Research Bureau, *A Report on Advertising Revenues in Canada,* 1981.
3. SOURCE: *Royal Commission on Newspapers,* Research Studies, Vol. 1.
4. SOURCE: Culture Statistics: Newspapers and Periodicals #87-625. Data are incomplete to a significant degree.
5. SOURCE: CRTC Annual Report, 1978-79.
6. SOURCE: Statistics Canada #87-601.
7. The six largest are CBS, WEA, RCA, MCI, Thorn-EMI, and Polygram. SOURCE: for data: StatsCan unpublished industry survey.
8. SOURCE: *Canadian Film Digest,* 1982.

3. Formally Constituted Institutions

The implications of technological configurations of the media cannot be discussed for long before a consideration of their associated industrial structures must be included. The mass media do not exist without industrial structures for the production and processing of content as well as the construction and maintenance of a physical plant. Media institutions have developed to provide the infrastructure needed to operate the media. These institutions may be private corporations owned by shareholders or publicly owned corporations or state enterprises – in Canadian terms, Crown corporations.

Private-Sector Institutions. Private media may be defined as corporations owning media enterprises for profit. Their primary purpose, obviously, is to gain the maximum revenues at minimum cost. This principle of action guides the entire scope of their operations; however, it is a principle that must be and is applied in a sophisticated manner.

Media institutions must build audiences. They do so by spending money to provide content of interest to their target audiences. Revenues come either from the sale of content to audiences (newspaper), the sale of audiences to advertisers (newspapers and TV), or both. Secondarily, sales of content to others who must similarly build audiences (network TV to affiliated stations) can bring revenue.

On the expense side of the ledger, the major cost in operating a broadcasting station, newspaper, book publishing house, or film studio is creating or purchasing content. Table 2.2 provides some sense of the magnitude of the costs involved as well as a comparison between different types of programming. They have increased substantially since 1978.

The economics of content creation are parallel to the economics of most commodity manufacturing. The greater number of sales of the content produced, the lower the per unit cost. In the case of newspapers, owners form groups or chains of newpapers in different cities. They can then hire certain personnel, such as columnists, to produce content for the whole chain of papers and thereby achieve economies of scale. In the case of broadcasting the same principle applies. It is clearly cheaper to purchase programming that has been or will be used in a variety of different markets rather than to make one's own programs with an equivalent audience appeal – hence, the formation of national networks. Internationally, the purchase of U.S. programming for showing in the Canadian market is inexpensive because most of the original production costs have usually been recouped in the U.S. market. It is customary for Canadian broadcasters to pay the equivalent of about 10 to 20 per cent of the production cost of an equivalent Canadian program for the national market rights for a U.S. program to show in Canada.

The common situation is, as Table 2.2 shows, that domestic productions cannot possibly match these prices and still cover the production costs. Thus, the economic incentive for Canadian private broadcasters to produce Canadian programming is extremely weak. Only with specific types of programs where audiences are highly interested – sports, news, and some public affairs programs where production costs are considerably less than, say, for dramatic productions – is there sufficient incentive for private broadcasters to engage in production.

In some cases privately owned media are induced to consider their social contribution over the bottom line. In the case of newspapers, *Le Devoir* is an example, as are *Le Monde, The New York Times, The Times of*

TABLE 2.2

Average Cost and Revenue of Canadian Programming by Program Category, 1978

	No. of Programs	Costs*	Revenues**	Audience† Actual	Break-even
English-Language Market					
Drama					
serials	4	$114,750	$59,536	921,500	1,776,300
short films	1	137,160	78,166	1,210,000	2,123,200
teledramas	2	112,830	46,318	717,000	1,746,000
Variety	2	115,620	74,452	1,152,500	1,789,800
Game shows	2	18,900	57,882	896,000	292,600
News	6	36,887	68,301	1,057,300	571,000
Documentaries	1	20,768	26,098	404,000	321,400
French-Language Market					
Drama					
soap operas	3	25,860	51,390	1,380,600	440,800
Variety	2	38,925	44,448	794,900	716,200
Game shows	2	21,090	42,620	708,500	193,400
News and information	2	29,730	36,025	687,500	567,400

*Costs are the average cost of a 30-minute program for a sample of programs in each category.
**The average revenue was obtained in the following manner: The minimum 30-second rate during prime time viewing for a network which had broadcast the program was multiplied by twenty time periods. This gave the revenue for a half-hour of programming for which the 15 per cent agency commission was subtracted. This income was divided by the average audience of the network during prime time, which gave the income per viewer. The average income by category of program was then obtained by multiplying the audience of each program by the revenue per viewer. The data are for rates and audiences in Fall, 1978.
†The actual audience is the audience observed for each sample program. The break-even audience is the one necessary to cover production costs.
SOURCE: Audley, *Canada's Cultural Industries,* which used: A Lapointe and J. LeGoff, *Television Programs and Their Production in Canada* (Department of Communications, May, 1980), Tables 1.25 and 1.26.

London, and at certain points in their histories, *The Globe and Mail* and the *Jerusalem Post.* In fact, in its testimony to the *Royal Commission on Newspapers* the Southam chain made clear that it placed a high value on journalistic quality, not solely a healthy bottom line. In broadcasting, the conditions of licence define the contribution the licencee is expected to make in return for being granted a broadcasting licence.

In these cases, the forces of economics and the conditions of licence or the pursuit of journalistic quality oppose one another. In newspapers, it has made each of the above named examples vulnerable to collapse or radical change of editorial policy. In the case of Southam it has made the company vulnerable to takeover. In broadcasting this opposition between regulatory conditions and economics tends to produce obedience to the letter of the law, as opposed to the intent of the overall broadcasting system.

Public-Sector Institutions. The other major type of formally constituted media institution is the public-sector institution. As noted in Chapter 1, in Canada these institutions are confined to the electronic media.

In Western nations, public media corporations are usually operated at "arm's length" from the control of government (although the length of the arm varies greatly). In socialist countries, public ownership of the mass media is achieved by means of state institutions not unlike government departments – a pattern that is also emerging in the developing countries.

In Canada, like private-sector businesses, public-sector corporations must also balance revenues and costs. The advantage public-sector institutions have is that they receive revenues from government. However, these revenues are not unconditional gifts. They are funds to assist them to fulfil the special public service responsibilities they have been given in the Broadcasting Act. For example, the CBC must attempt to make its signals available to all Canadians in both languages. Its programs must appeal to all ages, not just those audiences in which advertisers have an interest. As a result of government grants, which can be generous or miserly, the publicly owned media have a greater but still limited freedom to produce programming of value to the community.

Public and Private-Sector Institutions. Whether the media are owned publicly or privately is obviously a major factor affecting the relationship between the media and the state. Thus, the political role of the mass media in a specific society, as discussed in Chapter 3, is of considerable importance. Where private ownership is dominant, considerations of profit-making and advertiser interests tend to prevail over considerations of public service. (It is, of course, pos-sible for private ownership of a mass media system to be organized on a non-profit basis, but this is relatively rare.) Where public ownership prevails completely, potential advertisers complain of an inability to get information to consumers, while consumers sometimes complain of the lack of escapist programming that allows them to forget the issues and concerns of the day.

Distinguishing state ownership from private ownership is useful in understanding major differences in media operations, but it is also too simple to provide a full understanding of the role of the media in various societies, especially in the case of Third World or developing countries. To appreciate fully the role of the institution as part of a social and industrial infrastructure one must have some understanding of the nature of the society, capitalist or socialist, within which the institution exists. The operation of both private or state-owned media in a politically stable and tolerant state such as Canada is much less encumbered than is either form of ownership in many other countries, whether capitalist, social-ist, or communist. The rule of both capital and the state can be extremely harsh and intolerant. Salter (1988) has provided a useful paper on this issue within the context of how Canadians have come to conceive of the public interest in public broadcasting.

4. Certain Laws, Rules, and Understandings

The technology and institutional form of mass media systems, including the role of the industrial infrastructure and its ownership, are significant factors in the performance of these systems. However, they are far from the only factors involved. Almost all media systems operate within specific national societies and, as such, are subject to formal legal constraints as well as less formal patterns of expectations.

On the formal side, in the case of broadcasting, the relatively limited number of radio frequencies available to each nation-state oblige national governments to exercise some control over the frequencies used within their borders in the form of licensing requirements. In the case of publishing (newspapers or magazines) most developed countries exercise little overt control. No licences are required and media content is not restricted, except by such broad laws directed at libel, sedition, and pornography. However, various indirect controls, such as taxation, subsidies, business policies, and distribution subsidies, can be and are employed.

Several laws or, more formally, statutes have a major impact on the mass media. They will be discussed in full in Chapter 6 and introduced briefly here. First is the Broadcasting Act. The pre-eminent statute in Canadian broadcasting is the Broadcasting Act (1991). There is no equivalent statute for Canadian newspapers, magazines, books, or recorded music. The reasons why broadcasting has received such particular attention in legislation are partly constitutional (the federal government has clear, undivided power over "radio communication," which includes broadcasting) and partly social (a widely held belief in Canada is that broadcasting is particularly important to nation-building).

In addition to other formalities such as defining broadcast undertakings, who can participate, technical matters, and the like, the Broadcasting Act outlines what Canadians deem broadcasting should do for society. In other words, it provides a framework for policy. The Act addresses accepted values and ideals of Canadian society and the means by which broadcasting can contribute to their achievement.

The Broadcasting Act also sets up an agency to ensure adherence to the Act. This organization is called the Canadian Radio-television and Telecommunications Commission (CRTC). It is the CRTC's task to administer the policies and provisions enunciated in the Broadcasting Act. The CRTC translates the principles of the Act into rules for broadcasters. It mediates between the ideals and values outlined in the Act and the practical realities of running broadcasting undertakings. In this mediation many issues have arisen, some short-lived and others recurring. As will become apparent throughout this book and especially in Chapter 6, the recurring issues are valuable indicators of critical points of tension in Canada's broadcasting system.

A second key statute is the Copyright Act, which creates **intellectual property**. It transforms the material reality of one's intellectual efforts, for example a script or a movie, into a piece of property that can be owned by someone. Moreover, it attaches certain rights and privileges to that ownership. Copyright stimulates creators to create by providing a means for them to require payment for their efforts and prohibiting the use of their creation without their permission and/or paying them for it. Copyright does not protect ideas; it protects the expression of ideas.

Other acts also influence the way in which the media operate, but the Broadcasting and Copyright Acts are of primary importance. Both these acts have resulted in the creation of certain concrete **rules** that are consistent with the principles of the legislation. For example, the CRTC requires AM and FM radio stations that specialize in popular music to play at least 30 per cent Canadian selections. Publishers pay royalties to authors in return for the right to publish and distribute their books. Persons who make movies based on books buy the movie rights for the book.

The laws and rules that govern the behaviour of the mass media have developed from certain

understandings that society has of the potential value of the media. At the most general level, in Western societies, the media are encouraged to provide "continuity, order, integration, motivation, guidance and adaptation" (McQuail, 1983, p. 64). To reach this multifaceted goal, the media must know the values and goals of society. However, in any liberal democracy these values and goals are a matter of continuing debate. The presence of this debate gives the media substantial latitude within which to make their social contribution. It also raises the question of how one determines whether the media are contributing appropriately. Certain media spokespersons claim that if people are watching television, because they have the freedom not to watch, the television station is obviously making an appropriate contribution to their enjoyment of their leisure time. At the other end of the spectrum, others will claim that the media should set for themselves much more ambitious goals, to provide, for example, enlightening rather than escapist entertainment. This debate, which will receive further attention in subsequent chapters, is a debate over the **public interest**.

5. Persons Occupying Certain Roles

The number of people involved in the mass media and the number of roles people play are vast. The most obvious players are the journalists. But there are also owners, editors, technicians, actors, administrators, secretaries, designers, advertisers, members of regulatory bodies such as the CRTC, politicians who control the purse-strings, lawyers, public interest group members, and audience members. To keep the discussion to a manageable size we discuss five categories of persons and roles. Our emphasis is on how these roles are played out by individuals. Four of the categories are outside the operating structure of the mass media - business,

government, the legal system, and the audience. One – media professionals – is inside.

Business Influences. The influence of businesses on the mass media is largely exercised through advertising. Decisions by businesses on where to advertise and how much to spend collectively affect the fortunes of individual media enterprises. For example, decisions by major department stores to advertise in only one of two local daily newspapers and to favour the one with the larger circulation are likely to lead to the demise of the weaker paper. Similarly, decisions by Canadian branch-plant companies to reduce advertising budgets for television because the ads of their parent companies can reach Canadian audiences through the U.S. networks can lead to reduced revenues for Canadian TV stations and may even cause some stations to be only marginally profitable.

A less direct, but equally significant, effect of business is on the non-advertising content. Media managers try not to offend (or potentially offend) advertisers by ensuring that the content does not clash with the advertisers' messages. (See the example on the following facing pages of content and ad complementarity.) Such clashes may be specific, whereby a consumer-oriented article or program criticizes the products of a particular advertiser, or they may be more diffuse, such as descriptions of a non-consumer or anti-consumer lifestyle. Neither would fit well with the consumerism promoted in advertising.

To avoid offending advertisers media enterprises must tailor their program content to fit with the advertisements. The mythology of the mass media suggests that the two types of material – content and ads – are managed quite separately and that journalists or program producers are insulated from advertiser influence. In reality, as the Report of the *Royal Commission*

This development company sought prestigious placement of its ad to solicit the "right" clients, i.e., those who can afford Mercedes and who can't afford to waste time on the freeway. A different version of the ad was also placed at the end of the Top 1000 listings (opposite). The ad was also placed in *The Financial Post 500* annual publication. *Created by Destiny Media Ltd., Toronto and used with their permission.*

Courtesy The Globe and Mail's Report on Business Magazine, July, 1990.

on Newspapers (1981) points out, it does not work that way. Bagdikian reported that in 1978 Air Canada notified newspaper advertising managers that the airline's ads would be cancelled if they appeared anywhere within two pages of news stories about crashes or hijackings on any airline (Desbarats, 1990 p. 70). In the summer and fall of 1990 an informal boycott of the *Kingston Whig-Standard* by local real estate agents took place in response to an article outlining the advantages of self-selling by owners.

Government Influences. The influence of government, exerted from outside the mass media, has several dimensions. These will be explored in Chapter 3 and introduced briefly here. In a federal state such as Canada, more than one level of government influence is at work. Within any one government, we can also distinguish between bureaucratic (or departmental) structures and political structures.

At the bureaucratic level, the government is a major source of information for the mass media; in many instances it is the only source for specific types of information. The flow of information from government to the mass media benefits both parties but also, of course, has drawbacks. The government needs access to media outlets to inform the general public of its programs and expenditures. The mass media need the information supplied as a readily usable source of media content for news, current affairs, and public affairs .

Because of time constraints and limited resources, media workers rarely have the opportunity to collect this kind of information directly from government personnel, so they tend to rely heavily on news releases and handouts prepared by the government. By failing to look behind these announcements, the media outlets run the risk of acting as the propaganda arm of the government. The drawback for the

government is in the sheer volume of materials pumped out by numerous departments, agencies, and ministries. The mass media cannot publish or broadcast all of it, so the selection of items can be quite arbitrary from the government's viewpoint.

The government's influence on the mass media also exists at a political level. Politicians are news, and daily coverage of political events is an essential part of mass media content. Rivalries between individuals and parties are extensively portrayed in the mass media and balanced coverage between the government party and opposition parties must be handled carefully by media practitioners.

Related to both the bureaucratic and political levels of government is the phenomenon of government advertising. Advertisements can provide information on government programs, can be straightforward political campaigning, or can be in the grey area of general promotion of the federal or provincial government. Total advertising revenues from government sources form a substantial part of the revenues for mass media in Canada; the federal government outspends any one commercial advertiser.

In addition to being a source of information, the subject of "news," and the source of advertising revenues, government also has an influence on the mass media through the power to regulate and control. Both at the federal and provincial levels, government has the authority to approve legislation, to impose taxes, and in various other ways to affect the means by which mass media organizations conduct their operations. Private corporations have a strong tendency to resist or seek to reduce government controls over their operations by raising the banner of "freedom of the press." Restrictions on their freedom under legislation related to competition, for example, are more apparent than real. There were no successful prosecutions of media companies in recent history under Canada's anti-combines legislation. Nevertheless, mass media owners continue to argue that the freedom essential to a democratic press is threatened by excessive use of government power. Canada now has a relatively new Competition Act that appears potentially more effective. Until 1990, however, no major cases had been pursued under the provisions of the Act.

The tensions between mass media institutions and government exist at many levels and are not likely to be resolved by allowing private corporations a free hand to operate mass media outlets. The position of public corporations and their relationships to government are also complex, although the tensions tend to focus on areas other than freedom of the press, such as public funding and accountability. The CBC in particular has a long history of difficulties in maintaining the proper balance between political freedom and public accountability.

Legal Influences. A third influence on the mass media is that of the legal system, in particular the decisions of the courts. One obligation of the courts is to interpret existing statutes in instances where specific mass media practitioners or owners are thought to have operated outside the law. A much more widespread influence on content, however, has to do with various sections of the criminal and civil codes that cover such offences as sedition, promulgating obscenity, propagating hate literature, and issuing false messages. Court decisions on cases of these kinds tend to influence all mass media practitioners – particularly journalists – and are used as indicators to guide future actions taken in the selection of media content.

Audience Influences. The fourth outside influence on the mass media is the audience. Denis McQuail (1983, pp. 168-70) has suggested that the audience can influence media content in six different ways.

1. *As critics and fans,* audience members can comment (often approvingly) on the nature of specific content pieces or content producers. Numerous publications exist to reflect critics' opinions and the preferences of fans regarding media content. Such material is now becoming more common on television and radio, not just in print. The extent to which critics or fans influence future actions is debatable; it seems more likely the value of both is to endorse the present practices of mass media operations.

2. Through *institutionalized accountability* audience members can seek to influence mass media organizations. This is often easier to do with public corporations than private corporations. In Canada, the CRTC is obliged to regulate the broadcasting system "in the public interest" and, in doing so, seeks the opinions and preferences of viewers and listeners across the country. For the printed media, press councils – made up of representatives of owners, journalists, and the public – can act on behalf of readers who complain about specific content in newspapers.

3. Through the *market,* audience members can choose between media outlets and, through such choices, determined by ratings data, exert some influence on the mass media. However, any individual audience member acting simply as a single member of the audience cannot exert much influence by this means. So far, it has proved to be impossible for audiences to organize collectively and speak with a united voice on their preferences.

4. Through *direct feedback* to mass media outlets audiences can make their views known and hope to influence future actions. "Letters to the editor" are the standard form of feedback for the press while broadcasting stations rely on phone calls. The representative character of this feedback to indicate overall audience satisfaction or dissatisfaction must be questioned, since

editors select the letters to be published and radio station talk-show hosts, for example, choose who will get on the air and who will not.

5. Through the use of *audience images* formed in the minds of content producers the audience can influence media content. However, these images are constructs formed by the producers out of what may be very limited or non-existent contact with significant numbers of audience members. Producers may construct images of audiences similar to themselves and thus take insufficient account of the needs or preferences of other kinds of people.

6. Through *audience research* mass media practitioners can gain a more precise idea of audience interests and responses to specific media content. However, as McQuail points out, the type of audience most likely to be influential is that which can be delineated with statistical findings (audience size and breakdown) and conducted by the media organization itself. Qualitative research or that done by outside bodies is much less likely to affect the behaviour of mass media practitioners – especially if the research findings do not match the practitioners' own views about audience preferences.

The Influences of Media Professionals. To this point we have been looking at outside influences on the operation of mass media organizations. Of course, the internal structures of these organizations and the people who work in them also exert considerable influence on the mass media systems. Journalists and other media professionals are directly engaged in the production and processing of media content. They do this within an organizational structure, operated by media management, that may have several levels to it.

Above the managerial levels are the ultimate owners of the media corporations (or the owners' representatives). In the case of public corporations, the owners are the taxpaying public, but through Parliament and other governmental bodies responsibility lies with a governing board of some type – usually a board of directors. In the case of private corporations, the owners are shareholders or individual entrepreneurs (usually the former). Shares may be widely held among many investors or closely held by the members of a particular family. Owners may be actively involved in management of the media corporation or may rely largely or even entirely on senior managers. Internally, media corporations can be viewed as social systems with their own structures and history.

Besides these general internal role categories, many specific roles are played out, sometimes in print but more often in broadcasting organizations. The program directors, producers, executive producers, program assistants, editors, technical people, and sales managers all have at least a dual allegiance to their profession and to the company for which they work. How they play out these roles, and the social system that emerges within the corporation, can influence greatly the resulting output of the station, network, or paper. Of particular interest is the way creative people are attracted to organizations that must use, but inevitably restrict, their creativity. Gallagher (in Gurevitch *et al.,* 1982) provides an insightful account of how these individuals and their organizations negotiate in such a way that there is control and predictability over programs and at the same time room for creativity.

6. Information and Entertainment, Images and Symbols

We cannot afford to be ambitious in an outline of what constitutes information and entertainment, images and symbols. All four terms have dozens of different meanings and usages that we might discuss. Information theory, for example, might be claimed to be the very foundation of communications as a discipline. Our discussion of these four terms therefore will be limited, providing only the simplest of outlines of their meaning.

The inclusion of the four terms is meant to distinguish the activities of the media from other industrial activities. As a group the terms tell us that the media do not distribute material goods such as washing machines, soap powders, or clothing. While media products may have a materiality in the sense that they may be videocassettes, tapes, records, books, magazines, etc., their materiality is incidental to their central identity, the information (in the broad and formal sense of the word) they carry.

The words **information** and **entertainment** are to be taken in a narrow sense. On television, for instance, we are given information (news and current affairs) and entertainment (sitcoms, drama, etc.) programming. In newspapers, the same two words cover, on the one side, news, opinions found in editorials and columns, advertisements, and even the comics, and on the other, travel, leisure, gossip, columns, and the comics. Similarly, the words can be stretched a bit to cover, say, a mixture of non-fiction and fiction articles in a magazine such as *Saturday Night*. The content of the mass media brings us direct reports on the real world in information programming and indirect reports on the warp and woof of living in entertainment programs.

To say that the mass media convey **images** and **symbols** is to look at content from a different angle. Whether through words or pictures, in print or electronically, the mass media present us with images of the world. There are two classes of images, both of which we discuss in Chapter 4. The first is **denotative**, i.e., those which are explicit, objective, there for anyone to see. A descriptive analysis of a photograph identifying the various elements or a rational argument presents us with denotative images. The second class of images is the **connotative** associations that are implied and/or that we infer from the context that surrounds the denotative images. The focus of our discussion, and the emphasis in communications literature, is on connotative images. Such images may arise from rhetorical argument. They may have a visual base and derive from the composition of a still photograph or from the timing and juxtaposition of a series of video shots, or even from the layout of a printed page. Although very different in their sources, all of these can be considered as connotative images.

Symbols can include everything from the letters of the alphabet to something as complex as an icon. Here we use the term in a general sense, stressing the interpretive tendencies of the audience. Thus, at every level of our existence from the biological through the psychological, the social, the cultural, the political, and so forth, the meaning of a symbol is an interaction between the composition of the image and the interpretive predispositions of the audience. A death mask has a biological base; a flag has a socio-cultural as well as an aesthetic base; an appeal to democratic rights has a political base. A synonym for symbolic meaning is connotative value.

The images the media present are rich in their symbolic meaning or connotative value whether or not the media intend them to be. To some degree, the success of all media products, from movies through books to television stations and newspapers, depends on the presentation of images that are layered with symbolic meaning.

Without proceeding too far into a discussion of the significance of images and symbols, we should note that the sum of the meaning of the images and symbols presented to us by the media represents the ideological currents of society, at least those ideological currents that find their way into mass media form. Given that, the media play a fundamental role in articulating and consolidating ideological control in society.

7. The Mass Audience

The word "mass" implies large numbers. In some sense it might be best for us to leave the meaning of the word at that. However, like information, entertainment, images, and symbols, the word carries much more with it in the many uses to which it is put. At a basic level there is a value connotation; the negative is related to the mob, the positive, to the wisdom of the aggregate.

In an early article Blumer (1939) contrasted a number of different kinds of collectivities to arrive at a meaning for "mass." Simplifying and adapting Blumer's ideas somewhat, we can say that in a **small group** all members know each other and are aware of their common membership. The **crowd** is limited to a single physical space, is temporary in its existence and composition, and if it acts, it does so non-rationally. The **public** is customarily large, widely dispersed. It is often represented by largely self-appointed "informed" people who speak publicly and in rational discourse to validate their statements and appointment. As McQuail (1983) summarizes Blumer on "mass":

> The term 'mass' captures several features of the new audience for cinema and radio which were missing or not linked together by any of these three existing concepts. It was often very large – larger than most groups, crowds or publics. It was very widely dispersed and its members were usually unknown to each other or to whoever brought the audience into existence. It lacked self-awareness and self-identity and was incapable of acting together in an organized way to secure objectives. It was marked by a shifting composition within changing boundaries. It did not act for itself, but was rather 'acted upon.' It was heterogeneous, in consisting of large numbers from all social strata and demographic groups, but homogeneous in its behaviour of choosing a particular object of interest and in the perception of those who would like to 'manipulate' it.

The above differentiations of collectivities are useful for an understanding of the mass audience, especially in an historical context. While a discussion of various schools of thought on society and culture is outside the realm of this text, one school of thought, the **Frankfurt School**, saw the media as weaning the mass or common folk away from their "organic" society and, in so weaning them, depriving them of their place in a rich and stable culture. Other theorists on elite culture have also seen the media as debasing culture, as pandering to the uncritical side of the common person. The Soviets, of course, see the term "mass" in a favourable way at least for public and Western consumption.

In this book we attempt to go beyond the notion of the mass audience as an amorphous collectivity while nevertheless attending to certain undeniable aspects of its identity as outlined by Blumer. This treatment falls close to the notion of mass culture as popular culture, for the activities and tastes of the mainstream of society are communicated through its dominant institutions. Media-audience relations are a particular focus in Chapter 5.

THE MASS MEDIA IN CANADIAN SOCIETY

A conceptual definition, such as the one preceding, is absolutely necessary for understanding the nature of the mass media. However, the mass media are not global institutions. Nor are they organized haphazardly, sometimes crossing international boundaries, sometimes not. Nor are they run by renegade individuals who have no relation or allegiance to any society. The mass media are nationally organized private and public-sector institutions that, in comparison with each other, have both distinctive and shared characteristics.

To add to our understanding of the mass media we will examine one example – the mass media of Canada. We will discuss major elements of their formation and operation, such as their technological make-up, economic size, and cultural sensitivity. In doing so we will lay the groundwork for an understanding of how other national mass media interact with the societies in which they exist.

A Distinctive Communication Challenge

At the beginning of any introduction to or overview of communication in Canada we are told that Canada has a set of distinctive characteristics that are relevant to the understanding of the communications system that has evolved in the country. The first characteristic is the *vastness of the country*. This vastness is tied to a second element, the *small size of Canada's population*. Together and separately these two variables are particularly significant in the development of communications systems. On the one hand Canada's geography has required expensive per-capita transmission systems so that the country can stay in touch with itself. For example, following the establishment of a transcontinental railway in 1885 came a transatlantic radio link in 1901, a trans-Canada radio network in 1927, a trans-Canada telephone network in 1932, a transcontinental television service in 1958, a domestic geostationary communications satellite in 1972, and the first

nation-wide digital data system in 1973 *(The Challenge of Communication,* DOC).

Each of these developments was cause for some rejoicing and some sense of pride. But in another sense they were comparatively insignificant. One would hardly expect major objections to a microwave link capable of bringing national television to over 70 per cent of the country. But what of a service for other Canadians, those who live beyond the ribbon of population within 100 miles of the Canada-U.S. border? Perhaps a cause for greater celebration has been the commitment by Parliament through the CBC to provide Canadian broadcasting for all Canadians. This is such a significant achievement because the provision of broadcast services to such a widely dispersed population represents a firm national public cultural commitment – it is a commitment that can never be paid for by those who benefit from it.

A third significant characteristic, derivative in part from the size of the country, is our *regionality*. Canada is not just a country of physical geographic variety; it is a country of regional cultures. It is instructive to think back to Confederation to realize that Canada is an amalgam of communities. To the original four colonies to join Confederation – Upper Canada, Lower Canada, Nova Scotia, and New Brunswick – were added in later years other distinct colonies and communities, such as British Columbia and Newfoundland. A national will to develop a country separate from the United States and late nineteenth-century settlement led to other communities in Prince Edward Island and the Prairies joining Confederation.

For these disparate communities to thrive within a nation required means of internal communication and of initiating communication with other regions of Canada. Messages could not be generated from a central point and merely fed to outlying regions. The regions themselves needed to generate their own information for internal use and for the edification of the country as a whole.

Canada is also a nation of *two official languages*. The right to speak either English or French is now enshrined in our constitution. But Canadians have committed themselves to more than a freedom for individuals. They have committed themselves to providing various federal government services, including broadcasting, in both official languages. As with the example of the North, in certain communities no one could ever expect that the audience would pay for the cost of service in its own official language. The criteria guiding these decisions were not economic but rather political and cultural. Bilingual government services and French and English broadcasting channels (not just programs) are a symbol of the right of any Canadian to live and work wherever he or she may wish. They are also a continual reminder to all that we are a bilingual country.

The natural extension of the respect for plurality built into the notions of regional cultures, the extension of broadcasting services to the far reaches of our country, and bilingual services, given the extent and patterns of immigration to Canada, is a *multicultural policy*. Although it is long in coming and still severely underfunded, we are beginning to see an acceptance of the desirability of tailoring programming to various ethnic communities. While these television services are mostly distributed by cable rather than broadcast (and are therefore not available to everyone), ethnic radio services are broadcast. Together these services represent a beginning commitment to what is accepted general government policy, a commitment to multiculturalism.

A final, never-to-be-forgotten characteristic of Canada's communications environment is its *proximity to the U.S.* Together with our acceptance of much the same basic political and economic philosophy and the resulting fairly open border, this proximity has led to a massive interpenetration between our two countries of both products and ideas. More American television programming is available to the vast majority of Canadians than is Canadian programming. On most private radio stations, more American material is available to listeners than Canadian material. On virtually all magazine racks in Canada more American magazines are available to the reader than Canadian magazines, in spite of the fact that over 200 magazines are published in Canada. More American authors are read by the average Canadian school child than Canadian authors. And on the story goes. Our proximity to the U.S. and the resultant spill-over of American cultural products comprise a major factor to be taken into account in considering Canada's communications environment.

Historical Roots

A large part of the early history of the media in Canada focuses on newspapers and journalism. In W.H. Kesterton's *A History of Journalism in Canada* we learn something of the role of newspapers and journalism in the formation and development of our nation. To provide an overview, Kesterton describes press history by means of an organic metaphor that includes four stages of growth. The first period, 1752-1807, he calls the "Transplant Period," a transplant of a New England adaptation of a British activity. The second period, 1807-1858, is "Thickening Growth," the third, 1858-1900, "Western Transplant and Spreading Growth," and the fourth period, 1900-1967, "The Mutation." This last period constitutes a mutation because it was characterized by a dramatic decline in the number of newspapers although not a parallel decline in overall readership and became, essentially, a mutation into mass communications. Large-scale corporations developed on the achievements of a host of idealistic entrepreneurs and built distribution to large populations.

It appears from Kesterton's study that the basic principles of press operation in Canada evolved from struggles fought elsewhere. These principles were not then critically re-examined for their appropriateness to the Canadian environment. Rather, it was more a case of trying to find a way of adhering to the principles in spite of the lack of journalistic evolution within Canada. The situation was most apparent, for example, in the operation of the principle of **freedom of the press**.

Freedom of the press reflects an acceptance of an underlying principle that competing elites should have access to the general audience. Viewed from the perspective of the audience, it enshrines the principle of exposure to an ideological spectrum within which individual ideas and policies can be considered. Struggles to establish freedom of the press do not arise from considered allegiance to abstract ideas. They evolve out of distinct elites, each of which feels the need for press access and access to the public. Similarly, although historically later in the development of the press, the call by journalists for the recognition of their ideals as distinct from the interests of owners springs not so much from insightful analysis but rather from the establishment of a profession independent and distinct from an owning group. What owner-editor-reporter, however philosophical, is going to call for a recognition of the distinctive set of interests for each of the many roles she or he plays?

Liberal Principles in a Conservative State

Canadian press history is distinctive because of the acceptance of liberal principles of press operation and press freedom prior to the evolution of sufficient power by the relevant groups to demand and enforce recognition of these principles. Thus, while printers were still dependent on government printing contracts, the principle of free comment (meaning, often, anti-government comment) by newssheet printers was, at times at least, given grudging recognition. The achievement that characterizes Canadian press history over the years is the establishment of administrative arrangements that restrain the tendency of those with power, governments especially, to act in their own narrow and short-term interest. To be specific, there were just not enough printers to serve the various competing interests Canadians could recognize but which had yet to establish themselves. This principle of action, which runs through much of Canadian communications history, might be called an **enlightened keeping up with the Joneses**. That is, as a colony of Great Britain, dominated by a political elite enfranchised by their class connections to England, Canada and Canadians strove to remain abreast of the progress toward modern liberal democracy – specifically, the liberal political thought and social policies as they were being written about and put into practice in the mother country. When the enactment of liberal principles became too slow in Britain, Canada turned to the United States for models. Translated into principles for press policies, certain groups were continually having to constrain their potential power to act because of broader principles reflective of the interests of the community as they were being articulated in other countries in the writings of liberal theorists. Perhaps on the basis of this principle a case can be made that we Canadians have a distinctive perspective and thus a unique contribution to make within a discourse on technology (see Kroker, 1984).

THE CONTEMPORARY CANADIAN MASS MEDIA

As should be apparent, there is a dynamic tension in an "enlightened keeping up with the Joneses." At times enlightened liberalism may hold sway; at other times, keeping up with the Joneses by itself may claim the day. The complexity of the modern mass media is sufficient for both these tendencies to be in play.

A Technological High Road

The Jones side of the principle appears to manifest itself in our actions with regard to technology. The Canadian government, in co-operation with Canadian communications industries, has committed Canada to a technological high road – to remaining abreast of the most advanced communications systems available. This commitment is not entirely intended to serve the cultural needs of Canada and Canadians, in spite of rhetoric used to justify each new major expenditure. It is intended, rather, to serve industrial development interests. In keeping up with developing technologies the government has a showpiece of national unity and also a job creation program of considerable power. Jobs are created directly and numerous spin-off technologies lead to the creation of new industries, products, and hence jobs in the information sector. Not insignificantly, it also is a vivid demonstration to the average Canadian that he or she has access to an equal or superior range of programs and services than does the average American.

However, in pursuing such technologies, Canada finds its hardware commitments and industrial and economic needs taking precedence over its cultural needs. The result is an information environment that at once keeps us abreast industrially of the most advanced nations and at the same time opens us to inundation by their cultural products. Our hardware commitments mean that we end up oversupplying ourselves with channels for other people's information.

In face of this technological overcapacity we are encouraged to allow any producer who can assemble an audience for any message that does not run counter to basic political or social beliefs to claim the right to be granted access to a channel of communication and to sell the assembled audience to any buyer. This is a magnanimous gesture only beginning to be tried out by some other countries such as France and Britain. And as they remove restrictions on cable and satellite telev ision and loosen non-tariff barriers in other media, they discuss their actions as "Canadianization."

Some would claim that our approach to technology and unimpeded access for program producers to Canadian audiences does not err on the Jones side of the equation but is a good balance between the Jones side and the liberal side. Their justification is based on the argument that keeping abreast of technology has stimulated and will continue to stimulate the Canadian economy, and Canadian society has thus reaped benefits. While economic benefits can be identified, the present state of Canadian cultural industries, together with surveys of television viewing, challenges such an interpretation.

A Cultural Low Road

In 1983 Paul Audley wrote a report for the Canadian Institute for Economic Policy called *Canada's Cultural Industries*. In his report he provided an exhaustive analysis of the production, distribution, and consumption of cultural products in Canada. The four areas he concentrated on were publishing, film, records, and

TABLE 2.3

Publishing, Recording, Film, and Broadcasting: Estimated Canadian Market, 1980* ($millions)

Daily newspapers	advertising	987.3
	circulation	266.1
		1,253.4
Periodicals	advertising	276.3
	circulation*	400.0
		676.3
Books		931.7
Records/Tapes		265.1
Film	NFB (net cost of operations)	37.4
	private distributors:	
	a. theatrical	115.3
	b. television	103.7
	c. non-theatrical	26.9
		283.3
Radio (private)	advertising	392.0
	production and other	5.7
		397.7
Television (private)	advertising	510.0
	production and other	52.1
		562.1
CBC (radio and television)	advertising	100.9
	net cost of operations	542.9
	production and other	3.7
		647.5
Cable television		352.2
Sub-totals by source	advertising consumption,	2,266.5
	production, and other	2,522.0
	government subsidy	
	(film and TV only)	580.3
Total expenditure		5,368.8

* Estimates are derived as follows: Total spent by Canadian advertisers by medium plus *wholesale* revenue by medium form total sales in the Canadian market, plus government expenditure for broadcasting and NFB.
** Periodical circulation revenue is difficult to estimate. The estimate of $400 million is a cautious estimate based on reported revenue for Canadian periodicals of $121 million and imports valued for customs purposes at $277 million.
SOURCE: Paul Audley, *Canada's Cultural Industries* (Toronto: James Lorimer, 1983).

TABLE 2.4

Domestic Share by Origin of Content*
(percentages)

	Original Canadian Material	Adapted Foreign Material	Foreign Material
Newspapers			
Domestic coverage	close to 100		
Foreign coverage	0-5		95-100
Magazines	29.0	25	46.0
Books	16.1	4.4	79.5
Records	6.8		93.2
Radio**			
AM-music	30.0		70.0
talk	90-100		0-5
FM-music	10-30		70-90
talk	95-100		0-5
Film***			
Theatrical market	1.8		98.2
Television market	7.3		92.7
Non-theatrical	41.2		58.8
Television English****			
News information, current affairs	90.5		9.5
All entertainment	11.6		88.4
Dramatic entertainment	4.0		96.0
All viewing	30.5		69.5
Television French****			
News, information, current affairs	100.0		0.0
All entertainment	39.8		60.2
All viewing	54.2		45.8

* Figures for newspapers and radio are estimates based on general industry studies.
** Based on percentages of air-time.
*** Based on distributors' royalties, rentals, and commissions.
**** Based on audience viewing, 1978.
SOURCE: Audley, *Canada's Cultural Industries,* which used: Statistics Canada for books, records, and film; CRTC for radio and television; Audit Bureau of Circulations for magazines (consumer only); and the Davey and Kent Commission for newspapers.

broadcasting. In his final chapter he provides an overview, with recommendations, based on two summary tables of data and projections. Those two tables are reproduced here.

At first glance both of Audley's tables seem to be too general for our purposes. Table 2.3, which shows the extent of expenditures Canadians make in consuming cultural products, gives us only the size of the overall market. Table 2.4, which tells us the degree to which we produce content for our own domestic market, breaks down the data into categories of content only to a certain degree. How, therefore, can we look at regionality, bilingualism, multiculturalism, vastness, and dispersion with such gross figures?

The figures themselves provide part of the answer. While Table 2.3 gives us an estimate of the size of each medium, Table 2.4 tells us how much foreign material is to be found in each. If newspapers and radio talk and information programming are excluded, the average amount of foreign content is just over 75 per cent. Where this 75 per cent rule does not apply is in talk shows and information programming, i.e., the news and commentary we produce about ourselves and the world. Talk shows speak for themselves as contributors to the community. With regard to information programming, lest we be too optimistic, it is important to remember that we rely heavily on global and U.S. news wire and television news-gathering systems, a reliance that is not reflected in Audley's data.

How then can we be said to have designed a communications system to respond to our distinctiveness? Our response, it would seem, has been a massive program of importation of foreign cultural products. The distinctive attributes that characterize Canadian communications are to be found within the 25 per cent margin and within information programming.

Our regionality and our particular form of multiculturalism are continually underplayed, while our proximity and commonality with the United States, its culture, and its regionalism and multiculturalism are continually overplayed. Our dispersion is dealt with through hardware and the national broadcasting system commitments mentioned earlier, and our bilingualism by a dual national broadcasting system in English and French, a system that at once emphasizes our linguistic distinctiveness and separates us internally.

Even from a perspective that uses such gross figures as those of Audley, we can already see how major distinctive features such as regionalism and multiculturalism are bound to be influenced by notions of these factors as they exist in foreign countries, notably the U.S. The U.S., after all, has three times as much access to Canadian audiences as we give ourselves (i.e., 75 per cent versus our 25 per cent). Even with the "system commitment" we have given to bilingualism or population dispersion, such factors as regionalism, for example, have to compete for the attention of the viewer. That competition takes us immediately into the economic reality of program production, that is, the amount of money we can afford to invest in programming, an economic reality euphemistically referred to as quality of programming or production values.

These issues have been discussed in two papers, one by Alison Beale and the second by Robert Babe. Beale provides an overview of how Canadians have transformed a vast geography into a social space. Babe identifies patterns in the history of communications in Canada and concludes that the telegraph, telephone services, and broadcasting have all led not to national integration but to integration with the United States (Lorimer and Wilson, 1988).

Junior Partners in Our Own Cultural Enterprise

Audley's data point out that we are junior partners in our own cultural enterprise. Uniquely Canadian viewpoints expressed through Canadian creative artists hold a consistent minority position not just in comparison with foreign expressions but specifically with American cultural expression. Nor is there any saving grace in aspects of cultural production that Audley did not examine. In the arts themselves, such as the visual arts, dance, or theatre, the ratio of Canadian work to foreign and American work is no better (see Crean, 1976). In education (see Mathews and Steele, 1971; Symons, 1975; Symons and Page, 1984; Lorimer, 1984) the situation is again the same. The degree of commitment of all levels of government to the development and communication of social science and humanities knowledge is paltry compared to what comes into the country on purchase. One other aspect of our junior partnership needs mention. With so much cultural spillover Canadian cultural creators cannot help but be tempted to address particular themes selected, by repetition if nothing else, as salient by foreign, i.e., American, cultural producers. Audley's data do not address that manifestation of our proximity to the U.S.

We always have been and we probably always will remain a net importer of information. We survive, as other nations survive, as a net importer because the saving grace of any community or sovereign nation is that culture and cultural sovereignty are founded to a significant degree in the day-to-day personal relations and interactions each of us has with our fellow nationals. We survive also because we have the power, in some cases in our own minds and in some cases through business and government, to transform the information we import

and use it to our own advantage. Polls consistently show Canada gains enormously from the knowledge of other nations, especially the United States, primarily because the U.S. is such an open society. We have almost immediate access to much American-produced information, whether on the weather, international affairs, market projections, historical analysis, or even entertainment. As luck would have it, we also have the economic resources to set our minds and our computers to make that information work for us. But we still remain net importers of information and cultural products, products that each day influence our ideas, priorities, politics, personal ambitions, and sense of the world.

INFORMATION NEEDS, COMMUNICATIONS ACTUALITIES, AND THE UNITED NATIONS

Because of our proximity to the U.S., many Canadians equate international relations with Canadian-American relations. We tend to assume that other foreign countries behave more like the United States than they do like Canada. We also tend to believe that the U.S. behaves in a manner consistent with its ideology of free enterprise and free trade. We tend to be surprised when other countries are similar to Canada and not surprised when they are similar to the U.S. We are often surprised to hear that other countries have stronger restrictions to the importation of cultural goods than does Canada.

Most of the time these assumptions are wrong. The United States is only one of many sovereign nations and an extremely unusual one at that. It is a leader of one way of looking at the world, a perspective that emphasizes the freedom of the individual to act as he or she pleases and specifically to engage in business enterprise of any kind without interference of the state on behalf of the general or community interest.

Because the United States is such a large and powerful nation it is in a position to benefit from the energies of its citizens as they pursue their own economic self-interest. Given a hospitable climate, a rich resource base, the freedom to pursue one's own interest without fear of interference from the state, a large home market, a place at the leading edge of technology and of consumption, it is very much in the interest of the United States and Americans as a whole to pursue an ideology of freedom of enterprise and of free trade in goods of all sorts. Basically, this allows them to sell goods developed for the American market in foreign countries. The development of the technology is already paid for. All that is required is run-on production or perhaps the shipping of manufacturing equipment to another country.

The structure of production and marketing in cultural products does not differ significantly from the production and marketing of any other product. The consumption of cultural products does. While any product has a cultural component in its very existence, but more noticeably in its style (think of Italian-designed furniture or automobile bodies), a cultural product is almost pure information or pure culture. In consuming it we consume attitudes, perceptions, ideas, a world view, and so forth. To the extent that these products are created by other cultures, they may clash with our own cultural values. In some senses, as noted earlier, they may threaten to extinguish local culture. In fact, even if they do not clash with our own visions, when they seem to fit right into our own cultural viewpoint, they may twist and pull our culture in directions that only years from now we come to understand were not in keeping with other fundamentals that we hold dear.

Such issues do not reflect merely a Canadian paranoia. Recently, for example, we have begun to hear Americans crying out against foreign inundation of their country through purchases of key businesses in such fields as entertainment and real estate. In early 1990, for instance, the U.S. was considering legislation to restrict foreign ownership of cable companies. We do not hear Americans crying out about the inundation of foreign ideas (unless, of course, they are Communist ideas), because the United States dominates the information and entertainment markets internationally and imports a very small percentage of content. If we assume that few other nations share our concern it is not surprising because that information never reaches us. But virtually every other nation of the world, including the U.S.S.R. and China, is concerned by the inundation of its culture by foreign ideas, especially American ideas. This concern does not mean that they hate the Americans or even that they are anti-American, but rather that they are committed to the preservation of their own culture and nation. Their position is that if their citizens are fed a constant diet of American cultural products they will want to live like Americans; they will tend to assume that their own institutions are equivalent in function and intent to American institutions and if they are not that there is something wrong with their institutions. This perspective may be defined as pure political self-interest. But it may also be seen, more idealistically, as a commitment to a pluralistic world society in all its heterogeneity. It can readily be argued that in such heterogeneity is to be found a different level of human freedom, the freedom of communities.

Canada's Concerns and the Concerns of UNESCO

The similarity of Canada's position to that of other foreign countries (except the United States) provides any Canadian examining United Nations research studies with a sense of recognition. What those documents reflect is that every country has a distinctive cultural environment to which it can respond with the design of a particular communication system. Each country must design its communication system with elements of domestic production and elements of foreign production in mind. Accordingly, each must take into account a parallel set of distinctive qualities and production capabilities as we have put forward here in considering Canada's communication environment.

Because our fate is a common one (internationally), considerable discussion has been generated within the United Nations about communications needs, communications problems, national sovereignty, and so forth. Much of this discussion has taken place under the auspices of UNESCO and is specifically included in the MacBride Report on communications problems and prospects. As the MacBride Report indicates, *each nation needs a national information generation policy*. A nation must have the capacity to take information produced by the world community and analyse it according to national needs and priorities. While Canada has not fully committed itself to this need, along with a few other developed nations, Canada is in the happy position of being economically able to work toward an information infrastructure oriented to its national needs and the maintenance of its independence. Being already committed as we are to hardware development and hence technologi-

cal sophistication in communications, being economically well-off, and being the forward shock troops for the U.S. cultural barrage, we are in a position to lead in such an endeavour for our own ends and for the benefit of other nations.

SUMMARY

This chapter began with a conceptualization of mass communication. From an introduction that emphasized historical examples, we then turned to modern society. Following others, we proposed a model of social behaviour and media process in which the two were interlinked to a degree that the media could not be separated from the rest of society and said to be a self-contained set of entities. We concluded this first section with a formal definition of mass communication.

We then turned to the mass media, in some sense the set of institutions that are the backbone of modern mass communication. We set out a formal definition of the mass media and spent the bulk of the chapter explicating the basic elements of that definition. The mass media were put forward as a distinct set of activities, involving particular technological configurations, associated with formally constituted institutions, acting according to certain laws, rules, and understandings, carried out by persons occupying certain roles, which together convey information, entertainment, images, and symbols to a mass audience.

With this formal definition in place, in the context of mass communication in general, we then moved to a description of the particulars of the Canadian mass media – how they respond to the geographic, demographic, and historical realities of Canada, the degree to which Canada has committed itself to the use of advanced technology, and the degree of commitment to the production of content in broadcasting and the cultural industries. The chapter concluded with a brief discussion of the relation between Canadian concerns and realities in communications and those of other nations.

REFERENCES

Audley, Paul. *Canada's Cultural Industries.* Toronto: James Lorimer, 1983.

Babe, R. "Emergence and development of Canadian communications: technology, industry and government," in R. Lorimer and D.C. Wilson, eds., *Communication Canada.* Toronto: Kagan and Woo, 1988.

Beale, A. "The question of space," in Lorimer and Wilson, eds., *Communication Canada.*

Bennett, Tony. "Media, 'Reality', and Signification," in M. Gurevitch *et al.,* eds., *Culture, Society and the Media.* Toronto: Methuen, 1982.

Berger, Peter, and Thomas Luckmann. *Social Construction of Reality: A Treatise on the Sociology of Knowledge.* New York: Doubleday, 1966.

Blumer, H. "The Mass, the Public, and Public Opinion," in A.M. Lee, ed., *New Outlines in the Principles of Sociology.* New York: Barnes and Noble, 1939.

Canada, Department of Communication. *The Challenge of Communication,* videotape.

Canada. *Report of the Task Force on Broadcasting Policy.* Ottawa: Ministry of Supply and Services, 1986.

Canada. *Royal Commission on Newspapers.* Hull, Quebec: Canadian Government Publishing Centre, 1981.

Crean, S.M. *Who's Afraid of Canadian Culture?* Don Mills, Ontario: General Publishing, 1976.

Curran, James. "Communications, Power, and Social Order," in Gurevitch *et al.,* eds., *Culture, Society and the Media.*

Desbarats, P. *Guide to Canadian News Media.* Toronto: Harcourt Brace Jovanovich, 1990.

Eco, Umberto. "The Multiplication of the Media," in Eco, *Travels in Hyperreality.* New York: Harcourt Brace Jovanovich, 1986.

Gallagher, Margaret. "Negotiation of Control in Media Organizations and Occupations," in Gurevitch *et al.,* eds., *Culture, Society and the Media.*

Hall, Stuart. "The Rediscovery of 'Ideology': Return of the Repressed in Media Studies," in Gurevitch *et al.,* eds., *Culture, Society and the Media.*

Kesterton, W.H. *A History of Journalism in Canada.* Toronto: McClelland and Stewart, 1967.

Lorimer, R. *The Nation in the Schools: Wanted – A Canadian Education.* Toronto: OISE Press, 1984.

Lorimer, R., and Donald C. Wilson, eds. *Communication Canada.* Toronto: Kagan and Woo, 1988.

Mathews, R., and J. Steele. *The Struggle for Canadian Universities.* Toronto: New Press, 1971.

McQuail, Denis. *Mass Communication Theory: An Introduction.* Beverly Hills: Sage Publications, 1983.

O'Sullivan, T., J. Hartley, D. Saunders, and J. Fiske. *Key Concepts in Communication.* Toronto: Methuen, 1983.

Salter, L. "Reconceiving the public in public broadcasting," in Lorimer and Wilson, eds., *Communication Canada.*

Smythe, Dallas. *Dependency Road: Communications, Capitalism, Consciousness, and Canada.* Norwood, New Jersey: Ablex Publishing, 1981.

Symons, T.H.B. *To Know Ourselves: The Report of the Commission on Canadian Studies, 2* vols. Ottawa: Association of Universities and Colleges of Canada, 1975.

Symons, T.H.B., and J.E. Page. *Some Questions of Balance: Higher Education and Canadian Studies.* Ottawa: AUCC, 1984.

Williams, Raymond. *Television: Technology and Cultural Form.* New York: Schoken Books, 1975.

STUDY QUESTIONS

1. What seven elements are there to a definition of the media? Explain them and comment on the appropriateness of such a definition.
2. Do you think the content of media messages penetrates our lives to as great an extent as Christianity or any other major religion does?
3. How does the Broadcasting Act impinge on your own television and radio watching and listening?
4. What are the defining characteristics of Canada's information environment?
5. Why is it important for Canada or for any other country to have control over its own system of communication?

CHAPTER

3

Politics and the Mass Media

INTRODUCTION

MUCH OF THE information disseminated by the mass media is political in the broad sense of being concerned with the political state. The main components of the state are: the legislature, the judicial system, the executive government, and the bureaucratic system that underpins the government, as well as state-owned corporations ("Crown corporations" in Canada) and other state-run institutions including prisons, hospitals, schools, transport systems, and so on. Other kinds of political information distributed by the mass media are usually regarded as partisan; they concern the political parties and their proposals for dealing with current public issues. In democratic countries with multi-party political systems, the government in power is always interested in conveying both its executive decisions and its partisan viewpoint; these two kinds of information are often difficult to disentangle.

The mass media are an indispensable part of a modern society's information system. The political significance of mass media in modern societies comes from their role in gathering, analysing, and managing current information on the public affairs of the nation. Individual citizens, social organizations, and businesses rely on the mass media to tell them what is going on in the political world. At the same time, the state apparatus relies on the media to be informed about what the society (variously described as "the people," "the nation," "the business community" and so on) believes about, and wants from, the state. Thus, the mass media are at the core of an interdependent information system that encompasses a whole society.

In *Politics and the News,* a basic reference for this chapter, Edwin Black (1982, p. 4) illustrates this perspective as follows:

> Significant political data, such (as) particular occurrences of political injustice, are communicated to a number of points in the circuit (citizens), dissatisfaction grows, and the system is unbalanced. Demands for change are generated and conveyed to a central accumulator or legislature. If the charge is great enough, it stimulates appropriate reactions and information flows until the system is balanced once again.

The concept of the mass media as a vital conduit between government and people in managing the political life of a society may seem to imply that the mass media are neutral conveyors of information. The media can appear to have no political agendas of their own (see Chapter 4), but this would be an incorrect conclusion to draw. As social institutions, the mass media are participants in the political and economic power of their society. It is often useful to regard the mass media as acting as extensions of government. On occasion, the mass media are unwitting allies of the government, at other times they are critics. In Western societies, the mass media are usually privately owned; where that is so, their owners' main concerns are with profits, advertisers, audiences, and entertainment. Whether privately or publicly owned, the mass media are an integral part of the political processes of government.

The concept of the mass media as the vital conduit of information between government and people can also be assumed to mean that the two-way flow of information works perfectly and equally in both directions. This would also be an incorrect conclusion to draw. The information from government to the citizens is generally vastly greater than from individual citizens to government. Powerful groups in society usually do not depend on the mass media to convey their points of view to government whereas the general public often does.

In a more closed society, the mass media are the only officially legitimized source of political information for the people. However, if the mass media are used by the government to convey only the information that makes the government look good, the people inevitably recognize the mass media for what they are – government information outlets – and may cease to believe what they are being told. In the long term, this can be dangerous for the state, as we have seen recently in Eastern Europe. What appears to have happened there is that people relied on friends and relations to relay more reliable information, or they turned to other mass communication sources (such as churches) thought to be untainted by association with the state. Other examples are the use of street posters, the publication of underground newspapers and books, and the organization of mass rallies in the streets of major cities. When people cease to use the mass media, the state can have great difficulty in finding out what the people are thinking because the mass media have been used for so long as one-way communication channels. In such a situation, a major political crisis only becomes apparent when mass rallies and other forms of protest become unstoppable.

The more open a society is to all voices, the more vital is the role of the mass media to keep it open and accessible. However, the mass media alone cannot create a more open society. Nor should they be expected to do this. The mass media do not stand aside from the social structures and expectations of the society in which they exist. The democratic traditions of a society have a great deal of influence on the precise role played by the mass media in that society. The political legitimacy of the mass media in a society such as Canada depends on a set of beliefs about the proper role of the mass media and on the actual performance of the mass media through Canadian history. As part of the Western world, Canada draws on the political history of Western European democracies; the Canadian mass media have grown out of that history also.

The purpose of this chapter is to provide the reader with a number of different perspectives from which to begin to analyse the complex relationships between the mass media and the government. Our first concern is with how democratic societies evolved in Western Europe and how "the press" acquired an identity and evolved as part of the democratic process. In this section, the particular social history of Europe is discussed from the liberal-pluralist, neo-Marxist, and Foucauldian perspectives. The second section discusses the four theories of the press first summarized by Siebert, Peterson, and Schramm in the 1950s. These theories, and more recent variants of them, are still widely used in Western countries to give a perspective on the role of the news media in different countries.

The third section of this chapter looks briefly at the structural-functional perspective on the relationship between mass media and Canadian

society. This is followed by an examination of the more specific relationship between "the press" (i.e., the news media) and the political sphere in Canada on which the press provides daily reports. A final section discusses the structure and functioning of the modern nation-state, such as Canada, and its use of the mass media for its own purposes.

EUROPEAN DEMOCRACIES AND INFORMATION

Modern Western democracy arose in Europe between the seventeenth and the beginning of the twentieth centuries, replacing the feudal system based on the concept of divine right of rulers. In the case of state rulers, democracies replaced feudalism both in monarchies, such as England and Denmark, and in republics, such as France. In the case of church rulers, divine right was effectively challenged by an informed individualistic or democratic ideology proposed as early as the sixteenth century by such Reformation leaders as Martin Luther (1483-1546). However, as the continuing existence of the Catholic Church attests, it was not replaced but only diminished in influence by the growth of the Protestant churches.

Democracy brought many changes to society, including an important change in the conception of who had the right, or who was fit, to rule. In more concrete words, it changed the concept of the qualifying attributes of rulers and thereby changed the qualifications necessary for membership in the ruling class.

Within feudalism the right to rule was passed on from father to son – rarely to a daughter – in a particular blood line that could be traced back to traditional rulers, who were ultimately "chosen by God" and were believed to hold the inherent ability to rule. Democratic societies, by contrast, are organized according to the belief that the people should rule and thus that a ruler should act in the name of the people. Therefore, a ruler must inspire the majority of the people with the confidence that he or she will govern in their best interests. When a leader and his/her government can no longer maintain that confidence (formally speaking, the confidence of the House of Commons or of a provincial legislature), the government resigns and an election is called.

This change in the concept of government was brought about largely by an expanding, materialist, prosperous, and educated bourgeoisie, which also urged the separation of church and state. These changes were only a part of a massive upheaval in European society as it evolved from an agrarian to an industrial society.

The profound political change from feudalism to democracy was based on the spread of knowledge, which allowed certain citizens enough education to govern affairs in the name of their peers and enabled other citizens to make an informed decision on who ought to rule. As a consequence, information institutions became, and have remained, essential to democracies because they inform the public about the important issues of the day and the various solutions proposed by the competing elites who wish to rule.

Early and Modern Democratic Information Institutions

Early political information institutions, especially in Western Europe, were owned and therefore closely aligned with political parties. In Britain, various newssheets and pamphlets were published by individuals and groups who wished to inform the public on political matters. A wealth of documentation prior to and including the beginnings of copyright tells us much about the various attempts by those in power to control the output of information by their rivals. One of the more ingenious devices was a tax on cheap paper.

The alignment of information production with particular political interests is no longer the dominant form, either in Western Europe or in Canada and the U.S. In the name of "objectivity" or freeing the press and the media from undue political influence, business has assumed an ownership role.

In summary, the West generally has seen control of information institutions come into the hands of large, private-sector corporations. This shift in control can be seen as (1) an evolution leading to a differentiation of political activities *per se* from information activities, as (2) the bringing of information creation and distribution into the sphere of the ascendant class in a capitalist society, the business class with its market orientation to production, distribution, and consumption (see Murdock, 1982), or as (3) a more complex phenomenon in which owners have come to exert some influence through their financial control while professional journalists, audiences, and the state also exert influence based on the role each plays in society.

The evolutionary view is consistent with a **liberal-pluralist** perspective; the emphasis on business reflects a **neo-Marxist** perspective; the more complex view is here termed a **Foucauldian** perspective, based on the writings of Michel Foucault (1978, 1980, 1982).

Perspectives on Mass Media and Government

The liberal pluralist perspective sees the Western mass media as one set of institutions and interests within the plurality of interests and institutions that make up a democratic society. From this perspective, journalism is often referred to as the **fourth estate** (the first three estates being the Church, the landowners, and the bourgeoisie). The interest of the fourth estate is the pursuit of information in the name of the public good. This role is legitimized by notions of free speech. (Note that political parties pursue power in the name of the public good!)

From a liberal-pluralist perspective, the Western mass media function to preserve liberal democracy – in other words, the political system within which they now exist. As watchdogs, they monitor abuse of power and attempt to ensure that the will of the people is carried out. This role assists in making governments and institutions flexible and sensitive to the changing needs of society. The media provide the information necessary for public participation in the political process and aid in the dissemination of information about public programs and services. In short, they provide citizens with information about matters that are part of the political and socio-economic system in which they live, yet which most citizens otherwise could not know from personal experience.

Neo-Marxists view the same activities quite differently, for this perspective does not assume the preservation of the present political system of Western democracies. Neo-Marxist analysts see the mass media as promoting the dominant ideology of a society. In the neo-Marxist framework, the media propose revisions to improve the existing political system rather than opting for a new, more equitable system.

In putting forward a limited range of ideas and analysis, the media, according to neo-Marxist theory, present different manifestations of the same basic ideology and, therefore, reinforce that ideology. The political alternatives they take seriously are the ideas of one of several entrenched but competing elites, all of whom are members of the same (ruling or dominant) social class. In short, they reflect the interest of their capitalist owners in maintaining a politically stable society.

According to Curran (1990), Foucauldians claim that many different power relationships are at play in different situations. "These cannot be subsumed, according to Foucault, within a binary and all encompassing opposition of class interests or traced to the mode of production and social formation. . . . The role of the media is (still) considered within the wider context of social contestation." As an example of this perspective, Curran cites the writings of John Fiske (1987, 1989a, 1989b, 1989c).

The liberal-pluralist, neo-Marxist, and Foucauldian views need not be seen as contradictory except in their assignment of fundamentals. Once their ideological stances are understood, they can be seen as describing the same phenomena from differing points of view. The conclusion one would draw from analysis of all three views is that the mass media serve to preserve and adapt particular versions of the democratic system by maintaining faith in its ideals while seeking, by exposure, to correct imperfections in the institutions that represent those ideals.

A WESTERN PERSPECTIVE ON PRESS SYSTEMS AROUND THE GLOBE

Views on the role of the mass media can also be applied more specifically to the press (i.e., the news media organizations). In representing a Western view of world press systems, the following perspective highlights assumptions built into the liberal-pluralist view of the role of the mass media. In *Four Theories of the Press*, Siebert, Peterson, and Schramm (1956, 1971) describe four different approaches to media ownership and control and the relation of these approaches to various political theories of press operation. The four theories they identify are:

- authoritarian theory
- Soviet Communist theory
- libertarian theory
- social responsibility theory.

Authoritarian and Soviet Communist Theories

The assumption of the **authoritarian theory** is that all power should rest with those who rule. Control of information can be seen as an extension of the power to rule. The government can explain how it sees things and why its policies are good ones. Such control can be exercised directly through ownership of the means of communication or indirectly through laws of various kinds, including taxes on paper or ink as well as censorship laws. Distribution channels can also be controlled through licences or quota requirements. It is interesting to know that, for a considerable period of history in England, the only means whereby an author could gain access to publication was through the patronage of some reputable person who also had the desire and means to underwrite the publication.

The **Soviet Communist press theory** is seen by these American theorists as an extension of the authoritarian theory. It developed both out of Marxist-Leninist understandings of the media in combination with current understandings of the role of media in society and out of a rejection of the mode of operation of the Western media as counter-revolutionary. In this theory, the purpose of the media is to support the efforts of the party and hence the government to administer society. It supports society as a whole, as opposed to the individual, but more specifically it supports the ruling elite.

In the Soviet system, the mass media are owned by the state while individual journalists must interpret events from the point of view of the state-owners. With respect to TASS and *Isvestia,* this means the government leaders. With respect to other papers, as in Western nations, the papers examine issues from the perspective of the sponsoring body, for instance, a union of workers.

In light of political challenges to the monopoly of power historically enjoyed by the Communist Party of the U.S.S.R. and Eastern Europe, it is interesting to speculate on how the role of journalists and the functions of the mass media are changing, and may change further, during the 1990s. Accounts at the beginning of the nineties suggest a newfound freedom and westernization of journalism. Yet as the Gorbachev revolution matures, what appears to be freedom may turn out to be an alliance between reformers and the mass media. That is, there may be a continuing close relationship between government authorities and the mass media that – only for a time – emulates Western pluralist values. Alternatively, it is possible that a relatively autonomous journalism profession is emerging and will be able to establish its independence in each of the Eastern European countries, including the U.S.S.R.

If we compare press systems on the basis of the representation of the interests of the state versus capitalist owners we do not find as large a difference as one might anticipate on the basis of the names given them in *Four Theories of the Press.* Because the interest of the state is to govern and that of the governors is to keep themselves in power, we can understand why the state-owned Soviet papers are filled with state-based and state-biased analyses of domestic and international events. For example, the failure to report troop losses in Afghanistan was understandable in this context even if such censorship seems unnecessary to a citizen of a Western democracy. More recently, coverage of all kinds of events (previously considered taboo) by the Soviet media outlets may indicate the future possibility of claims of media ownership by the program producers, on behalf of the people.

Turning to the West, if we understand the interest of the owners to be capturing and maintaining audiences, which can then be sold to advertisers, as we outline in Chapter 7, and if we understand the relation of the content of the media to the general prevailing attitudes of the population, as will be discussed in the example of Enoch Powell in Chapter 5, then we can also understand why the pages of Western newspapers are filled with the extraordinary, drama, human interest, business information, and sports updates. Both the state and capitalist owners are served well by the content each produces.

In stating that the Communist press theory is authoritarian, the authors of *Four Theories* mean that the press is aligned with state authority. In equivalent fashion, they might call the Western press business-dominated.

Nonetheless, the differences between press operations in the Soviet Union and the West should not to be underestimated. One example may illustrate how very different are the news values in the Soviet Union as compared to here. This particular example was related by a Canadian professor of journalism, the late Richard Lunn.

Toward the end of a visit Lunn and a number of students from the journalism program at Carleton University were making to the Soviet Union, he was talking to the guide the Soviets had provided for the group. He asked, "If that ferry crossing the river overturned, would it be reported in the news the next day?" The guide's answer was blunt. "No," she said. "Why not?" said Lunn. "Why would it be?" said the guide. "Those that were involved would obviously know about it

and their relatives would eventually find out. Why would it be of interest to other people?"

Traditionally, the Western press interprets such lack of coverage as a coverup, as a gigantic attempt by the government of the Soviet Union to hide any imperfections in their system. But might it not also be the case, as it would appear from the remarks of the guide, that those who control the media do not deem such human interest events newsworthy? And is this really very much different from the habitual way Western news media use events for their news programming? That is, the Western media assume that any disruptive or violent event is automatically newsworthy, especially when numbers of people are killed. Many parents of young children do not appreciate the frequency with which such events are used to lead off the 6:00 p.m. television news. Changes introduced by Gorbachev seem to have led to increased reporting of violent events in the Soviet Union, perhaps in an attempt to hold the state more responsible or in reaction to many years of suppression of so much information.

Libertarian Theory

The **libertarian theory** of the press derives from concepts of liberty and the free will of individuals, which in turn derive from such liberal philosophers as John Locke (1632-1704), John Stuart Mill (1806-1873), and David Hume (1711-1766). The fundamental assumption of liberal philosophy is that individual freedom is the first and foremost goal to be sought, and that the ultimate goal of society should be to impede the freedom of the individual as little as possible. The state exists in service to individuals rather than the reverse. In serving the freedom of the individual, so the liberal philosophers maintain, the state will create the most advantageous situation for all.

It is easy to understand what role might be conceived for the mass media in such a theory. Rather than being arms of state enterprise, the libertarian theory sees the mass media as the watchdog of government, the fourth estate. The mass media are to be an independent voice keeping government responsible to the people by feeding information to people so that, come election time, performance can be rewarded or punished.

In striving to ensure distance between the government and the mass media, the libertarian concept of the press places the press in the hands of the private sector. The basic problem in this is that the private sector necessarily has its own interests – accruing profits – to consider above the interests of the people or the government of the day. As a consequence, rather than having a corporation beneficently allowing journalists to dedicate themselves to "serving the people," the privately controlled press has sought to maximize profits.

The usual example of the extreme of a libertarian press is the exploitation of sex to sell news. However, as we will see in Chapter 7, the general pursuit of profits sets quite fundamental constraints on the extent to which information is pursued and the *kind* of information that is pursued, which is of far greater importance. The seeking after profit is no guarantee whatsoever of a socially valuable press.

Social Responsibility Theory

The **social responsibility theory** arises from the failure of the libertarian arrangement to produce a press that is generally perceived to be of benefit to society. It was developed by a non-governmental U.S. commission, the Hutchins Commission on the Freedom of the Press (1947).

A Canadian inquiry, the Kent *Royal Commission on Newspapers* (1981), explained the

social responsibility theory well, pointing out that as newspaper publishing began to be taken over by big business, thereby heralding the end of a libertarian press, the notion of social responsibility was born. It was born of a need to fight against the potential of new authoritarianism brought about by big business ownership of the press. The Kent Commission (p. 235) defined the concept of social responsibility as follows:

> The conjoined requirements of the press, for freedom and for legitimacy, derive from the same basic right: the right of citizens to information about their affairs. In order that people be informed, the press has a critical responsibility. In order to fulfill that responsibility it is essential that the press be free, in the traditional sense, free to report and free to publish as it thinks; it is equally essential that the press's discharge of its responsibility to inform should be untainted by other interests, that it should not be dominated by the powerful or be subverted by people with concerns other than those proper to a newspaper serving a democracy. "Comment is free," as C.P. Scott, one of the greatest English-speaking editors, wrote, "but facts are sacred." The right of information in a free society requires, in short, not only freedom of comment generally but, for its news media, the freedom of a legitimate press, doing its utmost to inform, open to all opinions and dominated by none.

FOCUSING ON CANADIAN SOCIETY

The shortcoming of the various viewpoints discussed so far is a lack of consideration of the mass media within the context of a particular democratic society. In this book, our focus is the Canadian society. The interests of particular societies can enter through two routes. First is through the concept of **developmental journalism,** in which the specific needs of cultures and national communities have been taken into account from within an evolutionary perspective, from lesser to greater industrialization.

However, this model still leaves aside the specific cultural makeup and history of a society that might call for a particular mass media system. Consideration of these elements of society enter the equation in the electronic media through **government regulation**. While the print media consider government regulation anathema to their free operation, television and radio have lived within a regulatory framework almost since their inception.

In Canada, government regulation of the broadcast media is enshrined in the Broadcasting Act (1991). The Act empowers Canada's broadcasting and telecommunications regulating agency, the Canadian Radio-television and Telecommunications Commission (CRTC), to oversee the broadcasting system with the purpose of achieving public policy goals established by Parliament. The public policy framework affecting Canadian mass media is discussed in Chapter 6.

A Macroview of the Functioning of Mass Media in Canadian Society

The mass media can be looked at in the way they function in relation to the overall structure of society, that is to say, other social institutions. Such a perspective is called **structural functionalism** (see, for example, Coleman, 1973). This perspective tends to be allied with a liberal-pluralist viewpoint although it need not be. The model suggests seven political functions inherent in the running of society, and the mass media can be examined for their contribution to each. They are:

1. the articulation of various interests that span a range of the political spectrum;
2. the aggregation of interests through the identification of common assumptions, values, or beliefs;
3. the socialization of new members of the community into the political structure and values of the community;
4. the making of rules or laws by which members of the community are meant to abide;
5. the enforcement of those rules;
6. the adjudication of those rules;
7. political communication.

The mass media are clearly the main agent of political communication. As such they can be seen as contributing to the prior six functions. How they contribute to the first three seems relatively obvious. By making known and discussing the political environment, they bring to the attention of the audience the various interests of groups in society and their alignment on various issues. No doubt this contributes to a certain coalescence among both new and continuing members of society. By reinforcing collective symbols, by multiple coverage of the same issues (thus giving individuals the confidence that they know which are important), and by the more usual building of consensus, recruiting people to the political process, supporting existing institutions, and casting criticism within the dominant political framework, the mass media play a sizable political role.

The mass media's contribution to making, enforcing, and adjudicating the rules of society is less direct. For example, by monitoring the behaviour of society, publicizing rules and their enforcement system, and publicizing and commenting on adjudication, the mass media contribute indirectly to the nature of society's rules and how they are created, observed, and amended. Given this, it should not be surprising that, whatever the role of the mass media with regard to the general public, they play a key role in communication between elites in society. The most avid consumers of political news are senior civil servants and elected politicians. True, a certain amount of their consumption can be put down to egoism since the mass media deal in their daily affairs. But what the mass media report about them, and others of their kind, is functionally necessary to their jobs.

The contribution of the mass media to society, and a justification for press freedoms, can be seen in the political functions outlined above. In overview, the mass media maintain a two-way flow of information, a multiple feedback system from a variety of communities of interest that makes government efficient and sensitive to the popular will. It aids government in assessing the adequacy of programs, first, through media commentary, second, by reporting the opinions of special publics, and third, by reporting the reactions of the general public. It helps the government interpret its performance when there are few of its electorate in contact with its programs, for example, in international affairs. The mass media also create a general openness that allows for messages to reach legislators, which they then may or may not act upon.

More specifically, the mass media – especially the electronic media – have contributed to the nationalization of politics. The vast majority of political reporting during election campaigns (81 per cent in one instance, according to Black) deals with the activities and statements of the leaders of the political parties and their families. By following the leaders as they hopscotch across the country, the mass media are as much the agents of a national campaign as are the parties themselves, galvanizing local support for the party that then spills over to the local candidate.

Another way in which the mass media are playing an increasingly active role in the political life of Canadian society is in the use of public opinion polling, both in election campaigns and at other times. Not only do political parties conduct polls, the government also commissions them fairly continuously for administrative and political purposes. The results of government polling may be provided to the mass media or may become public through the investigative activities of journalists. Lastly, the larger mass media organizations – such as the CBC, *Maclean's* magazine, *The Globe and Mail,* and the Southam newspaper chain – are commissioning their own polls on broadly political issues, such as attitudes toward the environment, or on more specific topical issues, including the failed Meech Lake amendments to the Canadian constitution. The reporting of all these polling results forms part of the ongoing political debates in Canadian society.

In general, the mass media play a regular and important part in the governance of society, yet they have no political coherence or unity of purpose in a narrow sense. They inject themselves into the process of making public opinion and hence, over the long term, affect basic values as well as help to shift attitudes and opinions about discrete issues.

A MICROVIEW OF THE FUNCTIONING OF PRESS AND POLITICS

The above perspective of the functioning of mass media and Canadian society constitutes a broad overview or macroview. Now we turn to a microview, an inside look at press functioning within a political context, to form a more thorough picture of the political role of the press. In this section we use the term "press" to refer to news organizations as a subset of the mass media generally.

The influence of three different sets of variables will be discussed:

- institutionalization
- media processes
- business dynamics.

The Political Effects of Institutional Organization

The press is not composed of a great number of individual reporters whose reports covering the world are carried by one or other station or newspaper. The press has an industrialized institutional structure complete with control systems, institutional policies, occupational routines, a personnel organization, particular technologies of production and distribution, and so on. Each of these impinges on the political role the press plays.

In both the electronic and print media there are clear internal hierarchies and structures. These must be flexible enough to allow for the creativity and individuality of commentators, opinion-makers, and program creators (see Gallagher, 1982), but their presence is nevertheless forceful. For example, a reporter is given certain responsibilities by an editor. If the reporter should come across what he considers to be a great story, he must persuade that editor to allow him the time necessary to research the story.

Nor does the news organization sit on top of a world full of information, all of which gets on the air or into the paper. Slow news periods provide good examples of the way that news and commentary depend on the interests and inclinations of the editor, how he or she perceives his or her publication or program, how she or he perceives its audience

and even the news sources to which the organization subscribes.

The politics of the press also depend on information-gathering structures. **News** is gathered by a fairly standardized beat system. The reporter covers certain beats or sources that customarily turn up stories. The beat might be nightclubs, city hall, the police station, or a host of other institutions, such as universities, hospitals, social service organizations, large corporations, and labour organizations. In covering these beats in search of stories, the reporter tends to identify with the source of the stories rather than with the individuals who may make the story significant: in the case of the police station, for instance, the police rather than the accused, or with a large corporation, the corporation rather than its customers or employees. This tendency has led to the creation of counter-beats, such as labour and environmental groups to balance business.

Knowing how this system of information-gathering works, politicians as well as other newsmakers can feed the system to make stories. The most obvious example is the leaking of stories to individual journalists who frequent Parliament. Politicians may wish to get an advance reading on a proposed policy or to throw another party into disarray. Or they may want to puff a story so they leak a dramatized version. By leaking a story they can issue information without responsibility and, like the arsonist who watches his own fire, anonymous in the crowd, can assess the subsequent reaction.

The press has an implicit hierarchy of coverage that differs between the electronic and print media. Pronouncements by a Prime Minister from abroad always seem to receive special attention. The perception that the Prime Minister is still thinking about the home front when tour-

John Turner: the politician in unflattering pose. *Courtesy The Globe and Mail, Toronto.*

Bill Vander Zalm: the politician as hard-working friend. *Courtesy Slicko Studios, Vancouver, and the B.C. Social Credit Party. Photograph by H. Fry.*

ing the world may be a boost to our collective ego. (When one realizes that he has a bevy of reporters travelling with him and tracking his every move and word, the magic of his attention is diminished.)

In yet another example, a government can be assured that almost any policy announcement will be displaced by "explosions" of any sort, whether physical or political. The press is also sensitive to power in a broadly defined sense. Knowing this is to know the likelihood of the press sustaining its interest in a particular issue.

The Political Effects of the Press as Media

Each medium has its own "technique" and therefore its own bias. The print medium allows for a lot of words and very few pictures. However, the one picture used can create the whole tone for an article. For example, during the federal election campaign of 1984, a picture of John Turner, which had in the background an insignia that looked like the devil's staff or as if Turner had horns, was printed in *The Globe and Mail.* Complaints were made charging *The Globe* with potentially creating a subliminal bias.

In contrast to the negative image in *The Globe* example is the more usual, positively biased publicity shot, such as the one presented here of B.C. Premier Bill Vander Zalm. Note the simplicity and even the purity of the image, coupled with its informality, its reaching out, and yet its beckoning, the rolled-up sleeves suggesting a willingness to be directly involved in hard work.

The more usual example of print bias derives from the form of the printed story. The story is the creation of the reporter in his or her words, and is usually built around statements by a newsmaker. The potential for inaccurate, incomplete, or wrong contexts, misquotations, and inappropriate headlines is considerable. However, one method of minimizing such problems is to issue news releases or give news conferences that lend themselves to clear and logical analysis and restatement.

The problem of context is further exacerbated by the form of newspaper stories. As we will see in Chapter 4, newspaper stories have an inverted-pyramidal structure. The basic facts of who, what, when, where, and why are outlined at the outset. The details of the story are then filled in. The necessity of this kind of structure came from fitting stories into spaces. Layout editors had to be able to lop off the ends of stories without losing any of the essentials. The top-heavy inverted-pyramidal structure was thus created. This structure has also allowed for the development of fluffy tabloids, where all one gets in the story is the basic points with little but sensational elaboration.

In a farewell comment to the press, Pierre Trudeau captured with irony the vulnerability of the politician to these and other sorts of potentially undermining inadvertences, techniques, and tricks the press can play. He turned Richard Nixon's complaint on its head when he noted that he was sorry he would not have the press to kick around any more.*

In contrast to print, television news is dominated by the picture and few words. The words of a television newscast can fit on one newspaper page. Newsmakers oriented to television must therefore create media or television events to ensure television coverage. The contrived "photo opportunities" of Prime Minister Mulroney, or President Bush, which have no substantive news value, are cases in point. The television stations themselves find that audiences respond well to different stimuli from those offered by print. For a newspaper, being the first with the news may be the major goal. For a television station, bringing in a set of fresh pictures may once again revive interest in an event already discussed in the print media. Visual excitement can readily replace speed of news coverage.

Most television news is planned by both the news team and the newsmakers, which suits the needs and preferences of both the station and the politicians. During one provincial election in Quebec, so keen was he to avoid "live" coverage that Robert Bourassa ran his television campaign by issuing videotapes. In broader perspective, with television the politician is engaged primarily in political-visual image-making, in symbolic representation often devoid of the nuts and bolts of policy.

Radio deals more in sounds than in words or pictures. In its heyday and even now, the ability

---

*Nixon's remark about the press no longer having him to kick around was made at a press conference after he lost the 1962 California gubernatorial election. As it turned out, of course, Nixon did return to public life, as President of the U.S., and once again became a prime target for press criticism.

to recreate the actual sounds of a scene, be it a battle or a concert, drives both news reporter and creator. Sound recording, whether music, drama, reportage, or interview, is a staple for radio. The pun, alliteration, the one-line verbal quip all play very well into radio form.

All these technological biases are interwoven with press-perceived audience dynamics to form something we might call **media bias.** Thus a *Globe and Mail* and an *Edmonton Sun* are worlds apart in their newspaper form. The former enhances the basic bias of the printed word, milking it as best it can, while the latter attempts to match on the printed page what other media, predominantly television, offer. CBC radio uses the spoken word to extend our verbal understanding while most commercial stations are more interested in sound signatures (meaning recognizable noise patterns) in both voice and musical form. Most commercial television stations have more in common with glue companies than with attempts to reflect a culture in audio-visual form to a people.

With all this the politician must cope. What emerges is what Altheide and Snow (1979) have termed **media logic.** Events in the political realm are better understood as feed for the media than in terms of their political (in the sense of a policy) or informational ends.

The Political Effects of the Press as Business Institutions

Some might argue that, from a perspective of how the uses of information and communication ought to be situated in society, we are living with a quirk of history in having a "free press" operating clearly within the power base and dynamics of the business class. Others would contend that the basic functions of the press are intimately connected to industrialized

society and therefore to business dynamics. Whichever side of the debate one cares to favour, there is no doubt that the political role of the media is affected fundamentally by the media's placement in the business sector.

The press, whether public or private, deals in audiences. Its audiences must be of a size and type that either advertisers or Parliament deems valuable. The information it creates must be consumable and must be consumed on a regular basis. The information environment it creates must not interfere with advertiser messages, whether governmental or commercial. The press must also operate in such a way that it continues to have access to information as well as access to audiences. These and other constraints derive from the press being, essentially, a business operation.

Alternatively, the press could apply a number of potential levels of analysis to politics. The most abstract level is political theory, followed by ideology, policy, and then practice. It might be claimed that only with a full discussion of each of these levels are the mass media fully informing their audiences of their political environment. In its place we have reportage that concentrates on personalized, concrete events whose interest is further enhanced by formulae centred on simple thematics such as dichotomies, conflict, hubris, and the like.

For example, around election time the major story is winning and losing. This basic story is personalized by backgrounders on the leaders' families, their well-spent or misspent youth, their advancing age if appropriate, and so forth. Once these crude variables have been exhausted, the press moves onto only slightly more subtle themes. Fletcher and Taras (1984) use the example of a leadership cycle specifically as it was played out with regard to Trudeau's 1983 peace initiative. The press treated the initiative with considerable cynicism, a shame

A cartoonist's conception of the business leanings of the press. Roy Petersen, Vancouver. *From Royal Commission on Newspapers, 1981. Repro-duced with permission of the Minister of Supply and Services Canada.*

when the stakes in such a matter are so high. Black, in another example of the rule of theme over content, quotes Robert Stanfield, thrice-defeated national Conservative leader, as saying that if he walked on water the press would suggest it was because he couldn't swim.

Such topics keep ideology, policy, and, in fact, any discussion out of the abstract and within the realm of the concrete and the personal. Why? To ensure large audiences. The difficulty is that fresh thought about new phe-nomena becomes not only difficult but, at times, impossible. In the midst of the constitu-tional patriation debates in the early 1980s, the press engaged in a great deal of speculation about the exact amount of personal animosity between Prime Minister Trudeau and Premier René Lévesque. One might claim that the whole issue was, if not irrelevant, then certain-ly diversionary.

To consider only the level of political prac-tice, and, consequently, the concrete and the personal, has a number of other implications. Some on the political right attempt to claim that they "are not ideological but practical," thus making an unsubstantiated claim to being ideologically dominant since we tend to assume practicality accepts basic givens. Because of press avoidance of discussions of ideology, it is not difficult for anyone with few ideas to make such a claim. To counter such a claim requires background context that cannot be introduced to an audience overnight, as it depends on an already existing level of sophistication.

Dwelling in established images and especially personal dramas may make for a kind of political stability: new faces, but the same old policies. But as the press, especially television, distances itself through both technique and content from all sides of the political debate, the distinctive fabric of the nation may be endangered in favour of an apparent global homogeneity. This matter will receive more attention in Chapter 10.

Keeping matters personal and concrete leads to other unfortunate consequences. Patrick Gossage (1985, p. 21), reviewing an article from *The Bulletin of the Atomic Scientists,* notes that the Canadian mass media have been completely unwilling to do thorough research and discuss nuclear strategy. He quotes from the article: "such reporting as there has been on strategic doctrine has largely accepted policy declarations at face value. Coverage has tended to ignore the fact that declared policy represents the facade of a complex strategic agenda."

The above biases may arguably be traced to the business orientation of the press and therefore to the necessity to deal in audiences. This is not a big-business conspiracy to gelatinize our minds in political gossip. It does, however, play to a fairly low level of political thought and calls into question the adequacy of the press as a key democratic institution.

STRUCTURES OF INFORMATION AND THE MODERN NATION-STATE

The Need, Use, and Abuse of Information

Given the notion that the modern nation-state is a sophisticated information apparatus, with government and the mass media as two of its major arms, what are some of the details of that information structure and functioning? To represent the whole, the state gathers information in the name of the greatest good for the greatest number. It must seek to achieve this end but it must weigh its achievement against other communal goals and ends.

For example, the interests of the community may be very well advanced by the collection of information on every individual from birth onward. The right to individual privacy, however, is potentially in conflict with the right of the state to collect information in the interests of the community. In a greyer area, the state may design sophisticated information systems that work for government but also allow large business enterprises to have a distinct advantage over small enterprise because the former have the technology, scale of production, and monetary capability to make better use of the information. If the state fosters the creation of such information systems, it might be considered to have created a counter-obligation to small enterprise and perhaps to workers because small enterprise is a great deal more labour-intensive than large enterprise.

The Press in Relation to Government: The Parliamentary Press Gallery

Western society has created structural responses to the potential power of the state to abuse its trust not only in gathering and acting upon information but also in the general abuse of power. The first response in Commonwealth countries such as Canada has been the institutionalization of "Her Majesty's Loyal Opposition." The second response has been the development, in general terms, of an independent or free press and mass media systems whose function is to gather information about all aspects of society, including government. Specifically, the parliamentary press gallery is the primary press institution with a responsibility to monitor government policy and action. (See, for example, Fletcher, 1981.)

In one sense, the parliamentary press gallery is the sum total of all journalists who are working on political stories in Ottawa or the provincial capitals who apply to become members of the Ottawa or provincial capital galleries. On the other hand, as the federal Task Force on Government Information (1969, vol. 2, pp. 115-19) noted about the Ottawa gallery, it is "the most important instrument of political communication in the country." The gallery performs two essential roles: to disseminate government information; to assess the wisdom of government policy and action by reporting and analysing House debate between government and the opposition.

The Press as a Political Information Institution in a Controlled Environment

The press, and specifically the parliamentary press gallery, makes an important contribution to modern democracy by gathering information and monitoring government. However, the press does not have free rein to carry out this role without the formal constraint of law or without informal constraints. The press exists and acts within its own political environment. Just as the government must balance one goal with another, so must the press in pursuit of its ends. The difference between the two is that the government controls itself (subject, over the longer term, to the wishes of the electorate). The press is self-governed only to a limited extent and its self-governing mechanisms, such as professional ethics and press councils (discussed in Chapter 8), control its behaviour far less than the governmental mechanisms discussed in this chapter.

The best-known law controlling the press is **libel law**. Libel law is not a small matter used only to settle disputes between muckraking journalists and shady characters. Fundamentally, it represents an attempt to achieve a balance between two goods. On one side are the rights of individuals to such things as a good reputation or a fair trial. On the other are the rights of the press to speak freely about public affairs and to speak in such a way as to sell papers.

The trial of a Vancouver radio personality, which played in the media for approximately 18 months, is pertinent here. On the basis of press reports a reader would probably have expected a conviction on arson charges. The man was, however, acquitted, and not on a technicality. The question is, does he still enjoy a good reputation? According to Canadian libel law, the press did not overstep its bounds in this case. Were the trial held in the U.S. the press would have been even more within tolerated limits, and might have sensationalized, speculated, and implied far more than Canadian journalists did. Had the trial been in Britain, however, the press would have been far more circumspect in its coverage. The point here is that there is *no absolute interpretation of what is libelous and what is not.* It is a matter of time and place, a matter of the balance that each society considers appropriate.

A second set of constraints on the press role as monitor of society and government is that the press, like the public, traditionally has *only the right to speak or to publish but not the right to know*. The right to publish is the right of free speech. With the emergence of a greater emphasis on the press as an information institution rather than an extension of political parties, pressure has been brought to bear on governments to provide information to the press. Increasingly, in Western countries, this has led to legislation dealing with the right to know.

In the United States, for example, this pressure has resulted in **freedom-of-information** legislation. Under such legislation the onus is on government to demonstrate why government information should not be released. This legislation derives from the notion that government is representative of the interests of the people and has no separate interests of its own. As a result of this principle, much information has become public that heretofore was hidden. Often a Canadian reporter will seek information from the U.S. government about the Canadian operations of a company that operates in both Canada and the U.S. Indeed, the Canadian government has been known to take that very course of action itself.

In Canada and Britain, principles of confidentiality and secrecy produce almost the opposite effect. In both countries, government documents traditionally have been assumed to be only for government use unless cleared for release. In keeping with this tradition the Canadian legislation is much less powerful than American legislation and is called, significantly, the **Access to Information Act** (1983) rather than being legislation dealing with freedom of information.

The early experience of journalists with Canada's Access to Information Act seems to reflect this tradition. In general, restrictions on the release of information seem to be tightened up rather than loosened by the administration of the new Act. A 1986 report by the Canadian

Daily Newspaper Publishers Association noted that in 1984 in the U.S., 91 per cent of requests for information under the Freedom of Information Act were granted without any deletions (McElgunn, 1986, p. 5). In the same year in Canada, the comparable figure was 42 per cent. In addition, 25 per cent of requests were granted with deletions while 33 per cent were denied or delayed. The same report noted that there were wide variations between government departments with respect to both cost and co-operation and thus recommended a variety of remedial actions. More recent reports indicate that the government is gradually liberalizing access to non-political government information.

Another aspect of this subject concerns the public's right to know (as opposed to the press right). Thus we need to look at the adequacy of journalists, and especially of the parliamentary press gallery. Fletcher (1981) has provided such an assessment in his background study for the Kent *Royal Commission on Newspapers*. He notes that the galleries have emerged in recent decades as independent from the control of government, and consequently they have become more professional than previously was the case. Some journalists still remember the retainers of the Duplessis era in Quebec and the slightly earlier period in English Canada, with the preferred access and perks federal governments conferred upon "their" reporters. However, independence from government has not created a full independence of copy. **Pack journalism** is common (just as much the result of the expectation of editors as of the herd instinct among journalists) and creating possibilities for interesting television coverage has introduced its own homogeneity and diversionary potential. Vast areas of government activities are inadequately covered, such as the courts, regulatory agencies, and policy-making and adjudication within the civil service.

The parliamentary galleries have generally increased in size with the addition of the broadcast journalists and freelancers, yet the gallery perspective is now more clearly dominated by a few larger papers and services. Most noticeable is the decreased number of regional members whose sole function was to report on matters from the perspective of the region they represented.

Fletcher found also that the Canadian Press (CP) reporters played an interesting role. The large and respected CP bureau in Ottawa (to which virtually all Canadian papers now subscribe) has freed the multi-person Ottawa bureaus to specialize and investigate. However, any decrease in the size of the CP bureau, as happened with the closure of the *Ottawa Journal,* lessens the effectiveness of this CP function. In either instance, the use editors make of their press gallery copy is often limited because their surveys tell them there is limited interest in political affairs.

Fletcher's view is that the galleries are clearly understaffed and tend to vary in their effectiveness depending on such variables as the vigour of opposition parties and the expectations of editors and publishers. Competition does not produce necessarily better coverage, but without competition the discretion of editors and publishers can be seen. The turnover rate of journalists is high, essentially because publishers are not prepared to commit sufficient resources. Finally, the range of ideological perspectives is narrow, primarily because there are too few national columnists. Such an assessment is not inclined to give one faith in the press as a fundamental instrument of democracy.

To return to access to information, the above discussion may give a false impression. The government is not consistently miserly in its provision of information to the press. At times it is positively garrulous, as when the government wishes to boast about its achievements, or when it wants the public to know about a new program or to abide by a new or old set of laws. The government then depends on the press to inform the public of such programs both in discussion and by means of government advertising.

Even here, though, the information the government releases is only of a certain type. Canadian and other British-derivative governments are extremely reluctant to release context and planning information, that is, predecision information, especially when such information is contained in cabinet documents. All governing parties seem to feel strongly about the protection of cabinet secrecy.

Society and government place a variety of other normal controls on the press. Some, which are not particularly political in their effects, will be discussed in later chapters. Those with more direct political consequences are discussed here.

Most controls could be termed performance requirements. Various statutes, taxes, and regulations attempt to keep the media within the boundaries of good taste and to prevent undue exploitation of their position of power. Requirements concerning a balanced perspective affect political commentary in the electronic media. Regulations also control certain aspects of political advertising, excluding dramatization and forbidding political ads to be broadcast within 48 hours of an election. During elections, the electronic media must be especially careful to provide equal coverage of all political parties. The print media, however, are free to cover elections as they choose. Interestingly, what has evolved in the print media, especially in big city newspapers, is editorial coverage supporting one chosen party and news coverage aimed at equality but usually slightly favouring the government. Soderlund *et al.* (1984) provide a more thorough and detailed discussion of normal press controls.

Canadian content regulations, a reflection of cultural ethnic diversity as well as regionalism, and the pursuit of Canadian identity and unity are also represented in performance requirements that apply not only to public broadcasting but to the privately owned broadcasting licences.

In overview, the mass media are continually restructuring the political information environment away from one that extends from personal experience of the local through the regional and national to the international. Increasingly, we are immediately and continually in secondary or mediated touch with the centre, with the hub of the nation, while our next door neighbours seem to be hours or days away. They only appear in our political purview at times of crisis, often at meetings in the local school auditorium.

As the mass media impress these fundamental changes on our political system, society is challenged to design a set of freedoms and constraints so that our collective interests are best served. In this section we have seen some of the constraints intended to do just that.

UNUSUAL POLITICAL CONTROLS ON THE PRESS

The desire, indeed the necessity, of the press to carry information between people and their government makes for extremely close relations between government and the press. The government's desire to keep the press away from certain information, such as predecision information in cabinet documents, gives to that close relationship a certain ambivalence. The desire of the press to maintain its independence and to demonstrate periodically its separate integrity transforms that ambivalence into a love-hate relationship on the part of politicians. Also, the dependence of the press on government for information makes that love-hate relationship mutual. (Three sources are particularly good for understanding this rela-

tionship: Clive Cocking's *Following the Leaders* [1980], Michel Gratton's *"So, What Are the Boys Saying?": An Inside Look at Brian Mulroney in Power* [1987], and the proceedings of the Canadian Study of Parliament Group, *Seminar on Press and Parliament* [1980].)

Governments and the mass media exist in continuous tension. Both are the focus of the most basic and broadest public trusts to act on behalf of the people in the name of the collective whole. A great deal rides on carrying out that public trust. As a result, mechanisms have arisen that, when they come into play, indicate a serious lack of agreement between the mass media and government. In Canada, such mechanisms are rarely used but they are not unknown. These mechanisms are either *directed at journalism or directed at press owners.*

In recent history, these mechanisms were used most often during the Trudeau era, in part because of the times in which he was Prime Minister, in part because of his personality. During that period, specifically during the Front de Libération du Québec kidnappings, the War Measures Act was invoked along with a certain level of press and public censorship. In addition, as the CBC program *The Press and the Prime Minister* documents, Trudeau was continually engaged in matching wits with the press. On a day-to-day basis, he was neither an unsophisticated nor a mute observer of the role and failings of the press in Canadian society. At election times he was a master of media manipulation in his presentation of issues and persona.

However, the actions of the press owners brought about a clear but contained confrontation at the end of the Trudeau years. When one major newspaper chain, Southam, shut down the *Winnipeg Tribune* on exactly the same day (August 27, 1980) as another major chain, Thomson, shut down the *Ottawa Journal*, leaving each with a monopoly in one of those two

CLOSET

AISLIN 81

Aislin offers one version of press competition. *Reprinted with permission – The Toronto Star Syndicate.*

cities, the Liberal government responded in one week by setting up the Kent *Royal Commission on Newspapers*. In setting up the Commission the government subjected the chains to public examination of their operations, and by appointing Tom Kent, a former journalist, it set the journalistic community against the owners over the quality of journalism the owners were willing to pay for. The affair ended in a standoff, with ample warning given to the Thomson chain that the government would not allow it to increase its already substantial market share of newspaper holdings in Canada. More recently, when Southam bought a number of weekly newspapers in and around Vancouver, the House of Commons Standing Committee on Communications and Culture decided to hold hearings on the matter. These hearings were later cancelled.

The Political Power of the Press

The power of the press in political matters is far more constrained than one might at first think. Often the press seems to hound a good many politicians from office. Whenever governments are defeated or elected, somehow the press seems to be implicated. For example, a former leader of the British Columbia New Democratic Party, Dave Barrett, once gave a radio interview and mentioned that he would not extend wage controls to civil servants. That statement, which some have seen as costing him the election, was seen as a radio scoop rather than an extremely bad (albeit, perhaps off the cuff) policy error on the part of the former premier.

When set against the powers of government, the press seems to have little more than the power of the pen (and the camera). Yet, at its most interventionist, the press can leave behind any notion of mirroring the opinions of society and become an actor-crusader. It can mount saturation coverage, exposing and arguing, coaxing and cajoling, in the hope of changing government policy or persuading the people to change government. Not incidentally, when the mass media are engaged in such a power struggle, audience ratings and readership rise. Even where the press is not seeking policy changes, the journalists' direct involvement in events – as in the Oka confrontation – can be seen by the government as making the problem worse. Over several months, the government and army authorities tried hard to get journalists away from behind and in front of the barricades.

If government sees its own control and authority threatened, it can unleash a variety of devices. The most obvious is direct criticism. The authority vested in government makes its direct criticism of the press a powerful instrument, unless government can be seen to be looking after its narrow self-interest. When its self-interest is involved, it can set up arm's-length bodies such as royal commissions to call the press to account. Other mechanisms include judicial harassment, setting up or encouraging others to set up competing enterprises, and withdrawing patronage. Since government is the largest advertiser in the country, the withdrawal of advertising can quickly bring the press to its knees.

A more specific example of government-press conflict occurred toward the end of the Oka crisis, in September, 1990. As the final siege evolved, the army made it increasingly difficult for the journalists to do their job; for example, by limiting the amount of food crossing the barricades and by reducing opportunities for journalists to send out tapes or receive equipment supplies such as batteries. The final restriction involved the drastically reduced use of cellular telephones by Mohawks and journalists alike. The Sûreté du Québec got a court order requiring cellular phone companies to make inoperable the cellular phones that were behind the barricades (a few inexplicably remained in operation to the end). Although it was claimed by the police that the court order was not aimed specifically at the journalists, the effect was to curtail severely their ability to report on conditions and events during the siege.

The government can seek to control journalists by giving selective access to people or information, and can exercise favouritism in its monopoly over government-created information. For example, inconsistencies in dealing with access to information can easily be exploited for political motives. Releasing news at 4:00 p.m. allows processing in time for television news but not for the evening paper. (The soft form of this sort of manipulation by government is termed "news management.")

The government can also mount, or cause to have mounted, campaigns of harassment that undermine the fundamental trust between the press and its audience. Dependent as the press is on advertisements, it need only be accused of being, in a variety of ways, in the hands of its advertisers to be put on the defensive.

Finally, the government can always invoke the national interest or censorship. In invoking the national interest, any attack on government can be construed as an attack on the national community and, in the most extreme cases, tantamount to treason. When a government feels that it can no longer tolerate a free press, it can use censorship to prevent by rule of law what is otherwise impossible to prevent.

Many of these devices may seem unrealistic, extreme, and rare. This is both a tribute to the relative harmony among the various elites in Canadian society and, if one views press ownership as far too concentrated, an indictment of the Canadian government for failing to control press owners in their search for wealth. However, these devices are used in many countries of all political stripes around the world.

SUMMARY

Politics can be seen as an information enterprise and both the mass media and government can be seen as political and information institutions. Information and knowledge are foundations of the development and operation of democracy and information institutions have arisen to support those foundations. How the relationship between the mass media and government is thought to operate depends on the ideological and theoretical viewpoints used to describe and assess events.

The structures of information in modern nation-states and the place of the mass media in those structures are defined by a number of variables, including libel laws, the right of free speech, the right to know, government need of the press, various performance requirements, and so forth. Given those structures, the press and politicians, and their comparative power, are closely related. The considerable power of government appears to exceed that of the mass media, as witnessed by not only formal mechanisms but also the exercise of power by the government in recent years.

The macro-political functioning of the mass media in a democratic society is constrained by institutionalization, media processes, and business dynamics. Government processes such as administrative agendas, patterns of policy generation, and the anticipation and creation of public opinion by politicians also restrict the influence of the mass media on politics.

Information institutions, specifically the press, are important in modern democracies, yet they are limited in the scope of their operation. A "free" press is something of a misnomer because the press is closely integrated with other social institutions, especially business institutions, and is constrained by real or potential controls. Still, the mass media do make a social contribution and are key to the operation of government through the pursuit of the public interest on the basis of a separate set of interests from those of government. (Those interests are discussed further in Chapters 7 and 8.) Essentially, the role the mass media play in the political affairs of an open democracy is substantial but imperfect.

REFERENCES

Altheide, D.L., and R.P. Snow. *Media Logic.* Beverly Hills: Sage, 1979.

Black, Edwin R. *Politics and the News: The Political Function of the Mass Media.* Toronto: Butter-worths, 1982.

Canada. Canadian Study of Parliament Group. *Seminar on Press and Parliament: Adversaries or Accomplices?* Ottawa: Queen's Printer, 1980.

Canada. *Royal Commission on Newspapers.* Ottawa: Supply and Services, 1981.

Canadian Broadcasting Corporation. *The Press and the Prime Minister: A Story of Unrequited Love.* Directed and produced by George Robertson. Toronto: CBC, 1977.

Cocking, C. *Following the Leaders: A Media Watcher's Diary of Campaign '79.* Toronto: Doubleday, 1980.

Coleman, J.S. *Power and the Structure of Society.* New York: Norton, 1973.

Curran, J. "The new revisionism in mass communications research," *European Journal of Communication* (June, 1990).

Desbarats, P. *Guide to Canadian News Media.* Toronto: Harcourt Brace Jovanovich, Canada, 1990.

Fiske, J. *Television Culture.* London: Methuen, 1987.

Fiske, J. *Reading the Popular.* Boston: Unwin Hyman, 1989.

Fiske, J. *Understanding Popular Culture.* Boston: Unwin Hyman, 1989.

Fiske, J. "Moments of television: neither the text nor the audience," in Ellen Seiter *et al.,* eds., *Remote Control.* London: Routledge, 1989.

Fletcher, F. *The Newspaper and Public Affairs.* Vol. 7, Research Publications, Canada, *Royal Commission on Newspapers.* Ottawa: Supply and Services, 1981.

Fletcher, F., and D.G. Taras. "The Mass Media and Politics: An Overview," in Whittington and Williams, eds., *Canadian Politics in the 1980s,* 2nd edition. Toronto: Methuen, 1984.

Foucault, M. *The History of Sexuality.* Harmondsworth: Penguin, 1978.

Foucault, M. *Power/Knowledge.* Brighton: Harvester, 1980.

Foucault, M. "Afterword: the subject and power," in Hubert Dreyfus and Paul Rabinow, eds., *Michel Foucault: Beyond Structuralism and Hermeneutics.* Chicago: University of Chicago Press, 1982.

Gallagher, M. "Negotiation of Control in Media Organizations and Occupations," in Gurevitch *et al.,* eds., *Culture, Society and the Media.* Toronto: Methuen, 1982.

Gandy, O.H. *Beyond Agenda Setting: Information Subsidies and Public Policy.* Norwood, New Jersey: Ablex, 1982.

Gossage, P. "The media-government mouthpiece," *Media Magazine* (September, 1985), p. 21. The referenced article is W. Dorman, "The media: playing the government's game," *The Bulletin of the Atomic Scientists* (August, 1985).

Gratton, M. *"So, What Are the Boys Saying?": An Inside Look at Brian Mulroney in Power.* Toronto: McGraw-Hill Ryerson, 1987.

McElgunn, J. "Publishers urging reform of the law on access to information," *Media Magazine* (May, 1986), p. 5.

McPhail, T. *Electronic Colonialism: The Future of International Broadcasting and Communication.* Beverly Hills: Sage, 1981.

Murdock, G. "Large Corporations and the Control of Communications Industries," in Gurevitch *et al.,* eds., *Culture, Society and the Media.* Toronto: Methuen, 1982.

Siebert, F.S., T. Peterson, and W. Schramm. *Four Theories of the Press.* Urbana: University of Illinois Press, 1956, 1971.

Soderlund, W.C., *et al. Media and Elections in Canada.* Toronto: Holt, Rinehart and Winston, 1984.

STUDY QUESTIONS

1. Discuss the role the mass media play in affairs of state.
2. What kind of a press system is best for Canada?
3. Should Canadians have equal access to information that Americans have in their country?
4. Are there sufficient mechanisms to balance the power of the mass media with that of government?

CHAPTER

4

The Design
of Information

INTRODUCTION

PERHAPS THE MOST obvious area of study in communications is the study of content, that is, what is said and how it is said. At one level, that of personal interaction, we can study the content of what one person says to another and how. By examining the content of this interaction we gain some idea of the interaction and of the two individuals involved.

A concern for content is an important focus of study in material intended to have a lasting existence and a broad significance in our literature and arts. The study of the ideas expressed in the literature of a particular epoch, by authors of a particular nation, even in one piece of writing of a particular author, provides insight into the society from which these works emanate as well as the creative process of the individuals involved in their creation.

Content is also important in material that has a large audience but which is not specifically designed to have a lasting significance. For example, the information reaching us each day via the mass media must be analysed for its content if only because we live on a steady diet of it. In such content we are liable to find repeated ideas, information, and interpretations. These repetitions and their variations provide insight into the society of which they are a part and into the institutions that manufacture media programs. This content reveals the dominant themes, set of ideas, or ideology of a society. It also reveals subordinate or alternative interpretations or ideology.

Communication as Representation

When we study content, we study **representation**, sometimes also called **encoding**, or, loosely speaking, the creation of symbols. Representation combines the "what" and the "how" of communication. The study of representation is by no means confined to examining the so-called truth of statements. That is, it is not limited to commenting on whether a set of statements exactly corresponds to what it purports to describe. Indeed, as researchers have focused attention on the process of representation, it has become apparent how difficult it is to adjudicate questions of accurate representation. Representation literally re-presents the matter. Different representations re-present ideas differently. They are competing forms of representation or competing interpretations. At times, some are obviously better than others, perhaps because one or other is incomplete or inaccurate. But the more interesting cases are those in which the matter is much less clear. One representation brings a certain background set of ideas or ideology to its task and draws out certain elements, while another brings other background ideas and draws out other elements.

The study of representation, especially the representation of human affairs, is a study of indeterminate systems that have no boundaries.

In other words, there can be any number of ways of representing an object or event. Take, for example, a political event such as the signing of a peace treaty. Each side has reasons of its own for signing the treaty. It means different things to each of the signatories. Then there are the subgroups within those bodies who sign. For some the treaty may represent a good bargain, for others a sell-out. For the people living near the centre of hostilities no doubt it will represent a return to a less violent, if not a normal, life. For those aligned with the various signatories, the treaty will also have various meanings. For political scientists and historians yet another set of meanings will be generated.

A treaty may seem like an unfair example because it is a rare event and comes from the uncertain world of politics. Perhaps something in science would seem more determinate. Let us return to an example from Chapter 1, $e = mc^2$. That seemingly innocent formula changed the whole way matter and energy were conceived and transformed our understanding of the universe. For certain groups of scientists and politicians it represented a potential military weapon. For other people it has represented a potential destruction of human life on earth. For those near nuclear energy establishments it has meant a whole new set of worries and work opportunities. For Derrick de Kerckhove it is a key to total and absolute information.

Even if we choose a less significant event, such as the utterance of a particular sentence, we can similarly discuss the various meanings that can be taken from that sentence as well as the various assumptions that went into its composition, i.e., what it represents. "John hit the ball" contains within it most profoundly an assumption basic to human understanding, the notion of causality. But it also contains less fundamental meanings: our habit of placing the agent before the verb; the popularity of "John" as an Anglo-Saxon first name; the tendency for common words to be monosyllabic. As well as the **denotative** meaning of the statement, a meaning related to a male striking a sphere, there exist a multitude of **connotative** meanings such as the ones suggested above.

The discussion of the indeterminacy of representation does not end here. Different systems of meaning derive from different media. In all that has been said so far we have been dealing within one system of representation – language. We might want to argue that language is a most powerful and flexible system of representation, but that does not detract from the independent nature of other systems of representation, such as music and the visual arts. Nor can one system of representation encompass the full spectrum of the meaning of another. A painting cannot be translated into a prose essay, nor even poetry. In short, as well as a multiplicity of meanings capable of being generated within one medium, meaning can be generated within further sets in the multiplicity of media. Overall, because these meanings can multiply indefinitely, we are dealing with an indeterminate system.

THE IMPLICATIONS OF THE INDETERMINACY OF REPRESENTATION

The indeterminacy of representation tends to lead the study of communication content away from what has been taken to be the foundations of philosophy, science, and social science and more toward the foundations of interpretation we find in the humanities. It leads to an emphasis of what Frye (1971) has called a truth of concern versus a truth of correspondence. In other words, it is concerned more with rhetoric than with reason. In the study of communication the importance of a

statement is not limited to whether it predicts events, can be refuted by others, or generates other interesting hypotheses, all standards of science and social science. What is interesting in the study of representation is what gives a particular representation its force, its ability to persuade, or its attractiveness. Whatever makes a movie more powerful than a novel, one author or painter more popular than another, even one movie more popular than another, cannot be satisfactorily discussed by reference to the relative "truth" of each communication. They are more interestingly discussed in terms of their (rhetorical) force. In so discussing them we can compare movies with books, paintings of battles with portraits, cars with clothes, or rock music with Greek society. Do they "click" with their audiences?

Umberto Eco chose to express his accumulated knowledge of medieval society and the control of knowledge in the form of a mystery novel, *The Name of the Rose,* and the book became a best-seller. More recently, he has repeated his success with a second book, *Foucault's Pendulum.* It is probably incorrect to claim that he has demonstrated the interest of vast numbers of people in medieval life; his success is perhaps rather the result of the power of the mystery-drama form to attract significant audiences. Put differently, Eco's success illustrates the degree to which the packaging of a product can supersede the attributes of the product itself. On a more metaphysical plane we can speculate as to whether the "product" remains constant with variation in packaging. Is the knowledge contained in T*he Name of the Rose* equivalent to what Eco might have said in a scholarly text on medieval history?

By the time we reach such a level of discussion, we run directly into what has been a fundamental problem in the study of representation. In the history of communication studies, and to a greater degree in other social sciences, there has been a bias in favour of physical objects over verbal entities. Physical objects were seen as having a greater claim to an independent existence than representations of those objects. In fact, at times, representation has been subordinated to hypothetical entities, as in the case of language (representation) versus thought (a hypothetical entity). In the same way that the physical object was seen as somehow more fundamental than its representation, thought was postulated to be something that language only partially expressed. As a result, until recently in certain disciplines, representation was only studied as a secondary matter.

Signification

The postulation that the "real world" and the world of representations exist on different planes, with the latter having secondary importance, led early writers to assume that there were true portrayals as opposed to biased portrayals. Bennett's (1982) discussion of George Orwell's *Homage to Catalonia* is pertinent here. The more modern approach to the issue is to assume that physical objects and representations are two different but related aspects of the world. Both are seen as "real," but neither is subordinate to the other. The reality of objects has been taken as given. The reality of representation has come from the identification of systematic patterns of behaviour that are employed to collect and organize information. These patterns of media behaviour are a good example of **signification**, the articulation of a structure for determining meaning.

The beats that editors assign to reporters guarantee the presence of certain information and certain perspectives in the news rather than others. That pattern of presence and absence leads to the evolution of a point of view in the paper's overall operations. The current tendency to do away with beats merely replaces one set of biases with another. Similarly, what a television crew can obtain in the way of news is vastly different from what a single reporter writing news stories can present. Although the television equipment is invisible to the viewer and the television news seemingly puts forward a "true picture," anyone who has been the subject of a news report is well aware of the obtrusiveness of the cameras and the degree to which they interfere with, influence, and distort an event, or more accurately, how they mould an event (to what the technology and its users determine to be the demands of the medium). The work habits of communicators and the signification process that derives from these are as real as physical objects.

METHODS OF STUDY

In recent years a great deal of attention has been given to representation in the context of an indeterminate and ever-changing meaning system, especially in Britain. In an article entitled "Messages and Meanings," Janet Woollacott (1982) provides an especially useful summary of such work. She notes that one school of thought, typified by Hall *et al.* (1978), is that the media inject meaning into and consequently transform events in such a way as to reproduce the ruling-class or dominant ideology. One method by which they do this is through their choice of individuals or **primary definers** to define the issue under discussion. Hall *et al.* see the media as a key terrain where social consensus is won or lost, and as such the media become a field of ideological struggle. While we will leave this literature for more advanced study, it is worth noting that because the media are in the business of producing meaning, which cannot be produced outside of some context, it would be surprising indeed if the common context of media messages was not that which reflected the dominant interests of society and the interests that allow for the existence of media institutions themselves.

Our exploration here will be oriented to a basic introduction of two methods of analysis, **semiotics** and **content analysis.** Following their introduction we will look at several more recent analytical frameworks. Finally we will turn to examples of media forms.

Semiotics

There are three basic elements to semiotics. They are: **sign, signifier, signified**. The sign is a concept meant to stand for a full and complete representation of an object or event or, according to Roland Barthes (1968, p. 38), the union of **signifier** and **signified**. The object or event as we conceive of it is the thing signified and the signifier is the device used to represent what is signified. The sign encompasses both. The **signifier** exists on the plane of expression (e.g., aural or visual representation) whereas the **signified** can be said to exist on the plane of content (that to which the expression refers). However, if we examine this distinction too closely we find a contradiction. For example, in semiology, that is, the discussion of the theory itself, signifiers (expressions) become signifieds (content) by virtue of being the objects of discussion.

Sign-signifier relations have absorbed most of the attention of researchers who apply semiotics to practical studies. In focusing on these relations researchers show a great concern for a complete accounting of the meaning contained in various signifiers. In a sense a semiotician could easily write a book on the use of one word in a particular tract. Semioticians do not usually go that far. However, one French semiotician, Barthes (1970), has written an interpretation of a work that is longer than the work itself. Other essays he has written illustrate perspective on matters (such as wrestling, cars, etc.) we normally do not consider part of communication but which, as he points out, are profoundly communicative.

The primary focus of the semiotician is on the relation of meaning within and surrounding the piece. It is the job of the semiotician to demonstrate how his or her interpretation of a piece reverberates throughout. Nothing can show up that runs counter to the interpretation being put forward and a variety of elements must be demonstrated to be in keeping with that reading of the material.

The analytical device used to explain immediate context is the dyad (pair). By presenting a concept and discussing it in terms of its opposite, semioticians aim to clarify its meaning within the structure of the work in which it occurs. At the simplest level, by introducing the opposite of a term (e.g., light/heavy as opposed to light/dark), we can clarify its meaning. But, again, to emphasize the point, the semioticians are dealing with the meaning of a term, idea, or set of ideas *within the context of the piece as a whole.* They may then cast that meaning within a broader social context in a semiotics of society.

An Example: A Semiotic Analysis of a Black Label Ad Series

The following award-winning ad series was a multimedia blitz on television and radio and in print in Ontario and Quebec. The television and print ads had a tremendous impact. Not only did the sales of Black Label beer double, but also the world of advertising was effusive in its praise for the campaign. We will discuss the print ads that appeared in newspapers, magazines, and on public transit in Ontario and Quebec beginning in June, 1988.

Tattoos, jeans, and plain T-shirts, grainy black-and-white photographs with a single red highlight, billiards, bars, a waitress in a short, black leather skirt, reflective sunglasses with colourful frames, black vinyl LPs, western string "bolo" ties, single figures, at times no figures, a partial view of the product label, legend, black: these are some of the elements or signifiers drawn from a selection of the print ads that the agency, Palmer Bonner, created for Carling's Black Label. What do they mean?

Think in dyads, that is to say, opposites. Once you know the above images are from a beer ad, think of the beer ads of the dominant labels, Labatt's Blue and Molson Canadian. Most often they depict groups of fresh young men and women on the scene (and on the make). The men are handsome and muscular and exhibit strong male bonding, and at the same time they seem, if not driven to them, then certainly desirous of the women. The women wear tight or revealing clothes, keep company with other beautiful women, and await the sign of approach from one of the hunks. The ads spare no expense and present both human props and product in the most lush production that money can buy and video and computer technology can produce. The setting is well lit and everything is crisp, clean, life-embracing. Front and centre in the picture in full living colour is "the product." And if the viewer is besotted with the beauty of the actors and the set, then the music blasts the message in his/her ears.

All this works for the mainstream. But other groups in society reject or at least do not respond to these ads and drink other beers. Carling Breweries and its advertising agency, Palmer Bonner, began this campaign with the

knowledge that on Queen Street West in Toronto and St. Denis in Montreal there appeared to be one such non-responding group. How did they know? Because Black Label was not advertised and it had a high market share in those locations.

Corporations don't obtain such information out of idle curiosity only to dismiss it with a shrug. Most often, when sales figures show unusual patterns, they seek to find out why and to define, if possible, the characteristics of the consumers behaving in this way. This is exactly what Carling and Palmer Bonner did. With this distinctive pattern of sales they set out to find who was drinking Black Label and why.

A few visits to the bars in which Black Label had high sales, combined with the knowledge of their beer of preference (which had an extremely low advertising budget), gave the companies a sense of the consumer group. While reluctant to label the group, because to do so would create a mindset that might steer the company in the wrong direction, it was apparent to the ad agency early on that the group was somewhat anti-commercial. The agency felt, probably quite rightly, that this group was not about to throng to focus groups at the request of a market research firm and for the promise of a few dollars. Thus, they hired some students to hit the bars, talk to these people, find out a little about them, and find out a little about why they drank Black Label. This initial technique gave Palmer Bonner a bit more information, but it was not enough. However, it was enough for the agency to hit upon the idea of using the bartenders to recruit the Black Label drinkers to focus groups. The bartenders did their job. The focus groups were set up and the needed information obtained.

Black Label drinkers, it turned out, came from two groups. The first group was comprised of individuals who were some or all of the following: creative, non-conformist, individualist, intellectual. As well, they tended to be anti-commercial, not inclined against homosexuals, inner-city oriented. Their lives allowed them to play out these traits either through their employment or their unemployment. The second group of Black Label drinkers were the hangers-on to the first group, those who, for the most part, lived other lives but longed for and sometimes visited their ideological brethren on Queen Street West and St. Denis. What was more, it appeared that while the membership of the first group was small, the second group was potentially large. Indeed, the agency came to believe, partly as a result of their focus group work, that a little of the focal values of the first group could be found in all of us.

The identification of the characteristics of Black Label drinkers was interesting and illuminating, but it presented a conundrum. If, as the research showed, one of the major reasons people drank Black Label was because it wasn't advertised, how could one ever hope to advertise the brand and increase sales? The agency and its client elected for a strategy that seems obvious in retrospect. They would advertise the lifestyle of the drinkers; flatter those who lived it; understate the product identity; avoid too frequent exposure of any single ad; involve confirmed consumers and others in the ad by mental participation (filling in missing elements); and ensure that the creative elements of the ad reflected aspects of the lifestyle and were consistent with the values of the brand loyalists.

Why go to all this trouble if an identifiable population was already loyal to the brand and take the chance of alienating them? Because, the agency and the brewer reasoned, many more of the second group and perhaps some of the first group could be sensitized to the brand without alienating the brand loyalists. And, perhaps, the ads might strengthen the loyalty of the first group to Black Label.

The message of the ads was simple. If you look closely at this ad and you really know what is going on you'll know who we are depicting, that they are a real group in society, that they stand for something, and that they drink a certain brand of beer. You, too, can show your alliance with the values of this group by adopting elements of their lifestyle you don't already share, starting with drinking the same beer they do.

On to the elements of the ads. First, starting with the ad we have labelled #1, but in the context of the whole series. The ads are black and white, albeit with a red highlight. Second, they're grainy. Why? The lack of full colour immediately distinguishes the ads from all other beer ads. The graininess assists. Third, brand identification is obscured, not obscured enough for anyone who has been in a beer store not to know what it is, but visually obscured. Yet, by colour and placement the brand label is the focal point of the picture. Fourth, the beer label is in the form of a tattoo – now there's loyalty and commitment. Fifth, no beer bottle is in sight. Sixth, if you even notice it, in thin, white, broken letters sans serif (meaning without such little elements as the platform and small horizontal line off the top of a lower case "l") that don't impinge on the eye, The Legend is Black. Finally the model, in-style "of a type" but certainly not mainstream.

Each of these elements, led by the black-and-white grainy and red-highlighted photo, complements the others to add up to a whole-picture depiction of the brand loyalists and their preferred brand of beer. Of course, there is no one to challenge the company on whether the group it has identified actually drinks more Black Label than any other beer. No other company has identified the group and its associates as a target market.

Number 2 presents a grainy, black-and-white photograph of a black billiard ball in the

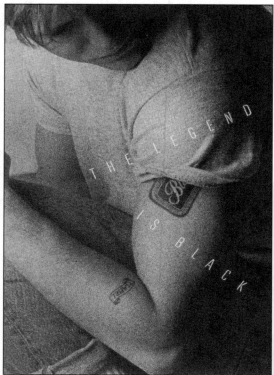

1.

Advertisements reproduced courtesy of Molson Breweries.

2.

foreground, slightly out of focus with part of the Black Label painted on it complete with red, presented upside down with only the first four letters of the word Black visible and with the last letter disappearing around the curve of the

ball. The photograph was taken at slow speed with two balls apparently moving in the background. Around the curve of the ball, again visually understated in white, broken, sans serif letters, The Legend is Black. Legend? Why leg-

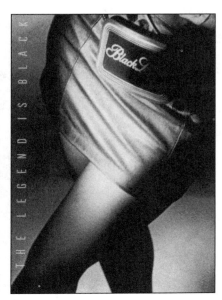

3.

4.

end? Why not a straight-out simple and direct, non-ambiguous, The Beer is Black Label?

Number 3 shows a grainy, black-and-white photograph of a tall woman, cropped across the hip and waist, apparently a waitress in a black leather miniskirt standing so as to decrease her height (as if serving a customer) and wearing a Black Label (sort of) belt buckle/clasp, deliberately partially obscured by a black shadow to show only "Black L." Her legs are crossed in such a way as to lead the viewer to the beer label buckle/clasp and the miniskirt is, of course, tantalizing. Note that we have yet to see and will not ever see the full unobscured face of a model. Up the left-hand side of the picture, in white, broken, sans serif letters is The Legend is Black. Legend?! With mini-skirts that harken back over two decades, black-and-white graininess that is reminiscent of black-and-white TV, even the red, white, and black of the label in contrast to the pastels of postmodernism that have been picked up by some of the alcoholic "coolers" – there is a suggestion of

history: the overall style seems to echo a form of industrial art.

In number 4, the grainy, black-and-white extreme close-up is of a male model wearing reflective sunglasses in which "Black" is mirrored in the tell-tale script of the label. The photograph is cropped vertically on the left across one eye after the "B," up through the forehead into the hair, horizontally across through the hair and down on the right-hand side just in front of the ear, allowing the line of the arm of the sunglasses to disappear in a curve over the ear. The letters of The Legend is Black – which, by the way, plays on "the legend is back" (and reviving itself in the marketplace) – are at about a 45-degree angle down from left to right to the less radical off angle of the sunglasses, which are at about 15 degrees, running up from left to right. The angles are such that the letters again do not impinge and play against the more common "radical growth curve" running up at around

5.

6.

45 degrees from left to right. The model's face is unexpressive.

Number 5 is the same type of photograph, this time of an LP with "Black" in the place of the record label. Its minimalism and the predominance of the black of the LP leads the eye more readily to the white, broken, sans serif letters printed following the curve of the LP about one-third of the way through the playing surface. This is simplicity itself – no beechwood chips, dryness, liteness, champagne-likeness, or endorsements of stars.

Finally, in number 6, we see an extreme close-up of the chest of a male model in the standard photograph typical of the series. His obscured face is on one arm, which adds a visually interesting top border. The shirt is well worn and "of a style" and the model is wearing three western string or bolo ties, all slightly askew. The top tie has a Black Label slide presented typically, where only the word Black is visible. The red, customarily visible on the

label, has been placed on the tie string. The Legend is Black is in the standard letter and colour form but radicalized somewhat by its angle of presentation and by being in the form of an upper case "L."

The campaign – whether consciously or not – was also playing on black as a sign (in the semiotic sense of the word), just as were the brand loyalists. Obviously the whole campaign would have been different if the brand was Green Label. Black is oppositional, of the night, associated with evil, rejection, danger, rejection of colour. Our everyday language is full of allegory carried by black, as a black mood, a blackened reputation, a black mark, a black sky, a black sheep, and so on.

With black at the centre of the campaign, adding understated signifiers of the lifestyle of the brand loyalists oppositional (in dyadic relation to) both to mainstream culture and mainstream beer ads, Carling (later Molson) and Palmer Bonner (later Bozell Palmer Bonner) had a winning campaign. It was not based on demographics – that is, it did not try to reach as great a percentage of 25- 35-year-olds as possible – and it was not intended to knock Labatt's Blue out of its top place. Rather, it was based on psychographics, designed to pick up market share by appealing to a segment of the market that possessed a certain set of attitudes. It was not without its "legendary" roots in certain historical art forms. The Russian constructivism it built on appealed, no doubt, to the cogniscenti. It also helped Bozell Palmer Bonner get established and, for a while, become the talk of the industry. What it "signified" was that people who shared the values of the brand loyalists would share their beer.

Content Analysis

Content analysis is quite a different technique, but in some ways it is a quantified version of an incomplete form of semiotic analysis. The content analyst sets up categories that appear to be salient to a particular piece of communication. They may be salient on the basis of the focus of the author or on the basis of the interests of the analysis. With categories in place, analysts then count various types of occurrences. On the basis of frequency of occurrence they then provide a reading of the article. In providing this reading, that is, setting up and interpreting their categories, their activities approach those of the semiotician.

An Example: A Content Analysis of the Media Treatment of the Shooting Down of a Korean Airliner in Soviet Air Space

The example we will use to illustrate content analysis was conducted by Robert Hackett (1983) on *Newsweek, Time,* and *The Globe and Mail* in the period immediately following the shooting down by the Soviets of Korean Airlines Flight 007 in Soviet air space over Sakhalin Island on the Kamchatka Peninsula.

Hackett begins by setting the context for his analysis. He tells the story in the abstract and then informs us that his abstraction is not of the KAL incident but of a previous incident in which the Israelis shot down a Libyan airliner over the Sinai, ten years previously. Having posited a parallel between the two events and at the same time a divergence – the one involved a capitalist nation as the aggressor, the other a Communist nation – he contrasts the amount and character of coverage of the two incidents over a ten-day period: one page and some letters to the editor for *Time* and *Newsweek* for the Libyan-Israeli incident, two consecutive cover stories and 45 pages for the Russian-Korean altercation. For *The Globe and Mail,* 11 articles were devoted to the Sinai incident, 103 to KAL 007, including two weeks of front-page placement.

What explains the difference? Hackett asks. He answers: Israeli contrition versus Soviet stonewalling; the direct involvement of a super-power; ethnocentrism: "the Israelis killed only one North American passenger, the Soviets, dozens." Beyond these common-sense factors, he points to the scholarly literature on news coverage, noting that the Israeli action contradicted the pre-Lebanon media image of the Israeli David fending off the Arab Goliath. Such an inconsistency does not tend to promote extensive coverage. In contrast, the Soviet action was able to be portrayed in a manner consistent with one of the predominant media images of the Soviets, "as a brutal totalitarian threat to world peace." Building on that established media image was easy.

Hackett bolsters this interpretation of a differing amount of coverage of the two events by citing other surveys that support the notion that the Soviets are often portrayed as a "totalitarian threat to world peace." Zwicker, he notes, in carrying out a six-month, Toronto-based survey (approximately one year prior), concluded that in coverage of the U.S.S.R., "There is virtually no human face, but a dehumanized ideological abstraction." He cites Dorman's interpretation of U.S. coverage of Soviet intentions and behaviour as "in the darkest possible shades." He concludes by casting a more general statement from Chomsky and Herman to the effect that "As one of hundreds of examples, two Soviet dissidents on trial gathered more press attention in 1978 than 20,000 Latin Americans tortured or killed by U.S. client states."

With the above as context, Hackett then sets the content categories of his analysis. They are three. First is the Soviets as "the evil empire." Second is "Soviet justification." Third is "a call for a reasoned response" in view of various Soviet and American realities. He then notes that credibility and ideological effectiveness demand an appearance of balance implied in "a call for a reasoned response." This is a way of informing us, prior to the presentation of the data, that we ought not to look for simple-minded bias. His counts support this notion: "Of the *Globe's* 129 articles in the three weeks after KAL-007, 18 seemed directly to support the 'evil empire' frame, and 21 the 'reasoned response.' Twenty-nine articles advanced the 'Soviet justification' (mainly in the Soviet's own statements, which were the main topic of 12 articles), and 23 contained explicit refutations of the Soviet spy/provocation line."

"Yet," Hackett continues, "the 'evil empire' frame was often privileged." By "privileged" he means that he is now moving beyond quantitative categorical phenomena. For example, he notes that *Time* claimed "that the loss of 61 U.S. civilians in a military attack may have been the greatest since Pearl Harbor." Note *Time's* speculative verb and the impossibility of comparing the two incidents. *Newsweek* cast the event as a confirmation of Ronald Reagan's warnings of the Soviet Union as the "evil empire." And so he continues with other examples.

Hackett then turns to whom the media used to "define the issues." They were government officials, politicians, and intelligence experts. *Newsweek* used one anti-nuclear activist while one *Globe* article gave the reaction of the peace movement. In contrast to the Sinai incident (where there was little coverage), victims had a prominent place. Hackett notes that victims of military action rarely receive such attention.

Hackett draws his analysis to a close by noting the complementarity between Reagan's scare-mongering politics and the news treatments he discovered. In addition, the underplaying of the Soviets' legal rights suited the Reagan government admirably – an illustration of the alignment of the press with government. His conclusion is that the media treatment of the incident did not contribute to world peace and understanding.

Hackett's analysis is useful and insightful and provides a good example of both the value and shortcomings of the technique of content analysis. Hackett sets categories in the context of both common sense and scholarly literature. He proceeds through his analysis weaving reason with categories of occurrences in order to provide us with an overall picture. He introduces comparative data so that we can see the distinctiveness of the patterns. He complements his category analysis with other data, such as sources used and themes underplayed. This latter device could be seen as "negative content analysis" in that it identifies, at least from Hackett's viewpoint, what was missing. The only questionable rhetorical trick he uses is the dismissal of the balanced treatment of the themes he identifies as necessary for the maintenance of press credibility. Certainly there is a supporting literature suggesting that balance does maintain press credibility, but to discuss its occurrence as nothing but a move to maintain credibility is probably a trifle cynical. The alternative would be to accept the attempt at balance as a way of leaving the door open for further information, such as the whole thing being a genuine misunderstanding or CIA set-up. It can also be interpreted, following de Kerckhove, as a responsible attitude toward a nuclear power.

At the same time, his analysis poses several important questions, as must any limited content analysis. What is the common pattern of media treatment of any act of aggression or defence by the Soviets against the West and its allies? Since there is no denying the "rivalry" at that time between the U.S. and the U.S.S.R., is there a common pattern of treatment of allies as opposed to "enemies" in the Western press, and what role do these patterns play in the governing of relations within and between the two camps? What are the temporal patterns of the themes Hackett identifies? An increasing frequency of "evil empire" stories would surely be much more alarming than an initial spate of such articles followed by the reporting of Soviet justifications and reasoned responses, even if the earlier articles do set the initial framework of understanding.

Was the story dead or did new themes emerge after Hackett completed his analysis? If memory serves, the Western press generally came to the conclusion that the KAL flight was somehow connected with U.S. spying, that a U.S. spy plane had been operating in the area that night, and that the whole incident was mired in nefarious motives and undertakings by the U.S. Given this conclusion, what then is the significance of the pattern of coverage and the credibility of sources that the media presented? It might easily be that by giving them full rein, the media revealed how untrustworthy such sources are in such cases and that we, as the audience, have seen how administrations such as Reagan's may attempt to stampede world opinion. The difficulty, as with the little boy who cried wolf, is to know when the threat is real.

Such questions almost always arise from any content analysis. A parallel set of questions arises less often in semiotic analysis because semioticians do not seek to put forward alternative interpretations of events or to illustrate bias in media treatment as content analyses often do, and as Hackett's certainly does, although implicitly. Semiotic analyses place events and most often the media treatment in a larger context so that we can see the connection of one to the other and to prevailing sets of perspectives in society.

A semiotician might begin with a statement of the role of the media in society, to represent the dominant myths of society animating members of society around significant events, thereby encouraging allegiance to a political whole. S/he might continue to discuss boundary incidents as symbolic transgressions. An additional element would be the necessarily different treatment of "we" and "they" and hence, "our transgressions" (unintentional, minor, unprovocative) and "their transgressions" (intentional, major, provocative). The event would then be examined as an illustration of such basic themes in any society and the opportunities that existed for the media to introduce real information within such mythic structures.

To be fair, Hackett is aware of at least some of the issues we have raised here and of broader concerns about the limitations of content analysis. In an article entitled "Decline of a Paradigm? Bias and Objectivity in News Media Studies" (1984, pp. 241-42), he notes that:

The growing interest in ideology and the consequent devaluation of bias have been associated with the emergence of new methods for reading ideology in media texts, notably those inspired by semiotics and structural analysis. . . . content analysis is limited to the manifest attributes of the text.

Comparison and Analysis

There are two basic limitations with both the semiotic approach and content analysis.

1. As semioticians have begun to identify internal structures of media content they have found themselves in need of making reference to broader theories of society to explain the structure of the ideas embedded in the content. Very quickly their analysis comes to be a commentary on the veracity of these broader theories of social relations, commonly called ideologies. As that happens the semiotician must adopt a theory of social relations.

To put the matter slightly differently, **semiotics is a theory of structure of content**. For a reasonably thorough treatment of its subject matter it must be wedded to a theory of content. Semioticians thus take up political, sociological, or economic theories of content, which they wed to their structural analysis. These theories propose to describe the consequences of real economic or social relations in terms of basic human values. They are thus theories of the meaning of content rather than theories of the structure of that meaning as is semiotics.

Content analysis is also oriented to the structure of content, only it is a **technique** rather than a theory. Content analysts must also, if they carry their analysis far enough, make reference to theories of the content of society. The major difference between semiotics and content analysis is that often semioticians immediately and explicitly take up theories of content

before they commence their analysis. In content analysis it is often the last act, after the empirical phenomena have been fully discussed. In the example given, Hackett's analysis of the treatment of the KAL incident, his closing comments imply that the role of the press is to promote international peace. While that is an admirable ideal, it is not a realistic portrayal. Had Hackett begun his analysis with the tacit assumption that the role of the press is to consolidate social ideology, his interpretation of the sequence of the coverage would have been quite different. In short, content analysis often fails to declare its alliance with a particular social theory.

The second basic limitation of both approaches concerns a different aspect of the content. Both tend to emphasize generalities that emerge out of the particulars contained in the material being studied. In fact, accusations have been levelled, especially at semiotics, that it cannot distinguish the banality from art. Eco (1986) has attempted to refute this claim. His argument is based on the notion that distinctions emerge in the detail of the analysis, in what the work does with the central signs and the complexity and subtlety of their embeddedness in other signs. This refutation notwithstanding, it is true to say that the identification of the sign system rather than its richness is the primary focus of the analysis. In the same way, the pattern of categories used is the primary focus of content analysis, not the originality of the interrelationships between categories.

The shortcomings inherent in the focus (as opposed to the capacities) of semiotics and content analysis have been addressed in theoretical frameworks that have gained recent recognition in a variety of fields, including communications. The five we will outline briefly are discourse analysis, Foucauldian analysis, cultural studies, post-modernism, and deconstructionism. Note that each perspective is not completely distinct from every other. Rather, they overlap and, in some cases, merely use different words to describe the same phenomena.

Discourse analysis derives from the notion that any discussion or discourse about any phenomenon makes reference to an already established framework of analysis. If we explain to a child why a hockey puck slides across the ice in the way it does, we work within established discourses, both of physics and about the capabilities of the comprehension of children. Discourse analysis identifies the discourse within which a particular analysis exists and what modifications this particular example brings to it. The analysis can then proceed to discuss the context out of which the discursive structures were developed, their assumptions, limitations, and so forth.

As mentioned in Chapter 3, Foucauldian analysis attends to the many different power relationships at play in the construction and interpretation of media content. Content producers and members of the audience construct their own meanings based on their own experiences and on their membership in various subcultures and groups. For instance, a lawyer viewing a program such as *Street Legal* might focus on the nuance of legal manoeuvres proposed in the show. A teenager viewing the same program might be more interested in whether the person accused "got away with it." A member of the police force viewing the same program might be most interested in how the police were portrayed. On the basis of their subcultural membership and their focus of attention each would interpret the program differently.

The approach of cultural studies attempts to build in a sensitivity to the cultural surround, the warp and woof of daily living in the particular time and place being studied with its particular institutions, economic and social dynamic, political orientation, and so forth. It does not deny the basics of a semiotic approach but rather points to the cultural system within which the sign system develops and operates. The cultural milieu, often termed lived experience, is seen to be an organizer of ideas, attitudes, and behaviours. Put in ways related to other schools of thought, lived experience can be seen as a selector or filter for the operation of signs or, to put it another way, within which discourses are built and modified.

Deconstructionism focuses on the details of analytical frameworks. Any communication is constructed or put together. If we take it apart and identify its elements together with the implied and explicit relations among those elements, we come to understand the logic and assumptions as well as expose the paradoxes and concealed contradictions of the constructed whole. Of the four frameworks, deconstructionism focuses most keenly on the elements and particulars as opposed to the composite and the general. Deconstructionism is also the framework diametrically opposed to a notion of one universal true explanation of a phenomenon.

Post-modernism can be thought of as building on the concern for the particular represented in the above frameworks. Modernism may be seen as a revolt and overthrowing of traditions as well as an attempt to affirm life in its present form. The phrase in architecture "less is more," used to describe the simplicity of the skyscrapers built by such architects as Mies van der Rohe, provides a sense of that tradition. Post-modernism can be seen as a boredom with pure form, as an attempt to add elements from whatever tradition that are not necessarily functional but pleasing, evocative, or decorative. Archways and pastels are typical of post-modern buildings just as music and art may be brought in as either the subject of analysis or as analytical elements in a post-modern essay. It is difficult to define boundaries for post-modernism and for post-modern analysis.

THE MEDIUM AND THE MESSAGE: MEDIA FORMS AND MEANING STRUCTURES

The foregoing analytical frameworks provide one level of understanding of the structures and implicit meaning of content. Another level comes about through the constraints of the medium itself, which forms and carries content.

In the day-to-day world of journalism, journalists, newsmakers, and news consumers alike have realized that the various media consistently select certain elements for emphasis. That selection leads to a bias about events that varies across each medium. The best example is the television news team as compared with the single newspaper reporter. Not only is the news team more intrusive on the event itself but also a television news story is uncompromising in demanding good visuals as part of the story. On the other hand, a newspaper story depends for its strength on various elements, including analysis. *Each medium organizes and encourages particular elements of content and particular relations between those elements.* These elements and relations are both distinct to each medium and forever shifting with the creativity of the practitioners in each: they provide the background to the effectiveness of any individual piece.

THE ADVERTISEMENT

The advertisement is an invention of profound significance to capitalist society. It lies at the very foundation of the commercial mass media, for it allows production and distribution of information and entertainment across a wide segment of the population at very little cost to the consumer. For a surcharge paid on every other consumer product, an advertising industry of immense size and power has been developed in the United States, and in other capitalist nations to a lesser extent.

In commerce, advertising has increasingly become the means whereby producers launch products and maintain sales. In the past the performance of a product and hence consumer satisfaction were supplemented by advertising to increase or maintain sales, but now markets are created by advertisers launching new products. Consumer satisfaction is anticipated, sometimes by means of market tests. As numerous commentators have pointed out, we are either threatened or tempted by advertisers into buying their products. The advertiser creates the need and then persuades us that this product fills that need. The accompanying photo of a billboard advertising Jolt cola illustrates how one company went about creating a market for its product.

Such ads as the Jolt cola ad customarily are created by ad agencies. During the twentieth century, these ad agencies have played a central role in the development of advertising as a persuasive communication process. The agencies taught producers about consumers, telling them how to pitch their product with the audience in mind, how to layer their goods with symbols structured to persuade the consumer to purchase and to feel satisfied with his or her purchase. On this basis ad campaigns are created. They are then followed up with audience research to measure how the audience is interpreting the pitch and responding to the product.

Because so much is at stake and the constraints of space or time are so great, there is an incredible investment involved in the making of advertisements. It is not at all uncommon for a 30-second ad to have cost more to produce

Did anybody need a Jolt before it hit the market? *Courtesy Jolt Beverage Co. Ltd.*

than the 30-minute program in conjunction with which it is shown. Millions of dollars of production investment in the advertised product hang in the balance. Moreover, no surface is safe from advertising. One example of an "untraditional" outlet is that of Stallwords of Boca Raton, Florida, which rents space in public restrooms, even on airlines, to corporations such as Holiday Inn and Rubbermaid. Their president boasts, "The only way not to read our ads is to close your eyes" (*Globe and Mail,* March 1, 1988, p. B19).

To summarize a general example of the process briefly, the producer first selects a target market. Some prized attribute of high-status members of this market, such as attractiveness to the opposite sex, is inextricably linked to consumption of this product. Using this process, the producer generates sales in the target audience. Sales are also made to people who envy and aspire to be like those who are part of the target market. Members of the target market essentially are presented with an idealized, supercharged image of themselves that they can consume through the purchase of a never-ending stream of products purported to be crucial to the lifestyle and values they represent. Consuming these articles not only feeds narcissism but also provides a means of gaining status.

One recent advertising phenomenon is the creation of opportunities to participate in real-life re-creations of ads. This phenomenon derives from a combination of presenting an image of an audience to itself and corporate sponsorship of various events, in this case sports. The Labatt company, some time ago, sponsored something it called "citizen races," a name that sounds like a direct and unmodified import from the United States. In one version, for a small fee a skier enrolled at the top of a slalom course. He or she waited for an hour or so consuming cold cuts and coffee, then ran the course, was timed, and was rewarded with a "Labatt's Lite on Ice" (the phrase in the ad of the time), or, in this case, Labatt's Lite in a snowbank, the beer having been already paid for in the entry fee. While the Labatt's Lite ads do not show these exact scenes, the ads with winter outdoor activities are aimed at exactly the same target market as would be found on the ski slopes of Canada's ski resorts, popular themselves at least partly as a result of aggressive marketing. (*Financial Post,* January 23, 1989, p. 11) This event brings the advertising, which purports to portray snippets of real life, full circle. Here real life mimics the advertising. Subsequent versions of this event have been taken up by Molson and called "Molstar races." They have dropped the word "citizen" and the food and extended the opportunity so generally that the races are a normal part of a ski holiday, if not of a one-day outing. The tie-in with the ads has also faded.

A different example of the same phenomenon has also occurred recently in a slightly different form. Again it involves beer. In the fall of 1984, Health and Welfare Canada issued an anti-drinking ad that showed a canoeist plying through peaceful waters clearly having an enjoyable workout. The canoeist was Olympic silver medal winner John Wood. The visuals drew the viewer into the picture by showing the canoeist in reflection in the water. The tone of the ad was that of a beer commercial. Then Wood said, "I like the taste of a cold beer on a hot day, but I certainly don't think you have to get the gang together with a couple of cases of beer just to celebrate the fact you've had a bit of exercise." The significance of this ad is that it addresses the ads of the beer companies as much as the drinking habits of the target audience. In addressing the drinking habits of the target audience it does so through the market research of the breweries and their discovery of that form of drinking as a valued activity of the target audience. (The background briefing materials obtained from Health and Welfare are extremely interesting. They show equal concern with the drinking habits of young people and the beer ads they see on TV; see Appendix A to this chapter.) The poster version of the ad, much less stunning in its effect, is shown here.

In the same spirit and using the same orientation toward both the target audience and the advertising image, the Non-Smokers' Rights Association has mounted a series of effective campaigns. These campaigns have made a significant contribution to the development of laws and regulation in Canada, which leads the way in the world. One of the organization's ads is included here for illustration.

Yet another interesting aspect of ads, specifically beer ads, is the relation of the product to the ad. The Black Label campaign discussed

Poster of canoist John Wood for Health and Welfare Canada's Dialogue on Drinking.
Courtesy Health and Welfare Canada.

The Non-Smokers' Rights Association, a lobby group with mainstream support from such organizations as the Canadian Medical Association and the Canadian Cancer Society, has had success in getting governments to place restrictions on smoking in public – and to tax tobacco heavily. Used with permission of the Non-Smokers' Rights Association.

earlier significantly increased its market share and turned Black Label into a premium beer in Ontario and Quebec, the two regions where the campaign was focused. Ironically, the same beer in the same cans (and later the same bottles) was a discount brand in western Canada.

In another example, as Labatt's marketing vice-president, Bruce McCuaig, has pointed out (Grady, 1983), a defining attribute of beer in advertising is not its taste. The taste of beer is usually not distinctive enough from one brand to another to be memorable. Besides, an emphasis on taste would risk alienating a significant sector of the market since there is no controlling people's taste. What is more predictable is their valued image of themselves. Product attributes that do not change the product's taste but rather change its image can then be manipulated to appeal to the target audience. For the launch of Budweiser beer in Canada, emphasis was placed on beechwood chips as ostensible elements of the brewing process that give the beer a distinctive taste. In fact, the chips were an element that appealed to the target audience's image of an ideal characteristic of the product they consume. They have no effect on the flavour.

The avid media consumer will note that all references to beechwood aging, predominant in 1983, were dropped not long after that date. No doubt, through market research, Labatt's found that the target market was beginning to be bored by beechwood chips. Consumer boredom, which may also be conceived of as the market's "neophilia," or love of the new, keeps the advertising world turning. Such boredom also influences the development of products and the application of technology to consumables. It is nothing more than the added "play value" the product gains that makes manufacturers consider putting holograms on cereals and chocolate bars. (*Globe and Mail,* July 14, 1990, p. A1).

Two final notes on beer: it should be apparent to any observer of the media that beer companies spend a significant amount more on their advertising campaigns than do manufacturers of other products. This, too, does not escape the notice of some consumers, nor does the surcharge aspect of advertising. These two factors have combined to create room for generic or no-name brands of beer. In objecting to consuming expensively produced images of themselves or others, certain consumers turn to non-advertised beer. But in so doing they do not avoid consuming images. Rather they consume a different and cheaper image, one that avoids advertising.

At the opposite end of the spectrum, the creation of a bland, indistinguishable product for the mainstream market has opened the opportunity for small operations to enter based on the very thing the large breweries avoid, distinctiveness of taste. As a result, microbreweries have sprung up across the nation that produce numerous interesting beers quite different in taste from the mainstream product.

Three other types of advertising are significant. The first includes advertisements for a company rather than its products. This type is usually called a **corporate image ad**. It promotes an image of the corporation rather than a particular product or product line. In some cases, such as the ads of the forest industries and oil companies, the responsible nature of the individual company or the industry as a whole is put forward explicitly on an issue about which the public has expressed concern. In British Columbia the fight between environmentalists and the forest industries has been particularly dramatic. The industry has spent millions of dollars trying to improve its image in the minds of the public by publishing such ads as the one following. In turn, the environmentalists have spent less money but more effort attempting to undermine the ad campaign. Partly in response to this and other parallel issues where corporations dominate the media with their information, an organization has been established called The Media Foundation. It publishes a magazine called *Adbusters* in an attempt to give the other side of the story to the public. The Foundation's counter-ad is reproduced on the following page, alongside that of the forest industry.

A version of the corporate image ad is the **advocacy ad**. It can be found in the ads of United Technologies, a company that obtains a good number of contracts from the American military. Over the years it has placed ads in an American magazine, *The Atlantic Monthly,* in which UT takes a position on a variety of public and social issues ranging from the so-called

FREE FOREST INDUSTR TOURS

For information and reservations, please
1-800-667-076

This summer a number of forest companies are inviting British Columbians to tour their operation Visit nurseries, sawmills, pulp and paper mills, logging sites... and reforested areas. Come and see our industry at work. We'd be pleased to see you, show you around and talk about our operations. Call our toll free number Monday to Friday from 8:30 am to 4:30 pm.

An invitation from forest companies in B.C. who believe in Forests Forever and for eve

LET'S TALK.
CALL B.C'S FOREST INDUSTRY THURSDAY NIGHT TOLL FREE
1-800-661-6622
(6 pm to 9 pm)

We want to hear what you have to say about the management and care of B.C's forests and B.C's forest industry. Call us on Thursday night and talk person-to-person. Professional foresters and industry specialists from around the province will be standing by to answer your calls.

WE'LL LISTEN AND WE'LL RESPOND TO YOUR QUESTIONS.

If we can't, we'll make sure someone who can, gets right back to you.
Phone Thursday night and talk to men and women who work in the forest industry and deal on a daily basis with issues of importance to forest companies and all British Columbians. Listed below are some of the people who will be on the other end of the phone when you call:

Sponsored by the forest companies in B.C. who believe in Forests Forever and for everyone.

Two sides of the forest story. *Ads used with permission of the Forests Forever Campaign and Adbusters magazine.*

governmental to the educational. As a piece of performance art, entitled "Reading Room: An Installation," done by Bruce Barber of the Nova Scotia College of Art and Design, points out, the position taken by United Technologies can be seen to be in the interests of the company at the very least, insofar as the position taken will encourage further expansion of corporations such as United Technologies. Advocacy ads are not a common feature of advertising in Canada. Perhaps the more central role of American business in American society encourages companies like United Technologies to place such ads.

There is also the ad that masquerades as a piece of reporting. It has been called a variety of names, one of which is **advertorial**. This is

Discover a wilderness that's a cut above the rest.

descriptive material on, for example, the contribution of the Port of Halifax to the Maritime economy, which is prepared for print publications, apparently written by a journalist, but in fact written by an employee or agent of the company or agency that is the subject of the article. In an article on the subject Michael Enright (1984) claims that readers are confused by advertorials because they do not know whether to read them as independent commentary or as ads.

The majority of readers, however, are unlikely to be confused by the advertorial. If they are attuned to the difference in content between normal journalistic pieces and advertorials they will probably be astute enough to understand how the piece came to be written as it is. However, more importantly, they may have no other information about the topic. If the media are filled with paid-for content by whatever company or interest group, the profits to be made by media companies serving as vehicles for such content will interfere with the ability of normal journalism to find its public and movie producers, for example, to produce "pure entertainment."

This leads to a last form of advertising, called **plugging**. Until the last decade or so, Hollywood producers portrayed themselves as putting out "pure entertainment." By this they meant that

An example of a corporation "advocacy" ad. *Courtesy United Technologies.*

they did not systematically attempt to promote products, take political stances, or teach public morality. This was not quite the case, of course. Billy Wilder's *One, Two, Three* (1961) blatantly plugged Coca-Cola, and the blacklisting from the industry of persons who were purported Communists demonstrates how ideologically sensitive Hollywood was. Also, Canada was persuaded that it did not need to build a Canadian

film industry of its own by a few plugs in numerous movie scripts (Berton, 1975).

Recently, according to Mark Crispin Miller (1990), the Hollywood product has become much more sullied. Miller (p. 48) reports that plugging products in movies is so rampant that some movies are being turned almost completely into advertising vehicles: "Friendly producers send scripts to [Associated Film Promotions] weeks and even months before filming starts, and the company analyses them scene by scene to see if it can place a product or advertising material, a billboard perhaps on, under or behind the stars." Miller adds that the plugsters choose projects that offer them maximum control, even telling the producers precisely where they want to see clients' brands. "The plug, in other words, must not just 'foreground' the crucial name or image but also flatter it – that is, brightly reaffirm the product's advertising." This is clearly exemplified by the plugs for Pepsi in the three *Back to the Future* movies, starring Canadian Michael J. Fox, who also appeared in Pepsi commercials on TV. The most extreme example, however, is the movie *Texasville,* in which 145 product placements were made.

The expansion of plugging in movies illustrates a more basic relationship between content and advertisement. In every medium, the content of the program or publication is closely allied with the perspective of the advertiser. No advertiser is going to support a publication or program with content adverse to the kind of values of possible advertisers. The delivery of large audiences who are alienated from advertised products is hardly going to gain the support of the advertiser. As a result the news media must wend their way between the discourses generated by all parties. They must balance what the various vested interests say with what other groups say, such as the public, the government, and the experts. Above all, they cannot forget advertiser sensibilities while, of course, not ignoring "undeniable facts."

THE NEWS STORY

The news story is a distinctive informational form that differs in its structure according to the medium within which it appears. However, all news stories share certain fundamental char-

acteristics. One Canadian study, *Visualizing Deviance: A Study of News Organization* by Richard Ericson, Patricia Baranek, and Janet Chan, developed a set of criteria to describe the characteristics of events that made them newsworthy. The criteria of newsworthiness they discuss have been usefully summarized by Desbarats (1990, p. 110):

- Simplification – an event must be recognized as significant and relatively unambiguous in its meaning.
- Dramatization – a dramatized version of the event must be able to be presented.
- Personalization – events must have personal significance to someone.
- Themes and continuity – events that fit into preconceived themes gain in newsworthiness.
- Consonance – events make the news more readily when they fit the reporters' preconceived notions of what should be happening.
- The Unexpected – unexpected events that can be expected within frames of reference used by reporters are newsworthy.

These criteria of newsworthiness are important to bear in mind as background to a consideration of the characteristics of news stories in individual media.

THE NEWSPAPER NEWS STORY

In print journalism the news story must be informative and interesting. To accomplish both of these goals, as we saw in the previous chapter, news stories are generally written according to a particular structure called the **inverted pyramid**. This means simply that a summary of the "important information" is put at the beginning followed by the development of the story and the context in which it happened. By "important information" journalists mean the five "w's," one "h," and one "s-w." That is to say, the story leads off with *"who, what, when, where, why, how,"* and then *"so what."* In more ways than one, that is just the beginning.

Journalists build into their stories a variety of other characteristics to try to make them both informative and interesting. First is **human interest.** A story with human actors, especially actors of some public reputation, is considered to be much more interesting than one that discusses policies or abstract ideas. A portrayal of Clyde Wells and Brian Mulroney battling it out over the Meech Lake Accord is much more interesting than a story listing the purported advantages and disadvantages of the Accord.

A second characteristic is **selectivity.** Information is important, but only if it is relevant. No matter how hard-earned the information is, if it turns out to be irrelevant it must be taken out of the story.

A third characteristic is **clarity**. The language must be simple and straightforward. Clarity is achieved by the avoidance of clichés, jargon, and excessively complex phraseology, more often called gobbledygook. In addition, the writing must make specific reference to people, events, and places.

Journalistic writing must also be **concise**. Neither unnecessary words nor redundancies should appear. Conciseness is also achieved through the use of the active voice: not "It was stated by the Prime Minister" but "The Prime Minister stated" Pace and tone are crucial. Ideas must be introduced at a pace the reader can understand. The tone of the story must reflect both subject matter and treatment of the material.

With regard to conciseness and clarity, it is shocking to a Canadian to read some of the up-market London papers. The length of sentences replete with subordinate clauses, all of which begin with "which" and prattle off on tangents that display more vocabulary than understanding, is, to say the least, noticeable.

Finally, **leads** are important to stories. Most often they are direct, sometimes giving the five "w's" in the first sentence. They must also serve to capture the readers' attention and orient them to the story. Delayed leads come in the second paragraph or sentence and exploit the curiosity of the reader established by an introductory delay.

Several points should be noted about the structure of a news story. The first is that, together with the headline, it allows the reader to get an idea of the news in a relatively quick fashion. With all the "important information" up front, readers can get a quick overview of the day's happenings. Given that they have some context of their own to bring to those events, they can choose to proceed through a story to its development of context and even analysis only if they so choose.

Tabloid versus Broadsheet Treatment

This story structure, as we noted earlier, has allowed the development of what are called tabloids, papers like those in the growing *Sun* chain, now in Toronto, Calgary, and Edmonton, and, to some extent, the *Vancouver Province*. In French Canada, the papers owned by Pierre Péladeau (who also owns the *Winnipeg Sun*) are the equivalent. They gain their name from the half-sized format of the pages, which makes them easy to read en route to work by public transit. But the characteristics of the writing in these newspapers are the cause for the disdain usually associated with the name "tabloid."

Besides fluff, that is, pictures of attractive young men and women, and low-level booster-ism of actual and potential advertisers, not much is to be found in any story besides the headline and a very quick relating of the five "w's." The format discourages lengthy analysis and detail,

A collage of weekly tabloid headlines. The degree of sensationalism, which is greater than in the dailies, is readily apparent.

and little context is provided. Events are often overdramatized and are interpreted as signals that things are either in control or, more often, out of control. As the accompanying collage of headlines illustrates, the unusual, unexplainable, and bizarre are often used as contexts, without analysis to make the events reported understandable in their occurrence and with regard to measures that will be taken to control future similar happenings. The world is presented in the tabloids as somewhat out of control and quite violent. At best, they can be amusing, the print equivalent of the Indiana Jones adventure series. Taken more seriously, they present a perspective that may encourage the notion that one never knows when such elements are going to invade one's own life. Consequently, the political bias of the tabloids is often right of centre and less liberal than that of the broadsheet papers.

Whether one sees them as vigorous and entertaining, or as intrusive, insensitive, and malicious, the tabloids' superficial treatment of stories periodically rouses disquiet in the U.K. about standards regarding privacy, libel, contempt, confidentiality, and slander. However, as an editorial in (Conrad Black's) *Sunday Telegraph* pointed out, if the government and, specifically, Margaret Thatcher really were outraged by the excesses of "the gutter press," why would she bestow knighthoods on its editors and elevate its proprietors to the House of Lords? (*Guardian Weekly,* July 1, 1990, p. 9).

The inverted pyramid and the medium of print mean that the journalist must tell the story, even if he or she uses liberal doses of quotations. This places the journalist and indeed the paper in a particular position in the mind of the reader. The angle taken on stories, what is brought forward and emphasized, is taken to be the perspective of the individual reporter and the paper. The discussion of context and the provision of analysis develops the

implicit position taken in the opening of the story. To assume that the angle taken on a story necessarily represents the view of the reporter, the editor, or the owner of the paper is, to a degree, the old problem of blaming the messenger, a problem around which neither journalist nor reader can steer. The reporter and editor are seen to be intervenors in the construction of the news even if they might not want to be. It is they who must tell the story. And while the press today is much less partisan than it has been in the past, the medium itself prevents the press from removing itself from this role as intervenor, interpreter, or mediator.

Events versus Issues

One further point, already mentioned in passing, must be emphasized. With the five "w's" up front, and with the constant emphasis on human interest and so on, what the news brings us is events rather than issues. As any public interest group knows (especially Greenpeace), any amount of informed analysis about a particular issue will never bring it onto the front pages. But an event, whether putting up a tent on Parliament Hill or barricading major traffic routes, will produce saturation coverage. Prior provision of information and analysis to a columnist is a good method of getting some of the issues discussed. But the event itself moves the issues to front and centre in the public agenda.

From the point of view of the public, and that of conscientious journalists, the irony of produced media events is that the produced event may obscure the importance of the real event. For example, the coverage of the 1988 meeting of the "Group of Seven" industrialized powers in Toronto focused on the helicopters patrolling the skies and the temporary housing of prostitutes and panhandlers in jail. Neither the issues discussed at the economic summit nor the city's ambition to demonstrate its ability to host the 1996 Olympics received much media attention (*Financial Post,* June 20, 1988, p. 25).

THE TELEVISION NEWS STORY

The most obvious difference between newspaper news stories and television news stories is the dominance of visuals. These visuals are not merely moving pictures that complement a text written up much like a newspaper text and then spoken by an announcer. The visuals structure the story and a text is built around those visuals.

The nature of the video camera is that while it is extremely intrusive for the actors of an event, it is quite invisible to the viewer. It claims by its ability to record sound and picture a veracity that no other medium can match. It apparently cannot lie. In its ability to record an event, barring intentional distortion, it brings the news to us from the mouths of the participants. What we see are snippets of the actual happenings, together with interpretations by on-the-spot observers and participants.

The trick for television news producers is to edit the material in such a way that the edits also appear unobtrusive. The visual coverage of the event must be simple enough to orient the viewer, but it must not appear incomplete. The sentences and phrases that are recorded and subsequently used in the final piece must be succinct and directly relevant. The speakers' identities must be obvious and they must have an obvious validity as observers or participants. On Parliament Hill, politicians who can speak in "clips" and who can move comfortably on camera are often the people sought out for background to stories. (*Globe and Mail,* April 6, 1988, p. A4).

A British Columbia television station once did a man-on-the-street interview of how Canadians felt about Pierre Trudeau's winter holidays. He was taking a few days on the beach in the South Pacific on his way to or from a diplomatic visit to the Orient. The street the news producers chose was the one on which was located the local Employment Canada office. The time was mid-February, 1982 – a year and season of high unemployment. However, in this case the plan backfired. The primary impression the news story gave was not of outraged people but rather of the artificial situation the news producers had created. The obtrusiveness of the news-constructing process was all too obvious.

What is primary in the television news story is not the interpretation of the story by the reporter out of all the information he or she can glean. Rather, it is the directing of the news crew interviewer and interviewees to create the elements of a story that can then be pieced together as a snippet of life.

Thesis, Antithesis, Synthesis

What television news presents to us is something that appears to be very direct and obviously true. But more than that, the television news story takes on a structure. In one sense it consists of two or more inverted, and many times incomplete, pyramids. First there is the visual summary of the event. Simultaneously or subsequently, one person provides his or her verbal summary. Following this is another perspective in a dispute, the story from the other side of the fence. The interviewer then steps back and brings these and other perspectives together, not to a resolution but more to a synthesis of the various positions or perspectives. In short, what is presented is **thesis, antithesis, and synthesis,** and all, often, in 30 to 90 seconds.

As with the newspaper news story, a number of attributes are crucial to high-quality TV reporting. To a large extent they are equivalent to preciseness, conciseness, human interest, clarity, pace, tone, and lead. But instead of these concepts being applicable only to the text, they are applicable to both text and visuals and the relations between the two.

The Camera versus the Reporter

The major difference between the newspaper news story and the television news story derives from the camera, the position in which the reporter or interviewer is placed as a result of the camera's ability to present facsimiles of real events. Instead of being in a position of messenger, the interviewer and his or her crew acts as a solicitor of information from others. Presenting that information and synthesizing it in the manner noted above, television news producers are apparently removed from a primary role of interpretation. They merely provide the means whereby the story and the participants can tell what they have to tell. In synthesizing the news, producers are apparently uninvolved. They merely manage the news by placing it in an understandable format. All this is a result of the dominance of the visual element. The camera never lies, or so we are led to believe.

However, it frames. It puts some things in the picture and keeps others out. It can emotionalize with the extreme close-up or provide a "more objective" panorama. It can present the authoritative distance of the medium close-up against a neutral cardboard backdrop or include an entire visual environment and attendant mood.

THE STUDY OF NEWS

In our discussion of advertising, specifically the Black Label ad campaign, we presented a simplified semiotic analysis. A content analysis of advertising would rarely be done on a single ad or ad series but would, more often, be used with many different ads to determine the frequency of use of certain categories of images, objects, types of persons, events, and so on.

The study of news does not differ a great deal from the study of advertising. Content analyses are often performed not on the individual stories themselves but on news programs. The tables included in Chapter 10 present the data of a content analysis that a group of us did on CBC national radio news from January to June, 1982. Many other content analyses of news exist (Berelson, 1972). The conclusions of such studies mostly have to do with the manner in which news is organized and what picture of the world is thereby presented to the reader, listener, or viewer. The discussion can then proceed to considering the implications of such a news structure.

Semiotic analyses of news can examine anything from a set of news programs to an individual news item, story, photograph, or visual. This type of analysis concentrates on the positioning of the various elements in the piece or the totality of pieces being considered. It works toward an articulation of the internal relations among those elements. For example, semiotic-type studies have drawn attention to the fact that labour is usually associated with on-the-street events such as recurring disorder, while management is often used to provide analysis in the context of the controlled, peaceful, quiet environment of a plush executive office. The implications of this way of using sources is that, even in a lockout, labour is shown as the instigator of the stoppage and management the patient victim. Semiological studies thus tend to show the signification process of newsmaking: what is deemed to be important and how it is placed within a meaning system. What is the nature of the news story? How does it reproduce the dominant ideology?

There are, of course, other studies of news, the most obvious being those dealing with what gets included in the news and what does not. While content analyses can enter into these studies as a first level sorting out of what is and is not there, these studies then tend to turn away from content and toward the process of news-gathering and the influence of professional ideals and the goals of owners (see Gans, 1979; Tuchman, 1978). These issues will be taken up in Chapter 7.

SOAPS

Radio soap operas were originally developed by an ad agency for its soap company client. They were designed to socialize a home-confined female audience with disposable income into the art of consuming. In a sense, soaps represented the life of the fictitious satisfied consumer whose worldly needs were entirely taken care of by the various products that she had purchased for her family. Once these needs were satisfied, she could turn her mind to dreaming of a richer, more fulfilling life found in the Gothic and romance novels of the thirties. However, pure fantasy was not the only powerful opiate. Not long after the soaps had established themselves, a kind of realistic fantasy was developed featuring professionals whose lives were made of the stuff of fiction. So was developed an illusion of reality that has carried through to the present day. Our discussion of the soaps will take us through this illusion into the dominant themes of present-day soaps and then into the grammar of the medium, the devices used to achieve the realistic illusion.

Soap Culture

Perhaps the most salient characteristic of the soaps is that, in contrast to movies, novels, or night-time television, there is no obvious dramatic patterning. There is neither a beginning nor a foreseeable end. This allows for the presentation of a set of characters in continuous narrative, a narrative that follows the seasons of the year and even the various festivities of mainstream Euro-North American culture. At times, world events can enter into the dialogue. Certain issues of the time definitely do. To prevent awkward particularities from discouraging a complete identification with the characters by the viewer, generic settings, usually inside rather than outside, predominate.

The characters in a soap become like neighbours who drop by on a daily basis. What distinguishes them as visitors is that they have the power, and seemingly the need, to confide their intimate secrets and feelings to the audience without the knowledge of the other soap characters. The lives of these characters are therefore separate from but continuous with the lives of the viewers. Like the lives of the viewers, there is no final climax to the play but rather a series of mini-climaxes in the ongoing action. There are occasions for the utmost joy as well as jealousy, envy, frustration, greed, and so forth.

The vehicle that allows for this continuity is the family. Without the family as the centre of every soap, all of the connivance, backbiting, jealousy, vengefulness, and so forth would be unbelievable. For only in the family is any individual burdened and blessed with permanent associations with other human beings. In any other social group, we have the opportunity to exit, to change our circumstances, to leave behind individuals with whom we are not compatible. The family is the vehicle for continuity; but it is also the vehicle for a concentration on character, the realm of the personal and the situational psychology that emanates from it.

By putting forward the family as the central focus, the illusion of reality can be maintained with scarcely a nod in the direction of the social, economic, and political environments. In the family, such realms of human striving and existence are more or less held equal. Internal family relations can, for the most part, be presented as if they were not determined or even affected by class economics and politics. Everyone is middle-class, or *nouveau riche,* or dandified middle-class. So the soaps can dwell on the personal without seeming to leave important levels of human existence out of the picture.

The British use soaps slightly differently. A constant diet of vulgar and semi-sumptuous materialism is not for them. Instead, they wallow in a more varied world of make-believe now dominated by poverty, now busybodies, and now class difference. It is difficult to say why the Americans insist on a greater homogeneity in their soaps, as in all things. It may be that the British are happy to have the naturalness of a layered class society confirmed. Perhaps, also, as a spent empire, they are more able to be entertained by the warts rather than the beauty spots of the modern condition.

A third version of the soap opera that enjoys phenomenal success around the world is the Brazilian "téléroman." Stories like "Heart of Diamonds" and "Isaura the Slave," with plot lines that play off everyday realities and focus on a multiracial mix of characters, have proven popular in countries as diverse as Nigeria, Morocco, and the Soviet Union. Other countries, such as Japan and India, also have their own soaps.

The Soap Vehicle

While the family is the vehicle for character continuity and a situational and character psychology, family dynamics in the sense of parent/parent, parent/child, and sibling relations

are not the primary thematic content. The primary dramatic content derives from individual character relations with both family and the world. To use *Dallas* as an example, how does a greedy person like J.R. Ewing survive day-to-day life? What are the various schemes a conniving person with a lot of money, such as Pam's sister, Katherine Barnes, might invent? What are the dynamics of women in business life? Here the soaps rely on male and female stereotypes for their character and plot outlines. Women are to be found in roles of power but they are there through the efforts of some man, usually their father. Women who have gained positions on their own merits are seen to be possessed with the curse of ambition or greed. They do not derive status from positive traits such as determination or talent.

Against a family backdrop, personal and gender politics provide primary thematic material. In both cases, emancipation from a basic identity given a character, whether that of personality or gender, is forever solicited but infinitely postponed. The case is the same with body type, especially for women. Fat, thin, short, tall, all contribute in a major way to the place of the character in the drama. Fat women are losers, as are women who are too short.

Nor are the themes contained entirely by the identity of the target audience. While the target audience still remains homemakers, young love has become wildly successful as thematic material. The decisive point for entry into family life (young love confirmed) could hardly be considered a boring subject. Its perpetual interest is confirmed by the success of Harlequin novels. Similarly, social relevance has come to be exploited by the soaps: prejudice, drug addiction, sexual repression, abortion, venereal disease, and so on all claim their hour on the stage. The soaps gain a certain notoriety by airing these issues (while never contributing seriously to the debate). But their popularity is hardly surprising when one thinks that the lives of most adults are touched twice by these potentially life-determining issues: once when the adult is in adolescence and a second time when his or her children reach adolescence. Another non-traditional market has been exploited with the success of *Lance et compte (He Shoots, He Scores)* in Quebec. There, audiences of 2.5 million confirm the centrality of hockey as part of local culture, while boosting the profile of the sponsor, Ultramar, an oil-refining and gasoline-retailing firm.

The illusion of reality and the ability to exploit these themes would not be possible without a cinematic code appropriate to the genre. That cinematic code is characterized by a number of techniques. Primary is the long, peering, extreme close-up, a framing technique that allows the viewer to search the face of the actor for its expression of emotion. This technique also encourages feelings of intimacy.

The long, peering shot is enhanced by being taken from eye level. The viewer becomes the eye of the camera, intimately involved and yet quite separated from and unaffected by events. Similarly, the slow pace of the drama allows the viewer time to read in a depth of emotion, and thus encourages the prediction of events and interpretation of reactions.

MUSIC VIDEOS

In a fashion similar to the soap, music videos, particularly rock videos, have emerged from the demands of producers to socialize an audience into an increased purchasing of their product. The difference between the soaps and music videos is that the product to be purchased is part of the promotional vehicle used to bring it to the attention of the audience. Music videos are visually enhanced versions of the records that the audience is intended to purchase.

The sudden explosion of rock videos and rock video television shows is not accounted for by the fact that these manage to express something that no other medium has done quite as well. Rather, rock videos make cheap television, just as playing records makes cheap radio. As of 1990, rock videos were distributed free to organizations that could assemble audiences, whether in pubs or through television. Suddenly, costs of a half-hour original television show dropped from $2,000-$2,500 a minute to approximately the same amount for a half hour. The beauty of the beasts was that they assembled quite sizable audiences whose attention could then be sold to advertisers.

Roots of Rock Video

As with each of the media forms discussed in this chapter, rock videos have evolved from other forms in the media. Movies featuring rock stars such as the Elvis Presley, Richard Lester's iconoclastic movies with the Beatles, and filmed recordings or concerts were the precursors of the rock video. Rock videos themselves were around the industry for several years before they exploded into television, first in the U.K. and then in North America (Laba and Lorimer, 1986).

Characteristics of the Form

In contrast to the soaps, rock videos are as fast-paced as any movie or television ad. They feature jump cuts, crazy juxtapositions, and an intense bombardment of images somewhat inspired by the song's rhythm and lyrics but certainly not constrained by its literal meaning. They appear to take their inspiration from the "visual effects" of movies, providing, again in contrast to the soaps, surrealism rather than realism. Their sets are often reminiscent of non-representational sculpture, and appear to represent reductions of modern living to an anticipated future without a clear reflection of human values and detail. They serve also to partition the rock market through easy visual identification of rock, heavy metal, rap, dance music, etc. Insofar as they take their lead from visual effects (which require more money than imagination), they allow the purchase of market dominance; such a situation places performers like Madonna and Prince, whose record companies will afford lavish extravaganzas to promote their songs, at a considerable advantage over less established artists. A carefully choreographed and staged video like Janet Jackson's "Alright" is certain to find heavy rotation on video playlists. This production is twice as long as the average video, a further extravagance that marks it as a special treat for fans.

Many videos are a means for the fan to engage in a rather straightforward voyeurism. The focus of the video is the individual artist or, in the case of a group, primarily the lead singer acting as chief protagonist. (The New Kids on the Block videos are a prominent exception: they offer five lead singers, one for every taste, democratically sharing lead vocals and video time.) The nature of the dominant vision in rock videos can best be contrasted with the literary, filmic, and choreography-based imagination apparent in Leonard Cohen's award-winning production, I am a Hotel (see Lorimer, 1988). There, while ample use is made of visual effects, the effects almost continually mean something in the ongoing narrative. In fact, rock videos, like the songs they promote, only occasionally represent the narrative form.

As with other communication forms, patterns of content can be seen in current rock videos. Bondage, especially of women, and restriction of all kinds are used to identify some of the more extreme forms of heavy metal. Violence, disembodiment, chaos, explosions, destruction are also present. Chase scenes, or their visual metaphorical equivalent, are occasionally used. The fragmentation and fetishization of the female body are matched by the aggressive phallic display of the male guitar players. A welcome contrast to such videos are those by the likes of Michelle Shocked, Melissa Etheridge, and Alannah Myles, which feature women in positions of authority.

It is interesting to speculate about the meaning and future of rock videos. While their sudden success is attributable to the economics of entertainment on television and in pubs, they are obviously not boring to their audience. The point to be made is that their key role in marketing, as with any promotional form, cannot help but influence the form itself. The form is also influenced by technology. For instance, one possible reason for the frantic cutting of music videos is that many people watch television with their remote controls at hand: the cuts are so quick that viewers do not even have the time to think of switching away.

Rock videos are similar in their structure to such movies as Graffiti Bridge, Purple Rain, and Flashdance. The notion behind these movies, according to the creator of Flashdance, Tom Hedley, is visual rather than narrative. Hedley sees 17- and 18-year-olds as involved in the creation of an interior musical that they act out, thereby creating the style they use to live their lives. He claims that such people take their inspiration from fashion photographs and magazine illustrations. They invest in such idealizations an individual interpretation and a dynamism built on popular music, thus ridding the pictures of their frozenness in time. The personal style of living results from this process.

Hedley's conceptions are founded (consciously or not) on the perspective developed by Goffman, which is foundational to the next chapter. They are also consistent with more recent research, such as that by Fornas, Lindberg, and Sernhede (1988). As Curran (1990, p. 154) remarks:

> The underlying assumption of this and similar research is that popular culture provides the raw material for experimenting with and exploring social identities in the context of a postmodernist society where the walls of tradition that support and confine them are crumbling. In this case, rock music is viewed as a laboratory for the intensive production of identity by adolescents seeking to define an independent self.

SUMMARY

The nature of representation or, as the semioticians would have it, signification is that it constructs meaning that refers to aspects of the real world and expresses that meaning within symbol systems such as language. It is a realm not subordinate to that of physical objects. Its study involves the study of indeterminate systems. The study of communication is thus closely aligned with interpretation, an activity more familiar to the humanities than to science or social science.

Two major methods used to study content are semiotics and content analysis. Both are oriented to the structure of content; the former is a fully developed theory, the latter a technique. The insights of semiotics lead to an understanding of the relations between a particular piece and the broader perspectives and theories of society from which it is derived. Content analysis allows us to see repetitive patterns that suggest underlying organizing assumptions built into the material.

Because underlying patterns and general structures do not comprise the whole picture for our understanding of communication, content analysis and semiotics are being supplemented and, to some extent, replaced by five other frameworks: discourse analysis, Foucauldian analysis, cultural studies, deconstructionism, and post-modernism. These approaches pay greater attention to the particular.

While all seven of these frameworks provide insights into the meaning system of any individual piece of communication in any medium, the medium within which meaning is expressed is also a determining factor in how meaning is constructed or how information is designed. Advertising emphasizes the complementarity of images. Newspaper news stories build on the standard inverted pyramid. Television news stories are organized primarily by the intrusion of the camera as opposed to the reporter. Soap operas have developed their own set of visual techniques to present an intimate, universal world. And rock videos bombard the viewer with technological gimmicks, bringing him or her back continually to the TV set and to the record store for a new hit.

APPENDIX:
DIALOGUE ON DRINKING

The Problem

Canadian consumption of alcohol has doubled since 1950. In Canada the annual bill for health costs and property damage directly related to excessive drinking is staggering. Fifty million dollars are spent on intensive alcohol treatment. And every year hundreds of millions of dollars are poured into paying for alcohol-related accidents.*

Today's youth is especially vulnerable. As adolescents make the difficult transition from childhood to adulthood, they are struggling to define their own identities. As they move farther into adulthood, they face a wave of new challenges: the pressures of maturing relationships, the responsibilities of marriage and family life, and fresh uncertainties about career goals in a period of economic insecurity.

They may respond to these pressures in a variety of ways. Drinking is one. According to a May, 1982, youth Gallup Poll, the average age given for trying alcohol is twelve. Sixty per cent of the young people polled stated that alcohol consumption "can make you feel part of the group." Sixty-five per cent said that it "can make you feel less shy," and 40 per cent noted that it "can help you if you are nervous." In other words, drinking is seen as a way of easing personal stress, especially on the social scene.

Recent research studies conducted by Health and Welfare are very revealing:

- The sharpest increase in (alcohol) usage occurs between the lower and upper teens for both males and females.
- Heavy drinking among teenagers tends to involve high levels of binge drinking.
- In 1981, 169,000 persons of all ages were charged with alcohol-related traffic offences, including criminal negligence, dangerous driving, and driving while impaired. Over 40 per cent of alcohol-related traffic offences occurred among persons 15 to 29 years of age.

* This Appendix consists of background briefing materials, edited slightly for inclusion here, for a government media campaign to combat overdrinking. Reproduced with permission of Health and Welfare Canada.

Background Research

Three major research tools were used to develop this campaign. The findings included the following:

- Young people, interviewed in Vancouver, Winnipeg, Toronto, Montreal, and Halifax, believe most moderation campaigns have been directed to older people.
- Awareness measurements of the phase one of Dialogue indicate that although the target group was 25- to 49-year-olds, 15- to 25-year-olds manifest the highest awareness.
- A Gallup survey, conducted in May, 1982, established that young people feel that alcohol use, like cannabis, is influenced by peer pressure.

New Program: Description

Against this background, development of the next phase of Dialogue has been undertaken. The intent is to build on the success of the media campaign and strengthen the community action strategy by:

- Focusing on high-risk groups and the issues associated with drinking.
- Using advertising and promotion to give a national profile, which will express federal government concern about hazardous alcohol use and provide an umbrella for community activity.
- Ensuring follow-through at the community level by working with provincial and territorial drug agencies to develop guidelines and resources to assist groups to initiate awareness and education projects.

Objectives

- To achieve a social consensus increasingly supportive of the safe consumption of alcohol.
- To stimulate self-examination of drinking behaviours in people aged 15 to 29.
- To stimulate collective examination of issues related to moderate and high-risk drinkers aged 15 to 29.

Target Group

- Males – 20 to 29 – predominantly, blue-collar workers and students.
- Females – 15 to 29 – white-collar workers and students.

Creative Strategy

Phase two of Dialogue plans to counter the beverage industry's lifestyle advertising with credible, modern messages about moderation. It should be noted that the beer, wine, and spirits industries spend over $100 million annually in Canada on advertising and promotion. It is vital, in order to effectively reach the target audience, to depart from the traditional and historical aspects inherent to the promotion of moderation. Therefore, a new term is proposed to describe alcohol abuse – *overdrinking.*

Since previous Dialogue ads have asked Canadians to think about and talk about it, phase two of Dialogue will suggest that the next logical step is to *take action on overdrinking.* This is in step with Canadians' growing concern on alcohol issues such as drinking and driving.

The individuals reached through this campaign will, by the end of the five-year program, become a new crowd of *real people who actively endorse moderation.* The people who will be selected to speak, in their own words, about moderation, will either be amateur sport champions or ordinary Canadian workers, all of the same age groups as the target audience. The visuals of these commercials will be based on the dynamics of action.

Media Strategy: Execution

Television is planned as the main vehicle of this campaign, with campaign support provided by transit/shelter and mall posters and limited print advertising.

Purchase

Since beer advertisers concentrate their media purchases on sport properties and direct their commercials to 18-29-year-olds, spots on sport programs, such as baseball and football, would be purchased to stretch the visibility of the campaign. The strategy is that one Dialogue ad placed with three or four beer commercials will receive more attention. The campaign would be on-air in the summer, when Canadian consumption of alcohol is at its greatest, and during the fall, when the festive season begins.

Dialogue on Drinking Creative Rationale: Another Five Years

The advertising segment of the Dialogue II program has a difficult mandate to fulfil. It must create positive awareness for Dialogue on strict advertising terms. And it must tie in nicely with existing Dialogue materials. It should be able to fit into any specific community's ongoing alcohol abuse programs, and indeed, be complementary to it. Dialogue II must offer something more, an extension of the existing Dialogue premise, the TALK ABOUT IT: THINK ABOUT IT theme. Additionally, Dialogue II must be flexible enough to be meaningful in all regions of Canada. It should be seen to have been conceived and executed in any community. It must be broad enough in scope and potential to allow its continuity to build over a five-year period.

At the same time, and perhaps most difficult, the advertising segment must appeal across the 15-29 age group, through the most turbulent and trying years of human development. These are just the specific program requirements.

The actual advertising of moderation in alcohol use is in itself not easy. The overdrinker is notoriously unaware of his or her habit's impingement upon performance, judgement, and the feelings of others. Teens, moving away from the smoky illegality of pot, may find alcohol a welcome legal high, endorsed weekly by parents, sipped at church, grand benefactor of baseball, hockey, and football, a high reinforced by handsome men and women after the slightest bout with sweat in TV commercials.

It's okay to drink.

It's the popular thing to do.

And alcohol has a great benefit over its running mate, tobacco. It makes you feel good.

It's fun.

It lets you forget.

Almost all present beer advertising uses beer as a reward for doing something. Whether it's "Jim and the boys getting together to launch a cottage raft, then sinking a couple of cases of Molson's" or "This Bud's for you, for all you do" or "Here's to playing hard and drinking easy," the theme of much beer advertising is that almost any activity is an excuse to party. And the set-up is not to have just one or two beers; the implication is that the beer at the end of the day is a celebration. Current beer advertising promotes the idea that if you walk, swim, crawl, or dance more than 10 feet, you deserve a beer in celebration.

The market to which the breweries pitch their reward advertising is similar to the one we are interested in, about 18- to 29-year-olds. Because of the high profile beer advertising receives on television, and because beer commercials appear in much sports continuity (baseball, hockey), the young end of the market scale, 18- to 29-year-olds, is particularly affected.

We believe we have an opportunity to take advantage of some of the weakness in logic of the breweries' reward appeal, to give impact and awareness to our new Dialogue II moderation campaign. As stated earlier, we have a tough job, but if we see it as making it all right to be moderate in drinking habits, and if we can give visible proof that moderation is practised by many people, especially people who are achievers, then we can make a positive statement for moderation.

But beer advertising, while capable of reinforcing a trend to partying, is not responsible for immoderate behaviour. And our advertising of moderation must try to address more basic issues of insecurity, boredom, peer pressure, and so on.

Our main advertising medium should be television, with support in posters and print advertising that can be used in specific communities. Television reaches more of our target market for less than any other medium and does it on the same turf used by the breweries. Television imparts glamour and the aura of excitement to a message and our moderation story can take advantage of this intrinsic television benefit.

An effective television campaign must make sense when applied to specific programs in different areas of the country. If a community group has a project to help reduce drunken driving, then our general advertising should be able to fit into the program and to help give it impetus and credibility.

Flexibility is the key.

But the problem with many flexible advertising themes is that they tend to be bland in nature, and therefore lacking in potency and memorability. So, our strategy would include a vehicle capable of carrying specific theme messages in a memorable way, while offering continuity that will build awareness and stature.

This vehicle should be able to operate for at least five years and be capable of being renewed, without significant wear-out. And it must be relatively inexpensive.

The television campaign must also be capable of translation into various print components, which can be applied to specific community projects. While the look may change to take advantage of the medium, the tonality should remain constant.

Our idea for a freshly defined and sustaining advertising campaign for Dialogue involves the dynamics of action. The program, to date, has created awareness of drinking problems, at least of the importance of bringing them out into the open, of talk being the beginning of understanding and remedy.

Now we feel we need action.

We need to translate the positive thoughts of moderation grown over the past years into action. We want people to think that they can actually do something to control overdrinking.

A simple theme that will fit nicely with the existing Dialogue theme apparatus is: TAKE ACTION ON OVERDRINKING. The word "overdrinking" tacitly states that moderate drinking is okay. It places the problem and the danger together in one word. It has connotations with overeating, etc., and it effectively removes us from the WCTU and teetotaler image.

"Overdrinking" is a useful word when selling moderation.

It defines a state of excess without resorting to a tangle of ounces or glasses or bottles per kilo of body weight.

It is easily understood by everyone, as is overeating, overworking, overtraining. It is something of which you have done too much.

It lets us stay away from numbers while getting our point across.

REFERENCES

Barthes, Roland. *Elements of Semiology.* A. Lavers and C. Smith, trans. New York: Hill and Wang, 1968.

Barthes, Roland. s/z Paris, Seuil, 1970.

Bennett, Tony. "Media, 'Reality,' Signification," in Gurevitch *et al.,* eds., *Culture, Society and the Media.* Toronto: Methuen, 1982.

Berelson, Bernard. *Content Analysis in Communication Research.* New York: Hafner, 1972.

Berton, Pierre. *Hollywood's Canada.* Toronto: McClelland and Stewart, 1975.

Curran, James. "The New Revisionism in Mass Communication Research: A Reappraisal," *European Journal of Communication,* 5, 2-3 (June, 1990), pp. 135-64.

Desbarats, Peter. *Guide to Canadian News Media.* Toronto: Harcourt Brace Jovanovich, 1990.

Eco, Umberto. *The Name of the Rose.* New York: Warner Books, 1984.

Eco, Umberto. *Travels in Hyperreality.* Orlando, Fla.: Harcourt Brace Jovanovich, 1986.

Ericson, Richard, Patricia Baranek, and Janet Chan, *Negotiating Control: A Study of News Sources.* Toronto: University of Toronto Press, 1989.

Ericson, Richard, Patricia Baranek, and Janet Chan, *Visualizing Deviance: A Study of News Organization.* Toronto: University of Toronto Press, 1987.

Fornas, J., U. Lindberg, and O. Sernhede. *Under Rocken.* Stockholm: Symposium, 1988.

Frye, N. *The Critical Path: An Essay on the Social Context of Literary Criticism.* Bloomington: Indiana University Press, 1971.

Gans, Herbert. *Deciding What's News: A Study of CBS Evening News, NBC Nightly News, Newsweek, and Time.* New York: Pantheon Books, 1979.

Grady, Wayne. "The Budweiser Gamble," *Saturday Night* (February, 1983), pp. 28-30.

Hackett, R.A. "Decline of a Paradigm? Bias and Objectivity in News Media Studies," *Critical Studies in Mass Communication,* 1, 3 (1984), pp. 229-59.

Hackett, R.A. "KAL: the Media Exploited Story," *Gateway,* Edmonton, October 25, 1983, p. 5. Reprinted as "Massacres and the Media: the KAL Story," *Canadian Dimension* (December, 1983), pp. 17-19.

Hall, S., *et al. Policing the Crisis: Mugging, the State and Law and Order.* London: Macmillan, 1978.

Heydon, Elizabeth. "The Land of the Soaps," unpublished paper, Simon Fraser University, 1984.

Laba, M., and R. Lorimer, prods. *Video, Vinyl and Culture* (30 min. video), Part 3 of Mass Communication in Canada. Burnaby: Simon Fraser University, 1986. Distributor: Magic Lantern, Oakville, Ontario.

Lorimer, R. "Canada in an Expanding, Industrialized Communications Environment," in R. Lorimer and D.C. Wilson, eds., *Communication Canada.* 1988.

Miller, Mark Crispin. "Hollywood: the Ad," *The Atlantic Monthly,* 265, 4 (April, 1990), pp. 41-68.

Olive, D. "Ads vs. Editorials: Have New Lines Been Drawn?" *Quill and Quire* (September, 1984), pp. 71-73.

Orwell, G. *Homage to Catalonia.* Harmondsworth: Penguin, 1974.

Pollack, D. "Mister Flashdance," *Saturday Night* (October, 1984).

Tuchman, Gaye. *Making News: a Study in the Construction of Reality.* New York: Free Press, 1987.

Woollacott, J. "Messages and Meanings," in Gurevitch *et al.,* eds., *Culture, Society and the Media.*

STUDY QUESTIONS

1. Semiotics is a basic technique of research and a basic point of view that every student of communications should understand. Provide examples of sign, signifier, and signified in the print medium, in painting, and in the movies. Specify the dyadic relations for each example.

2. Content analysis is another basic technique. Perform a content analysis of an individual article, then of an entire magazine. In the case of the magazine, you might leave it at setting up the analytic categories. If you carry the example through, you may be surprised at the results.

3. The power of an ad, a newspaper story, a rock video, a television drama, or even a newsmagazine derives partly from the uniqueness of each and partly from characteristics in common. Discuss, using examples.

4. In the CBC documentary *The Press and the Prime Minister,* gossip columnist Nigel Dempster refers to the storybook nature of newspaper content. One might say that the news content overlaps with that of soap operas. What advantages and disadvantages are there to that overlap?

5. Emphasis on design of information over content is extreme in ads. Discuss the image and the reality of the Black Label ads or Labatt's campaign for Budweiser.

6. One might suppose that a mass market would encourage a great variety of products. But in the example of beer, at least, all brands are fairly much the same in taste. Comment.

CHAPTER

5

The Media and
the Audience

INTRODUCTION:
THE LIMITATIONS
OF EFFECTS ANALYSIS

I N MANY TEXTBOOKS the topics discussed in this chapter are categorized as "effects." For example, the question of the effects of rock videos may be considered. Or, for example, what effect does the format of television news have on our views of the world, our political choices at the ballot box, or even our views of journalists? Similarly, are television soap operas a form of escape for people who are bored, and do they change the attitudes of their viewers, perhaps giving them unrealistic expectations that may lead to marriage problems, family problems, and, ultimately, social instability? All of the above are "effects" questions, and, of course, many more could be asked.

This manner of conceiving the interaction between the audience and the media derives from early research into the media conducted primarily by American social psychologists, such as Katz and Lazarsfeld (1955) and Klapper (1960). The primary question that interested these psychologists was the *influence of the media.* They were working to dispel the formulations of a set of European social theorists known as the Frankfurt School. The claim of the Frankfurt School was that the media were *destroying culture,* in the sense of culture as that which knits a nation or people together, including the common assumptions, behaviour patterns, and attitudes toward the world. These Europeans claimed also that the media were destroying folk culture, those traditions that were distinctive to the peasant and working classes of a nation or country (see, for example, Adorno and Horkheimer, 1972). The ideological assumption of the American psychologists who set out to counteract these notions was that the media were a marvellous democratic institution that brought all people into the mainstream of the culture. They set out to document the "effects" of exposure to the information and entertainment the media were able to bring into the homes and neighbourhoods of all Americans.

Conceiving of the link between the media and people as "effects" tends to narrow the scope of the kind of questions one might ask about media-audience interaction; also, it is difficult to point to the exact connections clearly and unambiguously. Formulations about effects can be clear and unambiguous only in cases that are simple and not of great social import. Thus, while experiments certainly can be designed to test the memories of members of an audience for some particular statement made as part of a television presentation, unless that statement is trivial or very specific in its detail, similar or related messages would have been encountered elsewhere in the social environment. Because of the impossibility of controlling the prior exposure of audience members to the message in question, let alone what they have made of that exposure, it is therefore impossible to isolate the "effects" of the media contribution to a wide selection of people's

opinions or behaviour. Even in cases when one finds the "smoking television set," a set belonging to some individual who has committed a heinous crime tuned to a channel that hours previously had shown a model of the crime committed, there is always more to the story. For example, what in the person's background could make him (or her) vulnerable to internalizing a message to act in such an aberrant fashion? Consequently, discussion of the "effects" of media on society becomes problematic.

MEDIA AND SOCIETY: AN INTERACTION OF MEANING-GENERATING SYSTEMS

Once we reconceive media-society interaction as a question of media content and audience behaviour, we move away from a limited, causal equation to a more open consideration of people and media messages and forms. In such a discussion we do not need to assume that the media program messages into people in the same manner that a computer is programmed. Nor do we need to try to make the case that, subject to the receptivity of individuals, the media can program in certain messages. The point is to discuss and compare media content to audience behaviour without assuming that a direct path connects the two and makes the latter dependent on the former.

Determination versus Interaction

As meaning- and image-generating entities, both individuals and the media affect one another, but they do not determine one another because the nature of the interaction is always multidimensional. Media and individuals interact with and affect one another because both generate meaning and each is an active part of the environment of the other. If one is not an active element in the environment of the other, then the relation does not hold. Once we accept that the nature of the relationship is interactional we can discuss the interaction between audience behaviour and the information presented by the media. They can be compared with one another and analysed for their relation to broader forms of social behaviour and concepts.

In general, as meaning-generating entities both individuals and the media select elements from each other, re-stylize those elements, and display them for possible reappropriation by others. The dynamics of this system are the basis for Eco's posed dilemma over the alligator on the polo shirt (see Chapter 2). Stated differently, *lived reality and media reality interact with one another through a constant process of mutual selection, re-stylization (or appropriation), and re-display.*

in a popular magazine article John Lekich (1982) provides an illustration (but not an explanation like Berger's) of media-audience interaction. Basically, in an amusing and vivid manner, he illustrates by example the role television played in his childhood. He talks of his mother's attention to the set as a valued piece of furniture. He talks of his early wonder about how so many people came to be inside the TV set. He recreates the child's wonder and naive embrace of mother figures like June Allyson, his literal interpretation of Camay ads, and his persistent if not desperate attempt to touch the people behind the television screen.

Perhaps what makes his piece so interesting is the detail of his memory. These details evoke memories and the images come rolling back to anyone who grew up in the same era or who has seen re-runs. The memories include not only the content of the programs but the entire family dynamic that the television programs created: what restrictions there were on viewing, how late one was allowed to stay up, parental differences in viewing habits, involvement in programs, and so forth. In short, he gives us access to his memory of the world created for him by his television set. Whether his model was June Allyson, Van Johnson, Jimmy Stewart, Robert Young, or Donna Reed, they and the situations in which they were placed, including intervening commercials, provided the fabric of his dreams. As he says, based on the television world:

> My wife would be ideal. She would have no cavities, an embroidered hanky for each day of the week, and a hairdo with crash helmet durability. She would never do the upsetting things that mothers did, like making you eat creamed corn or sticking name tags on the inside of your underwear. At night we would walk up a long staircase to our separate beds, and read books across to each other. Just like Donna Reed.

The power of the article is that it makes the futility of calculating the percentage influence of television versus social interaction versus movies versus books quite apparent. It forces upon us a recognition of the extent to which the material presented on television can become fodder for a child's imagination. Lekich and the various producers of the television shows he watched can be seen as **semi-autonomous, meaning-generating systems** each in interaction with the other. Lekich was in interaction with the programming through viewing. It was in interaction with him through his willingness, along with millions of others, to tune in each week to these various shows and through the sponsors' interest in having access to him and his fellow audience members. The nature of this interaction is that neither is free from the influence of the other, yet neither is determined by the other.

However, there is certainly not a lack of interaction. The dynamics of the interaction from the media side are not entirely invisible. They are the ratings game and all that transpires in the creation and presentation of programs. It is a game played constantly by the networks as they assess the audience shares of each of their programs.

In "How *Quest's* crew charted a suicide course," former managing editor Lynn Cunningham documents some aspects of audience-media interaction from the media side. As much as being killed by the owners, she maintains that the staff led the magazine down a suicide road. *Quest* offered writers, photographers, layout artists, editors, and other creative people a chance to do their best work. The result was that the magazine appealed editorially as interesting, exciting, and unpredictable, but from the point of view of media buyers, the people who locate vehicles for advertisers to reach known audiences in a known frame of mind, it was denounced. As Cunningham says: "good journalism . . . as media buyers are fond of pointing out, has little to do with good numbers." Michael Enright, the former editor, might have had a different opinion.

THE INVASION OF THE IMAGINATION OF AN INDIVIDUAL

For the audience, their interaction with the media has a longer-term aspect to it and probably more profound implications. What does it mean to have an imagination filled with the characters, events, and settings of the media? Because Lekich has given us such an engaging self-report, let us continue with the example provided in his article. First we will propose some elements of the identity of a viewer such as John Lekich. In doing this we do not pretend to be exhaustive in defining all the characteristics that make up the identity of a person. We will stick to a social identity and ignore the psychological, economic, and partisan political identities. Also, it should be pointed out that, as with readings of media materials, there can be as many readings of the identity of a person as there are people to do the readings.

For our purposes, let us propose three elements of a social identity for our fictitious viewer: he is young and male, Canadian, and of non-British stock. How might these elements interact with the content of the programs he watched as a child?

If what Lekich says might be considered to be typical, our viewer could easily have used the women he saw on television as the basis for idealized versions of two female roles, mother and partner. Rather humorously, Lekich points out how he made invidious comparisons between the television ideals and his own family. While this presentation of women the programs put forward was available to all viewers of both sexes, it has a particular significance to a growing boy. It provides a basis for a restricted view of women as home-based partners in a child-rearing enterprise or as ever-solicitous caretakers of one's every want and need. By implication (and at times explicitly) it puts forward a role model for the males as persons who can expect such solicitous behaviour from women.

A second element of our viewer's social identity is his nationality. In our discussion of soaps we noted how many of the shots were of interiors. We claimed that these interiors served the function of making the material "generic," as capable of happening everywhere but happening nowhere in particular. Generic material is not peculiar to soap operas. It is to be found in all mass-market materials, from ads to school textbooks. But, rather than actually erasing all specifics, it tends to erase only up-front cultural particularities, the kinds of elements that communicate that the story is set in the U.S. or Canada, Montreal or Vancouver, the Prairies or the Maritimes. But generic material does not erase cultural assumptions. Nor does it erase the background cultural particularities that require that the story could only have happened in one particular culture or country.

In the programs mentioned in Lekich's "Horizontal Hold," a great many cultural assumptions are intrinsic to the material:

- the authority of the father, father as breadwinner, mother as homemaker, all in *Father Knows Best;*
- woman as pretty if not beautiful seductress-servant in *I Dream of Jeannie;*
- the dream of being a millionaire in *The Millionaire;*
- the theatre of wrestling;
- the role of the lawyer for the defendant as opposed to the lawyer for the state in *Perry Mason;*
- the association of physical handicap with limited intellectual ability and the sexual and community politics of lawmen and madam in *Gunsmoke.*

The list could continue.

Hidden Culture

All these cultural assumptions are very much American assumptions. Some of them we share with the Americans as well as other nationals around the world. But some, such as being a millionaire as opposed to being well off in general, have a particular American flavour in the way they are presented. In *Gunsmoke* the background assumptions of relative lawlessness and in *Perry Mason* the presentation of the power

of oratory in the courts (which links back to Daniel Webster) are both quite American in their manifestation. These background cultural particularities are not erased at all but are actually infused into the programs. Canadian frontier towns did not have sheriffs as lawmen, nor was lawlessness a characteristic of the Canadian West. Madams and houses of prostitution were tolerated, but there were few saloons, most often only hotels with beer parlours. Similarly, while oratory is not unknown to Canadian courts, there is no strong oratorical tradition with known historical figures. Nor is there a strong preference for the sanctity of the individual over the state or the community, as *Perry Mason* would lead a viewer to sense.

In other words, while apparently generic, these mass media materials have built into them a host of cultural particularities of the producing culture. To an American audience they would appear to be culturally non-specific or generic. To any other audience they would appear as extrapolations or generalizations of the American world view onto events with no exact time, place, or culture. The further distant the viewer is from American culture, the more apparent will be the cultural roots or ethnocentrism of the material.

The third aspect of our viewer's social identity is his descent from non-British stock, as might be indicated by his last name. Consider the names of the actors and actresses and of the characters they play: Donna Reed, June Allyson, Jimmy Stewart, Loretta Young, Robert Young, Jane Wyatt, John Beresford Tipton, Mr. Anthony, the Andersons, the Nelsons, Perry Mason, Hamilton Berger, the Cartwrights, Mr. Dillon, Miss Kitty (not Pussy Galore), etc. All are British-derived, reflective of a melting-pot society whose only official language is English. Clearly, to be an acceptable member of society one must come from the right English stock.

Even a character meant to represent the fool, i.e., Chester, has a British name, which suggests a certain marginality. Similarly with Hamilton Berger, his Christian name, while casting back to the Declaration of Independence of the U.S., also connotes an excessive formality or a certain clumsiness that a monosyllabic or even disyllabic name lacks. The exceptions to this general rule are names with an element of the esoteric built into them, such as Shelley Fabares, Van Johnson, or, for that matter, Paladin. In contrast, with a character such as Ethel Mertz we have a symbol of a dowdy, raspy-voiced woman whose name tells us that, amusing as she is, she can never fully participate in the American Dream. All of these can be seen as variations on an acceptable English theme.

The Extent of the Invasion

Does the above analysis mean that our viewer would see women only as wives or mothers, that as a Canadian he would feel cast out of the American Dream, and, as a person with a non-British last name, forever marginalized? The straight answer is no. Were he a meaning-generating individual working solely from the elements of his identity we have put forward, and if he saw only those aspects of the programs we have emphasized in this analysis, then one might expect our analysis to be the basis for the meaning-generation we have outlined. However, media programs and individuals are very complex multidimensional entities rich in subtlety and attuned to a far greater range of meaning than any one book could ever identify. Our analysis cannot predict what our viewer would make out of his television childhood. But were we to know his opinions on all the matters we have discussed we could understand how these programs complemented or contradicted those

opinions. Moreover, were someone to report on the overall attitudes of his generation to these matters we would again have some idea of how television programming might have strengthened or weakened such attitudes.

THE INVASION OF THE IMAGINATION OF A CULTURE

The prospect of a generation or indeed a nation being tuned into the same set of programs is not terribly unrealistic. While currently we have a greater variety of programs and channels to choose from than Lekich did in his childhood, Canadians are still inundated with American programs, perhaps even to a greater extent than before. Moreover, with financial and ideological pressure on the CBC, it would seem that every time cutbacks are announced the likelihood of a significant level of Canadian program production in drama, the stuff of the imagination, becomes more distant.

What does it mean to have a whole nation tuned into the imagination of another? The general answer is parallel to what we described of the interaction between an individual and media programming.

Cultures as Meaning-Generating Systems

Cultures, like individuals and like media programs, are **meaning-generating systems**. They generate their identity from their history, their laws, various institutions that mediate interaction, governing structures, opportunities afforded by their cultural and physical geography, and so forth. They generate meaning through interacting on the basis of this identity in a particular style with the events of the day. How

Canada responds to famine in other countries is derived from our wealth, our history, and our present-day attitudes. It creates meaning at a cultural level by exemplifying principles of action for both Canadians and others to see.

In the context of media and culture there are at least two levels of interaction. On the one hand is the extent to which Canadians import cultural material. As Tables 2.3 and 2.4 indicate, the importation of cultural material is extensive by any standard. On the other hand is the effort our public bodies spend to discourage other nations from pouring their cultural overflow into our country. Specific questions that refer to the detail of these levels of interactions are as follows:

- How much and what kinds of foreign and domestic programming do individual Canadians choose to watch? Tables 2.3 and 2.4 provide valuable information here as well.
- When Canadians are given a choice do they watch Canadian programming?
- When Canadian musicians are given access to the airwaves do Canadian audiences respond by buying their records?
- How much effort and money do both public and commercial media spend making opportunities available for the creation of Canadian cultural products?
- What ratio of foreign versus domestic information do we allow, through our regulatory body, the CRTC, to circulate freely?
- When political parties suggest making cuts to the CBC how do Canadians respond?

These are questions we cannot answer in the space of a few paragraphs. They are addressed throughout this book, in describing the dynam-ics of Canada's communication system and environment, and in the nature of the analysis we provide of the various issues we bring forward. In depicting the interaction of media and culture as the interaction between meaning-generating systems such questions allow us to consider some of the mechanisms through which media and culture interact. And as we saw in Chapter 1, the interaction is at least eight-dimensional. What we do know is that while there is an amazing level of American programs watched by Canadians, there continues to be an even more remarkable resilience in the commitment of Canadians to maintaining a separate country and culture.

Three case studies that examine the interaction of media and culture are to be found in Lorimer and Wilson (1988). In that volume Laba examines both sound recording and broadcasting in the context of continental market organization, centralized national production, and local and regional cultures. McLarty's analysis contrasts to Laba's in her discussion of national televisual expression within the context of U.S. dominance in the industry. Valaskakis considers the influence of television on cultural integration in native communities in the Canadian North. She argues that while television's impact has been dramatic, native communities and individuals are now turning it to their own community and individual priorities and needs.

THE INTERPENETRATION OF MEDIA AND CULTURE: ENTERTAINMENT AND ADVERTISING

In the last chapter, in a discussion of beer commercials, we argued that the audience was sold an image of itself. Further, we claimed that the advertiser added the element of the presence of its product with high-status members of the target population and noted that at least one advertiser was sponsoring events in which members of the public were able to re-enact a commercial. In that series of ads and events is found an obvious interpenetration of media and culture. Advertisers identify valued behaviour of the target audience. They then portray it and adapt it to their needs to serve as a promotional vehicle for their products. They may even go so far as to establish audience behaviour (the slalom contest) that associates the product with recreational enjoyment.

The media interact with everyday life in various other ways. Catchy tunes played countless times or repeatable phrases that float through one's head at the oddest times are not infrequent, nor are they intended to be. And they are not confined to ads. The media teach us how to kiss, how to smoke cigarettes (Humphrey Bogart had a style that was immortalized in his movies and even reappeared in a popular song in the phrase, "Don't Bogart that joint, my friend"), how to rob banks, how to dance. The list is endless. But the interaction is not a one-way process. The media take their content out of the lives of real individuals and groups. Everything, from the surfing movies to portrayals of the life and times of F. Scott Fitzgerald, emerges not from a vacuum but from real life.

Annie Hall: A Case from Ancient History

A vivid but dated example of this interpenetration through selection, appropriation, re-display, and re-appropriation can be found in the relation between clothing fashions and movies. In 1977 a Woody Allen movie, Annie Hall, was released. In this movie the title character wore various versions of thrift-store derivative loose-fitting clothes (see photograph). These clothes were not the simple invention of the costume

designer* for the movie but rather expressed a growing trend for clothing like that worn by the hippies in the late sixties. Following Annie Hall a great many women and clothing designers, who had heretofore spurned such clothing as unstylish, adopted clothing derived from the movie and its roots. For a while such clothing was even dubbed the Annie Hall look.

What makes Annie Hall such a good example is that the fashion ten years later was still building on variations of what was introduced to the broad public in that movie. The point to take from this is not that Annie Hall transformed the designs of North American clothing, but rather that the fashion was brought out of a limited sector in society through Annie Hall. The movie confirmed the fashion and placed it firmly in the mass market. In other words, the fashion of a subgroup of society penetrated the movie, which in turn transformed and propelled it into mass fashion. It is also interesting that this process has not been repeated recently.

Valley Talk, Beachwear, and Ninja Turtles

The case of Annie Hall is unusual because the movie was such a clear turning point for clothing fashions, as in fact was Miami Vice, complete with its semi-shaved star, Don Johnson. More often elements from a variety of media creations combine with changing elements of fashion or behaviour to transform the latter. Take, for example, the craze for beachwear of

---

* The "costume designer" in this case was Ralph Lauren, a man who has shaped a whole career around making high-quality versions of classic designs from romantic periods of American history, first in clothing and later in furniture, soaps, towels, rugs, wallpaper, sheets, comforters, dishes, and so on.

Ralph Lauren's *Annie Hall* look in the Woody Allen film. *Canapress Photo Service.*

the late 1980s upon which have been built at least three very successful clothing operations – Quicksilver, Ocean Pacific, and L.A. Gear.

In the movie *Fast Times at Ridgemont High,* released in 1982, California valley talk, introduced to mainstream radio by Frank Zappa's daughter, Moonunit Zappa, was crystallized in the lead character, a thick, dope-smoking surfer played by bad-boy Sean Penn. Associated with this California-based teenage slang were beach fashions. The fashions were reminiscent of the drop-out, oppositional, surfing crowd of the early 1960s. However, they had been mainstreamed to attract urban dwellers and middle America by two phenomena. The first was recreational surfing typical of Californian coastal youth and of their cousins, the sons and daughters of middle America who found it easy enough to take holidays near surfing/holiday haunts in California, Florida, Texas, Hawaii, and Surfers' Paradise in Australia. The second was skateboarding, which planted the clothing in

JEANETTE CREATES THE "ANYTHING-BUT-ORDINARY" BLUE JEAN!

Take one ordinary maternity jean. Make sure the fabric is 100% cotton denim and bleached to supple softness. Style in two front pockets and double-needle stitching. Fashion a six-snap adjustable elastic waist. Cut the legs a little fuller up top for comfort, then taper them for a slim, flattering line. Now, gather the ankles in a mock-drawstring for the latest European silhouette...And voilà!

The "anything-but-ordinary" blue jean?—EXTRAORDINARY!!!

Our special waistband conforms to your changing body during pregnancy and after, for fashionability and wearing ease.

To top it off, add a sumptuous front-tie flannel shirt, then layer it with another for a dynamic dash of pattern and color. Now, watch **JEANETTE MATERNITIES** create magic for your spirited maternity wardrobe!

jeanette
MATERNITIES

Echoes of *Annie Hall* in contemporary maternity clothing. *Courtesy Jeanette Maternities.*

West Coast inner-cities if not throughout North America and into Europe.

The language and fashion gradually spread, as much by the activities of surfing and skateboarding and the beach-oriented, West Coast-based fashion industry as by media presentations. In the late 1980s the language received a giant prod from the creators of Teenage Mutant Ninja Turtles. Through the TMNTs in movie, cassette, comic, toy, and TV program form, highlighted in the character Michaelangelo (he of the whirling nunchakus), the language was picked up in caricatured form with his overuse of yoh, knarly, rad, cowabunga, dudes, surf's up, and so forth.

In addition, the beachwear and the lifestyle it represented were marketed in and out of the ads by beach volleyball, at first a vehicle for watching beautiful young women cavorting in bathing suits, which evolved into a convenient vehicle for all sorts of sponsors. By the late eighties and into the early nineties, beachwear was to be found thoroughly integrated into and even dominant in western North American mainstream fashion. Even the mini-characters sold by McDonald's in the 1990s to families of hamburger buyers presented the surfing motif.

Nor were the seasons to interfere. Snowboarding has also gained prominence with complementary fashions, separate from downhill skiing and with echoes to their surfing roots. All of these elements are, of course, rooted in post-modernism, with its penchant for recombining eye-pleasing elements from any tradition.

Elvis Presley and Béla Bartók

As the above examples illustrate, both movies and recordings, in fact, all forms of media presentation, can carry fashion from a segment of society into the mainstream. The best example in popular music is Elvis Presley. Elvis Presley took southern black music and transformed it into something white teenagers would consume, largely by simply being white, because mainstream white North American radio stations did not play recordings by blacks in this genre. That is not the sum total of what Presley did, but it was the basis of his fame. Lesser-known examples of the same thing come from any popular singer taking musical material from its folk origins, stylizing it, and offering it up for mass consumption, for example, Carl Perkins, Jerry Lee Lewis, and even Sinead O'Connor. The phenomenon is known equally in popular music and in classical music. Béla Bartók was a pioneer user of sound recordings to collect folk music, which he then used as the basis for his classical compositions. Anton Dvorak's *New World Symphony* transformed

Miami Vice makes it to Sears. *Photo © Sears Canada Inc.*

southern black music, as did Gershwin's *Porgy and Bess,* into contemporary orchestral form.

In recent years one of the most noticeable mass market entertainers to bring forward music from non-mainstream cultures is Paul Simon. His album *Graceland* brought black South African music to the Western world in a manner that was enormously successful and compelling. Simon has a history of such success dating back to his use of traditional English balladry ("Scarborough Fair/Canticle") and to his hit based on a South American folk tune, "El

Condor Pasa." Besides being enormously successful and giving the world a feel for the music of black South Africa and a sympathy for black South Africans, *Graceland* provided a platform for black South African groups, notably Ladysmith Black Mambazo.

One point should be emphasized about this process of interpenetration. In picking up material from other sources the mass media transform it, whether it is clothes, music, or, as we will see in the next section, information. At a first level they stylize it for mass audiences, smoothing its edges and in general making it something distinctive – but not too much so, or else it would not have mass market appeal. They also transform it to suit the particular characteristics of the medium.

The movies, for example, require visual overstatement of a fashion style for that style to be noticed. In being picked back up in the world of mass fashions, that overstatement does not disappear. This process thus tends to encourage extremes. Consequently, when movie costumes emphasize aggressiveness (through military-inspired styles) or sexual characteristics (through the portrayal of high-class prostitutes), styles also follow that overstatement. Because fashions are purchased most often by the young and those with disposable income, class and generational differences are increased. However, so extensive is the feed of styles derived from entertainment into the production of other consumer products that few sectors of the population are left out. Children's clothing frequently is emblazoned with media personalities. Media-derived styles, many now coming from rock videos, are as easily found in The Bay as in Holt Renfrew, although their expression is somewhat different in these two markets. The photograph on the previous page illustrates the derivation from top-rated *Miami Vice* of boys' clothing.

INFORMATION AND INFORMATION PROGRAMMING: MEDIA AND AGENDAS

The interpenetration of culture and the media is not confined to the domain of entertainment. Real political, economic, and social events are reported in and affect the operations of the media. On the other hand, the media also have a considerable influence on the shape of events and certainly of ideas, as mentioned in Chapter 2 and as will be considered more fully in Chapter 8.

A tragic personal example of how the media shape events took place in 1983 in Alabama. According to *The Globe and Mail,* on March 4, 1983, Cecil Andrews, an unemployed roofer, phoned the local television station in Anniston, Alabama, and announced that he would burn himself in a Jacksonville square to protest the high rate of unemployment. The television news crew dutifully got itself together and travelled to where the man was going to enact his scene. As he doused himself with lighter fluid for his television crew audience (no one else was present) the cameras rolled. After setting himself on fire the news crew extinguished the blaze, but not before the man suffered considerable burns to his body. The man subsequently sued the television station and news crew for being negligent in not having tried to prevent him.

A fuller account of the incident is contained in an article in the *Journal of Communication* (Bennett, Gressett, and Haltom, 1985), which we will introduce in our discussion in Chapter 8. However, in the context of our discussion here, bizarre as that example is, it brings up two issues. The first is the idea that the man was performing for television. Had the crew not shown up, it is questionable whether he would have burned himself. But the second issue is the responsibility of the crew in such a circumstance. Should the media intervene actively in ongoing events? We know that they interact with them and cannot help but be a factor in them as they go about their job collecting and organizing information, but do they also have a responsibility to intervene?

Even more unsettling is the case of Pennsylvania's state treasurer, the late R. Budd Dwyer, who, facing a number of criminal charges, called a press conference, read a half-hour statement, admonished camera crews who began to dismantle their equipment, and then killed himself with a shot to the head while the cameras rolled – a media induced event? – who is to say? (*Globe and Mail,* January 23, 1987, p. 49).

The Press and Prime Minister Trudeau

Less bizarre and more broadly significant examples of the interaction of the media and culture are numerous. The political life of Pierre Elliott Trudeau is surrounded with media-culture issues worthy of some attention. Richard Gwyn reports in *The Northern Magus* an event that occurred early in Trudeau's career as Prime Minister. The incident arose from a reporter's question on Canadian policy regarding Biafra and its many starving people. Trudeau's reply was "Where's Biafra?"

Gwyn notes that most of the media interpreted Trudeau's remark as arising from a mixture of ignorance, inhumanity, and arrogance. How could any Canadian Prime Minister not bother himself to know where thousands of people were starving to death? Gwyn claims that Trudeau posed the question as a means of asking a larger question: what should Canadian policy be toward a region of which most Canadians know little? More recently, other authors have claimed that Trudeau asked the

question to see if the reporters knew the location of the country they were questioning him about. The charge of arrogance, if not inhumanity, may still stand.

In the heat of the pursuit of stories, journalists tend to believe that they are on top of all the major stories of the day. However, after cool reflection only the rare journalist will not admit to a woeful inability to cover even major world stories. For one thing, they may simply be unable to obtain visas to enter a region where millions are dying of starvation. Several years ago, had the Ethiopian government refused visas to the West or to media, the famine there would never have captured world attention.

Trudeau's point can be seen as derived from the presence of information-gathering services governments have in their external affairs departments. Biafra may very well have been only one of many regions that External Affairs, if not Trudeau, knew was experiencing food shortages at the time.

A second example is better known to Canadians. In shooting some news footage at the time of the October crisis of 1970, during which a British trade commissioner and a Quebec cabinet minister were kidnapped, Trudeau took up the issue of the role of the media in ongoing events. He pointed out to the reporters that their interviewing him about the presence of troops in Ottawa was playing into the interests of the FLQ (Front de Libération du Québec). By publicizing the situation the media were giving publicity if not legitimacy to the concerns of the FLQ. The media were aiding the FLQ in terrorizing the population by reporting the feared possibility of more kidnappings and other forms of violence. This footage has been used many times, including in the CBC documentary, *The Press and the Prime Minister.*

Subsequent information and analysis of the events of October, 1970, suggest that the government itself, by invoking the War Measures Act and calling out the troops, contributed to the view that the FLQ was a broadly based terrorist organization. On reflection it also appeared that a remark of Trudeau's was the most significant aspect of that interview. The remark, made in reply to a reporter's question on how far Trudeau was prepared to go in infringing on the civil liberties of Canadians, was "Just watch me." Rather a bald statement of autocratic power.

Nearly two decades later the Canadian media and all media were still discussing how they ought to respond to terrorism. On April 2, 1985, *The Journal* broadcast a panel discussion on the subject in the wake of a threat by some Armenian extremists to bomb the Toronto transit system. The conclusion of the panel appeared to be that the media should not heighten the tension, for example, by putting through phone calls to the terrorists. Nor should they play into the theatre of terror the terrorists attempt to create. But given Western news values, it appears that the media will continue to respond to terrorist activities by using them to bring forward a broader discussion of the issues behind what the terrorists are fighting about, at the same time condemning the means and co-operating with the police in bringing them to the courts. It was recognized that, to an extent, this plays into the hands of terrorists, but the majority of the panel could not see a way around this problem without the creation of a new set of problems just as serious as those created by reporting terrorism.

By the 1990s it would appear that either the media and/or governments have devised reasonable mechanisms for placing themselves on the sidelines of terrorism, or there is a welcomed lull in terrorist activity. Whatever the cause the media are being less frequently used as publicists for terrorist causes.

The Press and Prime Minister Mulroney

More recently, we have come to have a different sense of the influence of the press on the events of the day. As a book written by a former press secretary, Michel Gratton, notes, Prime Minister Brian Mulroney is a media junkie. He cares about what journalists say about him. This led to the book's title, *So What are the Boys Saying?* But as his career continues, Mulroney's concern about coverage has not stopped him from setting up a PMO designed to keep an upper hand on the media, to provide access selectively and at the convenience of the Prime Minister and his government (Gray, 1990).

Another issue, political polling, has also taken the spotlight. More than ever before, political actors are taking polls of public opinion on all kinds of issues. The difficulty with increased polling is that it can compromise political leadership. Faced with an electorate of one opinion, even with the most noble goals in mind, a government must be courageous to ignore that opinion, especially when the public knows its polled opinion. More importantly, polls can allow politicians to attempt blackmail of one group with the opinions of another, with no allowance for the transience of opinion or the dependence of opinion on a current and perhaps passing interpretation of circumstances. Mulroney's attempt to pass the Meech Lake Accord, based on the polled views of Quebecers, is a case in point.

An interesting element of Mulroney's career has been his extremely low popularity in opinion polls, especially during his second term of office. By the fall of 1990 the Prime Minister appeared to have made up his mind that since his popularity could hardly sink lower – it registered at about 15 per cent approval – he was free to do as he pleased. In late September, falling back on a never-used clause in the

British North America Act, he appointed eight new senators to give the Tories more Senate seats than the Liberals, though not a majority, in a successful attempt to ensure passage of the controversial Goods and Services Tax.

The view Canadians had of Pierre Trudeau seems to have been derived from many of these interactions between the press and the Prime Minister that accumulated over the years. The same is true of Brian Mulroney. Whatever Mulroney does is coloured by the scandals that have surrounded him, his honey-smooth baritone voice, even the way he walks up and down the marble staircase into and out of scrums of reporters. To what extent these opinions influenced the voting patterns of the press or their attitudes to government or even their fellow countrymen and women is indeterminate. In terms of our earlier discussion, while the effects are not clear, very significant interaction obviously takes place between the press, the PM, and the populace.

Media and Notable World Events

A number of events of global significance have happened in recent years and have provided opportunities to watch the interaction of the media. First was the Falklands War waged by Britain against Argentina. In that altercation Britain put strict control on the media, yet Margaret Thatcher still lashed out against the BBC for its unpatriotic coverage that was critical of British actions. Then the Americans invaded Grenada and froze the press out entirely. Following Grenada, realizing that the United States was not beyond invading a country on the excuse of protecting even one American life, Nicaragua waged what might be termed an information war against the United States. In a public manner it asked Soviet advisers to leave, did not import advanced Soviet weaponry, and general-

ly attempted to avoid any actions that could be construed as a provocation for invasion. These very public acts were moves in a media-based information war in which the Sandinista government attempted to make it a greater embarrassment for the U.S. to invade than it would be a victory to oust the Sandinistas. The Sandinistas won the information war and, indeed, the military war. They could not, however, win the economic war mounted against them by the United States. In February, 1990, a rival party, with $40 million in assistance from the U.S., was elected to office.

Our introductory example of the Chinese in Tiananmen Square shows yet again the role of the media in social and political agendas. Both the expulsion of Western journalists and the clampdown on information sources indicate a perception on the government's part of the potential influence of the media. More recently there has been the invasion of Kuwait by Iraq.

As with Nicaragua, we appear to be entering yet another information war, albeit, at the time of writing, somewhat unfocused. Several developments are notable. First, at the time of the initial invasion the Iraqi army was portrayed by the Western media as one million strong and a powerful force equipped with advanced weaponry and liable to use such instruments as poison gas. Then the U.S. began its psychological operations, or "psych ops." It portrayed the army as large but bedraggled and exhausted. It emphasized the fire power and training of U.S. troops. U.S. President Bush attempted to appeal to the Iraqi people through televised news statements in which he was careful to declare that his quarrel was with Saddam Hussein, not all Iraqis. On the other hand, on a daily basis, Hussein waged a counter struggle for the hearts of his people and released to the Western world a number of videotapes that portrayed him as a caring, fatherly figure. He was careful to call the Westerners that forcibly remained in the country his guests rather than hostages.

On yet another front, the U.S. managed to get all other countries, with the exception of Cuba, to condemn the actions of Iraq in the United Nations. Nations such as Britain, France, and Canada committed troops to the region while others, such as Japan, supplied support funding. Meanwhile, after the initial invasion, Western journalists were granted visas to visit Iraq and report on the growing support of the country behind its leader. Once the war started, however, media reporting was largely controlled by military and government censors on both sides, and the U.S.-led forces used the media in a massive disinformation campaign.

Finally, with recent events in the Soviet Union and Eastern Europe, the role of the media seemed to be far from central except, perhaps, in the case of Romania. The action was in the streets and the coverage somewhat hesitating. Faced with a determined populace, the governments of Eastern Europe, in a tribute to humanity and to democracy, stepped aside. Even in the Soviet Union, the government itself brought in a multi-party system. At no time did the media serve as instigators or central rallying points. However, they were certainly not far behind in responding to new freedoms, especially in the Soviet Union.

In Romania the situation was different. Living under a Stalinist dictatorship that had good relations with the West, an uncomfortable fact that may yet cause the West shame, the media seemed to serve as a confirmation of a dramatically changed reality. The trial and execution of dictator Nicolae Ceaucescu and his wife Elena in a television studio appeared to be a necessary symbolic purge of the old regime. Even afterward instability continued as no organized moderate group came forth to take command of the situation.

Each of these situations appears to indicate that the media play a not insignificant role in major events. In Eastern Europe, the Soviet Union, and China, it seems that the media were not a critical factor in bringing about dramatic political reform. But it also appears that, in the case of Eastern Europe and the Soviet Union, they played an important role in consolidating change. In China the control of the media by government seems to have been instrumental in the government's ability to hang onto power. In the case of Nicaragua, Grenada, and the Falklands, the desire to control public opinion through controlled access to information and opinion was apparently high on the agendas of the involved governments. Whether a lack of interference would have been just as effective is difficult to judge. But certainly the judgement made was that freely operating media were potentially deleterious to the intentions of government. In taking the broadest of overviews we cannot forget the neo-McLuhanesque perspective of de Kerckhove (outlined in Chapter 1) and his view of various regions of the world as dominated by different media and therefore different social processes. The effects of the actions of the media in China, the Soviet Union, and Eastern Europe might have been quite different had those same actions been taken in North or South America.

THE FREEDOM OF THE MEDIA TO CREATE MEANING

The examples given in the previous section concern the role or interference of the media as they go about their task of collecting and disseminating information. However, these examples do not address the limitations that exist on the media to define issues, or to **create a discourse** within which issues are defined (see Mitchell, 1988).

Enoch Powell and the Consensus on Race

In Birmingham, England, in 1968, a Conservative politician, Enoch Powell, made a speech designed to sweep away an artificial consensus on race that had been constructed by the media in alliance with the politicians and the civil service of Britain. That consensus was really to ignore any racially oriented protestations. In the words of Jeremy Issacs, a television producer:

> Television current affairs deliberately underplayed the strength of racist feelings for years, out of the misguided but honourable feelings that inflammatory utterances could only do damage. But the way feelings erupted after Enoch Powell's speech this year was evidence to me that the feeling had been under-represented on television, and other media. (Quoted in Braham, 1982, p. 280)

It would appear that Issacs was right. Powell received 110,000 letters containing 180,000 signatures in the days following the speech. Only 2,000 did not express approval for what he had said. The majority of the letters of support contained reports of real and imagined sufferings that white Britons had experienced as a result of the immigration of "black" workers from Africa, India, Pakistan, and the Caribbean. They were allowed to immigrate by virtue of being citizens of the Commonwealth, in other words, citizens of former British colonies.

Enoch Powell opened the floodgates to an outpouring of feeling that had had no means for representation in the media. The principle the situation illustrated is the potential peril the media court in defining issues purely on their own terms, or on terms developed with those other than their readership.

Carving Out and Serving Up a Monopoly

The Enoch Powell incident is quite unusual. A parallel has not occurred in the Western media since 1968. Certainly in North America it is extremely rare for the media to suspend "news values" for "the greater good of the country." More often we are presented with an array of styles that play to the known attitudes of various sectors of the population. McCormack (1983) argues that the newspapers of large urban markets seek out separate population subgroups for whom they are in a monopoly position as sources of information. This may occur through a realignment of a newspaper, as happened with *The Province* in Vancouver. It became a morning tabloid (while not totally giving in to sensationalism) where previously it had been a morning broadsheet. Or it may happen more dramatically through the closure and subsequent opening of a new paper with new owners. For example, not long after the demise of the middle-of-the-road *Toronto Telegram* the sensationalist morning tabloid *Toronto Sun* arose. Similarly, soon after the middle market, evening broadsheet *Winnipeg Tribune* closed, the tabloid *Winnipeg Sun* opened for business.

History supports this interpretation of the behaviour of newspaper proprietors. The most vivid example of the search for or creation of market monopolies can be found in the history of Roy Thomson's empire-building (Goldenberg, 1984). Thomson sought out and purchased newspapers that were operating in small towns as the single print news source. He did the same with radio stations. By forming these papers into a chain, using copy in more than one paper, underpaying his employees, penny-pinching on supplies, and avoiding such niceties as pension schemes, Thomson turned these properties from marginal enterprises into cash cows.

He applied the same formulae to other media properties and ended up with enough wealth to invest heavily in the North Sea oil bonanza. More recently his son Ken has divested himself of the oil properties and reinvested in information industries. At the time of this conversion he was quoted as saying that he didn't think there was any publishing operation in the world that he could not purchase.

In pursuing market monopolies, the media search for formulae that appeal to their audiences. *The Globe and Mail* can be contrasted with the *Toronto Sun* to illustrate this point. A study done by Sullivan (1982) provides the basis for the following analysis. *The Globe* seeks readers who have responsibility for running elements of society. To *The Globe,* teenage gang conflicts are not the stuff of news until they begin to threaten the peace of the community. When they do become news *The Globe* attempts to provide an understanding of the reasons for their occurrence and what is being done to re-establish control. In other words, it plays to the interests and perspective of their readership.

The advertising in *The Globe* further reinforces the target reader's comfort with the publication. A typical ad is understated, one that lets the reader know the advertiser is a member of the club of the (Toronto-based) businesses that advertise in *The Globe.*

The *Toronto Sun,* on the other hand, is a typical tabloid intended for readers who have very little power in society. The *Toronto Sun* bombards the reader with an unordered melange of events that are at once trivialized and at the same time symbols of a profound disorder. For example, typical Sun headlines read, "235,000 JOBS VANISH" or "THE BUDGET'S A BUST."

The juxtapositioning of completely unrelated stories in conjunction with a treatment that emphasizes the dramatic, the unexplainable, the bizarre, the futility of trying to make sense, in general the lack of patterns and the randomness of events, trivializes all subject matter, from the Sunshine Girl to the federal budget. Such treatment is not unlike the bombardment of images that are the stock in trade of television. If Gerbner's studies (see below) can be generalized to the tabloid press, what they may be producing is a low-grade paranoia because, just as one never knows when one might win a lottery, one never knows when the lottery that dishes out disasters might deal a wild card. In keeping with this presentation of news, Sullivan argues that the *Sun* attracts ads that encourage its readers to exert the only power they have, the power of spending money. They are encouraged to comfort themselves through the purchase of the trinkets of the marketplace. A typical ad is a two-page spread on a stereo equipment sale lasting only the weekend and filled with items from top to bottom.

The *Sun* presents to its readers a fragmentation of consciousness. Nothing is related to anything else. There is no pattern that connects, only a series of random, threatening events. One's date with fate can never be anticipated. One might best wait it out buffered by technological playthings. In contrast, *The Globe and Mail* presents an integration of consciousness. Each event is placed in a context of understanding. It is made clear how the occurrence will be managed and who will manage it. In due course all will be right with the world and those who should rule will continue ruling.

A final example of the manner in which the media create meaning and of the limitations on their ability to do so deals with television news. Television news, merely by its format, gives the impression that everything one really needs to know is included. The familiar pattern – a dramatic beginning, followed by more significant but less dramatic middle stories, followed by a lighter ending – has the comfort of a bedtime story, squalid as it may be. For example, one-line summaries or other summarizing devices are rarely used. The viewer is treated as someone who has no real interest in knowing about the multiplicity of events that might be going on in the world. Rather, she or he is treated as a person who wants to be entertained by what the television station can do in packaging the events of the day into an entertaining and informative program. It is more important that the producers get cheers for the production than that the audience come away as informed as possible.

Similar to entertainment programs, information programming takes events of the real world and transforms them into "programs." As with entertainment, it, too, stylizes content while seeking to inform. Information programming is involved in a trialogue with its audience and with world events upon which it comments and of which it is a part. It assigns meaning to events, but not arbitrarily. Information programs tend to read events back to their audience in the categories that suit the audience. At the same time, they maintain the dominant order. They court disaster only in the long term, if their categories of analysis contradict life's experience.

MEDIA AND REALITY

Here we consider the interaction between signification or representation and the events themselves. Let us start the discussion with literature to provide some background for consideration of the basic issues.

Literary Devices and Real Life

When a novelist kills off someone in a novel he or she is using a convenient literary device to advance the plot or shape the plot in ways that otherwise would be impossible or at least difficult. The death of a person provides opportunity for all manner of human action and drama. However, the meaning of this device for the reader may be quite different. It is not unusual for the average reader to be distraught or indeed to cry at the death of a character. The reader has suspended disbelief and in so doing may identify with some or all of the characters and, as a result, become emotionally involved. Indeed, to some extent this is exactly what the novelist is trying to accomplish in writing a tale for the reader. While few people in this era would identify so strongly with the characters and interaction of a novel that they would confuse the world of the novel with their day-to-day world, in past times such an intermingling has not been unknown.

Intermingling of the Media and the "Real" World

In our times such intermingling is more likely to happen in other media. Soap opera characters, for example, regularly receive letters advising them of the intent of other characters or giving them gifts for their upcoming television marriages. Some observers have suggested that this means the viewers do not distinguish between real life and the soaps. It may be more the case that they want to test the system. If they send gifts, will their gifts be included in what the couple received? Or if they warn the character of the intent of another, will a warning be built into the plot somehow?

When we move out of literature and into other media, whether radio, television, or movies, the distance between reality and signification shrinks. To take another example, in 1939 Orson Welles produced a radio play called *The War of the Worlds* in which he presented, in pseudo-documentary style, an invasion of Earth by Martians. Great numbers of listeners phoned in, some as the program was being aired, reporting sightings of the landings of other Martians. Some listeners seemed genuinely in fear of their lives.

Other producers have attempted to use this intermingling of reality and media to their commercial advantage. The makers of everything from laser guns to controversial documentaries are delighted by serious academics decrying the denigration of human values illustrated by some aspect of their commodity. It is publicity that translates into a larger audience. Canada's National Film Board and the makers of a short documentary on nuclear war entitled "If You Love this Planet" were delighted to have the work labelled foreign propaganda by U.S. authorities. It helped win them an Oscar.

Chernobyl and *Challenger*

Two other recent events, which stand the *War of the Worlds* phenomenon on its head, appear to demonstrate a considerable intermingling of the real world with media fictions in everyone's mind. In 1986, the U.S. space shuttle, *Challenger,* blew up shortly after takeoff. Later the same year a nuclear plant at Chernobyl, in the U.S.S.R., underwent a partial core meltdown sending radiation throughout the Northern Hemisphere. In both cases, the pattern of coverage was considerably different from that for a normal news story. In the case of *Challenger,* for example, for the following hour or so, almost nothing else could be seen or heard except pictures or commentary on the tragedy on every North American channel. And for the following days, it was the lead story on the newscasts and in the newspapers. Approximately the same pattern of coverage emerged subsequent to Chernobyl.

The point to be drawn from these events and their coverage is that when the unanticipated but not to be unexpected happens, when "our worst fears materialize," the media recognize the special identity of the event with saturation coverage and thereby signal to us that this is no fictitious event. In other words, they make a special effort to signal to us that the event is real. Without such signals of verification, the event is not assumed to be necessarily fictitious but rather, like a rumour, is in a limbo somewhere between truth and reality.

"Freeze, buddy, or you're dead!"

In the early eighties a group of teenagers broke into a house in Sackville, Nova Scotia. One boy was shot and killed in the darkness as he apparently turned to run back down the stairs when the man of the house said something like "Freeze, buddy, or you're dead!" In his judgement in the case the judge, while finding the man not guilty of murder, severely chastised him. He pointed out that the manner in which he had held the gun, the position he took before firing, and the language he used in talking to the boy were derived directly from the gun culture the man lived within as a result of, among other things, subscribing to gun magazines.

The dominant mode of the presentation of information in our electronic society is dramatic. Ads are mini-dramas; entertainment is rarely anything but drama; news and information programming is increasingly presented in a dramatic style. Investigative television programming is more a detective story that happens to be non-fiction than a presentation of the results and the consequences of an investigation. The investigation is presented in dramatic form complete with a star, the intrepid reporter, like *60 Minutes'* Mike Wallace, who runs into various adventures as he or she seeks out the villain and demands to know the truth. The scene is reminiscent of the confrontational but crude CBC program *This Hour Has Seven Days* as opposed to the more exploratory *the fifth estate*. Superimposed on this dramatic form, whether fiction or non-fiction, is often graphic realism. Breakthroughs in the graphic portrayal of sex and violence are regarded as great achievements.

The difficulty with graphic realism combined with a dramatic form is that it succeeds too well. It transforms violence into a sensory bombardment that is at once repulsive and attractive. At a second level is the frequency with which members of the audience encounter these dramatic devices. There are two views of what appear to be the results of this overencounter with dramatic realism. The research of George Gerbner presents one view, research on children points to another.

Research Findings

Gerbner has concentrated his research over the years on the portrayal of violence on television (see, for example, Gerbner, 1977). He has argued that the frequent use of violence results from its being a cheap way to portray power. But his central concern has been the effects this constant use of violence has had on television viewers. In his studies Gerbner has pointed out how people who watch a great deal of television overestimate the amount of violence in society. They tend also to have a "bunker mentality," to protect themselves from what they perceive to be a violent world.

In a variety of studies of children's play, Bandura (1976) has shown that those children who watch a great deal of television tend to engage in more aggressive play than those who watch less or see none at all. Also, following a television session in which aggression has been shown, there is an increase in the amount of aggressiveness in the interactions between children. Tannis Macbeth Williams (1986) has done similar studies in Canadian communities newly exposed to television. She has found an undeniable change in children's play after the introduction of television. One of the noticeable changes is an increase in aggressive play.

In all of these studies, obviously, only a certain amount of control over the exposure of the subjects to the media can be achieved, and only a certain level of confidence in the results is appropriate because of other such uncontrolled variables as socio-economic status. There is also a difficulty in interpretation. Is an increase in aggressive play a bad thing? Does it translate into increased aggressive or violent adult behaviour? Obviously, the violence of previous centuries was not brought about by the media. So do media role models of today have a unique burden of guilt to carry? In any case, there is little doubt that Bandura's work points to effects that make sense if one takes a more analytic perspective, as we have done in postulating persons, cultures, and the media to be meaning-generating systems in interaction with one another. Let us return to that perspective and return once again to signification or media presentation on the one hand as opposed to real life on the other.

Pornography and Erotica

In discussions of pornography a distinction is often drawn between pornography and erotica. The former is put forward as unacceptable, the latter as permissible. The argument usually goes something like this: there is nothing wrong with having literature that is designed to stimulate the sexuality of males and females; there is, however, something wrong with portraying the exploitation of females or children, or, in fact, anyone.

While such a distinction can be made, another position questions the acceptability of erotica. This position is useful for viewing all activities of the media. Erotic magazines for men do two things. They idealize the female body. Only attractive women are photographed and, in addition, the photographs are touched up to remove what are regarded as imperfections. Second, they give men easy access to (pictures of) naked women in poses intended to encourage fantasies and masturbation. We must take into account a third point as well. Much of the erotic magazine market is accounted for by young men who have not yet formed a permanent attachment to a woman.

By virtue of providing erotica for the young, unattached male market, its producers have the potential to encourage unrealistic expectations on the part of young men. When this idealized form is combined with an unimpeded visual access, a rather dramatic rift emerges between community norms and the norms of the medium. The presence of such erotica is a continual challenge to the norms of the community. If one were to assume a direct effect of these materials, one would assume that rather large numbers of young men walk around in a state of wonder as to why they can have easy visual access to beautiful women in magazines whereas they have no such thing in real life. To carry the matter one step further, it might be similarly argued that rather large numbers of young women compare themselves to the idealized form presented in these magazines and must deal with the environment created by the circulation of nude pictures among their male peers.

In the same manner in which sexual portrayals challenge community standards, so do other portrayals whether they are violent, idealizations of family, or dramatic or even humorous portrayals of the life of anyone the media care to portray. The positive side of such portrayals is that they provide the viewer with another view of life besides the one he or she lives.

Such a view may encourage the striving for excellence, or the movement from the farm to the city, or vice versa, in order to take advantage of what is offered in a milieu other than the one in which one has grown up. On the negative side, they may discourage an allegiance to community values in favour of the values of a world of signification.

SUMMARY

There are inherent limitations in seeing the interaction between the audience and the media as "effects." Audience-media relations are better seen as the interaction between meaning-generating systems in that both interact with and affect the other. Since neither system can be fully defined or understood *a priori,* audience-media interaction can be well understood but only predicted within broad categories.

The imaginations of many individuals may be filled with the pantheon of characters and situations television provides. Further, a television-dominated imagination can lead to unrealistic expectations or to feelings of marginalization. However, for that to be the case depends on the identity of the individual and his or her relations with lived culture.

Whole cultures, too, may be bombarded by the imaginative output of other cultures. Specifically, Canada's pattern of importation of programming as opposed to its domestic production makes our culture vulnerable to living inside the media-based collective imagination of the United States. Its actual effects, however, depend on the programs we are willing to put in place to build our own culture.

The mass media select images and symbols out of lived culture, transform them, and display them in a restylized form to mass culture. In doing so they contribute both to the fashion and to the political agenda. Here again, however, their influence can be circumscribed by the redefinition of the significance of events by key personages such as, in the political realm, prime ministers.

The freedom of the media to create meaning or to define the elements of a discourse, for example, on race, is fundamentally limited by the lived experience of their audiences and the attitudes, social processes, cultural institutions, etc. that are created by such a life.

What the media say about the world and what the world is are two quite different things. While pornography denigrates, erotica is accepted by greater numbers of society; however, it challenges the world of normal social relations.

REFERENCES

Adorno, T., and M. Horkheimer. *Dialectic of Enlightenment.* New York: Herder and Herder, 1972.

Bandura, Albert. *Analysis of Delinquency and Aggression.* Hillside, N.J.: L. Erlbaum Associates, 1976.

Bennett, W.L., L.A. Gressett, and W. Haltom. "Repairing the news: a case study of the news paradigm," *Journal of Communication,* 35, 2 (Spring, 1985), pp. 50-68.

Braham, Peter. "How the Media Report Race," in Gurevitch *et al.,* eds., *Culture, Society and the Media.* Toronto: Methuen, 1982.

Canadian Broadcasting Corporation. *The Press and the Prime Minister,* directed and produced by George Robertson. Toronto: CBC, 1977.

Cunningham, L. "How *Quest's* crew charted a suicide course," *Quill and Quire* (January, 1985), pp. 18-19.

Gerbner, George. *Trends in Network Drama and Viewer Conceptions of Social Reality, 1967-76.* Philadelphia: Annenburg School of Communications, University of Pennsylvania, 1977.

Globe and Mail. "Burned man sues station over filming," January 31, 1984, p. 5.

Globe and Mail. "Pennsylvania official shoots himself dead at news conference," January 23, 1987, p. 49.

Goffman, Erving. *Presentation of Self in Everyday Life.* Garden City, New York: Doubleday, 1959.

Goldenberg, Susan. *The Thomson Empire: The First Fifty Years.* Toronto: Methuen, 1984.

Gratton, Michel. *So What Are the Boys Saying? An Inside Look at Brian Mulroney in Power.* Toronto: McGraw-Hill Ryerson, 1987.

Gray, Charlotte. "Massaging the beast," *Saturday Night* (January-February, 1990), pp. 9-10.

Gwyn, Richard. *The Northern Magus.* Toronto: McClelland and Stewart, 1980.

Katz, E., and P. Lazarsfeld. *Personal Influence: The Part Played by People in the Flow of Mass Communications.* New York: Free Press, 1965.

Klapper, Joseph. *The Effects of Mass Communications.* New York: Free Press, 1960.

Laba, M. "Popular culture as local culture: regions, limits and Canadianism," in R. Lorimer and D.C. Wilson, eds., *Communication Canada.* Toronto: Kagan and Woo, 1988.

Lekich, J. "Horizontal Hold," *Vancouver* (April, 1982), pp. 48-53.

McCormack, Thelma. "The Political Culture and the Press in Canada," *Canadian Journal of Political Science,* XVI, 3 (September, 1983).

McLarty, L. "Seeing Things: Canadian popular culture and the experience of marginality," in Lorimer and Wilson, eds., *Communication Canada.*

Mitchell, D. "Culture as political discourse in Canada," in Lorimer and Wilson, eds., *Communication Canada.*

Sullivan, Edmund. "Mass Media and Political Integration: Thematizing Three Major Dailies in a Canadian City," unpublished, 1982.

Taylor, S. "Sifting U.S. statements for the facts," *Globe and Mail,* November 7, 1983, p. 10.

Time magazine, November 7, 1983, p. 44.

Valaskakis, G. "Television and cultural integration: native communities and the Canadian North," in Lorimer and Wilson, eds., *Communication Canada.*
Williams, Tannis Macbeth. *The Impact of Television: A Natural Experiment in Three Communities.* Orlando: Academic Press, 1986.

STUDY QUESTIONS

1. How do the media capture the imagination of the individual and whole cultures?
2. Describe a meaning-generating system and how such a system impinges on the interaction between media and audiences.
3. "The media create their own realities." Discuss.

CHAPTER

6

Communications Policy in Canada

INTRODUCTION

I N CHAPTER 3 we described how communications is intrinsic to the functioning of modern nation-states. As happens with many other key industries, governments have created laws and rules over and above the general laws that govern the way communications corporations operate within their jurisdiction. Public policy about communications is concerned with the particular laws and regulations governing the behaviour of the communications industries. Such policy is in addition to the laws of libel and access to information already mentioned in Chapter 3.

The legal and regulatory framework within which Canadian communications industries operate explains a great deal about why Canadian communications corporations behave the way they do. That framework, which in total is called the field of communications policy, can also provide an understanding of the economic and cultural importance attributed to communications systems by Canadian society.

In this chapter we touch on **telecommunications, broadcasting** (including cable TV and pay

TV) and **cultural industries** policy, all of which are parts of communications policy. Although these three communications policies are treated separately in what follows, the industries they refer to are not insulated from each other. For example, while cable TV has historically been regarded as an adjunct to over-the-air broadcasting, the cable industry has always been a technical hybrid that shares features with both television and telecommunications services. Also, while film production has long been treated as a cultural industry, the production of film and video content is clearly related to – and crucial to – a viable Canadian broadcasting industry. Finally, the technical differences between the telephone and radio broadcasting may not be as great as we often assume when we look at their subsequent development into separate industries.

As each communications technology has been introduced in Canada and corporations have been established to exploit the technology, specific laws and regulations have been developed to manage the new industry that appears. Consequently, there has been put in place a substantial body of laws, regulations, and licensing decisions affecting one or more of the various industries within Canada's communications sector.

Historically, public policy has not been consistent between communications industries. That did not matter particularly as long as the industries operated quite separately from each other. However, as the technologies of communications transmission become increasingly interconnected and can be used equally well by different communications industries, the need for overall coherence in communications policy has grown. The term used for the increasing interdependence and linkage of different communications industries is **technological convergence**.

Each country has its own particular patterns of communications development and its own legal and regulatory structures to control the communications systems existing within its territorial boundaries. (Rather different rules apply to transnational communications systems; these are discussed briefly in Chapter 9.) The complex structures of communications policy in Canada have their parallels in other developed countries, such as Australia, Britain, France, and Italy. In most developed countries – with the notable exception of the United States – national policy-making is based, to varying extents, on the determination to exert **economic control** and **cultural sovereignty** over industries that, it is believed, would otherwise be dominated by foreign corporations and by commercial and cultural controls outside the country.

Two particular features of Canadian communications policy are worth noting: the relative openness of the policy-making process, in contrast to most other countries, and the obsession with technology.

For over twenty years, it has been the practice of the federal government – and more recently of some provincial governments – to open for public discussion the current issues requiring policies to be formulated. Under the procedures of the Canadian Radio-television and Telecommunications Commission (CRTC), policy questions, broadcasting licence renewals, conditions of service, and rate structures for federally regulated telecommunications companies and broadcasters are all considered at public hearings in cities across the country. In addition, the federal Minister of Communications may encourage public discussion and reaction on various proposed policies.

Besides these hearings, on a number of occasions since the mid-1960s, task forces, commissions of inquiry, and special committees have been set up to examine particular problems and the reports of these bodies have been made available to the general public. Indeed, since 1928, it has been the practice of the federal government to employ the inquiry processes of royal commissions and parliamentary committees on many occasions to examine aspects of the broadcasting system and to obtain public comments. This public involvement, as well as the more usual consultations with industry associations and between government agencies and departments, provides the federal government with a considerable range of information for developing policy.

The second notable feature of communications policy is technology. "Technology" is difficult to define yet its influence in industrialized societies is undeniable. As Langdon Winner has observed, it is useful to distinguish between three different levels of meaning in common usage (Winner, 1977). First, there are pieces of apparatus (tools, instruments, machines, appliances, gadgets), the "physical devices of technical performance." Second are the techniques needed to operate the apparatus and accomplish tasks (skills, methods, procedures, routines). Third is the type of social organization that can encompass various technical activities (networks, factories, bureaucracies). In the following discussion, all three levels of meaning are intended.

In scholarly discussions of communications technology, the most prominent topic is that of technological change – especially the supposedly rapid rate of change. The meaning of technological change and how it relates to society is a popular subject for analysis and theory-building. This subject also has application to the policy sphere since assumptions about the actual relationships between technology and society must underlie any public policy action. Technological change appears to be proceeding at an ever-increasing rate in recent decades and this trend is attributed mostly to the development of computer technology. Its widespread diffusion throughout manufacturing, processing, and service industries, as well as in communications networks and computer-communications processes, has made the computer the key technology of this time. The short term often given to this period of rapid change is the "computer revolution" or the "information revolution."

Canada today is said to be one of the technologically most advanced nations in communications, spending more per capita on communications equipment than any other country. As noted in Chapter 1, covering the nation with networks of radio stations and later of television stations, as well as encouraging the growth of a national grid of telephone (later telecommunications) networks, has been the primary preoccupation of Canadian communications planners and policy-makers. While these developments have encouraged equal access to services, critics have argued that the emphasis on hardware and distribution capability has been at the expense of production and programming capability – that is, the creation and packaging of the cultural and social messages these expensive systems carry. The question of what is the right balance between spending on "carriage" and spending on "content" is probably the most vexing one in Canadian policy-making on communications, and is discussed more fully in Chapter 9.

With respect to policy itself, responses to the perceived revolution in communications technology have been going on in various ways since the late 1960s, with the establishment of the Department of Communications, and the launching of the Telecommission studies, and – in more recent years – the Clyne Committee Report (Clyne, 1979) and the Broadcasting Task Force Report (Caplan-Sauvageau, 1986). Provincial governments have also produced studies and reports. The general tone of these documents is that the "revolution" is going ahead, with or without Canada's active contributions to it, and Canada must take account of (if not accommodate itself to) the changes that will occur internationally and, therefore, domestically. These changes are expected to occur in Canadian communications systems as well as in the economic system as a whole.

The federal government's conclusion, in response to these reports and studies, is that Canada cannot afford to be left behind in the technological race. The provincial governments appear to agree with this. The argument is that, if we are left behind, then the Canadian economy is fated to become increasingly dependent on foreign technology. This prospect does not make an appealing picture for a society that sees itself to be advanced.

Despite these concerns about the costs of not participating in the communications revolution and a general enthusiasm for technology, there is an ambivalence in Canadian policy attitudes toward communications technology. While the techniques can offer – and, it is usually argued, should offer – the opportunity to enhance political cohesion, economic growth, and cultural development, these systems are being used most often as additional carriers of non-Canadian information. It is frequently claimed by federal policy-makers that the increased diffusion of foreign information in Canada could decrease national unity and prevent economic and cultural development. So, communications technology is seen as both potential national saviour and potential Trojan horse.

GENERAL POLICY STRUCTURES

The policy assumptions about technology, as well as the particular character of Canadian society, are built into the numerous communications policy structures that have accumulated over time. These structures are represented by statutes (laws), regulations, corporations, commissions, boards, departments, and other government institutions at the federal and provincial levels of government (with a little still at the municipal level). Two structures that play a leading role throughout the policy field are the federal Department of Communications and federal-provincial negotiations.

The Federal Department of Communications

The federal Department of Communications and its minister have been playing an increasingly important role in the policy field since the early 1970s. The establishing statute is extremely short and gives the duties of the Minister as follows:

> The duties, powers and functions of the Minister of Communications extend to and include all matters over which the Parliament of Canada has jurisdiction, not by law assigned to any other department, branch or agency of the Government of Canada, relating to
> (a) telecommunications;
> (b) the development and utilization generally of communication undertakings, facilities, systems and services for Canada. (Department of Communications Act, RSC 1985, c. C-35, s. 4.)

Under the authority of the Radiocommunication Act, the Minister exercises regulatory authority over all technical licences for the use of the radio spectrum, including its use for broadcasting purposes. Related to his responsibility within Canada for spectrum management, the Minister is also empowered to negotiate international agreements to protect "the rights of Canada in communication matters."

However, the ministerial portfolio is not solely technical, and this has become more clearly the case since 1980. Basically, the Communications portfolio contains two elements, one technical and the other social or cultural. The former, which still needs most of the department's resources, is concerned with the technical matters of the radio spectrum and its usage, and advanced research and design of communications technologies. The latter is concerned with the development of communications (including broadcasting) policy and cultural policy.

In 1980, various duties and responsibilities were transferred from the Secretary of State to the Minister of Communications. Specifically, the Minister became responsible for the CBC and for a group of nine other agencies. In addition, a major portion of the Arts and Culture Branch of the Secretary of State was transferred to the Department of Communications.

It has been suggested that the Minister of Communications is "really six ministers in one" and the job is "an almost impossible one" (Fortin and Winn, 1983). Indeed, the Minister has a widely diverse portfolio, as can be seen in the range of the statutes for which he or she has some responsibility:

Department of Communications Act
Telegraphs Act
Canadian Radio-television and Telecommunications Commission Act
Teleglobe Canada Act
National Transportation Act
Telesat Canada Act
Radiocommunication Act
Railway Act
Broadcasting Act
Canada Council Act
Canadian Film Development Corporation Act
Cultural Property Export & Import Act
Social Science and Humanities Research Council Act
National Arts Centre Act
National Film Act
National Library Act
National Museums Act
Public Archives of Canada Act

The degree of control the Minister can exercise over the agencies in the portfolio depends on the scope of the statutes concerned and on the kind of control the Minister would like to exercise. For example, the Minister can determine the amount of money made available to the Canada Council but cannot influence directly who receives that money for book publishing. However, a publishing support fund managed by the Department of Communications is much more subject to ministerial supervision. All of the agencies operate at some sort of arm's length from the Minister and from department officials, but, as some have observed, the arm may not be very long at times.

From its inception in 1969, the department focused its attention on telecommunications, computer-communications, and the observed convergence of communications technologies that was leading toward the promised information revolution. The nucleus of the department's staff came from the Department of Transport and the Defence Research Board. The establishment of a task force (called the Telecommission), made up of public servants from various government departments, to collect and publish information about the imminent communications explosion helped to alert federal and provincial policy-makers to the importance of these developments for Canada.

In 1971, the Telecommission published a series of over forty studies and a summary report called *Instant World*. It was anticipated that the materials gathered and responses to the studies would allow the Minister to table in Parliament a White Paper on communications policy.* Twenty years later – and after the introduction of many different, discrete programs and policies – this still has not been achieved. The reasons for the inaction are complex, but one factor that stands out is the federal-provincial division of jurisdiction, a second structural factor that has a continuing influence over communications policy development.

The Federal-Provincial Dimension

Attempts made in the early 1970s by the federal government to develop macro-policies on communications for Canada ran afoul of provincial jurisdiction over certain elements of the telecommunications infrastructure, particularly the telephone systems in the Prairie provinces and in the Atlantic region. By March, 1973, the government was able to produce only a Green Paper for discussion (Minister of Communications, 1973). The Minister at that time, Gérard Pelletier, held the view there was a need, due to the technological revolution, for a national policy to co-ordinate federal and provincial regulations of telecommunications and to integrate that policy with the federal field of broadcasting. Somewhat to the surprise of the minister and his officials, the provincial governments strongly objected to the federal view, seeing it as an attempt to encroach on provincial jurisdiction and to override provincial priorities. A second Green Paper in 1975 was not well received either; consequently, no formalized "national" policy exists (Woodrow et al., 1980).

---

* In parliamentary language, a White Paper is a statement of *actual* government policy while a Green Paper is a statement of *possible* policy that is issued to elicit public response and suggestions for improvement.

Particularly prominent in the public disagreements between Ottawa and the provinces in the early 1970s were Quebec and the Prairie provinces. The Quebec government's objections were based on the argument that it needed to control broadcasting developments to meet the cultural objectives of the Francophone majority in the province. While the whole field of communications (understood to cover both telecommunications and broadcasting) was and still is of interest to Quebec, it concentrated for some years on the need for provincial jurisdiction over broadcasting, particularly cable TV. In 1973, the Quebec government tried to regulate some aspects of cable TV systems through the introduction of a licensing procedure administered by a regulatory board (Régie des services publics). This action forced the Quebec cable TV operators to deal with a dual licensing system and created acute problems for a few licensees. A series of court actions followed, which took until 1977 to be resolved by the Supreme Court of Canada when it confirmed that the federal government had exclusive jurisdiction over cable television (but not over closed-circuit cable TV systems that do not carry broadcasting signals).

The Prairie provinces were also concerned in the early 1970s about what they saw as the extension of exclusive federal jurisdiction from over-air broadcasting to cable television and the proposed intrusion of federal authority into what had been a provincially controlled area of telephone company regulation and ownership. As far as the Prairie provinces could see at that time, cable TV systems (not much was developed in Saskatchewan or Manitoba then) could become competitors of the telephone companies in the provision of pay TV and information services, for example. To prevent this, the Prairie provinces sought to exert control over the physical installation of cable TV technology.

While it would be incorrect to say that the Prairie provinces were not interested in the cultural arguments advanced by Quebec, they placed a higher value on arguments concerning their historic rights to own and control telecommunications carriers and systems in their territories. Any technological developments that threatened the provincial telephone systems and their economic viability concerned those provincial governments for social as well as economic reasons. As they saw it, changes in the availability of telecommunications services, especially in the rural areas, would affect the survival of small towns and farming communities throughout the region.

Since 1975, work behind the scenes by federal and provincial politicians and officials to develop nation-wide policies on telecommunications services and equipment has been slow, but good progress has been made in some areas through consensus. The effort toward developing national policies in telecommunications was greatly accelerated in August, 1989, when the Supreme Court made a landmark decision that will bring all major telecommunications and telephone companies under federal jurisdiction.

TELECOMMUNICATIONS POLICY

Telecommunication is defined in federal legislation as "any transmission, emission or reception of signs, signals, writing, images or sounds or intelligence of any nature by wire, radio, visual or other electromagnetic system" (Radiocommunication Act, RSC 1985, c. R-2, s. 2). In strictly technical terms, then, broadcasting is a type of telecommunication. However, in policy terms, broadcasting is treated separately. In less technical terms, the telecommunications sector refers mainly to the telephone industry and the services it provides. It refers, as well, to those telecommunications companies and services outside the telephone industry (for example, Unitel Communications – formerly CNCP Telecommunications), and to the satellite communications industry, the most significant part of which is Telesat Canada.

The Common Carriers

All of the companies in these industries are referred to as "common carriers." The basic characteristic of a common carrier is its obligation to carry whatever messages (i.e., content) any customer wants to have sent and to charge equitable rates for that carriage service. A carrier may not tamper with the message, nor is it involved in creating any of the messages carried for customers (although this requirement may be modified through changing technological opportunities). The creation of the "content" is what makes broadcasters different from common carriers; broadcasters are involved in content creation and are legally responsible for all the content they transmit even if some programming is purchased from other sources.

There are two nation-wide telecommunications systems and one international system, which provides telecommunications links overseas. The two domestic systems are Telecom Canada and Unitel; the international system is Teleglobe Canada.

Telecom Canada (which was known as the TransCanada Telephone System until 1983) is an unincorporated association of the nine largest telephone companies as well as Telesat Canada, the domestic satellite company. The Telecom phone companies are:

British Columbia Telephone Co.
Alberta Government Telephones
Saskatchewan Telecommunications
Manitoba Telephone System

Bell Canada
New Brunswick Telephone Co. Ltd.
Maritime Telegraph and Telephone Co.
Island Telephone Co. Ltd.
Newfoundland Telephone Co. Ltd.

Unitel is a partnership formed from what used to be the telegraph subsidiaries operated by the two major railway companies, Canadian National Railways and Canadian Pacific. In 1989, CN sold its half of the partnership to CP. Subsequently, in the same year, Rogers Communications acquired 40 per cent of the partnership. Unitel competes against Telecom Canada for the domestic market in telecommunications services although some services are provided by each of them on a monopoly basis. The competition is not exactly on an equal footing, however, because Telecom companies hold about 88 per cent of the domestic telecommunications market compared to the 4 per cent share held by Unitel.* The competition between them is keenest in the area of data communications.

Teleglobe Canada was established as a federal Crown corporation whose role is to provide telecommunications between Canada and other countries across the Atlantic and Pacific oceans (links to the United States and other American countries are provided through the domestic telecommunications carriers, mostly the telephone companies). Teleglobe is not competing against any of the domestic carriers. Its monopoly may be reduced with the further international development of satellite communications. In 1987, Teleglobe was sold to private owners as part of a shift away from public ownership and a government wish to deregulate as many markets as possible. At present, Teleglobe represents Canada in the operation of several international communications organizations; one example is INTELSAT, the satellite consortium owned by over 100 countries that provides international satellite services to most of the world outside the Soviet bloc.

Basically, telecommunications services can be categorized into five types: voice telephony; public message (telegram); switched teleprinter and other text services (Telex and TWX); data communications; and program transmission (audio and video signals, especially for broadcasting). Telecom Canada and Unitel compete in the provision of the last three service categories. In the first category, Unitel can compete only in the provision of leased circuits (private lines) and not in the public switched systems that we are most familiar with as a telephone company service. However, this may change in the 1990s since Unitel has begun an application to the CRTC for approval to provide this service in competition with the telephone companies. The second category, public message, is the monopoly of Unitel.

The National Telephone System

There are about 80 telephone companies in Canada but only a handful are nationally significant. There are also over 200 radio common carriers that provide mobile radio and radio-paging services in competition with the telephone companies. Recently, cellular radio service, provided by Cantel in competition with telephone companies, has been added. Even so, for most Canadians, telecommunications services are still provided by one of sixteen telephone companies. Some of these companies are privately owned while others are gov-

---

* The remaining 8 per cent is shared between many small telephone companies, Teleglobe Canada, and radio common carriers (Department of Communications, 1983).

ernment-owned at the federal, provincial, or municipal level.

The two largest entities in the telephone industry, Bell Canada (serving most of Ontario and Quebec) and British Columbia Telephone (serving most of B.C.), are shareholder-owned. The three largest public companies operate in the Prairie provinces, a region where distances between subscribers are often great and initial costs of building distribution networks are high. There are still some municipally owned telephone systems although most of them were taken over years ago by the bigger telephone companies. Examples of municipal telephone systems are 'edmonton telephones,' Thunder Bay Telephone System, and Prince Rupert Telephone System.

System interconnection to ensure compatible equipment and revenue-sharing agreements has been resolved partly by non-governmental means, such as Telecom Canada. First, through arrangements with the many smaller companies, Telecom Canada can provide telecommunications links from coast to coast and from the southern border to the North. For example, Telesat Canada (the Canadian satellite communications corporation, discussed below) and the major telephone companies also provide much of the cross-country distribution networks for the broadcasting networks. Second, system compatibility is also ensured by technical standards set by the federal Department of Communications and by provincial bodies responsible for regulating telephone services in their territories. The request by one carrier for the right to link its system with another is the subject of regulatory decisions at the federal and provincial levels.

Regulation of Telecommunications

Since its beginning in the 1840s, the telegraph industry in Canada has been under federal regulation; in turn, telephone companies were regulated when they began in the 1880s, but not necessarily at the federal level. Regulation of telephone and telegraph rates and service was deemed necessary for protection of the public interest because of the companies' operation as natural monopolies – that is, in the longer term, it was believed that only one company could provide efficient service in any one area. It is a moot point whether such monopolies could ever have been described as "natural" since they were authorized by statute and regulation (Babe, 1990). In any case, due to the proliferating technologies of communications transmission, it is no longer taken for granted that one large company should have exclusive rights to provide any telecommunications service in a specific territory.

The regulation can occur provincially or federally, depending on historical and jurisdictional circumstances (English, 1973). For example, the major Prairie telephone systems are owned and (to date) regulated by the province concerned. The two largest privately owned systems, Bell and B.C. Tel, are regulated federally. Transnational telegraph and data communications services provided by Unitel are the joint efforts of two private corporations (Canadian Pacific and Rogers Communications); Unitel is regulated federally. So also are Telesat Canada and a small telephone company operating in the Northwest Territories. Until 1989, the federal government regulated only five telecommunications companies. This does not seem to be much until one discovers that the five provided services to about 70 per cent of the entire Canadian telecommunications market. Bell Canada alone supplies 52 per cent of the market (Department of Communications, 1983).

However, the scope of federal regulation has recently been changed by the 1989 Supreme Court decision. The case concerned whether Alberta Government Telephones (AGT) fell under federal or provincial jurisdiction. The historical (and apparently rather haphazard) division of jurisdiction over telecommunications was based on a judgement of whether a particular company was a "local" or "inter-provincial" undertaking. If it was the former, it was deemed to be under provincial jurisdiction. If it was the latter, then federal jurisdiction prevailed. The interprovincial character of the undertaking was usually taken to refer to whether the company served customers in more than one province.

Historically, AGT had been regulated by the province of Alberta and this was not challenged until 1981, when CNCP Telecommunications sought to interconnect its network with AGT's. A series of court actions followed, culminating in the 1989 Supreme Court decision, which essentially extended the meaning of interprovincial by determining that all telephone and telecommunications companies whose technical facilities are interconnected across provincial boundaries are interprovincial undertakings. In particular, membership in Telecom Canada was regarded by the Court as an indication of the interprovincial nature of AGT's service.

The Court's decision has brought a number of telephone companies under federal jurisdiction for the first time. The decision potentially affects all members of Telecom Canada that have been regulated provincially to date. (In the summer of 1990, the Alberta government created Telus Corp., a holding company to be owned jointly by public shareholders and the provincial government. AGT is now a subsidiary of Telus Corp.) The provinces of Saskatchewan and Manitoba remain determined to continue exerting provincial control over their provincially owned telephone companies.

The basis for government control over a telephone or telecommunications company in Canada is regulation as a public utility with a view to ensuring that "just and reasonable" rates are charged to customers. The CRTC is responsible for regulating the rates of the federally regulated carriers, including Telesat Canada (as well as regulating all broadcasting licensees). However, having broadcasting and common-carrier regulation within one body does not mean the CRTC administers an overall communications policy. Further legislative changes are still needed, in the form of a telecommunications act, to provide a unified policy and regulatory framework at the federal level.

At the provincial level, each province has organized its regulatory function somewhat differently but most have a regulatory board responsible for the telephone companies that come within their jurisdiction. All provinces now have a minister responsible for communications policy, although only the Quebec government has a minister with a department solely concerned with communications. Several provinces have a department of transport and communications while others simply name any minister to be the government spokesman on communications matters and to attend federal-provincial ministers' meetings as the provincial representative.

Satellite Communications

Canada has been a pioneer of non-military satellite applications since the early 1960s; the possibility of improving trans-Canada communications links through the use of communications satellites has appealed to federal policy-makers since at least 1965. A White Paper on satellite policy was issued in 1968, in which the following statement was made: "A domestic satellite system should be a national undertaking stretching across Canada from coast to coast, north to Ellesmere Island and operating under the jurisdiction of the Government of Canada" (Minister of Industry, 1968).

In 1969, the Telesat Canada Act established the corporation given the responsibility to own and operate the Canadian satellite communications system and to provide communications services to Canadian locations on a commercial basis. Despite the fact that Telesat was established by statute and given a monopoly position, it is not a Crown corporation – as its officials have pointed out on many occasions. They often describe the corporation as "the carriers' carrier," a reference to the fact that most of the signals carried on satellite are being transmitted on behalf of another carrier, such as a telephone or telecommunications company. The ownership of Telesat is shared between the federal government (with 50 per cent) and a number of telecommunications carriers, principally the members of Telecom Canada.

Telesat's first satellite was launched in 1972 and shortly thereafter the company initiated the first domestic satellite communications service in the world. (In 1964, Canada joined INTELSAT, the international consortium that operated the first-ever commercial satellite service, but INTELSAT's mandate was to provide only international communications linkages.) By 1989, the corporation had launched several series of satellites and had five in operation, three Anik C satellites and two Anik D satellites.

Historically, the primary use for the satellites has been for telecommunications (mostly voice telephone and data communications) traffic. However, by 1987, it was apparent that broadcasting services were becoming at least as important to Telesat. By 1989, services to the broadcasting industry represented 58 per cent of Telesat's revenues. The vast majority of these services were for delivery of video signals across the country, with a limited amount for more specialized audio services.

Three types of network have been developed to provide or improve broadcasting service coverage in northern Canada, to take advantage of the existence of the Canadian satellite system and despite the high cost of leasing a full satellite channel (around $1 million per year). Since 1973, the CBC, with special funding from Parliament, has leased several full channels; part of this capacity is used to distribute a Northern Television service to communities in the territories. Since 1981, a broadcasting consortium known as Cancom (Canadian Satellite Communications Inc.) has leased satellite channels to distribute its package of Canadian TV and radio signals to remote and under-served communities across the country. In 1983, Cancom received CRTC permission to redistribute several American signals as well. In 1984, Cancom was given CRTC permission to provide service in more urban, southern communities. A third kind of system has been the Inukshuk TV network set up by the Inuit Broadcasting Corporation for a number of native communities in the eastern Arctic. However, this part-time network depends on federal funds and (until 1992) on access to CBC-leased satellite channels for its operation. While commercial radio or television networks in southern Canada make use of the satellite system, none has opted to abandon terrestrial links to use satellites only.

Telecommunications Issues

For telecommunications, the fundamental issue that guides public policy is always that of **fair access**. This revolves around the principle that individuals (households or businesses) are entitled to receive adequate service at equitable and non-discriminatory rates. While no one seriously expects that a person living in an isolated area will receive exactly the same range and price of services as someone living in downtown Vancouver or Montreal, there must be no deliberate deprivation of service and the rates charged must be shown to be "just and reasonable." This principle governs all telecommunications regulation on this continent.

Related to this is the principle that all customers in similar circumstances must be treated equally and the charges for services must be publicly known. This requires all telecommunications carriers to post their rates and to specify clearly who pays what for which level of service. Specific issues that arise in telecommunications are related to disputes about the equity of established rates, whether one type of customer service is being cross-subsidized at the expense of another (e.g., households by businesses, rural residents by urban residents, and so on), and whether the costs of service are being properly calculated by the carrier.

Another major issue in telecommunications that has become much more important in recent years is **competition**. As outlined above, telephone companies in the past were regarded as providing a "natural monopoly" type of service. This is no longer agreed upon because new distribution technologies allow for different ways of delivering essentially the same service (e.g., data communications) within any one area. The question here is the extent to which competition between telephone companies and others should be encouraged. In theory, full competition is better than monopoly but there are costs involved, especially for customers in less profitable regions. Competitors for market shares in large cities, for example, are eager to step forward, but there is no rush to compete in serving small towns and rural areas.

The benefits that may accrue to urban, business-oriented customers have to be balanced against the possibility of increased costs accruing to rural and other less profitable customers. In Canada, a high priority has always been placed on the widest possible availability of telecommunications services to all Canadians so there is no

presumption that competition is invariably beneficial. Arguments swirl around the question of who is going to win and who will lose in an increasingly competitive environment for telecommunications services. New technologies allow for new arrangements in providing service, but Canadian policy-makers are not necessarily in favour of deregulation without careful consideration of the likely consequences. These consequences can be effects on the telecommunications carriers themselves as well as effects on consumers and on new companies that would like to enter the telecommunications marketplace.

A whole series of issues that have been discussed and to some extent dealt with in recent years include the following:

- Will Unitel be allowed to interconnect its system with those of major Telecom Canada members even though they compete with each other?
- Under what conditions can customers buy their own communications terminals and attach them to the telecommunications system without the approval or knowledge of the carrier?
- Can the carriers be compelled to buy equipment from manufacturing companies not linked to themselves or their parent company?
- Can satellite systems or other new distribution systems be allowed or required to compete with telephone companies in providing data communications or voice telephony services?
- Can the satellite company be required to allow anyone to own an earth station and, if so, under what conditions so as to prevent unauthorized reception or transmission of signals?
- How can the monopoly services of the carrier be separated for accounting and

regulating purposes from the competitive services they offer?

- Can large telephone companies such as Bell Canada evade regulation of some of their telecommunications activities simply by reorganizing their corporate structure?

BROADCASTING POLICY

Since the establishment of the first royal commission into broadcasting in 1928, the federal government has regularly returned to the establishment of commissions or special parliamentary committees as a chief instrument of policy formulation in the broadcasting area. The 1932 Radio Reference case, heard by the Judicial Committee of the British Privy Council (then the final court of appeal for Canadian law), determined that the federal government had *exclusive* jurisdiction over radio communication in Canada. This was taken to include broadcasting, and no court case since has seriously challenged this interpretation.

The only role remaining to the provinces in broadcasting policy is in the area of educational broadcasting, although this was rather unclear for many years. In the early 1970s, it was finally agreed that provinces could set up educational broadcasting organizations as long as they were at arm's length from the provincial government itself. Thus, we have seen the establishment of Radio Québec, TVOntario, the Saskatchewan Communications Network, ACCESS Alberta, and the Knowledge Network of the West (KNOW) in British Columbia.

The legal definitions relevant to broadcasting are provided by the current Broadcasting Act, Section 2:

"broadcasting" means any transmission of programs, whether or not encrypted, by radio waves or other means of telecommunication for reception by the public by means of broadcasting receiving apparatus, but does not include any such transmission of programs that is made solely for performance or display in a public place;

"program" means sounds or visual images, or a combination of sounds and visual images, that are intended to inform, enlighten or entertain, but does not include visual images, whether or not combined with sounds, that consist predominantly of alphanumeric text.

These definitions are broader than those used in earlier statutes. In drafting the new Act, the federal government wanted to avoid defining the scope of broadcasting in terms of any one technology. Thus, cable television, pay television, satellite delivery of radio and TV services, and any future delivery system are now included within the broadcasting field.

Based on the 1932 judicial decision, Parliament has passed a series of statutes related directly or indirectly to broadcasting:

1932	Canadian Radio Broadcasting Commission Act
1936	Canadian Broadcasting Act
1958	Broadcasting Act
1968	Broadcasting Act
1969	Department of Communications Act
1970	Telesat Canada Act
1976	Canadian Radio-television and Telecommunications Act
1991	Broadcasting Act

Under these statutes, various federal institutions have been set up:

1932-36	Canadian Radio Broadcasting Commission (CRBC)
1936-	Canadian Broadcasting Corporation (CBC)

1958-68	Board of Broadcast Governors (BBG)
1968-76	Canadian Radio Television Commission (CRTC)
1969-	Department of Communications (DOC)
1970-	Telesat Canada
1976-	Canadian Radio-television and Telecommunications Commission (CRTC), an expanded version of the one set up in 1968.

Regulation and the CRTC

Regulation of broadcasting has taken various forms, mostly aimed at encouraging the production of Canadian programming content or at extension of service coverage to less urban areas. One type of regulation that has affected international control of the broadcasting system is the restriction on levels of foreign ownership. As long as the CBC was the predominant broadcaster, less concern was expressed about the existence of foreign companies owning broadcasting stations. However, by the 1960s when the private sector had grown and cable TV was expanding quite rapidly (often with the help of foreign capital), political concern about foreign control of broadcasting became greater. Direct and effective action was finally taken in 1969 when the CRTC was directed by the cabinet not to issue licences to corporations with less than 80 per cent Canadian ownership or where the corporation board was not made up wholly of Canadian citizens (CRTC, 1974).

Because of the strong federal authority over broadcasting, much attention is given to the body that holds this power on a day-to-day basis. The CRTC has a central role in the policy processes regarding broadcasting in Canada. Historically, the CRTC is the successor of a long line of state regulation of Canadian broadcast-

ing going back to 1932. In the first twenty years after 1936, the CBC exerted some regulatory control over private broadcasters through its organization of national networks to which the private stations belonged. Not until 1958 was a separate regulatory authority set up for non-technical regulation; this was the Board of Broadcast Governors (BBG).

From the earliest years of radio broadcasting (the years immediately after the First World War), technical licences were issued by the Minister of Marine and Fisheries; later the Minister of Transport had the job, which was eventually moved to the Minister of Communications in 1969. In the technical licensing process, considerations of signal coverage, signal quality, and potential interference with other users of the radio spectrum are the main criteria for issuance or non-issuance of a licence although the CBC, as the national broadcaster, has the opportunity to reserve specific frequencies for its own immediate or future needs in serving the country as a whole. Once having received a technical licence, a private broadcaster until the late 1950s had to meet some minimal standards and categories of programming content in his broadcast airtime; these standards were set by the CBC but apparently not strictly enforced.

In 1958, non-technical regulation was changed by the establishment of the BBG. However, the new statute under which this was done did not specify clearly what should be the relationship of authority between the CBC and the BBG. As a consequence, the CBC tried to continue its operations as it had in the past while the Board was left to exert whatever control it could over private broadcasters. This confusing situation was resolved by the next statute, in 1968, which set up the CRTC as the Board's successor and gave the Commission full regulatory powers over all licensees, including the CBC networks and stations.

The purpose of the Commission is to regulate and supervise the Canadian broadcasting system and to do this with the intent of achieving the social and cultural objectives of the broadcasting policy stated in Section 3 of the current Broadcasting Act. The basis for the CRTC's authority stems from this section, titled "Broadcasting Policy for Canada." Typical CRTC policy actions can be setting general regulations applying to broad classes of licensees (for example, AM radio, FM radio, TV, cable TV) or directed toward certain kinds of programming content (for example, political broadcasts, commercials, foreign-language programs, programs intended for children). The CRTC also engages in policy action through the attachment of specific conditions of licence on individual licensees. In addition to having the responsibility to implement the stated broadcasting policy, the CRTC is also obliged to act in response to direction from the Governor-in-Council (i.e., the federal cabinet) on certain matters specified in the statute.

Much of the CRTC's work on broadcasting revolves around public hearings on the issuance and renewal of broadcasting licences. The hearings are held virtually year round and across the country in the larger cities. Each year, the Commission has to decide on thousands of licence applications: new applications, amendments, renewals, securities-related matters (affecting the ultimate control of a licensee or changes in assets), and network licences. In 1988-89, the CRTC made decisions on 2,481 applications, of which 1,629 were on cable TV, 143 on TV, 225 on AM radio, 184 on FM radio, 226 on securities, and 74 on networks (CRTC Annual Report, 1988-89).

To say that the CRTC is merely regulating the broadcasting system to achieve policy objectives set by Parliament understates the extent to which the CRTC has been obliged to interpret the policy before it could draw up regulations. It also understates the extent to which the CRTC has established sub-policies of its own in areas such as cable television, which was not given a clear role in the 1968 Act. Section 3 in the 1991 Act is much longer than in 1968 but is still not explicit about all aspects of policy direction. The CRTC must determine the specific policies and regulations applying to any group of licensees.

While cable TV is the outstanding example of an area where policy-making by the CRTC has involved much more than simply implementing a statutory policy section, there have been other areas as well, some of which may turn out to be equally significant in terms of substantive broadcasting policy. One such area is concentration of private ownership in broadcasting licensee companies. Another is the introduction of pay television and other new broadcast-related specialty TV services. A third is the use of satellites for the distribution of broadcasting signals.

Since the mid-1970s there has been considerable discussion in the policy field about the degree to which the CRTC can and should initiate or resist policy action. There has also been discussion about the extent to which the federal government or Parliament should maintain policy control over the CRTC. One of the controversial aspects of the 1991 statute is the increased scope for cabinet direction to the CRTC. As well as making section 3 much more detailed, the new Act requires the CRTC to implement a stated regulatory policy (s.5) and also provides cabinet with the power to issue directions on how the CRTC is to interpret both policy sections. How often and in what ways the cabinet will exercise this power remains to be seen.

The Canadian Broadcasting Corporation

The CRTC is not the only important federal institution in broadcasting policy and the broadcasting system. Aside from the technical regulation administered by the Department of Communications, the Canadian Broadcasting Corporation must be considered. The CBC is now over fifty years old and, for many of those years, it has provided the major portion of Canadian radio and television programming. To do justice to the CBC's complex history and organization would require a substantial book – indeed, several books have been written largely about it (see, for example, Peers, 1969; Peers, 1979; Weir, 1965).

The mandate of the CBC is stated in the 1991 Broadcasting Act as:

3(1) (m) the programming provided by the Corporation should
 (i) be predominantly and distinctively Canadian,
 (ii) reflect Canada and its regions to national and regional audiences, while serving the special needs of those regions,
 (iii) actively contribute to the flow and exchange of cultural expression,
 (iv) be in English and French, reflecting the different needs and circumstances of each official language community, including the particular needs and circumstances of English and French linguistic minorities,
 (v) strive to be of equivalent quality in English and in French,
 (vi) contribute to shared national consciousness and identity,
 (vii) be made available throughout Canada by the most appropriate and efficient means and as resources become available for the purpose, and
 (viii) reflect the multicultural and multiracial nature of Canada.

This statement of mandate is a considerable change from that given in the 1968 Act, particularly with regard to the CBC's former obligation to "contribute to the development of national unity and provide for a continuing expression of Canadian identity." It is too early to say what effect the changed mandate will have on CBC operations.

The Corporation has six national networks, three in each official language; of each three, one is television, one AM radio, and one FM stereo radio. The English-language networks extend across the country although not fully in Quebec; the French-language networks are fully developed in Quebec but only partly available elsewhere. "Extension of service," as it is usually called by the CRTC, is a special obligation of the CBC (much more so than for private broadcasters). While only a small percentage (less than one per cent) of Canadians remain unserved by Canadian broadcasting, the CBC is obliged to extend its signals to reach these people whenever possible.

Aside from the six major networks, the CBC also maintains other services:

- northern radio and television services, including native-language program production in seven languages for radio and three major languages for television; the CBC also carries "access" programming by community organizations on both media;
- two national satellite-to-cable House of Commons networks, one for each official language;
- a TV captioning service for the hearing-disabled;
- a 24-hour, English-language news and information TV service distributed via satellite and cable (Newsworld);

- an international short-wave radio programming service in fourteen languages to countries around the world.

As well, it provides host broadcasting services for foreign broadcasters when international events occur in Canada.

Public ownership of broadcasting is usually considered to have started in 1932 with the establishment of the CBC's predecessor, the Canadian Radio Broadcasting Commission. It can be argued that the public broadcaster still dominated the broadcasting system until the early 1960s. In 1961, the first licensed private network of broadcasting stations (the CTV network) began operating. Until then, the CBC was the only broadcaster allowed to form permanent networks.

Statistics for comparison between the public and private sectors of broadcasting are difficult to get, partly because of their different purposes and corporate structures. Statistics Canada data on public and private broadcasters exclude non-commercial stations such as educational, community, and religious broadcasters so that the CBC alone is compared with the private, commercial broadcasters. Generally speaking, in 1986, the CBC represented about 40 per cent of the expenditures on programming and about three-quarters of technical costs (production facilities and distribution facilities) in the broadcasting system.

The policy significance of the CBC relates to several factors: its corporate size and history; the dependence on public funds for most of its revenue; the provision of radio and TV services to almost all Canadians in one or both official languages; and the large expenditures on program productions and creative artists' fees. The more than $900 million a year now received by the CBC from Parliament makes the Corporation the largest recipient by far of public funds assigned to cultural purposes.

Canadian Content

Canadian content regulations stem from the CRTC's obligation under the Broadcasting Act to ensure that each licensee makes "maximum use ... of Canadian creative and other resources in the creation and presentation of programming." The CBC's programming should also be "predominantly and distinctively Canadian."

The idea of requiring a minimum percentage of broadcast time to be used for transmitting Canadian productions did not originate with the CRTC but had been in place since 1959 under the Board of Broadcast Governors regulations. The Canadian content quota was never well received by the private broadcasters, who protested each rule and rule change vigorously and sought to minimize their carriage of Canadian material as far as possible (Babe, 1979). This is the case for both radio and television; cable TV, being almost entirely a carrier of other licensees' content, is not subject to the same sort of rules. The CRTC requires television licensees to have at least 60 per cent of all programming hours be given to Canadian productions (50 per cent in prime time for private broadcasters). Licensees for AM and FM radio stations must play at least 30 per cent of popular music from Canadian selections.

Canadian content quotas on radio are generally not a big issue, either with the broadcasters or with the general public (although there was much complaining when the regulations were first introduced). It is generally agreed that the Canadian record production industry has benefited enormously from the quota, which has given the companies and their artists some assurance of access to the Canadian audience. The major problems have always existed on television. During the 1970s, a good deal of evidence was produced to show that, while the majority of programs aired by Canadian TV broadcasters were "Canadian" in the regulatory definition, the Canadian audience showed a strong preference for American entertainment series and movies.

There was clearly a strong demand for TV drama yet very little of this was being produced in Canada. Independent producers said they would like to produce this type of program but were unable to persuade Canadian broadcasters to pay them adequately for their productions. The CRTC re-examined the Canadian content rules to see whether they could be changed to encourage the production of more and higher-quality entertainment for television. There was some hope expressed that the introduction of pay TV in Canada would open up a big new market for Canadian popular entertainment production. As is discussed in Chapter 9, this hope proved to be ill-founded when the Canadian pay TV services were first launched in the 1980s and did not attract enough subscribers to support the large expenditures needed.

Evolution of a New National Broadcasting Policy?

In 1982, the federal Minister of Communications announced he was developing a comprehensive broadcasting strategy. The strategy was revealed in March, 1983, in a paper entitled *Towards a New National Broadcasting Policy.* The paper was subtitled: "New policies and initiatives to provide Canadians with greater program choice and make the Canadian broadcasting industry more competitive: A response to new technologies and a changing environment." The broadcasting strategy was given these fundamental goals:

1. To maintain the Canadian broadcasting system as an effective vehicle of social and cultural policy in light of a renewed commitment to the spirit of the broadcasting objectives set out in the 1968 Broadcasting Act.
2. To make available to all Canadians a solid core of attractive Canadian programming in all program categories, through the development of strong Canadian broadcast and program production industries.
3. To provide a significantly increased choice of programming of all kinds in both official languages in all parts of Canada.

One key action taken by the federal government was the creation of the Canadian Broadcast Program Development Fund to be administered by Telefilm Canada (outlined later in this chapter). A second action was the declaration that the cable television industry would be the chosen means to deliver greater choice of programming to Canadians.

In May, 1985, the Minister of Communications appointed a task force to make recommendations on "an industrial and cultural strategy to govern the future evolution of the Canadian broadcasting system through the remainder of this century, recognizing the importance of broadcasting to Canadian life."* In 1986, the Caplan-Sauvageau Task Force produced its Report, which was discussed at length by a parliamentary committee. In 1988, the Minister of Communications introduced new legislation intended to replace the 1968 Broadcasting Act. The bill (C-136) did not receive parliamentary approval before an election was called and a

---

* For those interested in how the task force interpreted its mandate, the secretary to the task force, Paul Audley, has written "The Agenda of Broadcasting Policy: Reflections on the Caplan-Sauvageau Task Force," in R. Lorimer and D.C. Wilson, eds., *Communication Canada*: *Issues in Broadcasting and New Technologies* (Toronto: Kagan and Woo, 1988).

second version of the bill (C-40) was introduced in 1989. By early February, 1991, C-40 was approved by Parliament and had received royal assent.

Passage of the 1991 Broadcasting Act set the stage for a number of significant changes in broadcasting policy-making. One already noted is increased power for the cabinet to issue directions to the CRTC. Another is in the way in which the CRTC makes regulatory decisions on broadcasting matters; the change is from a collegial process involving all full-time commissioners to a system known as "they who hear decide," which permits only the commissioners at a public hearing to make the decision. A third change is in the chairmanship and presidency of the CBC, which has been split into two positions.

Broadcasting Issues

In telecommunications the key issue is access, while in broadcasting it is the production of Canadian programming **content**. As with telecommunications, the key issue is not isolated from others (in this case, they are choice and participation).

The issue in content production stems not only from the economics of the small Canadian production industry but also from the business relationships between Canadian producers and Canadian broadcasters, and the relative cheapness of acquiring programming from the United States that is familiar, popular, and attractive to Canadian audiences – especially to Anglophones.

It has often been observed that there is a strong Canadian demand for local, regional, and national news, current affairs, and sports programming on radio and television. In Quebec, there is also a strong demand for entertainment programming produced in that province for the French-language audience. However, English

Canada lacks a broadly based popular entertainment industry to feed content into the broadcasting system. At the same time, Hollywood and New York provide an overwhelming market presence in television and music entertainment; Canadian producers (English and French) have difficulty creating and maintaining a programming production industry that has economic clout and growth potential within the Canadian marketplace for broadcasting content.

The issues surrounding Canadian content are not solely concerned with balancing it with (or against) the quantity and quality of foreign content. Diversity within Canadian content is also important. Canadian content need not mean only Toronto productions for the English market and Montreal for the French market. Centralization of the meagre production resources in a few centres probably makes economic sense but most Canadians appear to expect that programming will also be produced in the region (and, often, the city) where they live.

Many questions arise in policy discussion about broadcasting content, and there are not many easy or widely acceptable answers that can be implemented through policy action.

- How much economic protection should Canadian productions receive (e.g., through Canadian content quotas), and for how long?
- What types of regulatory protection are appropriate and effective?
- Has the Canadian content quota outlived its usefulness? If so, what – if anything – would encourage the distribution of more Canadian productions on radio and television?
- If there are to be programming subsidies, should they be for production? To aid distribution? To aid exports to other countries?

- Should production incentives be more selective and aim at encouraging particular types of content (e.g., children's television programs)? Or at particular kinds of producers – e.g., independents, producers in particular regions of the country?
- How much are Canadians prepared to pay (in taxes or consumer purchases) to encourage the development of production centres outside of Toronto and Montreal?
- If the economic incentives for commercial broadcasters are ineffective in encouraging more Canadian programming to be broadcast, should policy be directed mainly toward affecting the behaviour of the public broadcasters, such as the CBC and educational broadcasters?

The second policy issue associated with broadcasting is **choice**, which refers to audience choice – and, increasingly, consumer choice, as audience members have to decide what type of broadcasting service they are willing to pay for. Historically, all broadcasting services were delivered to the home via over-the-air transmitters with relatively limited reception range and signal quality. By and large, the choices available to audiences were limited by the quality of signal reception and the number of signals that could be received.

In recent years, because of an increasing number of technological systems to deliver broadcasting-type services – over-the-air, cable television, satellites, VCRs, compact discs – there is a growing demand from consumers for greater choice between delivery systems for what may be largely the same programming content delivered at different times or more frequently. (One of the key advantages of VCRs, from the consumer viewpoint, is the ability to view selected television programs or films at times suitable for that individual or household.)

In choosing content in terms of source and diversity, consumers are also choosing between methods of payment. Of course, all broadcasting must be paid for. If it is a commercial service, we pay indirectly through the reception of advertisements and the purchase of advertised products or we pay directly as in pay TV. If it is a public or educational service, we pay through taxes. If it is non-commercial, then the community pays through local taxes or voluntary contributions of various kinds.

There are really two kinds of payment, direct and indirect. Increasing attention is being given lately to direct forms of payment in systems such as pay TV, specialty TV, and VCR cassette rentals. These are not necessarily better or worse than the older payment systems; they are different and we have to consider the different effects of their development on content and on consumer choice. Indirect payment methods tend to have a redistributive effect in that wealthier people, although they receive the same service, pay more through taxes than those less well-off. Direct forms of payment tend to discriminate against those with the least amount of disposable income. The policy choice between payment systems is a social one and cannot be made solely on technical grounds if the broadcasting services provided are regarded as an important and basic requirement of nationhood.

Participation is a third and usually much less publicized issue in Canadian broadcasting policy. It refers to the access permitted to people outside the professional broadcasting companies to the production decisions on programming content. Participation by the general public is often disparaged by broadcasters because it is seen as allowing "amateurs" to dabble in a "professional" activity. That public broadcasting should involve the public in direct participation is an argument advanced forcefully by Marc Raboy in *Missed Opportunities: The Story of Canada's Broadcasting Policy* (1990).

Ironically perhaps, access in the North for native people to the facilities of the CBC is actually a good deal better than is access for most southern Canadians to any broadcast facilities. Participation issues can be about the difficulties of using the local cable TV system's community channel for a discussion of local politics, about the problems of selling independent productions to any broadcaster (CBC or otherwise), or about the difficulties of regional CBC producers getting the opportunity to produce a nationally aired program series, not just a local news hour or current affairs show.

There are a few community radio stations in Canada, mostly in Quebec where the provincial government has encouraged their establishment and provided basic funding for their operation. There is the access policy in the CBC's Northern Service. There are, as well, an "ethnic broadcasting" policy and some third-language programming. Also, the picture is improving for independent producers to sell their products to TV broadcasters. But there is still a long way to go before most Canadians have a chance to use the broadcasting system to say anything to their fellow citizens.

CULTURAL INDUSTRIES POLICY

In recent years, broadcasting has been combined with the film, publishing, and recording industries to form what are called "cultural industries." The term derives from the fact that each of these industries is involved in manufacturing, distributing, and retailing cultural materials. In this section we will look at those cultural industries other than broadcasting.

As Audley (1983, p. 320) suggests in *Canada's Cultural Industries*, the major challenge for policy in cultural industries "is not that properly financed Canadian cultural materials are being offered to the Canadian public and rejected, but that as a general rule, they are in limited supply, have limited financing available, and receive inadequate distribution or exhibition." Why do these barriers to production, financing, and distribution exist? Audley identifies two reasons. First, cheap foreign content is available at run-on prices. Second, Canadian companies must compete with foreign-owned branch plants that supply such materials to the market.

Given such barriers to Canadian participation and the nature of cultural materials themselves, cultural industries policy has been founded on two rationales. The first rationale is an economic one. The standard market economics version of this position is that, because there are structural barriers to the participation of Canadian businesses, the "infant industries" in Canada need a certain amount of government intervention in the marketplace. The purpose of such intervention is to allow Canadian businesses to gain a foothold under protective or supporting legislation, then, eventually, to re-open the doors to international competition. (See Rotstein [1988] and Globerman [1983] for opposing views on this rationale.)

Another version of the economic rationale focuses on the crucial importance of copyright legislation. Canada has weak copyright laws that do not separate Canadian rights from either North American or British rights. As a result, foreign-owned branch plants can have exclusive and prior rights to the output of their parent companies. Thus, for the most part, Canadian companies are unable to compete for the right to manufacture and distribute cultural products in Canada produced by foreigners. Support programs help to counteract this restricted competition.

The second and perhaps more fundamental rationale used to establish cultural industries policy is a cultural one. This rationale has been cited by all the public bodies that have examined cultural industries and cultural policy – even those with a preference for minimizing state intervention. An example of this could be seen in the Nielsen Task Force on Program Review, whose task was to find where government spending could be cut. The study team charged with examining communications and culture programs stated:

> The analyses of this paper suggest that while the economic impact of cultural activity is positive, economic reasons alone are probably not sufficient to justify the allocations of public resources to culture. The study team suggests that the main rationale for public support has to reside in the political and social value of cultural activities and their ability to contribute to the definition of the Canadian character. (Nielsen, 1986, p. 45)

As reviews of policy have pointed out, it is important that both economic (sometimes called industrial) and cultural considerations be built into policy. The predominance of economic considerations can lead to culturally undistinguished products. However, if cultural considerations dominate, this can perpetuate the international dominance of foreign cultural industries.

Film and Video

There is no comprehensive policy for film and video at the federal or provincial levels. This is an area in which the provinces could play an active role if they so chose. In May, 1984, the federal Minister of Communications issued a National Film and Video Policy, but this was more a statement of intent than a program that has been actively pursued. The key goals of the

policy statement were given as: (a) the development of the private-sector Canadian film and video industry; (b) a more focused and smaller production role for the National Film Board (NFB). This latter objective has not been followed up yet, although some decisions may be made within the next few years. At present, the NFB absorbs about 40 per cent of federal government expenditures in the film sector so it is clearly an important part of public policy. Among policy-makers, there has been dissatisfaction with the NFB for some years, as well as increasing uncertainty within the NFB itself about what its proper role is, now that the private film and video production industry is growing.

With regard to the private-sector initiatives, the most important federal policies have been Telefilm Canada's Broadcast Program Development Fund and the development of the Capital Cost Allowance (CCA).* The Fund was intended to provide greater resources to Canadian producers so that they could produce "attractive high-quality Canadian programming in both official languages and of international calibre – Canadian programming that people will choose to watch." The Fund was to be $35 million in its first year of operation and would rise to $60 million in its fifth year. Since 1988, the Fund has been established on a permanent basis.

To receive funds, producers have to show their program will be exhibited by a Canadian

---

* The CCA is part of the Income Tax Act and allows investors in certified Canadian film and video productions to deduct 30 per cent of their capital costs annually from their taxable income. This type of policy action is called a tax expenditure; that is, the government forgoes collection of taxes in exchange for some other type of benefit. Both Ontario and Quebec introduced similar tax allowances in the late 1980s.

broadcaster and initially they had to raise two-thirds of the money from other sources. (This rule was later modified to allow Telefilm to contribute a larger share.) Further, the funds have been earmarked for three program categories: drama, children's programming, and variety. Since its beginning in 1983, the Fund has been well received by independent producers and has also been acceptable to the CBC and some of the private TV stations. Given the long lead-time needed to create high-quality television productions, it is still too early to say if the productions assisted by the Fund will form the basis of a strong TV production industry, as the policy-makers and producers have hoped.

Aside from the Broadcast Fund, Telefilm also provides support for the production of motion pictures intended for theatrical release. Other federal policies relate to the funding of the NFB to produce and distribute films, the support of film (and video to a lesser extent) as art by the Canada Council, and establishment of Cité du Cinema, which is a jointly funded federal and Quebec production facility in Montreal. While federal policies have been important to film and video producers for many years, the provinces have become active more recently. In all, seven provinces now provide some funding support.

Most of the policies focus on much-needed production and development support, but another major problem is the lack of screen time for Canadian production on Canadian cinema screens. About 2 per cent of screen time in Canada goes to Canadian films. This obviously makes the film production industry very weak in terms of its own "natural" market. The reason for lack of market access is the historic, structural relationship between the major American studios and the Canadian exhibitor chains (who own the vast majority of first-run, urban cinemas). There are only two major chains of Canadian movie theatres today, Famous Players

and Cineplex Odeon. They have established contractual arrangements with the seven Hollywood majors, who are both producers and distributors. From a business point of view, these agreements are beneficial to the financial security of all the parties involved. The problem is that the independent Canadian producers and distributors are largely excluded.

A policy solution is not easy to find. First, the federal government cannot act directly in this area because cinemas are a matter of provincial jurisdiction, and provinces have been reluctant to intrude on the business decisions of cinema-owners. Furthermore, such government action is often perceived as dictatorial interference with the open market – even though it can easily be demonstrated that there is no free market in this sector. On the other hand, efforts to get the exhibitors to agree voluntarily to give access to more Canadian films have not worked well. The access to the Canadian cinema audience for Canadian films is crucial to later access to the television and pay TV markets. So, even though the cinema audience is now much smaller than the TV audience, the initial cinema market remains important for structural reasons. No policies yet have been established to deal effectively with this bottleneck.

Publishing

Publishing, a term that normally includes book and magazine publishing but not newspapers because they are usually not seen as a cultural industry, has its own collection of policies attempting to deal with specific aspects of the sector. There is no comprehensive policy and this is another industry in which provincial governments can and do play a policy role.

Book publishing is generally regarded as having four kinds of markets: educational, trade, mass paperback, and scholarly. All of these kinds of publishing show structural weaknesses that harm their effectiveness both as transmitters of culture and as industrial sectors in Canada. Essentially, there are two separate linguistic markets for published materials (as well as many minuscule markets for other languages). This divides the country into a small French-language publishing industry based in Quebec, largely restricted to that province, and a somewhat larger English-language publishing industry, largely based in Ontario but also spread across a wide, relatively underpopulated country.

Foreign presences loom over both of these industries. In the case of the English-language industry it is the giant U.S. book industry, together with the British, with their lower per unit costs for published material and heavy promotions of best-selling authors. In the case of the French-language industry it is French publishing, with slightly higher than American per unit costs but still an ability to supply the Canadian market with books at run-on prices. In addition, because of foreign-owned branch plants and weak copyright laws, there are problems of poor access for Canadian-owned publishers to the Canadian rights of foreign works (such rights are usually already held by foreign publishers and their Canadian subsidiaries act as exclusive agents for distribution in Canada). Because of weaknesses in other cultural industries, such as film and broadcasting (already mentioned), the Canadian book publishers do not benefit much from the sale of subsidiary rights for their published works for movies or TV programs. This reduces their profit potential.

Altogether, Canadian-owned publishing companies operate under severe structural handicaps and both the federal and provincial levels of government have support programs that try to develop a vibrant (and eventually self-sufficient) book publishing industry. The latest program of support for book publishing entrenches the cul-tural support the Canada Council is able to provide for "culturally valuable" books. The Department of Communications policy is oriented to increasing the participation of Canadian companies in the more profitable areas of publishing: educational books and, to a lesser extent, mass paperbacks.

Periodical publishing also shows a division between different kinds of publications. In this case, the differentiation is between general interest, special interest, literary, and academic periodicals. Each type is supported by government programs designed to deal with the problems of that particular market segment. Most periodicals publishers have all the same structural weaknesses associated with the lack of an adequate advertising base. One federal policy that has given significant aid to periodicals published in Canada is postal subsidies. In 1989, this funding was cut and it was announced that it would end altogether in 1991. In its place, there will be direct grants to selected Canadian periodicals for up to 50 per cent of postal costs.

Government policies are usually intended to help only Canadian-owned publishers, but it is extremely difficult to design support programs that exclude foreign-owned publishers from benefiting as well. This is very much the case with postal subsidies, which are also used extensively by foreign publishers. Since this was never the intention of the policy-makers, a re-examination of the program seemed in order. The Nielsen Task Force recommended the gradual abolition of the subsidy and that another way to aid Canadian periodicals publishers would likely have to be developed, which has since been done.

Cultural Industries Issues

With regard to all the cultural industries, the issues are largely the same as for broadcasting, with the addition of the key issue of **ownership**. Unlike in broadcasting, foreign ownership of other cultural industries has not been limited by laws equivalent to the Broadcasting Act. Federal and provincial governments both have jurisdiction over various aspects of the film and publishing industries. These governments do not usually act in unison to implement a coherent policy. Many underlying problems of the industrial process of production, distribution, and retailing in the Canadian cultural industries relate to the small size of the domestic market and the strong presence of foreign-owned companies into that market.

The dominance of foreign companies in cultural industries (other than newspaper publishing) has significance not only because it weakens the cultural sovereignty of Canadian society but also because it clearly affects the **content** of the cultural products that are made available to Canadians. The industrial aspect of cultural products for the mass market shows that the flow of Canadian products from production through distribution to retailing is not a smooth process but is restricted by business practices that often favour large (usually foreign) corporations based outside Canada.

In terms of the international trade in cultural products, Canada is a very small player indeed and Canadian companies operate from a weak domestic base. In industrial terms, decisions about what kinds of content to develop and promote are affected by the market potential. The cultural industries face a tough choice of trying to sell Canadian materials to a small domestic market or aiming to produce "international" products that appeal to a world-wide audience accustomed to American mass culture products. Neither choice is particularly appealing in industrial or cultural terms, yet the choice has to be made.

SUMMARY

This chapter has looked at three main kinds of public policy affecting the communications industries in Canada: telecommunications, broadcasting, and culture. It is becoming increasingly difficult to treat them separately in technical terms because their production and distribution systems are converging in terms of usage. In policy terms, however, these systems are still dealt with separately even though newer technologies like satellite communications clearly affect more than one area of policy. While the specific uses of communications technologies that are of concern in broadcasting policy are somewhat different from those in telecommunications, there are increasing overlaps in services. In other cultural industries, film and video are becoming drawn more into broadcasting policy actions while book publishing remains largely dominated by foreign companies.

For the foreseeable future, the three areas of communications policy discussed in this chapter will continue to develop differently. One of the major reasons for these differences is the historic accumulation of statutes, regulations, and public corporations that are specific to certain communications industries and are difficult to change in the short term. Another reason for the differences is in the specific economic structure (including market structures and business relationships) found in each communications industry, not only within Canada but also in its connections to the transnational or global economy. A third reason is in the complex federal-provincial divisions of jurisdiction and in the differing priorities between governments regarding communications matters.

REFERENCES

Audley, Paul. *Canada's Cultural Industries: Broadcasting, Publishing, Records and Film.* Toronto: James Lorimer, 1983.

Babe, Robert E. *Canadian Broadcasting Structure, Performance and Regulation.* Ottawa: Economic Council of Canada, 1979.

Babe, Robert E. *Telecommunications in Canada: Technology, Industry, and Government.* Toronto: University of Toronto Press, 1990.

Canada, Task Force on Program Review (Nielsen Task Force). *Culture and Communications.* Ottawa: Minister of Supply and Services, 1986.

Canadian Broadcasting Corporation. Annual Reports.

Canadian Radio Television Commission. *Canadian Ownership in Broadcasting: A Report on the Foreign Divestiture Process.* Ottawa: Information Canada, 1974.

Communications Canada. *Canadian Voices: Canadian Choices – A New Broadcasting Policy for Canada.* 1988.

Department of Communications. *Canadian Telecommunications: An Overview of the Canadian Telecommunications Carriage Industry.* Ottawa: Minister of Supply and Services, 1983.

English, H. Edward, ed. *Telecommunications for Canada: An Interface of Business and Government.* Toronto: Methuen, 1973.

Fortin, Luc, and Conrad Winn. "Communications and Culture: Evaluating an Impossible Portfolio," in G. Bruce Doern, ed., *How Ottawa Spends: The Liberals, the Opposition and Federal Priorities 1983.* Toronto: James Lorimer, 1983.

Globerman, Steven. *Cultural Regulation in Canada.* Montreal: Institute for Research on Public Policy, 1983.

Minister of Communications. *Proposals for a Communications Policy for Canada: A Position Paper of the Government of Canada.* Ottawa: Information Canada, 1973.

Minister of Communications. *The National Film and Video Policy.* Ottawa: Minister of Supply and Services, 1984.

Minister of Communications, Consultative Committee on the Implications of Telecommunications for Canadian Sovereignty (Clyne Committee). *Telecommunications and Canada.* Ottawa: Minister of Supply and Services Canada, 1979.

Minister of Communications, Task Force on Broadcasting Policy (Caplan-Sauvageau Task Force). *Report.* Ottawa: Minister of Supply and Services, 1986.

Minister of Industry. *White Paper on a Domestic Satellite Communication System for Canada.* Ottawa: Queen's Printer, 1968.

Peers, Frank W. *The Politics of Canadian Broadcasting: 1920-1951.* Toronto: University of Toronto Press, 1969.

Peers, Frank W. *The Public Eye: Television and the Politics of Canadian Broadcasting, 1952-1968.* Toronto: University of Toronto Press, 1979.

Raboy, Marc. *Missed Opportunities: The Story of Canada's Broadcasting Policy.* Montreal: McGill-Queen's University Press, 1990.

Rotstein, Abraham. "The Use and Misuse of Economics in Cultural Policy," in R. Lorimer and D.C. Wilson, eds., *Communication Canada: Issues in Broadcasting and New Technologies.* Toronto: Kagan and Woo, 1988.

Weir, E. Austin. *The Struggle for National Broadcasting in Canada.* Toronto: McClelland and Stewart, 1965.

Winner, Langdon. *Autonomous Technology: Technics-out-of-Control as a Theme in Political Thought.* Cambridge: MIT Press, 1977.

Woodrow, R. Brian, *et al. Conflict over Communications Policy: A Study of Federal-Provincial Relations and Public Policy.* Montreal: C.D. Howe Institute, 1980.

STUDY QUESTIONS

1. Canada does not have a clear and unified national policy on communications. Discuss the pros and cons of developing such a policy framework.
2. It has been suggested in this chapter that assumptions about the power of technology have influenced Canadian policy-making on communications. Give two examples of how this influence has been exerted recently.
3. The most crucial issue in telecommunications policy today is the proper balance between competition and monopoly service provision. Why is this a policy issue at all and how do you think it will be resolved?
4. The Fowler Committee Report in 1965 began with this statement, "The only thing that really matters in broadcasting is program content; all the rest is housekeeping." Do you agree? Explain your reasons.
5. "Cultural sovereignty" is an important term used in policy discussions about the cultural industries. What does this term mean? How does it translate into policy actions regarding the film industry?

Cartoon by Jean-Marc Phaneuf, Beloeil, Quebec. *From Royal Commission on Newpapers, 1981. Reproduced with permission of the Minister of Supply and Services Canada.*

CHAPTER

7

The Structure and Role of Ownership

INTRODUCTION: PEOPLE AND PROPERTY

M ANY OF US grow up in blissful ignorance of the vast framework of laws and government policies that govern our lives. Simple laws governing traffic and crimes against people and property we know about. But general laws and policies governing communications and, especially, ownership of communications enterprises are distant from our minds.

In Canada, as elsewhere, we think of our houses and apartments as our homes. Their interiors are our private domain, a domain over which we control access. Their exteriors are the face we show to the world as both an invitation and a barrier. In the same way, a farmer's field becomes his in a personal and private way as a result of the years of toil he spends in it and his ability to know its behaviour under all kinds of circumstances.

Capitalism has no respect for such relations between people and property. Nor, in fact, does state socialism. No *economic* system does. In capitalist countries, at certain times, such as the Great Depression, vast numbers are expelled from their homes and denied the right of access to what is more humanly theirs than anyone else's. If the rent is not paid, if the mortgage is not kept up, the landlord or lender evicts. At other times in history, fewer feel the brunt of the owner's exercise of his or her property rights. But at all times, numbers of people live out their days with the conscious or subconscious realization that they carry out their private daily routine in surroundings that are granted to them at the pleasure of an owner. Where state ownership prevails those routines are carried out at the pleasure of the state and woe befalls the person who offends the state.

The other side of capitalism is that each citizen has the right to own property if he or she can find the money to buy it. Essentially, that right or privilege allows people to build houses, set up businesses, and own land for a variety of purposes: to live in, make money from, or rent to others; to respond to opportunities in the marketplace. Such an arrangement means that we do not have to depend on the state to discover needs, plan ways of meeting those needs, and begin programs to address such needs as reinterpreted by government study. And there is a magic to the marketplace. Capitalist societies, especially rich ones, do manage to manufacture and distribute goods and services fairly well.

However, while capitalism creates a certain amount of individual freedom in market-oriented activities and a certain level of distribution of goods and services, it also pits individual against individual for scarce resources. The price of a house is set, in theory, by market conditions. Market conditions are the variables that determine the price people in general are willing to pay for a house. Thus, while person A may need a house and house A may be empty and for sale, unless person A is prepared to pay market value, then he has no right to live

in the house. For a lesser short-term amount he may rent the house, but he may not even be able to afford that alternative.

Individuals are pitted against one another in the sense that they must compete in the marketplace. So person B may purchase house A and rent to person A essentially because person B has the money or capital to buy the house, although B may not need it to live in. Moreover, purchasing and renting it may just make B that much richer than person A.

In the case of larger properties, such as business institutions rather than houses, the little guy who cannot even afford his own home has no chance of participating in ownership. There is, of course, a group of reasonably well-off people who can participate, but not equally, with a third and richer group, those who own and control large business enterprises. Substantial numbers of Canadians can and do participate in ownership through the purchase of small blocks of shares in public companies. But as we will see in this chapter, they have very little say in what goes on in such corporations.

This third group of owners, who exert effective control, is made up of men (rarely women) with copious amounts of surplus resources that they invest to make more money to reinvest further. This group, which holds controlling ownership of a significant percentage of the larger business institutions of our country, consists of very few people.

Culture and Capitalism

Ownership of land and property is not quite the same as ownership of media institutions. Communication, as we pointed out in Chapter 1, is infused into every aspect of personal, social, and cultural life. It is a necessity of modern civilization. Just as a person's home or a farmer's field is the private domain and the public face of an individual, so a nation's communication system is essential to and an expression of the culture of which it is a part.

Yet communication in modern society is increasingly dependent on privately owned media institutions whose primary aim is to make money. Communication, therefore, takes place within the structures of an economic regime. In broadcasting, were it not for the CBC, the very fabric of our culture – what we have to say to one another, what insights our artists and writers have to share, our distinctive national imagination, our domestic reality – might depend for its dissemination on the pleasure, which is to say the profit, of a small group of owners of media institutions. Even the CBC lives within an increasingly parsimonious regime where it must weigh the value of the message against the number of viewers or listeners a particular program might attract.

Private Enterprise and the Public Purpose in Media

These two opposing forces, public good and private interest, are enshrined in the Broadcasting Act (1991) (see Chapter 6). A more recent discussion of them can be found in the *Report of the Task Force on Broadcasting Policy* (1986). Hardin (1988) has provided a useful commentary on that report from the perspective of public broadcasting. As the Act itself makes clear, while accepting the participation of the private sector as a complement to public enterprise, the primary purpose of broadcasting is cultural and is stated explicitly in Section 3(h):

> where any conflict arises between the objective of the national broadcasting service and the interests of the private element of the Canadian broadcasting system, it shall be resolved in the public interest but paramount

consideration shall be given to the national broadcasting service. . . .

The Act empowers the CRTC to oversee these opposing forces, giving it the job of persuading capitalists to spend their profits on items of cultural value, at times at the expense of economic gain.

This cultural function is taken up in the news and information media as follows. In large newspapers and magazines journalists take up the cultural issue. Owners represent business concerns. With small magazines and with many Canadian-owned book publishers, both owners and writers are concerned with cultural content.

In this chapter, we will review the structure and role of ownership, predominantly private ownership, as it exists in media institutions in Canada. The following chapter deals with the functions of journalists.

HISTORICAL BACKGROUND: FUNCTION AND OWNERSHIP

The roots of media institutions are found in social, cultural, and political opportunities. Gutenberg's press was an invention that responded to growing literacy, to an opportunity to make the Bible and other tracts available to a wider audience. The establishment of the press in Canada, in the sense of an institution rather than a machine, was a response to the opportunity to print under contract official government information, such as official records, and to make such information widely available. It soon evolved into an institution capable of responding to other social and political pressures for the distribution of information and ideas.

With such roots, the intensive involvement of government in the press and printing is not difficult to understand. In the case of the British press at least, which provided a model for Britain's colonies, while ownership was not exclusive to the public domain, numbers of laws and taxes were used to control press output so that it would reflect the interests of those who allowed its operation. However, as printers as a group became less and less dependent on government largess, and with the general economic and political rise of the bourgeoisie, intense, insistent pressure grew for the freedom of printers to pursue their economic interest.

Free Press, Free Market

As we saw in Chapter 3, the battle for the establishment of the economic interests of private press owners was not fought on economic grounds. Rather, the press put itself forward as an estate representative of a distinct set of interests, not those of church, business, or landowners but those of "the people." The press won recognition because the basis of its pursuit of its economic interests was in accordance with the generally accepted theory and practice of the day. That theory, which still holds sway in capitalist countries, posits that the pursuit by individuals of their own economic self-interest will maximize the economic interests of the whole. The mechanism that leads to this happy confluence of interests is Adam Smith's "invisible hand," named after the theorist who proposed it. The invisible hand guides individuals to pursue a social need through each response to a self-interested, economic opportunity.

The press asked for nothing more than any other business. But in dealing with information, which, even during the Industrial Revolution, was recognized as somehow different from other commodities, the press found it prudent to fight and win the battle on non-economic grounds.

The Public Role in Broadcasting

We can probably attribute public (i.e., government) involvement in broadcasting to government reaction to the capitalistic instincts of Guglielmo Marconi. Marconi was the first person to transmit intelligence electronically from one point to another without the use of connecting wires. As a result of this, and with other extensive experiments and achievements and considerable business acumen, Marconi was able to create for himself a virtual international monopoly of the airwaves through the patenting of his inventions, the lease rather than the sale of his equipment, and control over authorization of operators. Faced with that monopoly and the differences of interests between nations, which one monopolist would be hard-pressed to serve without rancor, the nations of the world were only able to break his monopoly by declaring the airwaves to be a public resource. They were then able, and to some extent forced, to regulate the airwaves.

Once in the business of regulation, governments needed to identify a guiding principle. That principle, in virtually every country, was that the airwaves should be regulated for the general public good. In the early stages of broadcasting in most countries, this principle led to the founding of public broadcasting institutions. But private businesses, especially in the United States, applied continuous pressure to be allowed to exploit the airwaves for their interests. They argued that market theory, i.e., Adam Smith's invisible hand, would ensure that the general public good was best served by the profit-seeking behaviour of individual businesses. In the U.S. they won the day. Elsewhere, private business was precluded from owning broadcasting undertakings or, as happened in Canada, was allowed to do so alongside public institutions. Of the developed Western countries, only the U.S. rejected the involvement of public institutions in the early years of broadcasting. The modern trend in countries where public institutions have held monopolies or near monopolies is toward increased private-sector involvement.

In both major areas of communication, broadcasting and newspapers, there was an early involvement of public institutions. However, in the Western world, pressure for private exploitation has never been distant from communications institutions.

Media Ownership in Canada

The nature of ownership has been especially significant in Canada. As we noted earlier, communications serve an important role in binding the nation together. They bring isolated communities and individuals into the nation and are intended to reflect our regional differences, our two official languages and cultures, and our multi-ethnicity.

The mesh of these public goals with private economic interests is not perfect. The Broadcasting Act recognizes that conflict of interests in assigning special responsibilities to the public sector. These special responsibilities include:

- attention to balance in types of programming;
- programming for all population groups;
- extension to all parts of Canada as funds permit;
- contribution to national unity and a Canadian identity;
- the primacy of the national system;
- provision for educational broadcasting;
- attention to technical advance.

The difficulty of meshing public goals and private interests has been recognized in other ways in Canadian communications. Foreign private interests have been especially problematic. In contrast to other industries, every encouragement has been given to Canadian entrepreneurs and corporations to maintain ownership of Canadian media. Following the sale in the late sixties of two venerable Canadian book publishing companies, W.J. Gage and Ryerson Press, governments, beginning with Ontario and followed by the federal government and other provincial governments, have reviewed ownership and granted direct subsidies to ensure Canadian participation in the Canadian book publishing industry. In an attempt to ensure a sound advertising and therefore financial base for other media, including magazines, newspapers, and private broadcasting stations, the federal government brought forward Bill C-58. Included in that bill were provisions now incorporated in Section 19 of the Income Tax Act, which prevent Canadian businesses from deducting as a business expense advertising in foreign-owned media destined for the Canadian market. Foreign-owned media are defined as those with greater than 25 per cent ownership by non-Canadians. The stipulations of Section 19 have ensured the maintenance of Canadian ownership in the newspaper industry and, along with other support programs such as postal subsidies, have allowed a variety of Canadian magazines to develop and thrive. They have also helped to control the growth of U.S. border television and radio stations. Tax breaks and direct subsidies have also been put in place to encourage the development of Canadian-owned film and sound recording industries.

In education, the production of educational programming has been a public-sector activity involving provincial educational authorities and the National Film Board. Such activities have been a major basis of resistance of the energetic export initiatives of the U.S.

In broadcasting, through licensing, while private ownership has long been a *de facto* element of the overall system, only in 1968 did the Broadcasting Act give formal recognition to the private sector as part of Canada's overall broadcasting system. Prior to 1968, it was still an open question whether the entire system should be in public hands.

These media traditions and initiatives were designed to allow Canadians to keep control of their communication system through public ownership, which was seen as the best means of allowing Canadians to use communications to pursue public, cultural desiderata. Private ownership of media, however, with its unavoidable pursuit of profits and audiences with whatever products work, has come to play a large role, in fact, has come to predominate communications in Canada. With the signing of the Free Trade Agreement between Canada and the U.S., the pressure to make private-sector opportunities available to both U.S. and Canadian enterprises has increased substantially.

FORMS OF OWNERSHIP

A variety of enterprises operate in the marketplace. We will differentiate between two major types and discuss the second in some detail.

The Single Enterprise

The **single enterprise** is a business form in which control rests with a group of shareholders who do not represent other companies. Examples of this form of ownership were plentiful in small Canadian towns until press barons such as Roy Thomson began buying them all up. Such purchases continue today as independent weeklies are bought out by large firms such as Southam and smaller chains such as Black Press, run by David Black.

The Chain: Horizontal Integration

The second major type of firm is the **linked company**. In this case, the nature of the links is significant. On the one hand, a company may be part of a chain of similar companies. The group of cable companies owned by Rogers Cablesystems Inc. and of newspapers owned by Québecor and Southam are examples of groups of companies that constitute chains. Each chain can also be described as **horizontally integrated;** the links do not buy or sell to or from one another but are a number of enterprises, usually in different locations, doing the same business.

Vertical Integration

Another form of linkage is through **vertical integration**. In this circumstance, companies under the same owner supply and consume each other's products. Thus, when the telephone companies purchase from equipment companies owned (or controlled) by the same group of investors, or when a major newspaper owns a newsprint supplier, such companies could be said to be vertically integrated. One example here was Selkirk Communications, which before it was purchased by Maclean Hunter owned radio stations CKKS-FM, CKWX, and Quality Records. Another is Western Broadcasting, which owns CKNW and the Vancouver Canucks and broadcasts Canuck games. Pierre Péladeau's Québecor, as of late 1989, published 42 weeklies and four dailies, thus being horizontally integrated, but it is also vertically integrated though its distribution companies. Eaton's ownership of CFTO, Toronto, the main CTV station, and of Glen Warren productions, the main CTV production studio, is yet another example.

Cross-Ownership

A further type of linkage more closely associated with horizontal than vertical integration is **cross-ownership**. Cross-ownership of media companies refers to companies that own more than one type of media company, e.g., a television station, a radio station, a newspaper, a magazine publisher, a book publisher, a cable company, a telephone company, etc. Maclean Hunter is an example of cross-ownership. It owns *The Financial Post, Maclean's,* and the Toronto, Calgary, and Edmonton *Sun* newspapers as well as several radio, TV, and cable companies.

The Conglomerate

The last type of linked ownership is the conglomerate, which combines a variety of linkages, usually inclusive of horizontally and vertically integrated companies. The conglomerate operates in more than one field, for example the media and travel, or oil exploration and retailing. It is a conglomeration of all sorts of different companies. Power Corporation, which owns, among other companies, Montreal Trust, Investor's Group Inc., *La Presse,* and radio interests is an example of a rather powerful Canadian conglomerate.

FORCES TOWARD INCREASED CONCENTRATION OF OWNERSHIP

Corporate Concentration: A Definition

When ownership within an industry shifts increasingly to the hands of the few rather than the many, the emergent business structure is said to have an increasing degree of corporate or ownership concentration. Corporate concentration in any single industry, such as the media, arises through a combination of chain ownership and cross-ownership, two different forms of horizontal integration. The resulting situation is that a small number of chains take on a national presence as information and entertainment providers and in some markets all media are owned by one of those few. Most markets are affected in some way or other by these dominant few. Industry in a country is said to be concentrated when chains and cross-ownership are combined with vertical integration. The economy is thus dominated by relatively few large corporations.

Statistics Canada's publication *Intercorporate Ownership* shows the linkages that exist among holding companies and subsidiaries, and is careful to report such factors as stock options, insider holdings, convertible shares, and interlocking directorships, as well as to replace nominee accounts with the names of the true owners. One of Canada's media giants, Télémédia, exemplifies a corporate size and cross-ownership typical of the industry. It is a private company and is second only to the CBC in combined audiences. With *TV Guide* and *Canadian Living,* it produces more copies of consumer magazines than any other Canadian company. However, Télémédia is no higher than 17th among Canada's largest media companies. It has no television, cable, or newspaper holdings, but it does own 22 radio stations in Quebec and Ontario, publishes eight magazines, maintains controlling interest in a Toronto-based promotion and marketing company, and holds equity investments in Canadian Satellite Communications Inc.

It is usually assumed that corporate expansion is stimulated by the expectation of greater efficiency. The first type of efficiency is derived from a greater number of companies doing the same thing under one overall owner (i.e., horizontal integration). The second derives from

TABLE 7.1

**Maclean Hunter's Growing Empire
($ millions)**

	1989	1987	1985	1983	1981
Revenue:					
Periodicals	355.7	316.8	238.8	184.0	159.4
Bus. forms &					
comm'l print.	353.6	293.6	134.9	100.2	82.9
Newspapers	312.2	213.3	166.0	140.5	26.1
Cable TV	255.9	19.5	162.1	115.1	70.6
Broadcasting	80.0	69.0	51.1	51.5	47.5
Communication					
Services	68.8	32.8	32.1	26.5	22.9
TOTALS	1,426.2	1,125.0	785.0	617.8	409.4
Consolidated					
net income					
(profit)	92.2	135.3	64.6	47.7	28.3

SOURCE: Maclean Hunter Annual Report, 1989.

cutting suppliers and those whom one supplies out of the market by becoming supplier and end-product producer oneself. If an owner can buy from another company he already owns and sell to a third he owns as well, then nobody but the one owner makes a profit. In addition, because the one owner knows the needs of one business and the output of another, the former is assured of continuous supply while the latter is assured of a known and reliable market. No need exists for a vast sales department, nor for the continuous processing of competitive bids from suppliers. Vertical integration is thus another level of efficiency.

The average person might consider efficiency to be the major reason for growing concentration, but a number of other reasons are no less significant.

High Profit Levels

Until the 1960s, newspapers and broadcasters had managed to persuade the government and the public that the profit levels of media industries were relatively low. With the publication of the *Report of the Special Senate Committee on the Mass Media,* headed by Keith Davey, that little fallacy was exploded. Davey found the highest profit level in one year to be 27.4 per cent for medium-sized operations. The overall after-tax average for all newspapers over ten years was between 12.3 per cent and 17.5 per cent. The comparable percentage for all manufacturing industries was 10.4 per cent and for retailing industries 9.2 per cent (p. 47). Regarding television in the 1960s, the Committee wrote:

It would appear from this Franklin cartoon that Maclean Hunter is not the only firm that grows for the sake of growing. *From The Financial Post, July 4, 1988; reproduced with permission.*

The other thing to note is how wondrously profitable some broadcasting operations can be. The largest revenue-group of TV stations, for instance, earned a before-tax profit (on equity) of about 98.5 percent in 1964. At that rate, even after taxes, shareholders would recover their entire investment in two years! The big TV stations' worst year was 1967, when pre-tax profits declined to 40 percent; in most other industries, that kind of margin would be considered fabulous.

Growth for Its Own Sake

A second reason for expansion of already established large corporations leading to industry concentration is simply that such firms are in a position to expand. Maclean Hunter, for example, has increased its revenue not so much by increased sales but from expanded activities (Table 7.1). According to company president Ronald Osborne, in 1985 "Maclean Hunter could comfortably handle a cable-television acquisition of $300 million to $400 million and a publishing venture of $100 million to $200 million" (Enchin, 1985). Nonetheless, the company does not have that much spare cash, nor does Maclean Hunter necessarily think it could manage things better than existent companies (at the time of the announcement apparently it did not even know who it would try to buy out). Simply, it has the borrowing power to take on such an expansion. Since 1985, Maclean Hunter has been very busy with acquisitions. The company increased its annual revenue from $973 million (profits, $64.6 million) in 1985 to $1,426 million (profits, $92.2 million) in 1989. (*Financial Post,* 1990).

Borrowing Power

Access to financial resources often results in corporate expansion. A small company may not be able to borrow enough money to upgrade its physical plant to remain competitive, but frequently a larger company will buy out the smaller company, even paying a premium to the owner, and then will be successful in borrowing the money for upgrading. The necessity of borrowing for technological upgrading can lead to corporate concentration. It is often easier and, for a number of reasons, cheaper for a company to buy an existing company than to build one up from the ground. And sometimes, just when an individual entrepreneur has brought an enterprise to the verge of real financial success, a conglomerate with the needed financial resources to provide the final expansion or marketing will buy out the entrepreneur and subsequently reap the profits.

Replacement of the Rich

People die, and shareholders are people. When shareholders die, their shares often come on the market. When these holdings are large, often only large corporations have the resources to take up the shares. Ownership thus becomes further concentrated. An interesting case of this type, which also represented a major cross-ownership issue, emerged in the fall of 1985 when Paul Desmarais's Power Corp. agreed to purchase controlling interest of Télé-Métropole through the purchase of 1.4 million class A and 6.2 million class B non-voting shares from the estate and foundation of J. Alexander DeSève and Ciné-Monde Inc. for $97.8 million. Obviously, few would be in a position to match the Desmarais offer

(Phillips, 1985). As it turned out, the CRTC refused permission for this Power Corp. purchase. The eventual purchaser was Télécable Vidéotron, the largest cable TV company in Quebec.

A Small Canadian Club

In some media, restrictions against foreign ownership lead to increased concentration of ownership. In broadcasting companies, no more than 20 per cent of shares can be foreign-owned. In newspapers and magazines, Section 19 of the Income Tax Act effectively prevents foreign owners from acquiring more than 25 per cent ownership of newspapers and magazines. In book publishing the so-called Baie Comeau principle applies, which requires divestiture within two years of acquisition of any book publishing company acquired by a foreign owner. This policy is overseen by Investment Canada and protection and mechanisms for compensation are set out in Articles 1607 and 2005 of the Free Trade Agreement. The result is that new foreign owners are effectively prevented from entering the marketplace. A change can be expected to this policy in the 1990s. Most likely, firms already in place will be allowed to stay and to change owners. However, new foreign owners will not be allowed to buy up Canadian companies, thus forming branch plants or new foreign-owned publishers.

Large blocks of holdings, however, are quite characteristic in the media industry, and only the rich few pension funds and large businesses have the necessary borrowing power to acquire available blocks of holdings when they come on the market. The point is not that Canadians do not have the money – as often as not the money comes from the accumulated savings of

Canadians. But the financial clout is organized by these financial brokers. Thereby they gain enormously, while others gain the crumbs, that is, the interest the banks are prepared to give to pave the way for these people to use the money of ordinary Canadians.

Large companies may also wish to buy into emerging industries because they represent potential competitors or outlets for products they are already producing. For example, the Famous Players movie theatre chain was an early investor in cable television, which represented a new and potentially dominant outlet for movies that might have ruined Famous Players. Similarly, in the U.S., Warner Brothers' investment in cable television represented a potential outlet for its products.

In Canada, just one of many examples is the Maclean Hunter purchase of *Media Scene,* a short-lived publication about the media. After a few years of publication, Maclean Hunter bought the magazine, kept it operating for a short period of time, and then closed it down, offering subscribers its long-running *Marketing* instead.

Media Ownership as Status and as an Ideological Vehicle

Certain media companies and media ownership in general can provide status. In England, Roy Thomson acquired *The Times* and the *Sunday Times* for reasons of status and for that reason his son, Ken, was able to sell them to Rupert Murdoch. Conrad Black's activities combine a pursuit of status and promotion of ideology. Black has always had some media holdings but his real wealth was acquired through a set of aggressive acquisitions and divestitures of Argus Corporation (a holding company), Dominion Stores (a grocery chain), and Massey Ferguson (at one time Canada's preeminent farm equipment dealer). In the 1980s Black set about increasing his media holdings. Using Roy Thomson's technique, he acquired many independent small-town newspapers, adding them onto his existing chain of newspaper holdings. In two major moves, he acquired the prestigious and conservative *Sunday Telegraph* of London, England, as well as the Canadian politics and current affairs magazine *Saturday Night.* Later, he acquired the *Jerusalem Post* and in late 1989 faced the ire of journalists over the apparently ideologically inspired moves of his newly appointed publisher, (Colonel) Yehuda Levy. Levy was quoted as saying: "I am not an editor. I do not want to be an editor." Yet, according to *The Globe and Mail* (January 3, 1990, p. B11): "Last month he informed a committee of Israeli editors that he planned to assume editorial control."

Newspaper ownership, especially in Britain, can bring owners considerable status and recognition. Two Canadians, Roy Thomson and Max Aitken, gained peerages. Thomson became Lord Thomson; Aitken became Lord Beaverbrook.

On the side of ideology, as far back as 1973, Black was contemplating the purchase of the perennial money-losing *Saturday Night.* At that time he was consulting with American conservative ideologue William F. Buckley, Jr., on the possibility of turning it into a right-wing magazine of political commentary to, in his words, "convert an existing Canadian magazine into a conveyance for views at some variance with the tired porridge of ideological normalcy in vogue here as well as the U.S.A." (Newman, 1982, p. 183). Once he acquired *Saturday Night* in the late 1980s, he obtained the resignation of the long-time publisher, Robert Fulford, and appointed an old-time school friend, journalist John Fraser, who has increased the breadth of the political spectrum represented in the magazine and paved the way for a further turn toward the political right.

The right turn of the *Jerusalem Post* has also not gone unnoticed. In face of accusations that he would transform that prestigious and left-leaning newspaper into a right-wing ideological vehicle, Black replied:

> I wish to make it absolutely clear that we are committed to making the *Jerusalem Post* more respected, more balanced and profitable all at the same time – and it will happen. It will not be the propaganda sheet for any faction . . . and we will have absolutely no problem proving to anybody who is fair-minded about it that we have not only maintained the quality and integrity of the newspaper, but enhanced it. It will be a good solid profit centre. (*Globe and Mail,* January 22, p. B1)

Balance, and fair-mindedness, of course, are all in the eyes of the beholder because, in a different context, Black has described the media as "an industry like the others, though more profitable than most, and *more strategic than any*" (emphasis added) (*Financial Post,* May 19, 1988, p. 16).

Sunset-to-Sunrise Industries

Traditional media industries may also buy up certain media properties as a means of diversifying for survival. The newspapers were lured into investing in Telidon for this reason, and Famous Players, in its original investments, undoubtedly

saw cable in the same light. The cable TV companies and the movie producers are both trying to set themselves up strategically so that whatever emerges as the dominant form of movie distribution, they will not be in a losing position.

The big do get bigger. For example, as of 1985, there were far too many players in the video rental business and we predicted in the first edition of this book that when some order was established in the marketplace and a way of predicting and buying success became apparent, the big boys would step in and make it impossible for the little guys to keep anything but a marginal place in the market. By 1990 that trend was amply visible. While there were still too many players, many of the independents had been replaced by franchises and chains. A pattern of consumer demand had been established that was sufficient to allow such large media corporations as Rogers to establish its own chain with an expanded range of titles imitative of the trend toward grocery super-stores.

Recent statistics on the recording industry demonstrate how difficult it is for the small companies to get a piece of the action once the big companies have moved in, even in an expanding market. Ten foreign-owned firms in Canada earned 82 per cent of the domestic profit in 1983. The remaining 18 per cent was divided among 84 Canadian companies (Off, 1985).

The CRTC Contribution

A final factor leading to increased concentration in cable TV as a regulated industry has to do with the manner in which the CRTC operates. While the CRTC regulates cable subscriber rates, it does not generally pass judgement on the price a company might pay to take over another company. Thus, one of the biggies – Southam-Selkirk, Rogers, or Maclean Hunter – might decide to buy out a small company at a high price and do it all with borrowed money. It can then go to the CRTC with a request for an increase in rates because it paid an exorbitant amount for the shares and must now keep up the interest payments on the borrowed money. It is not asking to make undue profit, just a reasonable return on its (unwise) investment. In other words, the subscribers are the ones who pay for the takeover. Because the company is protected by virtue of being a monopoly, it has only consumer resistance to worry about, certainly not competition.

Currently, in reviewing a takeover, the CRTC likes to see what it refers to as "significant and unequivocal" benefits deriving from the purchase. For instance, in 1989 Rogers was able to take over Western Cablevision of Vancouver, with 115,000 subscribers, for $55 million. Two earlier attempts, in 1981 and 1983, had been rejected. This time, however, Rogers put together a benefits package worth $11.2 million, more than twice the unofficial standard amount of 10 per cent of purchase price. The money is meant to go toward such things as new equipment for the community channel, as well as innovative programming, including a program called "Women and Media." The CRTC's acceptance of the offer effectively gave Rogers control of more than half of B.C.'s cable subscribers (up to 56 per cent from 46 per cent).

Discussion has begun within the CRTC to keep profit levels "reasonable." In 1990, the CRTC (*Canada Gazette,* Part 1, May 26) reported the beginnings of a discussion designed to replace the old guidelines dealing with economic need (ibid., September 18, 1974) and profitability with new, more quantitatively oriented, guidelines. The CRTC is proposing that the new guidelines set a range of profitability. Currently cable companies make around "the reasonable figure of" 24 per cent return on net fixed assets while their "competitors," the telephone companies, make about 15 per cent.

The CRTC is content to allow another monopolistic subterfuge by not requiring full disclosure of the finances of the parent and sister companies of the regulated company. Given this shortsightedness, arrangements can be worked out whereby profit is centred in unregulated companies while regulated companies become burdened with debt.

Policy on Ownership

Warnings regarding ownership concentration are not new. As far back as 1929, the Aird Commission registered concern about the ownership of media industries. Various committees and royal commissions have also sounded the alarm. Federal combines investigation officials have taken on a variety of cases (which they have consistently lost). The CRTC itself has expressed alarm at growing concentration but seemingly has lacked the will to take decisive action. The Kent Royal Commission's strongest point was that there was far too high a level of corporate concentration in the newspapers. In response, Trudeau's federal Liberal cabinet passed a now-rescinded order-in-council discouraging a greater degree of cross-ownership between newspapers and broadcasting. No other action has been taken by any government to enforce Kent's recommendations.

However, in 1986, the government brought in a new Competition Act, ostensibly to give more teeth to Canada's competition legislation. Certain noises have been made and in 1990

Thomson was being investigated for predatory pricing practices between 1976 and 1985. However, the tide has not changed in the movement toward greater concentration.

At the same time as these alarms have been raised, government policy has been to proceed without delay on the development of high-technology communications (see Chapter 9). But who benefits from such technology? While it could be argued that Canadians do through access to a wider range of services, the greater beneficiaries lie elsewhere. First, large enterprises get the information systems they need for world-scale operations. Firms able to pursue the manufacturing and marketing of these technologies in the world market also benefit. All the while, these same firms are going into partnership with the federal government for development of such technologies. The very firms that dominate the market are being placed in an even more advantageous position by the commitment of the Department of Communications to high technology. It would appear that Canadians both want and do not want these firms in their position of dominance.

IMPLICATIONS OF OWNERSHIP FORM

Public Enterprise

Public ownership has a long and distinguished tradition in Canada. As Herschel Hardin (1974) points out, we Canadians have made extensive use of public enterprise throughout our history. We have used public enterprise – its most common form is the Crown corporation – in instances when we saw that the market was incapable of adequately serving the needs of the country. At times, as in the case of CPR, we have combined public enterprise with private ownership to produce the same end, public service.

The prime example of public ownership in the media is hard to ignore. The CBC, originally a radio operation, was set up essentially in fear of inundation by programming from the U.S. As for television, in the face of the small costs of purchasing U.S. programming, it was not apparent how Canadian production and display could be a money-making venture. To bring information reflective of the variety that makes up Canada to the greatest number of Canadians in order that we might all see ourselves as members of a single nation did not look like a private-enterprise project. As a consequence, the CBC extended its activities into television.

The Ethic of Public Enterprise

Public corporations such as the CBC do not, like some public enterprises, go off on their own and act like private corporations, assiduously pursuing profit. To do so would be, in a sense, counter-productive. In the case of the CBC, this is not within its mandate.

For the public corporation, economics is only one factor to be considered in an overall equation. The amount of money exchanged must be considered within the broader reality of being able to provide a service to Canadians. In a democratic society, to provide national benefits to as many citizens as possible, in as attractive a way as possible, is extremely important. It is, to some extent, part of the fabric of a nation.

To bring radio and television services to every Canadian community of 500, even if those 500 people cannot ever consume enough to make them a market sufficiently attractive to advertisers to pay for the service, is surely a national achievement. Not to provide such services would threaten the maintenance of national sovereignty: if we find ourselves unable to provide services, another nation, most likely the U.S., will find it in its interest to provide them.

The central ethic of the public corporation is **public service**, to both the users of the service provided and to the population as a whole. Under such an ethic, charges are levied for services rendered, determined in part by what other Canadians must pay and in part by how much the service actually costs. Government corporations engage in scientific and technological research that is then licensed out to Canadian companies, largely to the benefit of the latter. Such an ethic, for example, justifies the creation of umbrella export corporations to aid private companies in developing foreign markets. The variety of such "transfers of technology" continues.

Public versus Private

The point in laying out the general *modus operandi* of the public corporation is that at times we assume that private corporations operate in the same way. Canadians tend to assume that public corporations are notoriously inefficient. While Crown corporations are vulnerable to such problems, there is no systematic evidence to suggest they are more vulnerable to mismanagement than private corporations. Rather, they are generally in business for a different reason. They aim at public service rather than profit.

While the private media outlets can talk about how they must scramble to attract audiences and sponsors, the CBC must weigh its special responsibilities, such as training top-level journalists and appealing to all ages and people in all locations, against audience size and type. The CBC can consider, on the merit of the case itself, whether it will or will not, for instance, carry children's programs without ads, develop socially oriented programs for the poor, underwrite programs for the aged, and so forth. The private station must consider such issues within the context of the long-term economic equation. It is responsible to its shareholders to do just that. But through regulatory insistence, an attempt can be made to force private enterprise to address public service concerns. However, to be effective, such an insistence must be cast within the abilities of such companies to make a profit, otherwise they will simply not abide by the regulations. For example, one of the ways the CRTC encourages cable companies to keep their equipment upgraded is by allowing them to recover half their costs of equipment upgrading through subscription fees. This means the public effectively pays for half the cost for any installation of fibre optic cable by a private corporation. While such an installation increases picture quality and channel capacity, it also, incidentally, makes the company more competitive with telephone companies in carrying long distance signals. CRTC policy on production of high-quality Canadian content has been much less effective. This is essentially because it and the industry have been unable to identify mechanisms that simultaneously encourage high-quality Canadian content and increase profits. Arguably, the establishment of other support policies such as the Broadcast Fund of Telefilm Canada assist in this direction.

Private Enterprise: The Private, Independent Media Corporation

The private corporation exists in a different world from that of the public corporation. Private corporations exist to make a profit. They perform a service in order to remain in business so that they can generate wealth for their owners. There are two major perceived social benefits of private enterprise. The first is that by virtue of Adam Smith's invisible hand, needed, desired, and affordable services are stimulated by economic opportunity. Second, because in some cases communication services are advertiser-supported, they are "free" to the consumer.

The prospect of a single independent media corporation operating a newspaper or a television or radio station, or publishing magazines or books, is not at all an unpleasant one. In all likelihood, the scale of operations is such that the owner lives in the community, is anxious for the development of the community, and attempts to provide a service to the community while seeking to make a healthy profit.

As with any independent operator, one expects a certain personal bias, a kind of bias toned down but nonetheless present as a result of the outlook of any managing editor, for example. One would also expect to find personal quirks of the owner reflected in the paper's or station's output. One might further expect that no stories denigrating the owner or the owner's close associates would be found in the company's products.

About the only unknown, given the present state of media industries and ignoring the spectre of a possible takeover for the moment, is the degree to which the owner might feel it necessary to purchase professional advice, for example, material and formats from outside. That is, as the CBC's *Inside TV News* points out, various consultancy firms exist to advise on nearly every aspect of the design of information services. The degree to which such services and their resulting formats interfere with a media company's responsiveness to the community in which it exists is considerable.

To put the matter bluntly, the community to which the company refers if it hires such consultants, or even highly specialized editors, managers, and the like, is the state-of-the-art media manipulators rather than the audience it has been licensed to serve. The responsibility for decisions passes out of the hands of the owners themselves and into the hands of those whose sole purpose is to develop formats that maximize audiences everywhere, especially in the larger media markets.

The Multi-Enterprise Media Corporation: Horizontal and Vertical Integration

Once we leave the environment of the independent media corporation and enter the world of companies related in ownership to other media and non-media companies, the whole scene, save the pursuit of profit, changes. Essentially, these dramatic changes are brought about because the emergent identity of the multi-enterprise corporation comes to be represented in the output of its media arm. That identity is affected by two types of internal integration, the first called horizontal, the second, vertical.

A simple horizontal combination of one media company with a non-media company can serve as a first example. With such a combination, normal horizontal relations suggest that taboo subjects are extended from the personal affairs of the owner to the business affairs of his (or her) other company. Court proceedings, labour practices, any news that might reflect on the owner become, if not taboo subjects, then subjects that are treated very carefully by the employees. It is rare for a multi-enterprise company or conglomerate not to make its overall holdings known to its employees to prevent the latter from pleading ignorance of these matters.

TABLE 7.2

An Hour in the Life of Ten 10
(7 to 8 p.m., November 11, 1981)

Time	Client	Length (seconds)	Cost $
1901	Chesebrough Ponds	30	1,417
1901	Dairy Prom CNL (M)*	30	1,319
1914	Aust Motoro Ind.	30	1,251
1914	Cadbury	30	1,026
1925	Angus and Coote (M)*	60	1,806
1940	United Permanent	30	1,159
1940	Malvern Star	30	1,352
1941	Waltons (M)*	60	1,990
1942	Cadbury	30	1,026
1947	Sportsplan P/L*	60	1,557
1948	Pulsar	30	1,382
1948	McDonalds	30	1,275
1949	Rose Music P/L*	60	2,151
1954	Unilever	30	1,275
1954	Norman Ross	60	1,450
1955	Beecham (M)*	30	1,275
1956	Meyers Taylor P/L*	30	1,224
2001	Mars Incorp (M)*	30	1,275

* The meaning of these terms was not specified in the source used.
SOURCE: *Financial Review,* 1982, p. 12.

The media company will ease the business atmosphere for the non-media company as much as it can without being charged with undue bias. The relation is parallel to any intra-company dealings. Related companies, while concentrating on their primary responsibilities, do what they can along the way to ease things for their sister companies. The apparent difference when one is a media company is that, in dealing with information, the media company is in a fairly powerful position to make matters easier.

For example, when the Australian Broadcasting Tribunal issued a gag order to Australian newspapers early in 1982 not to print the contents of a submission by a Murdoch-owned television station to the Tribunal, it neglected to send the order to Murdoch-owned newspapers, *The Daily Telegraph* (Sydney) and *The Australian.* Apparently it assumed, quite rightly as it turned out, that the Murdoch-owned papers would not print material of detriment to a sister company (*Sydney Morning Herald,* November 2, 1982, p. 2).

Vertical relations also come into play in a simple media/non-media association. To explain, most companies use advertising. While the placement and pricing of ads is standardized by rating cards, such cards are only the beginning of negotiations.

As the mistaken submission by Murdoch's Channel Ten 10 to the Australian Broadcasting Tribunal demonstrated, item by item (see Table 7.2) the amount paid by companies for advertising varies a great deal with the identity of the company concerned. Presumably, variations are normally based on the amount of advertising taken out by the company itself, the firm the ad is about, and so forth. But advertising by a related company can be discounted or overpriced depending on the wishes of the owner. Advertising or related companies can also be given space preference unavailable to others. As an illustration, figures from one hour of one day of Channel Ten 10 are included here. The station's logs also show the general level of advertising on a daily basis – rarely less than $200,000, most garnered at prime time, and little on such programs as children's shows.

The newspaper holdings of The Thomson Corporation and the advertising of the various retail (The Bay, Zeller's, and Simpson Sears) and travel companies Thomson also owns are a good case in point. It appears that no one has attempted to analyse the actual financial dealings between these media and non-media holdings. These would be internal company records. But Thomson must be careful not to be seen to exploit its advantage, because the potential for non-arm's-length relations are certainly undeniable. To exploit those advantages would earn the disfavour of those concerned with media and other business monopolies. It would also raise objections from Thomson's various competitors at each level of its operations.

Sony Corporation's 1987 purchase of CBS Records and 1989 purchase of Columbia Pictures illustrate the linkage of "hardware" manufacturers with compatible "software" producers. The prior owner of Columbia Pictures,

Coca-Cola, is reported (Miller, 1990) to have continuously plugged its products in movie after movie put out by Columbia.

Conglomerate Relations

When the simple association of media and non-media companies is extended into a reasonably sized conglomerate, the potential extension of self-censorship and insider financial relations also extends in lock step. What employee journalists find themselves able to talk about, what potential favouritism exists in advertising rates and placement, what potential abuse there is for tailoring soft news items to the travel and business interests of the conglomerate – all become major items of concern not only for employees but for the public and, in the case of broadcasting, for the regulator.

Said thus, it might appear, for instance, that a newspaper that is part of a conglomerate will be nothing but a propaganda tool for its sister companies. Thankfully, such is not the case. The primary role of the newspaper is to capture and maintain a market of readers to sell to advertisers of all types. Were a newspaper to be seen solely as a propaganda tool of a larger group of companies, it would begin to lose this readership and jeopardize its primary function as a company dealing in the capture and sale of audiences. That primary function significantly curtails narrow-minded, self-serving journalism done in the context of a narrow set of economic interests.

However, just as bigotry attracts its own audience, so the personal prejudices of media magnates can be found in various media. Rupert Murdoch is a prime example. When his papers have not reflected his point of view, he has been known to write editorials himself. Given that he owns a third of the U.K. newspaper market, the *South China Morning Post*, Twentieth Century Fox, and the Fox network, as well as the publisher Harper and Row, one might say his platform for editorializing is rather large. Similarly, Conrad Black has written for his own media properties as well as for those of others. The potential danger of backfire is that the opinions of the owner, if published with any frequency, might jeopardize the market penetration of the outlet, assuming that the outlet was not purposefully attempting to change its market identity and attract a new audience.

Matters such as these are both interesting and subtle. The human face or personality of a media outlet can go a long way to making outright bias and prejudice acceptable. The various writings in *Canadian Newspapers: The Inside Story,* which are documented in the following chapter, make that apparent (Stewart, 1980). But when such biases extend beyond those common in the community, as we saw in the Enoch Powell story, the journalistic integrity of the outlet is indeed jeopardized.

A Subtle Transformation in Content: Chain Journalism

The environment of the conglomerates is transforming journalism. In the atmosphere of an increasing number of media-related and non-media-related conglomerates, there is good reason to discourage in-depth investigative reporting. Media conglomerates have joined other global corporations, and as a group these are portrayed by their owners and managers as the harbingers of all things bright and beautiful. Investigative reporting into the unseemly behaviour or power trading of members of the global club or even into the business community as a whole is inconvenient at best and undermining at worst. Conrad Black has referred to those who follow this profession as the "swarming, grunting masses of jackals calling themselves 'investigative journalists' " (*Vancouver Sun,* July 7, 1989). In the environment of the conglomerates, journalists are encouraged to create soft news that is vaguely boosteristic of this or that community cause, and that complements advertising or expected advertising. Advertorials (sometimes also called informercials) create a complementary visual and ideological environment for other commercial products.

Journalists and other content producers working within the context of a media chain are well rewarded for their efforts. Beginning with the seven-figure salaries of the news anchors on the U.S. networks, it may be a long way down to the average journalist, but once such a person has established him or herself in the market, the process of bargaining for a salary takes on the flavour of negotiations of any other entertainment media personality.

These developments do not reflect a crude representation of a set of narrow prejudices but a change in function and approach of media industries. Most surprising is that, according to the Kent Commission, the journalists who work at the forefront of such a weakening of the ideals of journalism (e.g., the tabloids) are often more satisfied with their jobs than those who work on more traditional papers.

The problems of conglomeration become more apparent when the likely form of the conglomerate is examined in greater detail. It is rare to find a conglomerate with only one media company among a group of non-media enterprises. The more usual situation is a group or chain of media companies that are either unconnected to non-media companies or exist within a set of larger corporate holdings.

Economies of Scale

A chain, whether of media companies or otherwise, allows for so-called **economies of scale**. For example, a chain such as Southam can employ a columnist and use him or her throughout the chain for a fraction of the cost and arguably produce better-quality content. Beneath the surface, managerial techniques successful in one location can be adopted all along the chain, as can promotional strategies, special features, and the like. The Thomson chain is said to have a set of managerial techniques and other corporate guidelines that appear to define, among other things, the ratio of advertising to editorial content. These guidelines apply to all its papers except *The Globe and Mail* (Stewart, 1980). In another case, one radio station of the CHUM group, CFUN in Vancouver, switched its market from teenagers to yuppies. Once the formula proved workable, other stations in the CHUM chain followed suit.

In television, because of the network status of CTV, not strictly speaking a chain, negotiations can be carried out for the national market by CTV on behalf of all its affiliates. The bargaining position of the network is that much stronger than if the stations came to the negotiations singly. Programs can be acquired and production undertaken for the use of all affiliates. Such factors minimize costs. Similarly, consultants can be hired by a chain for all its stations rather than separately, treating each station as a unique instance.

Managers as well as managerial techniques can be transferred from paper to paper or station to station. With a chain there are opportunities for advancement within the company, a situation that encourages company loyalty in managerial echelons. If a loyal editor cannot get along in one location but appears to have tal-

ent, she can always be transferred to another location to have a fresh start.

Service to the Consumer

While all of these points have to do with production efficiency, they are only indirectly inspired by attempts to enhance the service that the media outlet is able to provide as a result of being a member of a chain. Media companies would argue that any economies of scale that can be achieved mean a higher level of service to the consumer. No single paper, for example, could afford to hire the number of columnists any member of a chain offers readers. In television, negotiations for city- and province-wide rights rather than national rights would introduce a great deal of uncertainty in the importation of foreign television programs. Similarly, were stations to be limited to an initial local audience, media companies would argue that little now produced would appear.

On the surface, these economies and qualitative improvements are not to be denied, but McCormack (1983) has argued that the pursuit of such economies distances newspapers from their traditional readership. In achieving such economies, the newspapers are neglecting content that would expand their readership. More concretely, it can be maintained that the mass media are contributing to the reforming of communities, making them much more oriented to national (i.e., chain-wide) content than local content.

In book publishing, it is particularly interesting to compare independent with chain-owned bookstores. The two tend to operate quite differently. The former are usually in the traditional mould of providing a wide range of books from the classics to the contemporary for their clients. The chains stock only fast-selling items that are given limited shelf life, depending on their computer-monitored sales. The cultural values of the two types of stores are vastly different. The possibility of a vibrant national literary community being maintained through the marketing practices of the chains is zero. Their mode of operation biases their selection against new writers, certain genres such as poetry, and books with only a regional appeal.

Cross-Ownership

Complementary to the media chain is cross-ownership of different kinds of media companies. The chain is constituted of a series of geographically distant companies, each operating in a separate market, but any one company is confined to a geographical boundary as a result of its distribution system. The physical delivery of newspapers and the strength of the local signal for broadcasting are the operative variables; today, however, both variables are being much changed by the introduction of satellite transmission.

With cross-ownership a newspaper and a radio station, for example, might operate in the same market and be owned or controlled by the same person or group of persons. The best-known example of cross-ownership in the media is the holdings of the Irving family in New Brunswick. The Irvings own all five English-language daily newspapers in the province plus a certain number of television and radio stations. Another example of extensive cross-ownership exists in London, Ontario, where the Blackburn family controls the *London Free Press* newspaper, AM and FM radio stations, and a TV station.

Monopoly Control

The central issue of corporate concentration is monopoly control. The two types of monopoly are a "natural" monopoly and effective monopoly. Economists and policy-makers define a "natural" monopoly, if one can ever be said to exist, as the result of limited technology. They apply the word "natural" to denote that competition cannot exist in the long run except by duplication of facilities. A licensing and regulatory structure is put in place to substitute for competition. The monopoly ensures that by avoiding duplication the greatest number of households can be serviced for the lowest cost. In Canada, the telephone and hydroelectric companies are principal examples of natural monopolies. It is interesting to note in this context that the "natural monopoly" of the telephone companies contains vestigial traces of earlier competition, when between 400 and 500 independent telephone companies existed. In fact, there are still 42 such companies in Canada, servicing half a million customers (*Financial Post,* July 31, 1989, p. 7). Babe (1990) has challenged the notion of "natural" monopolies in communications industries, suggesting that competition could have existed between technologies through the history of their development.

An effective monopoly, rather than being granted to a company by government, is gained by a company buying up or establishing companies that have control over the market in which they operate. In media, the combination of radio, television, and newspapers can provide a company with an effective media monopoly in a certain locale. In other, more common, instances, one company may have a newspaper or television monopoly, although all three kinds of monopolies are being weakened by one piece of communications technology, the communications satellite. Communications satellites are now being used to distribute both newspapers and television nationally and internationally. Such a situation makes local stations more dependent on purely local business for their advertising revenues.

When natural monopolies are granted, they are regulated in an attempt to ensure that the interests of the consumer and the public are looked after. When effective monopolies are gained, no such mechanism exists, although broadcasting licence renewals and commissions of inquiry can be used to attend to the worst monopolistic practices. If we assume, as a liberal pluralist might, that the ownership structure of each media enterprise leads to particular biases, with a multiplicity of owners at least some range of content can be expected. However, if all of the media are controlled by the same owners, then a potential for one predominant bias is hard to avoid.

So problematic is the potential for monopoly exploitation in the normal course of events that legislation has been put in place (formerly the Restrictive Trade Practices Act, now the Competition Act) to prevent such market monopolies from emerging. Faced with lack of success in the prosecution of the Irvings and subsequently Southam and Thomson in their simultaneous closure of the *Ottawa Journal* and the *Winnipeg Tribune,* the Liberal cabinet of Pierre Trudeau passed an order-in-council designed to discourage further cross-media acquisitions. However, during the time it was in effect (it was withdrawn by the Mulroney government), though it may have discouraged some new cross-media acquisitions, the CRTC was not single-minded in disallowing cross-ownership from continuing. Southam was allowed to keep 20 per cent of its holdings in Selkirk Broadcasting (reduced from 30 per cent) through the formation of a "voting trust" in which Selkirk voted Southam's shares (*Marketing,* 1982, p. 2).

Maclean Hunter was seen to be in contravention of the directive because it held 49.7 per cent of the Toronto Sun Publishing Co., publisher of *Sun* papers in Toronto, Edmonton, and Calgary. Its other holdings included CFCN Communications Ltd., holder of one television and two radio licences in Calgary. However, at the hearings, Maclean Hunter argued that it did not control the Sun papers because of a standstill agreement, part of which was that Maclean Hunter could only elect two of the twelve members of the board of directors. The CRTC renewed the broadcasting licences in question. In late 1989, Maclean Hunter also bought Selkirk Broadcasting from Southam. However, it then turned around and sold off most parts of it for a net gain of several millions. The CRTC disallowed some sales and required Maclean Hunter to turn over its net gain in dividing up the company to a production fund.

In a third and last case, involving the renewal application of CHSJ-TV, the CRTC ruled that the cabinet directive held because the licence holder, New Brunswick Broadcasting Ltd., was owned and controlled by the Irving group, publishers of two daily newspapers in the area. However, the CRTC saw fit, in spite of complaints that the station was not living up to its promise of performance, to renew the licence for 2.5 years (rather than five years) because there was no CBC station in the area and little likelihood of there being one within the next two to three years (Skinner, 1984).

Manipulation and thoroughness in coverage of the news are not the only problems created by media monopolies. Media monopolies have full control over advertising rates and can abuse that control. They also have a considerable advantage in wage negotiations with labour, and they know full well that what revenue they lose in one company will be picked up to a great extent by one of their other holdings.

CORPORATE CONCENTRATION: THE SOCIAL ISSUE

In an article in *The Financial Post Magazine,* Henry Knowles, former chairman of the Ontario Securities Commission, is cited for his comments on corporate concentration in Canada and its problems. His basic concern is that if the corporate barons become too powerful, Canadians may lose control of their economic destiny. If control is lost to an elite group of super-rich businessmen, who are not responsible to the public or who are too powerful for anyone to force them to live up to their public responsibilities, such a concentration of control may lead to social and cultural instability (Hatter, 1985).

Participatory Capitalism

Other aspects of corporate concentration in Canada deserve attention. As things now stand, some observers feel that Canadian stock prices are already too high because of the level of control exercised by major players in Canadian industry. The small shareholder stands to gain only by shifts in the price of the stock and by declared revenues. The controlling shareholder stands to gain beyond the small shareholder in any way he can use the company, its assets, and its production capacity to lever gains where he has holdings elsewhere. Many stocks are therefore worth more to the controlling shareholder than to the non-controlling shareholder.

In 1985, the degree of concentration in Canadian industry was conservatively estimated by establishing that only 78 of the 300 stocks on the Toronto Stock Exchange (TSE) index (a wide cross-section of Canada's major publicly traded companies) can be said to be widely held in that no more than 20 per cent of the shares are in the hands of any one individual, equity, or group. Further, 112 companies on the TSE index have single shareholders with 50 per cent of the stock or more, thereby giving that shareholder legal as well as effective control. Comparative American (1983) figures show that 85.2 per cent of companies listed in Standard and Poor's 500 index are widely held, that is, no shareholder controls more than 20 per cent.

Hatter reveals also that in 1985, eight major power brokers – two branches of the Bronfman family, Paul Desmarais, Ken Thomson, the Blacks, Galen Weston, Hal Jackman, and the Reichmanns – controlled 15 per cent of the TSE index. This figure does not include any of their private (i.e., not publicly traded) companies because such companies are not listed on the TSE index. Hatter's figures do not account for non-participation by the average Canadian by virtue of wholly owned foreign subsidiaries operating in Canada. Given the percentage of such corporations operating throughout the economy, it would be surprising if Canadians were not more greatly disenfranchised by them than by the Canadian super-rich.

Participatory Capitalism in the Media

Compared to industry in general, the Canadian privately owned media are even more highly concentrated in ownership. Robert Babe reports that in 1980 two chains, Thomson and Southam, controlled 59 per cent of the English-language daily newspaper circulation. In broadcasting, as of 1975, the four largest private broadcasters, Baton Broadcasting, Télé-Métropole, Southam-Selkirk, and Western Broadcasting, accounted for 40 per cent of private-sector advertising revenues. Further, again as of 1975, the 10 largest radio chains controlled 75 stations accounting for 44 per cent of private-sector revenues. The

TABLE 7.3

Selected Financial Data: Major Newspaper Groups ($000s)

	1979	1984	1988
Southam Inc.			
Revenue from operations*	484,235	1,084,329	1,653,654
Pre-tax operating income*	55,507	78,472	80,290
Equity**	159,406	253,653	661,033
Pre-tax return on equity	34.8%	30.9%	12.1%
Thomson Newspapers Ltd.			
Operating revenue*	335,561	811,757	1,207,778
Pre-tax income*	123,061	271,650	363,451
Equity	319,650	576,230	1,136,756
Pre-tax return on equity	38.5%	47.1%	31.9%
Torstar Corporation			
Operating revenue*	371,100	619,441	956,348
Operating profit*	51,996	60,919	139,354
Equity	105,484	146,926	564,330
Pre-tax return on equity	49.3%	41.5%	24.7%

* Pre-tax operating income/operating profit is given after depreciation and interest payments.
** A share swap with Torstar in 1984-85 injected $233,027,000 into Southam's equity, boosting it but driving Southam's ratios down.
SOURCES: Annual reports for each company.

largest, CHUM, owns 21 radio stations across the country, five television stations, and the cable video-music channel, MuchMusic. Finally, as of 1980, the top three cable television companies – Rogers Cablesystems, Télé-cable Vidéotron, and Maclean Hunter – accounted for about 50 per cent of cable subscribers. Tables 2.3 and 2.4 plus the ones that follow here (Tables 7.3 to 7.9) provide a sense of the overall degree of concentration of media ownership in Canada. While more recent figures are difficult to assemble, trends indicate that concentration is increasing with considerable speed.

Monopolies

In markets with monopolies, now the common situation for newspapers, the monopoly completely controls what news is covered, how it is covered, the ratio of ads to news, and the slant taken on the news, i.e., analytic and informative or sensational. The threats to such a monopoly are the possible alienation of its audience and the remote possibility of some other company taking a run at its market. The monopolist is also constrained to some degree by the other media in the same market, provided that it does not own those media outlets. The role of "other

TABLE 7.4

Share of Gross Advertising Revenue for Five Major Consumer Magazine Publishers, English- and French-Language, 1978 and 1979

	1978		1979	
	$000's	% of Total	$000's	% of Total
English-language				
Maclean Hunter	25,512	34.4	31,553	36.1
Comac Communications*	14,376	12.3	15,656	17.9
Reader's Digest	9,090	12.3	10,631	12.2
TV Guide Ltd.	8,582	11.6	9,949	11.4
Time Canada Ltd.	6,884	9.3	8,764	10.0
Total	64,444	87.0	76,553	87.6
French-language				
Maclean Hunter	5,557	40.1	6,807	44.3
TV Guide Ltd.	3,874	27.9	4,316	28.1
Reader's Digest	2,182	15.7	2,593	16.9
Comac Communications	1,622	11.7	1,639	10.7
Nous Magazine Ltd.**	633	4.6	Not available	
Total	13,235	100.0	15,355	100.0

* Comac, a subsidiary of Torstar, is involved exclusively in the publishing of controlled-circulation magazines.
** Includes *Nous* only.
SOURCE: Audley, *Canada's Cultural Industries*, which used: *Interim Profile of the Periodical Industry in Canada*, vol. 1.

media" is considerable and is increasing. With regard to newspapers, the presence of weeklies, magazines, and, in large centres, *The Globe and Mail* curtails the worst monopoly practices. In broadcasting, the multiplicity of radio and television stations available by cable, broadcast, and satellite also restricts monopoly practices to a degree.

Alienation is a very real threat, for the readership or audience is what the company sells to advertisers. It would be a mistake, however, to assume that media outlets are continually seeking ways to enhance the informative value of their product and thus please their audiences. More often they attempt to capture the audience with anything that works and is not too costly to produce, such as game shows. The advertorial is also a case in point. It fills the "news space" in that it is not advertising. Because it is not advertising, it costs the advertiser nothing. And because it is not written by a journalist, it costs the paper nothing for the generation of the content. Everyone gains, except journalists and readers (if readers expect reasonably independent commentary). Polling is also beginning to take its toll. Where media

TABLE 7.5

Revenue of Recording Industry by Source and Country of Controlling Interest, 1984-88 ($000s)

	Sale of Discs/Tapes		Revenue from Lease of Master Tapes	Revenue from Related Activities*		Total Revenue from Record Industry Activity	
Canadian-Controlled							
1984	29,685	11.26%	4,825	71.0%	22,153	25.87%	56,663
1985-86	32,488	12.64	4,922	64.6	16,907	19.13	54,317
1986-87	29,039	10.45	3,499	53.7	10,547	10.71	43,085
1987-88	43,865	16.18	10,155	75.0	26,299	16.38	80,319
Foreign-Controlled							
1984	233,732	88.74%	1.968	29.0%	63,472	74.13%	299,172
1985-86	224,398	87.36	2,697	35.4	71,443	80.87	298,538
1986-87	248,833	90.55	3,014	46.3	87,867	89.29	339,714
1987-88	227,220	83.82	3,372	25.0	134,184	83.62	364,776
Total							
1984	263,417		6,793		85,625		355,835
1985-86	256,886		7,619		88,350		352,855
1986-87	277,872		6,513		98,414		382,799
1987-88	271,085		13,527		160,483		445,095

* Related activities (column three) include distribution for others, custom disc pressing or tape duplicating, rack-jobbing operations, artist management, concert promotion and booking activities, renting of studio time to others, sales of imported finished goods (excluding imported master tapes).

Note: Revenue from non-industry activities
1984 $1,308,000 in grants to three Canadian-controlled companies.
1985-86 $529,872 in grants to 10 Canadian-controlled companies.
1986-87 $1,120,626 in grants to nine Canadian-controlled companies.
1987-88 $1,662,956 in grants to 31 Canadian-controlled companies.

SOURCE: Statistics Canada, Catalogue 87-202, Annual: *Culture Statistics: Sound Recording,* various years.

outlets have, through the years, often acted as social antennae, bringing emerging issues to the attention of the community, sagging audience figures are now often addressed with polls of the tastes and attitudes of the audience. Using such polls tends to turn the media into reactive rather than proactive entities, contributing more to a stagnation in community values rather than their growth.

A second concern, that of an emergent competitor, is minimal, because the chain-linked company has the financial resources to with-

TABLE 7.6

North American Theatrical Film Rentai Market Shares: 1970-1989

Year	Columbia	Fox	MGM/UA	Paramount	Universal	Warner	Buena Vista	Orion	Tri-Star
1989	8%	6%	6%	14%	17%	19%	14%	4%	7%
1988	3%	11%	10%	16%	10%	11%	20%	7%	6%
1987	4%	9%	4%	20%	8%	13%	14%	10%	5%
1986	9%	8%	4%	22%	9%	12%	10%	7%	7%
1985	10%	11%	9%	10%	16%	18%	3%	5%	10%
1984	16%	10%	7%	21%	8%	19%	4%	5%	5%
1983	14%	21%	10%	14%	13%	17%	3%	4%	–
1982	10%	14%	11%	14%	30%	10%	4%	3%	–
1981	13%	13%	9%	15%	14%	18%	3%	1%	–
1980	14%	16%	7%	16%	20%	14%	4%	2%	–
1979	11%	9%	15%	15%	15%	20%	4%	5%	–
1978	11%	13%	11%	24%	17%	13%	5%	4%	–
1977	12%	20%	18%	10%	12%	14%	6%	4%	–
1976	8%	13%	16%	10%	13%	18%	7%	5%	–
1975	13%	14%	11%	11%	25%	9%	6%	5%	–
1974	7%	11%	9%	10%	19%	23%	7%	4%	–
1973	7%	19%	11%	9%	10%	16%	7%	3%	–
1972	9%	9%	15%	22%	5%	18%	5%	3%	–
1971	10%	12%	7%	17%	5%	9%	8%	3%	–
1970	14%	19%	9%	12%	13%	5%	9%	3%	–

Notes:
Each year's largest market share percentage is shown in a box. Percentages do not add to 100% in any year; the residual amount is accounted for by smaller and/or defunct distributors.
1. MGM/UA means the present distribution company as well as the "old" UA, which took over domestic distribution of MGM product late in 1973.
2. Orion includes old American International Pictures (1970-79), and Filmways Pictures (1980-81). Name changed to Orion in 1982.
3. Tri-Star Pictures began operations in April, 1984, absorbed Columbia Pictures late 1987; corporate name changed to Columbia Pictures Entertainment. Col and Tri-Star retain separate sales staffs, but certain administrative functions are performed by Triumph Releasing, an entity which has no operational significance.
4. Embassy Pictures market shares as follows: 3% in 1980, 5% in 1981, 1% in 1983 and 1985, nil in 1984, insignificant in other years. Company bought by Columbia Pictures in 1985. Dino De Laurentiis acquired Embassy's theatrical production-distribution operations from Columbia later in 1985. Name changed to De Laurentiis Entertainment Group, distribution operations resumed June, 1986. Market share for 1986 just over 2%; for 1987, just over 1%.
Thereafter in fiscal reorganization.
5. Pre-'74, the "old" MGM market shares as follows: 4% in 1970, 9% in 1971, 6% in 1972, and 5% in 1973. Company exited distribution late in 1973.
6. National General Pictures (most of its release schedule being CBS-Cinema Center Films) market shares as follows: 7% in 1970, 8% in 1971, 3% in 1972, and 8% in 1973. NGP also released First Artists product under a commitment transferred to Warner Bros. in 1974 when NGP folded.
7. Cinerama Releasing Corp. (most of its releases being ABC Pictures product) market shares as follows: 3% over 1970-73 period. CRC folded thereafter.
8. Allied Artists Pictures had a 4% market share in 1974. Insignificant in other years. Lorimar acquired assets in 1981. Lorimar began domestic distribution operations in August, 1987. Warner Bros. acquired Lorimar in late 1988.
9. Buena Vista releases Walt Disney Co. pix from various production subsidiaries.
SOURCE: *Variety*, January 17, 1990.

TABLE 7.7

Numbers of Private Radio Stations Owned by the 13 Most Important Groups, 1985

Groups	Atlantic	Quebec	Ontario	Prairies	British Columbia	Canada	Stations Share %
CHUM	8	2	8	5	1	24	5.4
Telemedia	–	10	10	–	–	20	4.9
Selkirk	–	–	1	7	4	12	2.7
Maclean Hunter*	2	–	6	3	–	11	2.7
CUC Group	–	–	11	–	–	11	2.7
Moffat	–	–	1	6	2	9	2.0
WIC	–	–	4	3	2	9	2.0
AGRA Industries	1	1	3	2	1	8	1.8
Claude Pratte and Paul Desmarais Group	–	2	6	–	–	8	1.8
Eastern Broadcasting	7	–	–	–	–	7	1.6
Radiomutuel	–	7	–	–	–	7	1.6
Gordon Rawlinson Group	–	–	–	7	–	7	1.6
Standard Broadcasting	–	2	5	–	–	7	1.6
Number of Stations Owned by the 13 Groups	18	24	55	33	10	140	32.4
Total Number of Originating Stations in Operation	58	85	135	91	74	446	100.0
Relative Share of Total of the 13 Groups in Each Region (%)	19.0	28.2	40.7	36.3	13.5	29.8	

*Excluding shortwave stations.
Note:
1. Maclean Hunter purchased Selkirk in late 1988.
2. CKO/AGRA is presently non-operating.
SOURCE: *Report of the Task Force on Broadcasting Policy*, which used: CRTC, Financial Statistics and Analysis Division, *Financial and Corporate Analysis.*

TABLE 7.8

Number of Private Television Stations Owned by the 21 Most Important Groups, 1985*

Groups	Atlantic	Quebec	Ontario	Prairie	British Columbia	Canada	Share of all Canadian stations (%)
CUC Ltd.	–	–	7	–	–	7	8.6
CHUM Ltd.	4	–	2	–	–	6	7.4
Skinner Holdings	–	–	–	6	–	6	7.4
Pathonic Inc.	–	5	–	–	–	5	6.2
Selkirk Communications Ltd.	–	–	1	2	1	4	4.9
Moffat Communications Ltd.**	–	–	–	3	–	3	3.7
Newfoundland Broadcasting Co.	3	–	–	–	–	3	3.7
Radio Nord	–	3	–	–	–	3	3.7
Claude Pratte and Paul Desmarais Group	–	1	2	–	–		3.7
Number of stations controlled by nine largest groups	7	9	12	11	1	40	49.3
Baton Broadcasting	–	–	1	1	–	2	2.5
Canwest Communications	–	–	1	1	–	2	2.5
Cogeco	–	2	–	–	–	2	2.5
Harvard Developments	–	–	–	2	–	2	2.5
Huron Broadcasting	–	–	2	–	–	2	2.5
London Free Press Holdings	–	–	2	–	–	2	2.5
Monarch Broadcasting	–	–	–	2	–	2	2.5
Shortell Ltd.	–	–	–	2	–	2	2.5
"Marc and Luc Simard" Group	–	2	–	–	–	2	2.5
Télé-Métropole	–	2	–	–	–	2	2.5
Thunder Bay Electronics	–	–	2	–	–	2	2.5
WIC	–	–	–	–	2	2	2.5
Number of stations controlled by the 21 television industry groups	7	15	20	19	3	64	79.0
Total number of private stations in operation	8	17	24	24	8	81	100.0
Regional holdings by 21 groups (%)	87.5	88.2	83.3	79.2	37.5	79.0	

* Some of these stations may be termed rebroadcaster stations with a small amount of local programming and/or advertising sold locally; they file revenue reports with the CRTC and in this way are considered separate entities.
** Two of Moffat's three TV stations are 50 per cent owned through Relay Communications Ltd.
SOURCE: *Report of the Task Force on Broadcasting Policy*, which used: CRTC, Industry Statistics and Analysis Division, Financial and Corporate Analysis.

TABLE 7.9

Cable Ownership Patterns (1973, 1980, 1985)

1973

Holding/Cable Company	Province	Subscribers	% of Canadian Total	Cumulative %
1. Premier Cablevision	Ont., B.C.	300,200	14.2	14.2
2. Canadian Cablesystems	Ont., B.C.	291,700	13.4	27.6
3. Cablevision Nationale	Que.	189,000	8.9	36.5
4. Maclean Hunter	Ont.	187,000	8.8	45.3
5. Selkirk Holdings	Ont., Man., Alta.	100,800	4.8	50.1
6. Cablecasting Ltd.	Ont., Man., Alta.	91,500	4.3	54.4
7. Bushnell Communications	Ont.	67,700	3.2	57.6
	Total Canadian Subscribers: 2,116,000			

1980

Holding/Cable Company	Province	Subscribers	% of Canadian Total	Cumulative %
1. Rogers Cablesystems	Ont., Alta., B.C.	1,270,300	29.6	29.6
2. Vidéotron Ltée	Que.	500,100	11.7	41.3
3. Maclean Hunter	Ont.	339,600	7.9	49.2
4. Cablecasting Ltd.	Ont., Man., Alta.	156,800	3.7	52.9
5. Moffat Communications	Man.	133,300	3.1	56.0
6. Agra Industries	Ont., Sask., Alta., B.C.	131,300	3.0	59.0
7. Cable TV (CFCF)	Que.	130,000	3.0	62.0
8. Selkirk Communications	Ont., Man.	127,100	2.9	64.9
9. Cable West	Alta., B.C.	105,600	2.5	67.4
10. Bushnell Communications	Ont., Que.	104,800	2.4	69.8
11. Capital Cable	Alta., B.C.	96,200	2.2	72.0
	Total Canadian Subscribers: 4,293,000			

1985

Holding/Cable Company	Province	Subscribers	% of Canadian Total	Cumulative %
1. Rogers Cablesystems	Ont., Alta., B.C.	1,280,400	23.5	23.5
2. Vidéotron Ltée*	Que.	621,700	11.4	34.9
3. Maclean Hunter	Ont.	370,100	6.8	41.7
4. Shaw Cablesystems	Alta., B.C., N.S., Nfld.	319,300	5.9	47.6
5. CUC Holdings	Ont.	290,800	5.4	53.0
6. Cablecasting (excluding Greater Winnipeg)	Ont., Alta.	210,400	3.9	56.9
7. Selkirk Communications	Ont., Man.	177,100	3.3	60.2
8. CFCF	Que.	167,300	3.1	63.3
9. Cablenet (AGRA)	Ont., Alta., B.C.	161,600	3.0	66.3
10. Moffat Communications	Man.	142,900	2.7	69.0
11. Bushnell Communications (Standard)	Que., Ont.	141,500	2.0	71.0
12. QCTV Limited*	Alta.	110,700	2.0	73.0
	Total Canadian Subscribers: 5,438,000			

* QCTV has been acquired by Vidéotron, CRTC approval pending.
SOURCE: Report of the Task Force on Broadcasting Policy.

stand any kind of circulation or ratings war by virtue of its membership in a larger company. Another constraint on emergent competition is that for any company in the media business to undertake such a run would mean counter-pressures on some of its other holdings in other markets. For a new player to emerge with sufficient financial resources to make a go of it is unlikely because of the interlocking interests of the Canadian business elite. This leaves open the possibility of a foreign company. In broadcasting, as noted, foreign ownership beyond 20 per cent is not possible because of an order-in-council dating back to the 1960s. With newspapers, Section 19 of the Income Tax Act has managed to keep foreign owners at bay, although Robert Maxwell took a 25 per cent stake in Pierre Péladeau's attempt to take some of Montreal's English-language market away from Southam's *Gazette*. The tabloid *Daily News* lost money for 21 months and was closed.

The emergence of the tabloids in markets already served by broadsheets is a special case. It appears that they gained entry essentially because they targeted their publications at a different market of readers. The broadsheet publishers did not want to abandon their traditional readership. Once established, however, the tabloids became direct competitors for advertising dollars and for the sub-population of readers who are equally happy with either a tabloid or a broadsheet.

All of these dynamics are being played out in Vancouver in the boardroom of the *Vancouver Sun* and *The Province*. Having recognized the emergent competition just described and owning both Vancouver dailies, Southam decided to convert *The Province* to a morning tabloid and to create a style that would attract the untapped sensationalist tabloid market but not lose its traditional readership. Ten years after the conversion, *The Province* is growing faster

than the *Sun* and its existence prevents the emergence of a tabloid that would compete with the *Sun* for advertising dollars.

As for the third constraint, there is some real effect of the presence of other media (and media targeted at slightly different markets, as we just explained), as there is with the general level of rates across the country for similar-sized markets. No media outlet is in a very good position to gouge its advertisers and maintain good business relations.

A highly concentrated media industry also leads to a narrowing of perspective. This is not because journalists become narrow-minded but because the sources of news become fewer. As things stand, news is generated internationally by the global agencies (see Chapter 10). Within Canada, Canadian Press and its derivative, Broadcast News, generate national news for the vast majority of papers and for radio and television stations that do not have reporters in locations other than their home base. Local papers normally generate most of their own local news, which they then feed to other companies within their chain. These sources are supplemented indirectly and at all levels by the continuing investigative reporting of the CBC.

It is difficult to believe that sources can get much narrower, but it would work as follows. At the international level, as concentration increased, costs could be cut by subscribing to the global agencies and having no foreign correspondents and no subscriptions to secondary news agencies such as Tanjug. At the national level, as concentration increased, the owners of Canadian Press could decide that there was no longer any need for duplication of reporters between Canadian Press and its subscribing papers. Canadian Press could dispense with all of its reporters and adapt what local reporters write for their local papers. At the local level, the number of beats would be decreased. For example, after the *Winnipeg Tribune* closed, the *Winnipeg Free Press* dispensed with regular coverage of education.

For the present, and perhaps into the future, Canadian Press creates a margin of safety for its subscribers. It covers main events across the country, rewrites international Associated Press coverage, and does so in a straightforward, factually oriented format. Should a paper be unable to cover an event, or should its journalist provide an unacceptable account of proceedings, the subscribing newspaper can fall back on the Canadian Press account. The CP account can also be used as a cross-check on facts or interpretation. In short, there may be much to recommend the permanence of a national news service such as CP, even in a more monopolistic market.

Superconcentration: Beyond Monopoly Power

As mentioned previously, if the Kent Commission accomplished anything, it put the Thomson organization on notice that further expansion in the media field in Canada would not, if tolerated at all, be approved without a great deal of public debate. The matter was not so much quality of journalism, although Thomson newspapers compare unfavourably with those of the Southam chain, and not that there were not areas of the country that Thomson does not dominate, but rather that the Thomson organization was growing too large for Canada.

In 1989, recognizing what chairman Kenneth Thomson described as "a tendency to consolidate in the publishing industry," Thomson Newspapers merged with International Thomson Organization Ltd. to form the Thomson Corporation. At that point, the chairman could add, "I can't imagine any publishing company any-

where in the world that would be beyond our ability to acquire" (*Globe and Mail*, March 16, 1989, pp. B1, B4).

Another example of this same phenomenon occurred when Paul Desmarais's Power Corporation sought regulatory approval for its takeover of the TVA flagship station, Télé-Métropole. Power Corp. is an extremely large Quebec-based conglomerate with extensive interests in a variety of areas of the economy. As Peter S. Anderson notes in *The Canadian Encyclopedia* (1985), it is

a large diversified company engaged in newspapers, financial services, pulp, paper and packaging. Through its subsidiary, Gesca Ltée, Power publishes 4 daily newspapers, including *La Presse*. In addition, Gesca has 2 separate book-publishing operations. Its financial services include controlling interest in Great-West Life Assurance Co, Montréal Trustco Inc and the Investor Group. The company's pulp, paper and packaging interests are held in Consolidated-Bathurst Inc [now sold], a major Canadian pulp and paper firm. Total assets of all operations associated with Power Corporation exceeded $12.7 billion in 1983, with revenues exceeding $4 billion.

When Power came before the CRTC, as happened with Thomson and the Kent Commission, numerous individuals and organizations came forward to oppose the takeover. *Le Devoir* devoted a series of articles and editorials to the matter. On February 21, *Le Devoir's* editor-in-chief, Paul-André Comeau, noted that the CRTC had the responsibility to protect a pluralism in information sources in the name of the public interest. This approach was turned into an argument against the takeover (*Le Devoir*, March 18, 19, 1986). With newspaper and radio holdings in both Montreal and

Quebec City, the Power takeover would diminish the diversity of voices in Quebec. Citing the referendum crisis of 1980, *Le Devoir* on March 18 questioned whether a Power-dominated media would have allowed for the expression of separatist sentiments in a matter so clearly against the interest of Power. A third argument coming from this March 18 article was that since Power had suggested no improvements to the news programming, none would take place, and thus there was no public benefit from the takeover.

The judgement of the CRTC against the takeover emphasized some of the same arguments. But if one reads between the lines of all these various statements, it would appear that Power is simply too large to be allowed to expand further into more media holdings. As *Le Devoir* put it in a March 18 headline, "Télé-Métropole: une super-concentration injustifiée."

It would appear that a political will exists to resist monopoly power not at the level of one industry but at a level in which the power of private capital threatens political power. Thus, when no political action can be taken in a region or in an economic sphere (such as agriculture) that does not impinge on the interests of a single company, Canadian governments and their regulatory bodies apparently are prepared to take a stand.

Trends in Ownership

In this chapter, we have stressed the negative side of corporate concentration over the positive benefits. The positive benefits accrue primarily to the owners. But it is true that an independent city newspaper, based, say, in Vancouver and not hooked into the global agencies and Canadian Press, would not be much more than a local paper. For all the curses that world-wide news services bring, they do provide important information for an industrialized society. Without this information, our economy would disintegrate.

However, if corporate concentration brings certain advantages, an optimal level of concentration doubtless brings that advantage. A greater level brings into play the disadvantages we have discussed. Most observers see that the level of corporate concentration in the media in Canada is beyond the level necessary to obtain that advantage.

Faced with this situation, we perhaps could predict that trends in ownership patterns would be toward a lessening of corporate concentration, either by policy or in anticipation of the advantage of moving in front of policy. But no such trend is visible.

SUMMARY

Capitalism or private ownership deals with relations between people and property in a manner that has a limited capacity to encompass the full potential of communication media in society. Yet private enterprise has come to own and control much of this cultural domain in Western society and specifically in Canada. The nature of that control derives directly from the dynamics of the dominant business form in the mass media, the multi-enterprise conglomerate. Three major elements of those dynamics are horizontal and vertical integration and cross-ownership.

Increased concentration of ownership has been viewed with some alarm over the years almost universally by Canadian observers. Moreover, forces leading to increased concentration are clearly identifiable. They include growth for its own sake, acquired borrowing power, the greater ease of buying a company over starting one from scratch, providing capital to financially strapped entrepreneurs, taking over large share blocks from the estates of the rich, the limited number of wealthy people in Canada, buying up the competition, diversification, and a nurturing legal, tax, and regulatory framework. However, little has been done to combat continuing trends toward increased concentration.

The implications of ownership form, whether public or private, are many. The goals and operations of public enterprise are directed differently from those of the private corporation. They are, essentially, to serve the public interest. Private media enterprises cannot help but transform journalism, whether electronic or print, by their increased size and scope of activities. This does not mean that journalists will become the lackeys of big business. It is more that the style of journalism practised within large media companies will come increasingly to resemble the production of any other commodity by mass manufacturing for the mass market, a trend that does not appear to be of any great concern to our legislators. Yet, when the power of such corporations begins to rival the total power of the state, then there are indications that counteractions may be taken.

Two forms of ownership are not discussed in any detail in this chapter. The first is co-operative ownership, a form common enough in Quebec-based community radio stations but much less common in English Canada. It is a type of public ownership. A co-operative is open to any person who wishes to become a member. In that way it is public. Co-operative or community radio stations in Canada tend to be oriented to their local community and involved in cultural animation.

A second form of ownership, now evolving on the Canadian scene, is characterized by the identity and purpose of the owners. Whereas private stations are usually in business to make money, there are now groups, such as churches, interested in owning their own radio and television stations so that they will have greater access to audiences. The CRTC now allows such groups to hold a broadcasting licence provided it is jointly held by a number of members of a particular group. Vision TV is a case in point. As Salter (1988) points out, this arrangement represents a reconceiving of the notion of the public interest in public broadcasting.

REFERENCES

Anderson, Peter S. "Power Corporation of Canada," *The Canadian Encyclopedia* (Edmonton: Hurtig, 1985), p. 1464.

Babe, R. *Telecommunications in Canada*. Toronto: University of Toronto Press, 1990.

Babe, R. "Media Ownership," *The Canadian Encyclopedia* (Edmonton: Hurtig, 1985), pp. 1014-15.

Canada. *Report of the Special Senate Committee on the Mass Media*. Ottawa: Ministry of Supply and Services, 1976.

Canada. *Report of the Task Force on Broadcasting Policy*. Ottawa: Ministry of Supply and Services, 1986.

Canada. *Royal Commission on Newspapers*. Ottawa: Canadian Government Publishing Centre, 1981.

Canadian Broadcasting Corporation. *The Press and the Prime Minister,* directed and produced by George Robertson. Toronto, 1977.

Canadian Broadcasting Corporation. *Inside TV News,* directed by F. Steele, produced by H. Gendron and F. Steele. Montreal, 1982.

Enchin, H. "Southam Faced Total 'Destruction' if Taken Over by Maclean Hunter," *Globe and Mail,* October 11, 1985, p. B1.

Financial Post White card, February 4, 1990.

Financial Review, February 17, 1982, p. 12.

Hardin, H. "Pushing Public Broadcasting Forward: Advances and Evasions," in R. Lorimer and D.C.

Wilson, eds., *Communication Canada: Issues in Broadcasting and New Technologies.* Toronto: Kagan and Woo, 1988.

Hardin, H. *A Nation Unaware.* Vancouver: Douglas and McIntyre, 1974.

Hatter, D. "Corporate Concentration: Charmed Circle Still Firmly in Control," *Financial Post 500* (Summer, 1985), pp. 58-61.

Marketing, May 23, 1982, p. 2.

McCormack, T. "The Political Culture and the Press in Canada," *Canadian Journal of Political Science* (September, 1983).

Miller, Mark Crispin. "Hollywood: The Ad," *The Atlantic Monthly,* 265, 4 (April, 1990), pp. 41-68.

Newman, Peter C. *The Establishment Man.* Toronto: McClelland and Stewart, 1982.

Off, C. "Statscan Report Casts Doubt on Culture's Economic Clout," *Financial Post,* October 12, 1985, p. 11.

Phillips, F. "Rough Reception for Power Corp. TV Deal," *Financial Post,* September 28, 1985, p. 2.

Salter, L. "Reconceiving the Public in Public Broadcasting," in Lorimer and Wilson, eds., *Communication Canada.*

Skinner, David. Unpublished student paper, Department of Communication, Simon Fraser University, 1984.

Stewart, W. *Canadian Newspapers: The Inside Story.* Edmonton: Hurtig, 1980.

Sydney Morning Herald, November 28, 1982, p. 1.

STUDY QUESTIONS

1. The first Lord Thomson of Fleet said: "It is the business of newspapers to make money." What are the arguments for and against this viewpoint?

2. The mass media systems in Canada have specific organizational and ownership characteristics. What are they and how do they affect the content received by Canadians? Use examples from newspapers, radio, or TV (or all these media).

3. "Freedom of the press is for those who own one." Discuss.

4. Wallace Clement, in *The Canadian Corporate Elite* (Toronto: McClelland and Stewart, 1975), p. 235, has written: "The conclusion must be that together the economic and media elite are simply two sides of the same upper class; between them they hold two of the key sources of power – economic and ideological – in Canadian society and form the corporate elite." Do you agree or disagree with this statement?

CHAPTER

8

The Functions of Media Professionals

INTRODUCTION

THE MEDIA OF the Western world bring together in their production activities two groups of individuals – capitalist (or sometimes state or co-operative) owners and professionals of various types, including journalists, announcers, typesetters, camera operators, and so on. The focus of the present chapter will be on these **professionals**, specifically **journalists**, a group that makes up about 10 per cent of newspaper employees. Throughout this chapter, we will sometimes talk about print journalism, sometimes about electronic journalism. Unless stated otherwise, comments apply to both.

A PROFESSIONAL PROFILE

Drawing on the work of George Pollard, Desbarats (1990) presents a professional profile of Canadian journalists circa 1985. Pollard's work was based on responses to a questionnaire completed by 174 journalists working for English-language media in all regions of Canada. The following is a summary of his findings:

English-Language Journalists (1985)
Median age: 32.3; Range: 19-69 (note lowness of median given range, meaning few senior members)
Gender: Women, 18.6%; Men, 81.4% (This is changing.)
Education: 40%, some post-secondary; 60% of post-secondary did not complete; average completed years 14.4 (print 15.5, radio 13.9)
Avg. income: university grads, $28,476
Avg. income: others, $19,589
Mean annual income journalists: $26,764 print, $33,009; television, $32,367; radio, $22,593
Mean number of years as a journalist: print, 16.6; television, 9.3; radio, 9.3
Mean age: print, 38.7; television, 33.6; radio, 32.5
CBC journalists: older than average (36.3), better educated (15.5 years), and more experienced (14.4 yrs), much like print average.

Roughly comparable data from a less detailed study (Sauvageau, 1981) are also presented by Desbarats.

French-Language Journalists (1980)
Number of respondents: 240, working for nine French-language dailies
Education: 37% university degree
View of role of state: 64.2% noted state should intervene in the field of information to: prevent ownership concentration (about 50 per cent), assist deliveries to remote regions (about 33 per cent), ensure quality (about 20 per cent).
The most educated were the most critical. The least educated favoured private ownership and took marketing needs of employer into account.

THE IDEALS OF JOURNALISM

The journalistic profession, like the teaching, legal, and medical professions, has a set of ideals to which its members make primary reference. Contemporary journalism finds the basis of those ideals in the notion of **social responsibility**. Freed from the yoke of government through the achievement of a libertarian ideal (see Chapter 3), only to be constrained by large capitalist employer-owners (see Chapter 7), the profession has asserted this ideal as a way of establishing its right to seek information and to maintain a measure of independence from its employers. In the view of the profession, its quest for information is based on a commitment to treat "events and persons with fairness and impartiality, but also . . . [to consider] the welfare of the community and of humanity in general in a spirit devoid of cynicism" (Royal Commission on Newspapers, 1981, p. 24). Journalists see, and most declarations of human rights enshrine, this ideal of **freedom of the press** as an extension of the basic right given to all individuals, **freedom of expression**.

The 1960 Canadian Bill of Rights, brought in by John Diefenbaker's government, speaks to freedom of expression and freedom of the press in two different sections, Sections 1(d) and 1(f). The Canadian Charter of Rights and Freedoms addresses both freedom of expression and freedom of the press in Section 2 under the heading "Fundamental Freedoms":

2. Everyone has the following fundamental freedoms:
(a) freedom of conscience and religion;
(b) freedom of thought, belief, opinion and expression, including freedom of the press and other media of communication;
(c) freedom of peaceful assembly; and
(d) freedom of association.

...there are, however, certain indications from head office that ours is a troubled paper...

PUBLISHER
MOOSE CHIP TIMES

Cartoon by Phil Mallette, Winnipeg. *From Royal Commission on Newspapers, 1981. Reproduced with permission of the Minister of Supply and Services Canada.*

Journalists do not take the ideals of their profession lightly, nor do they consider those ideals and their profession as peripheral to the workings of Western democratic society. As Royal Commissioner Tom Kent points out, most journalists believe that press freedoms are the very reason we have responsible democracy, rather than vice versa. They see press freedoms as the prime mover.

The classic self-image of journalists is that of inveterate seekers after truth, devoted to the facts and to the reader. If they err in excess, it is in their view of the ideal reader who may bear a closer resemblance to an ideal self or ideal rational citizen than to the average citizen. At another extreme is the journalist who believes in attending to the public's wants and needs. Usually these wants and needs are prescribed by the market and therefore the corporate values of

the newspaper for whom the journalist works. They are, as often as not, measured in numbers of subscriptions, advertising lineage, and profits. The market logic is that if the consumers buy – subscriptions or advertising – a want or need has been demonstrated. But the wants-and-needs approach may also be found in those oriented to left-wing politics. There the journalist may see his job to be to combat a false consciousness, to persuade the public how to view various issues and events or how they are being duped into accepting false interpretations.

Two cases in British Columbia illustrate the normal split on what is considered to be appropriate professional behaviour. In one case, five people, who at the time of their arrest had in their possession a quantity of arms and ammunition, were charged with a variety of offences, including blowing up a hydro substation.

Almost immediately they were named the "Squamish 5" and local television news had a field day exploiting the situation and depicting them in the image of terrorists after the style of European groups. Other journalists were quick to sense this exploitation and monitored it. One CBC television program prepared an extensive item questioning the role of the media. To place this "field day" in a slightly fuller context, the trial judge later placed a ban on the use of the term "Squamish 5" for the duration of the trials of all of the accused, apparently because he felt that it was prejudicing the right of the accused to a fair trial by casting them as terrorists. On the other side, the news journalists who hyped the story saw their brethren as self-appointed media watchdogs.

In terms of the two general perspectives we spoke of above, those who were anxious to hype the five into modern-day political terrorists could be said to have been fulfilling the public's wants (if not needs) for intrigue and high drama. Those who were more circumspect could be said to have been playing out the role of rational, disinterested citizens, committed to the principles of justice for all.

A second case involved a man who was accused of killing members of two families in northern British Columbia and burning their car and camper. Once again, representatives of the media differed as to the appropriate course of action. Some explored every lead surrounding the accused once the man was arrested. Others questioned the wisdom of such story creation prior to the trial of the accused.

The two positions in both these cases express opposing views of the role of the journalist. One group espouses what could be called a traditional role: to seek after information surrounding any case and bring all the information that can be uncovered to the public eye. The second group sees the responsibilities for journalists as including a consciousness of the consequences of their own action. Inflammatory presentation of the accused as terrorists or amateur psychologizing on what might have caused an accused to do a terrible deed potentially may jeopardize a fair trial and certainly creates a problem for an innocent person after his name has been cleared.

When one looks back at the articles a scant five years later, one can easily see how both sides were wrapped up in the dominant social issues of the time. As the libertarianism of the sixties and seventies was dying, a certain level of moral panic was created by the possibility that, in defeat, those resistive of the current level of power of those who hold it in Canada might be serious about disrupting the execution of that power with genuine, organized terrorism. In calm Canadian tradition, the judge presiding at the trial of the "Squamish 5" was having none of either side and deflated the debate by robbing it of its vocabulary.

This point seems to have motivated a specific comment by one presiding judge. In an incest case reported in the *Vancouver Sun*, County Court Judge Peter van der Hoop found it necessary to say, "This is not just an acquittal based on reasonable doubt. This is a declaration of the innocence of the accused" (June 21, 1985, p. A3). As the accused in this case noted to an inquiring reporter, seemingly more in reference to the media than to the legal treatment, "I have no comment. This whole thing has already caused me too much grief."

The same division of opinion was apparent on a Journal program aired early in 1985 following a threat by a political group to place bombs in the Toronto transit system. A number of journalists from the print and electronic media, along with some representatives of the "oppressed" community to which the bombing was intended to draw attention, were interviewed as a group. Most of the Canadian journalists felt that while coverage plays into the hands of terrorists by giving them publicity, that coverage must continue in order that the public be informed. They believed that the responsibility of the media was to refrain from heating up the issue through its coverage, for example by opening a "hotline" to those doing the threatening. The extreme position on this side of the argument was that the media are responsible to pursue the collection of information to the extent that the law allows. That opinion was put forward by an American journalist and former White House adviser, and would seem to be indicative of a stronger adherence to libertarianism in the United States and perhaps to a willingness to use naked power. Several non-journalists argued for no coverage at all.

Another example of media-terrorist interaction emerged in the summer of 1985. In this instance, involving the hijacking of a TWA jet out of Athens, there seemed to be little leeway for the two perspectives on the role of the media, so powerless did they become as they were swept up in the events. Journalist Glenda Korporaal, writing in the *Australian Financial Review* (July 3, 1985, p. 1) under the title "How the U.S. media hijacked foreign policy," saw the event as a turning point in the role of the media in global politics. The hijackers realized very quickly what power the U.S. media had in producing movement in the Reagan administration. The hijackers stated: "The Central Press Bureau of the Amal declares that all the film taken of the hostages can be used freely by all press agencies and television networks."

Thus they milked the media for all the publicity they could get. But perhaps the hostages and their families had more at stake in the media treatment of the event. As Korporaal put it, the event established a precedent: television is both an essential part of an effective hijack-

ing and an important tool for the families of the hostages to keep the pressure up for the release of the captives.

In 1985 media coverage of terrorist events seemed to be at its height, but by 1990 such events were scarce. Whatever the reasons for the apparent decline of international terrorism, it is certainly true that the media have become far more peripheral to the exercise of terrorism. This does not mean, of course, that the media are not significant players in political events, whether, as we pointed out in the opening of this book, such events unfold in China, Eastern Europe, or Oka, Quebec.

In Oka, for instance, as we noted, several journalists chose to confine themselves within a siege of a group of Mohawks mounted by the Canadian army. Whether they saw themselves as taking sides, certainly the Mohawks, by issuing an invitation for the journalists to join them, saw their company as a method of protecting against a possible full-scale army assault. The media also played a significant role in presenting an image of each of the groups involved. Civil liberties advocate Alan Borovoy has called attention to the behaviour of the army in and out of earshot of the media (*Globe and Mail,* October 9, 1990, p. A17): for the media they were contained and calm; when the media were gone they evidently engaged in harassment.

In summary, while journalists operate under the banner of freedom of the press, in exchange for this right they undertake certain obligations. The major obligation is probably to "inform as fairly and forthrightly as possible, without fear or favour" (*Globe and Mail,* May 2, 1988, p. A7). As they attempt to fulfil this obligation journalists generally recognize that they are not neutral conduits of information (*Globe and Mail,* November 29, 1988, p. A7). They create the news based on issues they deem important as a result of their particular social, economic, and political histories. The public should be aware of this journalistic "subjectivity" and should also be aware that there is no such thing as pure objectivity. Journalists have influence ranging from setting the agenda for Parliament's Question Period to affecting election outcomes and stock prices. Again, generally, they accept the responsibility to declare any conflicts of interest affecting their work.

The perspective inherent in this balance of rights and obligations is what is meant by the notion of "social responsibility." Canadian journalists accept social responsibility as a guiding principle, but they are certainly nowhere near united in applying its meaning. They do agree, however, that no matter how social responsibility is applied, it is an extension of freedom of expression and is fundamental both to democracy and to press freedoms.

A further level of agreement among journalists is indicated by the Kent Commission. Journalists account for a fall in the prestige of the press by citing its lack of depth. If they were allowed to:

> get to the bottom of facts and events, go beyond the tip of the iceberg, grapple with difficult, complex, but important subjects, and expose them, explain them clearly to the public, bring out the deeper significance of events, in short, assume the responsibility of finding and publishing what the public should know rather than seeking to satisfy the lowest common denominator of public demand as determined by market studies and advertising surveys then the former prestige of the press would be regained. (*Royal Commission on Newspapers*, p. 31)

University professors sometimes feel that they, too, would be more respected if they had the freedom to pursue truth and knowledge to its very base and make it known to all.

Canadian Newspapers: The Inside Story

If the Kent Commission lays out the ideals of the journalistic profession, its realities are to be discovered in a growing number of books and other publications, including *Canadian Newspapers: the Inside Story,* edited by Walter Stewart, *Birds of a Feather* by Allan Fotheringham, and *Guide to Canadian News Media* by Peter Desbarats.

The strongest point that emerges from these publications is the extremely influential role of the owner on journalism as practised in various Canadian newspapers. There seem to be almost as many styles of owner influence as there are owners. The ideal is the rare case in which the owner has a fundamental respect for the profession of journalism and sees his role to be that of standing behind the decisions of the editor. This ideal passes on to the reporters through the editor in the form of respect for their judgements, and the reporters, in turn, must accept the responsibility of this freedom.

At the other extreme is the type of owner, personified by Beland H. Honderich of the *Toronto Star,* whose tastes and predispositions guide the entire operation of the paper. Stewart, writing about the *Star,* claims that the paper, although it has a readership of 640,000, is edited with one reader in mind at all times – the owner. He tells how series were dropped because it was anticipated that Honderich would not like them. In another instance, a *Star* book editor was removed from his post for no other reason than that Honderich did not want him there. The *Star* engages in Metro Toronto boosterism because that is what Honderich wants. Pictures of people in profile rarely appear because the boss has laid down a rule forbidding such pictures. With respect to other owners, Allan Fotheringham claims to have been fired by Southam for an anti-American speech given at the annual meeting of Southam in the presence of the American ambassador. A comparable owner to Honderich is Rupert Murdoch: his intrusions into his papers and TV stations are discussed in the hearings of the Australian Broadcasting Tribunal of 1981-82, as well as in many other places.

Other owners are no less idiosyncratic. For a very long time, almost into the 1990s, Halifax papers went in for highway safety and support of the monarchy on account of the predispositions of the owner. And intrusion on major issues is certainly not the exception. Back in 1955, Charles Woodsworth, son of J.S. Woodsworth, the founder of the Co-operative Commonwealth Federation, predecessor to the NDP, was fired as editor of the *Ottawa Citizen* by R.W. Southam mainly because he was the son of the famous socialist politician and to a lesser extent because his editorial policies were seen to be "socialist." Throughout the reign of the CCF in Saskatchewan, by reason of the views of the owner, the *Saskatoon Star-Phoenix* continually did battle with the government. It only made peace when Ross Thatcher's Liberals were elected. In the U.S., in parallel with American norms, the restriction on the journalist is a balder exercise of power. Lewis Lapham notes:

> I write a newspaper column twice a month for a syndicate and I am instructed by the syndicate never to write an article critical of the press. I can criticize the other institutions in American society, but if I criticize the media or the profession of journalism the piece isn't likely to make the paper. (Henry, 1988, p. 15)

Our point here is not the behaviour of owners but the behaviour of journalists in response to the realities of ownership. It is important to emphasize that the presence of the owner is, seemingly, the most strongly felt influence in the day-to-day lives of practising journalists. Wedding those influences with the ideals of journalism – truth-seeking, social responsibility, etc. – causes continual tension, intrigue, and self-censorship in the profession.

As to the ideals themselves, in Stewart's book and in other accounts of journalistic practices, it is extremely rare to find accusations of being handed orders to write on an issue from a particular perspective, contrary to the facts or to one's conscience. The kind of selection that takes place is more subtle. If an editor wants a certain perspective taken, s/he will choose the reporter who will give that perspective and will often inform the reporter about that perspective. In many other cases, the reporter is left with the "responsibility" to do something that fits in with the perspective of the paper. The reporter knows that perspective simply by having worked for the paper for some time, by having read it previous to employment, and by its general reputation in the profession. If a reporter turns up something that is not pleasing to the editor or publisher but cannot be faulted factually, the piece is either killed or pressure is applied to the reporter to produce something that balances the reporter's perspective with that of the editor or owner.

One example of the journalist as "hired gun" is an article called "The Corporation Haters" (*Fortune,* June 16, 1980), which argued that the Nestlé baby formula boycott had been engineered by corporation-hating radicals, not by those concerned about infant deaths in Third World countries. The author, Herman Nickel, received a $5,000 fee from a Washington, D.C., conservative think tank (Maclean, 1979) and ended up, not long after, as U.S. ambassador to South Africa, a handy man for the Reagan government to have in such a position. Nestlé, by the way, ultimately accepted some responsibility for the infant deaths by pulling back on its marketing efforts in underdeveloped countries.

Similarly, the U.S. State Department under the Reagan administration arranged news media interviews and concocted opinion articles opposing the Nicaraguan government that were placed in major media outlets. The investigative arm of Congress concluded that the activities were misleading and constituted propaganda, violating a ban on use of federal money for propaganda not specifically authorized by Congress (*Globe and Mail*, Oct. 5, 1987, p. A10).

Should reporter and editor or owner continually disagree, the reporter finds opportunities narrowing sufficiently to encourage him or her to move to another paper. Journalists who are uncompromising tend to become freelancers whose articles and programs are purchased as single items. The same kind of relationship, one level up, may develop between the publisher of a newspaper and the owner. While the journalist may find the opportunities of his assignments narrowing, a publisher may find the resources with which he has to work unduly diminished as the owner allocates fewer and fewer resources to create a good paper. (See Murdock, 1982, on allocation control.)

Some investigative reporters, such as John Sawatsky, operate as freelancers. To make ends meet, Sawatsky combines the teaching of journalism (currently at Carleton) with extensive research, and sells individual articles to newspapers as he develops a book, which is then published and excerpted in newspapers and magazines. The quality of work that Sawatsky and other freelancers produce would suggest that this is a good way around the limitations that journalists most often complain about, namely, the lack of the time or resources to do investigative reporting in any depth. The paper may not be interested in hard-edged investigat-

ing for fear of uncovering things embarrassing to its advertisers or setting a tone with which advertisers are uncomfortable. Or the paper may be interested enough but unprepared, purely for reasons of profit, to devote enough resources to the task.

Few institutions in society have an interest in providing journalists or anyone else with an increased freedom to pursue information and understanding regardless of its consequence. In fact, the Access to Information Act, whose basic principle, as mentioned in Chapter 3, is that most information should be available, is administered in such a way that exemptions frequently allow a bureaucracy keen on "efficient government" to prevent disclosure. Common criteria used for keeping information secret include national security, law enforcement, foreign affairs, federal-provincial relations, privacy of individuals, and the advice of public servants to cabinet ministers.

Television Journalism

It is rare for a television station owner to exert the kind of pressure common to newspaper owners over the shape, if not the content, of the news. The person who plays that role is the news director, whose opinions about what should be covered and how it should be covered or followed up shape television news. The documentary footage in the CBC's *Inside TV News* tells us as much about the role of journalists as does anything.

As that program points out, on the basis of agency feeds, morning newspapers, and other credible sources, a news program begins to take shape early in the day. The task for the central office is to get reporters and crews to the right places and to obtain the right information to construct visually compelling "on-the-spot" stories about what they already know is news. The task for the journalists is to obtain access to people and places in order to collect information in a way that can help to build the story.

In his *Memoirs,* René Lévesque told of his involvement in 1956 with the beginnings of the current affairs genre in Canadian television:

> According to the experts in program planning, it was hard to imagine anything more stillborn than my idea to introduce real stories from far-off lands into the family living room after the local soap opera. . . . Everyone was crazy about our little family dramas perpetuated on TV from one series to the next. As distant as they might be from Saint-Denis and Sainte-Catherine streets, couldn't the crises of world events be made just as captivating, given that the cast was made up of highly dramatic characters and the plot was fuller of jolts and surprises than anything Grignon or Lemelin could invent? . . .

Lévesque and his producer proceeded to construct a story on the Suez crisis in soap opera terms. Their basic notion was that Suez was "the joint tragedy of colonial empires and their humiliated subjects, of the unconscious arrogance of their rulers and, finally after years of resignation, the angry revolt of the subjugated."

> That night, signing off, I risked saying to the TV audience that from the look of things we'd soon be speaking of Suez again. The next day or the day after war was declared . . . and our friend Pearson was awarded the Nobel Peace Prize . . . on a more modest level I was considered to be something of a sorcerer. Or better still, a prophet in my own country, however minor. (pp. 143-45)

Similar stories unfolded with other CBC reporters as a tradition of foreign and domestic reporting and storytelling was built up. Luck

and informed judgement sometimes put the right people in the right spot at the right time. More often, and increasingly frequently because of budget constraints, the CBC's foreign correspondents, in contrast to the large American networks, are either confined to news hot spots or they are covering several countries or entire continents. However, the CBC backs itself up with the feeds of the major U.S. networks, which make it a point of pride to operate on their own resources, to be in the right place at the right time, and to be sufficiently informed that they are used by the U.S. government as a source of information. The U.S. networks also use feeds, but to a more limited degree.

Where the CBC, and to some extent Canadian broadcasters in general, shine, in comparison with the U.S. broadcasters, is in backgrounders, explorations of continuing issues, and follow-up journalism. In the case of CBC radio, because the telephone may be used for "phone-out" interviews, programs such as *Sunday Morning* and *As It Happens* can be much more immediate in their reaction to events. The fancy technology of *The Journal* also allows a certain amount of up-to-the-day coverage. But planned, in-depth documentary pieces that combine both issues and events by anticipating occasions of contemporary significance are particularly good opportunities for Canadian television journalists and producers to show their mettle. Such was the case, for example, with Lévesque's current affairs program, *Point de Mire,* in the 1950s.

Career Patterns in Journalism

One might not expect the career patterns of journalists to be relevant to an analysis of the broader significance of their role. Usually a profession has a slightly skewed distribution toward younger members, enough to give it new blood but not enough to set norms for the profession as a whole. The situation in journalism has been summarized with respect to the parliamentary press gallery (whose motto reads, "Afflict the comfortable, and comfort the afflicted") by Roy MacGregor. He wrote in 1980:

> If we could distill one composite reporter from the two hundred thirty or so that make up the present Parliamentary Press Gallery we would come up with one male, close to thirty years of age, middle-class background (perhaps slightly higher), university educated (rarely in journalism), earning in excess of $25,000 a year, somewhat concerned about his weak backhand in tennis, and frightfully testy about his lack of knowledge of political history. He would be fairly conservative in his soul, Liberal in print and NDP in the bar. (Stewart, 1980, p. 196)

Is the parliamentary press gallery a place where the relatively young congregate? Are older journalists found elsewhere? Not at all. Journalists tend to advance relatively quickly out of their basic role as reporters to become editors and columnists or, just as often, to leave journalism to work on the other side of the fence, for government or private enterprise as information officers. For example, Prime Minister Mulroney's former press secretary, Bill Fox, was lured away from his position as Washington correspondent for the *Toronto Star* when he was 36 years old (MacDonald, 1984, p. 230).

When journalists move on to private enterprise and to government, they often find positions that offer more money and less immediate day-to-day pressure. Such jobs involve designing and orchestrating information to be fed to the media. Knowing from their journalistic background what makes reporters pay atten-

tion, they design press releases so that certain information is bound to be emphasized in the papers. Or they cook up photo opportunities for television crews. Or they advise ministers on how to leak and whom to leak to in order to float trial balloons or achieve other secretive purposes.

The morale boost from working for an organization that depends on a journalist's ability to present information in the best possible way is substantial. Besides direct comments of appreciation that come from each successful project, seeing the advance of the interests of the organization for which one works gives the journalist the sense that s/he is making a constructive contribution. For most, such a position is socially and psychologically more comfortable in middle age, if not at any age, than continually challenging the exercise of power (afflicting the comfortable) in the name of the public, whose appreciation is difficult to assess.

As a consequence, the public is left with the relatively young and the idealists to pursue journalism on their behalf. On the other hand, for every orchestrating information officer working to create press releases, there is an equally and perhaps more competent editor assigning his reporters to uncover other aspects of the story that may not be immediately apparent. (A fuller account of the functioning of the parliamentary press gallery, following Fletcher, 1981, was provided in Chapter 3.)

One final point on the journalist/information officer interaction. It is quite interesting that journalists find themselves able to move back and forth between government, private corporations, and the media with relative ease. Such ease of movement illustrates the degree to which such institutions share the same basic viewpoint. It also illustrates a basic liberal pluralism to which they all adhere with relative comfort.

Relations between Journalists and Newsmakers

Journalists need information. Formally speaking, information can be acquired by interview and by virtue of the Access to Information Act. The journalist can also search through records that private companies, for example, are required to make public. Equally important to a journalist are informal channels of information.

Almost all outstanding journalists use a combination of officially available and informal information. Their ability to solicit information off the record from various unnamed individuals is often a key to their success. As columnist Allan Fotheringham points out in the CBC documentary *The Press and the Prime Minister*, there is in Ottawa a kind of incest between politicians and journalists. Journalists need politicians to give them good stories. Politicians need journalists to get things into the press. They extend favours to one another in exchange for return considerations. It is an intricate game played according to certain rules that could not be described as the pure pursuit of truth. The journalist must develop a host of relationships with a wide variety of newsmakers in order to get the occasional scoop and quickly check the veracity of, or get another opinion on, the many stories s/he must write.

In 1990, the relationship between CKVU reporter Margot Sinclair and B.C. Attorney-General Stuart "Bud" Smith led to the resignation of each from their respective positions after transcripts of taped cellular phone conversations between the two, indicating possible libel and obstruction of justice, were tabled in the legislature. After review, no charges were laid. The public airing of such "behind-closed-doors" conversations tellingly reveals the tangled web of relationships formed among media and political personalities.

In an intriguing book called *The Insiders,* John Sawatsky extends the discussion of how various groups in Ottawa, including lobbyists, trade information for personal and political gain. One complementary book to Sawatsky's is Stevie Cameron's *Inside Ottawa.* Her book explores the exercise of power and the role of various key groups, including both bureaucrats and politicians. She also takes advantage of sources privy to some very confidential information, such as image consultants and interior decorators whose services have been sought by the major power players. Yet another book, David Taras's *The Newsmakers* (1990), explores many of the same issues from a third perspective.

THE MANAGEMENT OF INFORMATION

Journalists are not hired as autonomous information seekers and given the freedom to pursue and reveal what truth they personally deem worthy of their efforts. Their activities are constrained by their bosses, owners and/or editors, news directors, or anonymous bureaucrats who lay down policy and allocate the necessary resources to do the job. Their bosses, if they are not owners, are usually former journalists who have advanced to the editorial stage in the collection and organization of information. The responsibility of these editors is to deploy strategically the troops at whichever fronts appear to be potentially active and then to sort through what information is gathered for the "best stories."

In carrying out this function, the editor-managers must provide a credible and attractive information product that attracts listeners, viewers, or readers to a great enough extent to stave off the competition. In other words, their jobs are to maintain a market penetration rate that does not leave room for a competitor to enter. They must assemble a large enough audience to sell to advertisers at a sufficient price to pay for production costs and to provide the requisite percentage of profit the owner demands.

The division of responsibilities between reporter and editor, or between the reporter and the person acting in the name of the publisher, is recognized by law in section 267 (1) of the Criminal Libel Act. In a 1981 libel case involving the CBC and reporter Chris Bird versus the deputy attorney-general of B.C., Richard Vogel, in which Bird, through the facilities of the CBC, accused Vogel of misusing his office, the presiding judge drew distinctions between the responsibilities of the journalist involved and his editors, who represent the institution. The judge wrote:

> Mr. Bird's conduct was in the course of his employment as a reporter. Had his employer exercised a reasonable degree of editorial judgment and control, that conduct would have caused no harm to anyone. The damage came, not from the investigation, but from the publication. The responsibility for deciding whether to publish rested with those above Mr. Bird. The most seriously reprehensible conduct was their abdication of that responsibility. That was an abdication not by individuals, but by an organization possessing a unique degree of power and influence.
>
> The circumstances of the case call for the award of an additional amount against the CBC as exemplary damages.
>
> That amount should not depart from the traditional moderate awards but should be sufficient to mark the court's disapproval of the conduct of the CBC and provide some element of deterrence from similar conduct. . . . The defendants CBC and Bird will be liable jointly for damages in the amount of $100,000. The defendant CBC will be liable for the further amount of $25,000.

Editors as Gatekeepers

The manner in which this judgement has been written leads us directly into what is perhaps the dominant way of seeing the functions of editors in the media, that is, as gatekeepers.

The notion of **gatekeeper** was originally conceived and coined by social psychologist Kurt Lewin in 1947 in reference to the consumption of food. The question he posed was, why do people eat what they eat? To answer his question he developed a "channel theory": food comes to the table through various channels, for example, buying in the store, picking from the garden, etc. Food moves step by step through a channel, from gatherer to processor, to wholesaler, to retailer, to family, to freezer, fridge, or cupboard, to table, to eater. He then questioned who controls the flow of food along those channels. In general, the answer is gatekeepers. He noted also that gate sections were either governed by impartial rules or by the decision-making of the gatekeepers (Cartwright, 1951, p. 186).

This model can be applied to just about any social phenomenon that involves gathering objects or materials and transforming them into consumable products. As Hester (in Wells, 1974, p. 210) points out in his study of international news agencies, the reporter selects from a universe of events:

- which are then selected for transmittal by a national agency,
- which are then selected for transmittal by the global agency,
- which are then selected for transmittal by the media users,
- which are then selected for reading or watching by the individual consumer.

While "gatekeeping" is an evocative metaphor, it is usually applied in academic literature only to

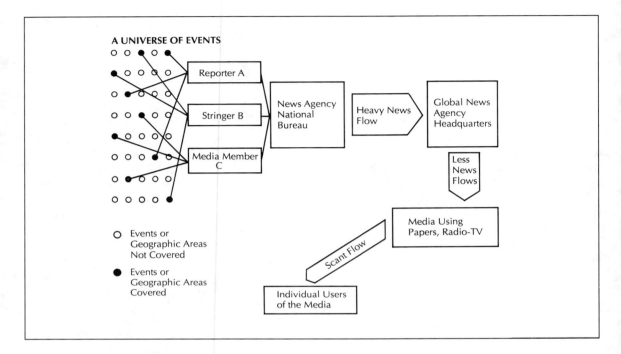

FIGURE 8.1 *International news flow via a news service.* Of the many potential news events, only some are covered by reporters, "stringers," or members relaying stories to the bureau of the global news agency. Editors there forward important news items to the world headquarters of the agency. Editors at world headquarters select what they think newsworthy. Finally, the individual reader, listener, or viewer decides what international news he will be attentive to. What began as hundreds of events and items has gradually dwindled to only a handful. SOURCE: Al Hester, "International News Agencies," in Alan Wells, ed., *Mass Communications, A World View* (Palo Alto: Mayfield Publishing, 1974). Reproduced with permission of the author.

some stages of selection, specifically not to the reporter's gathering and the consumer's choice. The selection process in which both reporter and audience engage is not considered to be "gatekeeping."

There are limitations to the metaphor of gatekeeping for describing the process by which newspapers and television programs are created. Nonetheless, the gatekeeper metaphor focuses our attention on the refusal or negative-selecting function of editors and owners. By implication,

truth and value are in the hands of the reporters or writers, and editors allow only acceptable truths through the gates. The Americans are the greatest proponents of the gatekeeping model. Some insight into why they should be comes from the comments of Brian Stewart, a Canadian journalist who has worked for television networks on both sides of the border. Stewart notes:

The Amnets [American Networks] are interesting places to work, in that they resemble

Three treatments of a power outage in Toronto. *Reprinted with permission – The Toronto Star Syndicate; The Globe and Mail; The Toronto Sun.*

courts of the Italian Renaissance – plots, factions, favorites, intrigue, and threats. Marvellous Theatre! Before going to NBC, I assumed those at the heights of network news were motivated by normal greed and ambition. I discovered the real propulsion was fear. Producers and reporters live in holy terror of even minor failures. Any setback is career threatening. . . .

Canadian news is quite the opposite. On foreign stories you aren't terribly concerned about what your Canadian opponent is doing. . . . CBC editors rarely had a clue what CTV had done. They were interested mainly in meeting our "mandate." The CBC was to do its thing regardless, which is a pleasant regime to work for most of the time. (Frum, 1990)

In the light of this analysis, gatekeeping, the arbitrary inclusion and exclusion of material, seems to represent a slightly abstracted description of the dynamic of American news production – just as editorial construction seems a more apt description of the dynamic of Canadian news production.

A major element neglected in the gatekeeping analysis is the construction or meaning-generating function that the editor, news director, or program producer serves. From this perspective, it might be argued that the significance of the editor or producer, or for that matter any others involved, is to help transform or construct something from the raw material, which reporters gather or writers produce, to form the greater whole of the program, magazine, newspaper, and so on. Only then does the material become fully contextualized and take on its full significance. What the three Toronto papers made of a power failure on April 25, 1990, gives not only a sense of the event but also an insight into how each constructs the news, with what flavour, for what kind of an audience, and with what intended effects. More generally stated, the editorial whole is greater than the sum of its "gatekept" parts.

Incidentally, owners, too, serve a construction function in providing the institution within which journalists operate and by allocating the necessary resources to the news-gathering and editorial processes. The challenge of the editor/producer role is to negotiate a place for material that is culturally valuable. It is to the construction function that we now turn.

The Editorial Construction Function

The Royal Commission on Newspapers provides a description of the workings of management in the newsroom. That description provides a sense of the mechanics of the construction of various elements of a newspaper and of the newspaper as a whole.

The *head of the editorial department* or *editor-in-chief*, who reports directly to the publisher, is responsible for the editorial content of the newspaper. S/he usually creates the character of the paper both in its day-to-day operations and in the context of its broader relations with readers, politicians, and other opinion leaders.

The *executive editor* or *editorial page* editor works under the editor-in-chief, as does the *managing editor,* the person who manages the newsroom, hires and fires, and negotiates editorial (i.e., news) space with the advertising department.

The *news editor,* as might be expected, looks after the news desk, sorting items for placement in the paper and on the front page, asking for rewrites, obtaining headlines, etc. Again here, this sorting process is influential in determining the character of a paper.

The role of the news editor comes closest to the simple notion of gatekeeper. But the news editor builds and creates an emergent reality as much as he excludes pieces. And even in his exclusion, it is not so much that he censors or refuses to let events interfere with his and the paper's world view, but rather that he requires of the reported events an interpretive context consistent with his sense of what his paper is all about.

Apparently the strongest negative editorial influence, which is potentially censoring, is related to the type of ownership of a newspaper. As the Kent Commission (p. 114) reported, from the testimony of Professor Henry Mintzberg:

> [Chain ownership] tends to insulate management from local pressures, local situations. The loyalty is to the corporation, the loyalty is to the bottom line, and there is a certain mobility built into the fact that, if you don't make in Montreal, then you can move to Toronto or Winnipeg or what have you, within the corporation. I think that creates certain tendencies to be less sensitive to local needs, and perhaps sometimes to be less in touch with them.

Beyond the Mechanics of Construction

Journalists and the entertainment industry have celebrated the construction function for some time. The "good editor/good newspaper" tradition and the reverence held for John Grierson of the National Film Board are elements of that celebration. So, in the entertainment field, are such awards as the Oscars, Genies, Emmies, Rockies, Junos, etc. The construction function has been discussed by Martin Knelman.

Knelman points to a Canadian tradition in documentaries, beginning with John Grierson, but his focus of attention is on *The Journal,* its executive producer, Mark Starowicz, and the other central figures involved in the creation of the program. More than a year and $10 million were spent in conceiving and developing the format and personnel for the show before any content was ever introduced.

While few shows are able to spend $10 million setting themselves up, it could be argued that the capital costs of setting up a newspaper are equivalent. However the costs are reckoned, a great deal of attention is paid to the matter of how one will present information, how one will construct and package information to appeal to one audience or another. Neither is this activity confined to the pre-production phase. Once in operation, all media maintain a constant surveillance of their audiences.

The editorial/management function is not confined to the broad design of the program as a whole. The gatekeeping view would have us assume that on a day-to-day basis editors are rather like St. Peter manning the gates to heaven. In fact, more often, at least in the Canadian media, the editor works with the journalist/writer to shape an initial draft into something suitable for the editor's particular program or series. The process involves much give and take, and has been described in *The Newsmakers,* a book of engaging interviews with Canada's top journalists by Linda Frum, star anchorwoman Barbara Frum's daughter.

This process is not confined to news and information programming. While much emphasis has been put on the gatekeeping function, constructive interaction is frequent. Writers, whether for television, periodicals, or book publishers, seek out the programs, magazines, or publishing houses respectively for which they anticipate they can write. They feel that they understand the approach and the style of the production. On that basis they develop scripts, pieces, or book outlines that they believe fit their target program or publication. After the material is submitted, if it is seen to have possibilities, the editor then sits down with the writer to try and maximize possibilities inherent in the script. Together they reconstruct the piece with regard to both the creativity of the writer and the contingencies of production or publication in the particular outlet.

The differences emerge between, say, book publishers and program producers in the degrees of freedom within which each feels it must operate. Clearly a publisher known for encouraging new and innovative writing has a much broader range of possibilities than do the producers and editors of *Lance et Compte* or *DeGrassi High*.

A More Academic View

Extensive research has been conducted into the function of editors, but from a more abstract perspective than the one we have been discussing so far. Some of it derives from a gatekeeping model but manages to move to varying extents into a discussion of the editorial construction function.

Take, for example, the claim introduced in Chapter 2 and extended in Chapter 5 that the media are an ideological control apparatus. That notion derives, to a considerable extent, from a view of the media as gatekeepers. According to this model, news is a constructed entity that reproduces the dominant ideology by numerous journalistic means, such as story format, use of beats, pursuit of accepted angles, use of authorities as primary definers of events, etc. Such a viewpoint de-emphasizes the creative act of making the world comprehensible – the work of consolidating or articulating culture – in favour of seeing such activities as an ideological reproduction process aimed at extending powerful and dominant interests. The gatekeepers, so the model goes, let in stories that conform or can be made to conform to acceptable themes played out in the daily news. When stories appear to but do not conform to the implicit definition of news that results from these procedures, as Bennett, Gressett, and Haltom (1985) put it, they must be repaired and made to fit.

Thus, in the example of the Alabama man setting himself on fire, the U.S. national media felt compelled to transform or repair that story from the one that the "victim" wanted told about unemployment, but for which he had no media-understandable credibility as a teller, to a story of journalistic ethics. Similarly, with other examples that we have cited – such as Trudeau's "Just watch me!" and "Where's Biafra?" – a senior journalist such as Richard Gwyn feels the need to repair the story to make it conform with our image of the Prime Minister as knowledgeable and sympathetic to human suffering.

Much of the academic work in this area tends to be slanted toward a basic gatekeeping model, e.g., Epstein (1973), Gans (1979), Gitlin (1980), Tuchman (1978). Such writings are not devoid of insight, nor is the reader steered away from any sense of the creative construction function that is basic to media functioning. Indeed, Gaye Tuchman's *Making News: A Study in the Construction of Reality* emphasizes this in its title. Some British work (see Gurevitch et al., 1982) has also been done on how the assigned work patterns of journalists, which are customarily defined by management, affect the information collected. Two major Canadian studies by Ericson, Baranek and Chan (1989, 1987) also emphasize media construction of news. However, this is conceived from within a larger system of maintenance of ideological dominance.

Tuchman points out that both editors and reporters are continually searching for frames of reference within which to present news. By identifying a frame or a perspective on an occurrence, as Tuchman says,

> an occurrence is transformed into an event, and an event is transformed into a news story. The news frame organizes everyday reality and the news frame is part and parcel of everyday reality, for, as we have seen, the public character of news is an essential feature of news.

In other words, news frames tap accepted social and ideological categories of lived culture for the frames of reference of their productions, and news consumers select, use, and transform those productions in the context of everyday life. Both the media and the audience construct meaning in interaction with one another.

In the British literature on the work patterns of journalists (see, for example, the Glasgow Media Group's *Bad News* and its sequels), much attention is paid to the daily beats of the reporters. The very existence of a crime beat – a daily visit or check with the central or local police – ensures that there will be stories centred on police matters. Moreover, in such a beat, the common factor is the police. Hence, their behaviour will not be worthy of note, but the behaviours they collect as a result of their law enforcement action will be seen as newsworthy. Other beats work in exactly the same way. A business beat without a labour beat ensures that labour will be treated continually as a disruptive force. Interestingly, in 1989, *The Globe and Mail* compounded its increasing business orientation by cancelling the labour beat (*Financial Post,* April 17, 1989, p. 17). Long-term labour concerns and initiatives are almost certain to be ignored. Conversely, a labour beat without a business beat would probably turn into a running grievance column.

The structure of beats comes together with the relations that journalists have with newsmakers, that cast of characters who are vehicles or agents through which the news is brought to the attention of the journalist or editor. The personal and professional adventures of these people – prominent citizens in political office, business, labour, law, etc. – become the background against which news is defined. But they also play off against one another to catapult the social behaviour of other groups into the limelight. In an imaginative book called *Folk Devils and Moral Panics,* Cohen traces the attribution of meaning and escalation in significance by those "in authority" of some relatively contained concrete action. They also point out the role of the media in helping certain groups extend their definitions of the behaviour of others to name and control the lives of those named.

An example that goes beyond content and delves into ownership and long-term marketing dynamics is to be found in a study on the presentation of welfare in the British press over the past 50 or so years. In *Images of Welfare: Press and Public Attitudes to Poverty,* Golding and Middleton identify four factors contributing to a definition of public attitudes toward problems of poverty:

1. four centuries of cultural history in which poverty was seen as a mixture of unavoidable misfortune and morally culpable behaviour;
2. the disappearance of an alternative, labour-oriented press in the 1960s;
3. the economic crisis of 1973 in Britain, which sent welfare costs soaring for both the unemployed and elderly;
4. how news-gathering organizations picked up the dominant, culturally based explanation of poverty in their regular beats with welfare bureaucracies, the courts, the police, and ultra-conservative British MPs.

The first of the Canadian studies by Ericson, Baranek, and Chain, *Visualizing Deviance,* analysed the restricted use journalists made of information available. They noted that

> while an enormous array of information was available – official documents, academic texts, survey and trend statistics, and direct observation – journalists tend to limit themselves to the 'performatives' of news releases and interview quotations from sources . . . as well as key spokespersons for particular bureaucratic organizations. (1987, p. 1)

The authors' *Negotiating Control* refined this analysis by documenting the processes of negotiation and struggle between sources and journalists. Here, Ericson, Baranek, and Chan concentrate on how large bureaucratic organizations organize themselves to produce news discourse and limit the terms of that discourse (1989, p. 2).

There is also an extensive literature on balance and fairness (e.g., Cook, 1984), which exists because there are formal (in the case of the electronic media) and informal (in the case of the print media) expectations of "objectivity" in news reporting. As a result, interest groups, regulators, and the media themselves often monitor the treatment of issues from these perspectives. The irony of such monitoring, as many academic researchers have come to realize, is that it is a very limited perspective on what one might call the constraints on discourse.

The work of Tuchman, the Glasgow Media Group, and many other researchers demonstrates the limitation of the notion of balance as an analytical category. What is deemed to be the other side of the balance defines the issue in a particular way, as the semiologists point out (see Chapter 4). Put somewhat differently, the choice of a **primary definer** of an issue is an interpretive act in itself and, inherently, is ideologically oriented. The **values of journalists** also play a role in how information is man-

aged. The degree to which the journalistic community is exorcised by a simple statement that, overall, they have a left-wing bias (e.g., Cooper, Miljan, and Vigilante, 1986) reveals both the probability of the truth of the statement and the degree to which they strive to avoid an explicit expression of it.

Equally interesting is why journalists would feel the need to defend themselves. In most definitions, the right wing is taken to be representative of business interests, other power elites, and law and order, while the left is taken to be the more general humanistic and social interest, leaning toward the common people, many of whom are wage labourers. If journalists seek truth in the name of the people, one would think that as a group they would be explicit in describing themselves as at least on the liberal left.

Perhaps the greatest lack in the literature is a sense of the media's contribution to the articulation and consolidation of culture. As Chapters 3 and 6 demonstrate, debates dealing with the establishment and support of media industries and those focused on licence renewals of both the CBC and private stations are an indication that Canadians see the media, especially the CBC, as major, albeit imperfect, contributors to the articulation and consolidation of national culture. Such testimony as is to be found in the various editions of Gzowski's *Morningside Papers* (1985, 1989) reveals the contribution that Gzowski's program makes to providing individual Canadians with a sense of the national community. Current conceptions of the media fail to address this community-building role adequately.

OTHER STRUCTURAL INFLUENCES

M edia editor/managers are torn between the ideals of their profession, the realities of the market, the politics of the market, and the structural constraints imposed by the owner or ownership form. In the previous section, we discussed how such individuals negotiated a constructive and creative course amidst such constraint. In this section, we will consider some specific examples of other structural influences that are part of the environment of the media.

The Law

As Peter Desbarats (1990, p. 156) notes:

> In the course of their work, journalists encounter a bewildering variety of laws and regulations that govern such activities as court reporting; access to court documents; news coverage of public hearings; reporting of, and response to, search warrants, injunctions, and subpoenas; police reporting; treatment of confidential news sources; investigative reporting techniques; coverage of elections; and invasion of privacy. This thicket of jurisprudence and government regulations is one of the reasons why every Canadian journalism school includes a course in law among its requirements.

> For most journalists, however, the laws that are of greatest concern in their day-to-day work are those relating to libel. According to the Royal Commission on newspapers, the law of libel "has a vastly more pervasive influence on the way journalists write" than do any other constraints.

The presence of libel laws is at all times a constraint on media content. The federal law of criminal libel (criminal defamation), not to be confused with provincially administered civil libel, defines (in Section 262 [1]) an offence as:

> matter published without lawful justification or excuse, that is likely to injure the reputation of any person by exposing him to hatred, contempt or ridicule, or that is designed to insult the person of or concerning whom it is published.

Conviction for publishing such libel is punishable by imprisonment for two years. Conviction for publishing such libel with the knowledge of its falsity is punishable by up to five years in prison.

Cases of criminal libel are extremely rare in Canadian law. More common are cases of civil defamation. More than half of Canada's dailies have been served with writs, but only one per cent of the cases have gone to trial and judgement (*Globe and Mail,* December 11, 1989, p. B1). The law varies between provinces and, as a result of many judgements, is fairly complex. As noted in Chapter 3, the complexity of the law can be accounted for by the necessity of balancing two basic rights, freedom of expression and the individual's right to his reputation. One of the difficulties for media professionals involved in potentially libelous content is that if the case comes to court, they have the unusual requirement known as reverse onus, meaning it is up to the media to prove that the story is true. This may conflict with the journalistic obligation to protect one's sources, who may have been consulted for any number of good reasons (*Globe and Mail,* December 11, 1989, p. B1).

The journalist's job is to collect information and to ensure its authenticity. However, it is also the responsibility of the publisher to account for the presence of any piece of information in his publication. Reporter, editor, and publisher thus share the responsibility of ensuring that what they publish is not libelous. An example is the case of the Toronto development family, the Reichmanns, profiled in a lengthy article in the November, 1987, issue of *Toronto Life* magazine. They mounted a $102 million lawsuit naming the author of the article, as well as the publisher of the magazine and the magazine's managing editor. Also named were the *Toronto Sun* and a columnist who had reviewed the article for the paper (*Globe and Mail*, December 11, 1989, p. B1). In February, 1991, the case was resolved with *Toronto Life* publishing a retraction in its March, 1991, issue that said in part, "Let us unequivocally and categorically say that any and all negative insinuations and allegations in the article about the Reichmann family and Olympia & York are totally false."

The easiest way of avoiding libel, of course, is to publish non-controversial material. Indeed, soft news, positive news, and boosterism get around libel in this very way. But there is a vibrant tradition in journalism of engaging in the critical and controversial, "of afflicting the comfortable and comforting the afflicted." The profession appears to believe that this approach attracts audiences. Journalists deem it to be the cutting edge of the duty of the media to inform, to pursue truth. While the law may seem to be a censoring device, introducing libel chill, it can be claimed that libel law does not censor but rather contributes positively to the reporting of what would be agreed upon by a community of fair-minded people as true.

The Media and Business

In two major studies of business and Canadian society (Porter, 1965; Clement, 1975), the argument is advanced that the Canadian media are closely interwoven with the Canadian and North American business elite. One manifestation of that interweave is that members of boards of directors of banks and other corporations are found regularly on the boards of directors of media corporations. In Chapter 3, we discussed the general influence of business on the press; here our interest is centred on the influence this has on media professionals and the significance of this influence for the media consumers, the audience.

The media see themselves generally as the fourth estate or as watchdogs, yet they watch government in an entirely different way from how they examine business. When particular policies are being developed or a controversial law is passed by Parliament, the media consider it a source of pride to hound it out of existence. At least one member of the media, Val Sears, explicitly stated that the job of the media was to bring down the government of John Diefenbaker (quoted in the CBC documentary, *Inside TV News*). The role they play is that of an articulate, informed citizen with independent ideas.

By contrast, the watchdog role toward business, in general, appears to be confined to identifying the transgressors of the law or of what is considered to be proper conduct. They do not voice, on a day-to-day basis, criticisms of the behaviour of business with respect to the public interest. Indeed, the business section and additional special regional or national development sections are customarily directed at informing the public of new developments. These sections are complemented by advertisements placed by the very companies that are crucial to those developments.

The newspapers, television, and magazines serve to some extent as the ideological arm of the business community. They provide the background within which the contribution of business to society is made to seem primary. The success of the CBC program *Venture*, which deals with business issues, and of PBS's most popular show, *Wall St. Week*, add to the momentum of the business pages in featuring the contributions of business. Even in television sitcoms, the job identity of the person is often placed up front. The adventures presented are derived from his or her function as a working person.

This orientation toward business creates an environment within which advertising is well received. An ad puts forward the accomplishments of an individual corporation just a little less critically, with just a little more specificity and a little more hoopla, than does the journalism that surrounds it. If this advertising/ journalism relationship is true of the "news" media, it is even truer of the media that do not see themselves as engaged in the pursuit of truth in the name of public interest. As fashion photographer Howard Fry points out in the video program, *The Fashionable Image,* in doing a photographic editorial piece his job is to enhance the environment within which the advertisers' ads appear. A journalist writing for the same magazine might say the same. Their job is to make the package within which the ads appear sufficiently attractive to bring to the ads an audience of a particular type.

In television, attracting and delivering a suitably prepared audience to advertisers has quite an immediate, temporal connotation. In the same way that a front page is designed to take the reader further into a paper, an evening of programs is designed initially to attract an audience and then deliver that audience in a frame of mind suited to the acceptance of the advertisers' messages from program to program throughout the night. Usually that is accomplished through the use of known quantities, i.e., programs that are part of familiar series and non-threatening but adventurous enough to capture the attention of the viewer.

In one class project at Simon Fraser University, about fifty students viewed a documentary dealing with the trials of a young teenage girl whose parents had recently separated. In mid-program, an ad for a charter flight to Las Vegas was shown. The self-indulgence implied in the ad hit a raw nerve with nearly all of the viewers. It was certainly the wrong ad for the program content. The example highlights the general situation rather well. Advertisers are not interested in having audiences delivered to them whose frame of mind is not open to a fairly non-critical acceptance of their message. As a result, there is a real constraint on programming not to involve the viewer too deeply in the subject of the program so that s/he resents the intrusion of the ad. Also, the subjects chosen must not show the ads in a bad light. This restriction in advertiser-supported communications argues most strongly against the privatization of the public media.

Many in business, not surprisingly, would disagree with the above analysis. For example, in the *Report on Business Magazine* published by *The Globe and Mail* in May, 1990, there was an article on direct mail. Some in the business saw it as a consumer-interest article full of misinformation about the industry based on the practices of some unsophisticated operators. It was their view that they had an even greater interest than do customers in increasing the sophistication of direct mail techniques and not upsetting anyone with unwanted mail, which would obviously not get them customers.

However, such an article, annoying as it may be to a particular group, serves the crucial purpose of communicating that business practice is not beyond criticism. In fact, it demonstrates to the general public, at the expense of one sector, that even the mild annoyance of receiving unwanted mail is given serious attention in the business community.

The CBC and Its Affiliates

In Canada, we have a particularly interesting example of the contrasting pulls within private and public enterprise. In the world of privately owned television production, just as in magazines and many newspapers, a station and network stay alive by delivering audiences to advertisers. This life-sustaining act is more obvious in television, radio, and controlled-circulation magazines (magazines delivered free in certain city areas, or to certain professionals or income groups) because there is no purchase price for access.

The CBC lives partly in this reality and partly in the reality of its annual parliamentary appropriation. However, it has a number of privately owned affiliates that do not get parliamentary appropriations and thus are continually pressing for the CBC to provide them with programming that will net the largest audiences possible. They object to Canadian cultural programming, which may develop part of the mandate of the CBC but garners relatively fewer viewers than would American dramas.

Their arguments have been successful enough to persuade the CBC to provide them with subsidies to carry its programming, to compensate them for the perceived loss of audience. (They are tied to CBC programming by the conditions of their licence.) This situation is rather like the tail continually threatening to wag the dog. The CBC has neither completely capitulated to its affiliates nor felt free to ignore their protests. The matter is continually in flux, and some stations have disaffiliated themselves to become private independent stations.

Community Politics and Standards

In a narrow sense of the term "community standards," the programmer or editor must at all times be aware of how content will be received by the target audience. The media play to or with community standards and with the politics of acceptability. A survey done in 1984 reported that violence was more frequently portrayed on CTV than on any other network, more than on the CBC, ABC, NBC, or CBS. Presumably this was because CTV buys programming on the basis of its ratings and pays less attention to

program balance and production cost because it does not produce the programs. But bringing the matter to the attention of the network would not necessarily lead to change. One of the many interesting revelations of Channel Ten 10's submission to the Australian Broadcasting Tribunal was an item-by-item description of how much each advertiser paid for each ad during the course of one week (see Chapter 7). The submission revealed that the station, owned by Rupert Murdoch, made very little money on advertising on children's programming. This led to increased pressure from parent groups to ban advertising from children's programming altogether. Murdoch would have none of it; the advertising stayed.

SUMMARY

The major point of this chapter is that in every medium a rather thick layer of organization affects the content we receive as consumers. Whether such a layer represents the ideals of a journalist/editor tempered by years of experience, the marketing orientation of a glossy magazine editor, or the attempt by a programmer to tailor a program idea to the image a particular client wishes to project, there is no doubt that it exists. The relative failure of community programming on community cable channels speaks to the necessity of that layer to produce "acceptable" programming.

In the same way that a symphony orchestra represents an extremely elegant, hierarchically organized use of the potentialities of the many musicians and instruments of an orchestra, so the production of a newspaper, a program or series, a magazine, is also a sophisticated integration of the talents and potentialities of the many crafts and interests of the production team. Yet, just as an orchestra excludes the untrained musician who might wish either to join in or to have a musical composition played, so media production excludes the single individual who may wish to communicate a simple idea. For that communication, the individual must rely on the co-ordination of the talents of a group of professionals who all have different but crucial roles to play in getting his or her message across in an effective manner.

The musical analogy is relevant in other ways. Both music and communication are social processes. Through these processes a community can express and enhance itself. If the mode of expression is layered with complexities, however, the ideas of a community have a rather limited possibility of being expressed in a manner that is true to their nature. They are professionalized along the way and, as this happens, some of the ideas become so transformed that they are extinguished. In the end, and to a significant degree, the very social nature of communication is lost to a particular class and a specific profession. In that loss there may be some damage to the community's ability to express and renew itself in order to adapt to its changing environment. The media may become alienated; they may no longer mediate but, instead, become semi-autonomous image-generating processes.

REFERENCES

Bennett, W.L., L.A. Gressett, and W. Haltom. "Repairing the News: A Case Study of News Paradigm," *Journal of Communications*, 35, 2 (Spring, 1985), pp. 50-68.

Cameron, Stevie. *Ottawa Inside Out: Power, Prestige and Scandal in the Nation's Capital.* Toronto: Key Porter Books, 1989.

Canada. *Royal Commission on Newspapers.* Hull, Quebec: Canadian Government Publishing Centre, 1981.

Canadian Broadcasting Corporation. *Inside TV News,* executive producer, M. Blandford, directed by F. Steele, produced by H. Gendron and F. Steele. Montreal, 1982.

Cartwright, E., ed. *Field Theory in Social Science: Selected Theoretical Papers, Kurt Levin.* New York: Harper & Row, 1951.

Clement, Wallace. *The Canadian Corporate Elite.* Toronto: McClelland and Stewart, 1975.

Cohen, S. *Folk Devils and Moral Panics: The Creation of the Mods and Rockers.* London: MacGibbon and Kee, 1972.

Cook, Peter. "The Concept of Balance in the Supervision and Regulation of Canadian Broadcasting," M.A. thesis, Simon Fraser University, 1982.

Cooper, B., L. Miljan, and M. Vigilante. "Bias on the CBC? A Study of Network AM Radio," paper presented at the Learned Societies meetings, Winnipeg, May-June, 1981.

Desbarats, Peter. *Guide to Canadian News Media.* Toronto: Harcourt Brace Jovanovich, 1990.

Ericson, R.V., P.M. Baranek, and J.B.L. Chan. *Negotiating Control: A Study of News Sources.* Toronto: University of Toronto Press, 1989.

Ericson, R.V., P.M. Baranek, and J.B.L. Chan. *Visualizing Deviance: A Study of News Organization.* Toronto: University of Toronto Press, 1987.

Epstein, E.J. *News from Nowhere: Television and the News.* New York: Vintage, 1973.

Fletcher, F. *The Newspapers and Public Affairs.* Vol. 7, Research Publications, Canada, Royal Commission on Newspapers. Ottawa: Ministry of Supply and Services, 1981.

Fotheringham, Allan. *Birds of a Feather: The Press and the Politicians.* Toronto: Key Porter, 1989.

Frum, Linda. *The Newsmakers: Interviews with Canada's Top Television Reporters.* Toronto: Key Porter, 1990.

Gans, H.J. *Deciding What's News: A Study of CBS Evening News, NBC Nightly News, Newsweek, and Time.* New York: Vintage, 1979.

Gitlin, T. *The Whole World is Watching.* Berkeley: University of California Press, 1980.

Glasgow Media Group. *Really Bad News.* London: Writers and Readers Publishing Cooperative, 1982.

Golding, Peter, and Sue Middleton. *Images of Welfare: Press and Public Attitudes to Poverty.* Oxford: Martin Robertson & Co., 1982.

Gurevitch, M., *et al.,* eds. *Culture, Society and the Media.* Toronto: Methuen, 1982.

Gzowski, P. *The Morningside Papers.* Toronto: McClelland and Stewart, 1985, 1989.

Henry, William A. *Media Freedom and Accountability.* New York: Gannett Center for Media Studies, 1988.

Hester, Al. "International News Agencies," in Alan Wells, ed., *Mass Communications: a World View.* Palo Alto: Mayfield, 1974.

Knelman, Martin. "Their Finest Hour," *Saturday Night* (March, 1983).

Korporaal, G. "How the U.S. Media Hijacked Foreign Policy," *Australian Financial Review,* July 3, 1985, p. 1.

Lévesque, René. *Memoirs.* Toronto: McClelland and Stewart, 1986.

MacDonald, L. Ian. *Mulroney: The Making of the Prime Minister.* Toronto: McClelland and Stewart, 1984.

MacLean, E. *Between the Lines.* Montreal: Black Rose, 1979.

Murdock, G. "Large Corporations and the Control of the Communications Industries," in Gurevitch *et al.,* eds., *Culture, Society and the Media.*

Porter, John. *The Vertical Mosaic.* Toronto: University of Toronto Press, 1965.

Sauvageau, Florian. "French-speaking journalists on journalism," in Robert Fulford *et al.,* eds., *The Journalists.* Royal Commission on Newspapers, Research Studies on the Newspaper Industry, vol. 2. Ottawa: Ministry of Supply and Services, 1981.

Simon Fraser University. *The Fashionable Image.* Videotape, Communications Department, 1985. Distributor: Magic Lantern, Oakville, Ontario.

Stewart, Walter, ed. *Canadian Newspapers: The Inside Story.* Edmonton: Hurtig, 1980.

Taras, David. *The Newsmakers: The Media's Influence on Canadian Politics.* Toronto: Nelson, 1990.

Tuchman, Gaye. *Making News: A Study in the Construction of Reality.* New York: Free Press, 1978.

Vancouver Sun, June 21, 1985, p. A3.

Vogel vs. CBC/Bird. #C802500 Vancouver Registry, in the Supreme Court of Canada, 1981.

STUDY QUESTIONS

1. The label "gatekeeper" hides much of the creative side of the work of editors, news directors, and program supervisors. Discuss the role of the information manager in the context of the aims of information seekers.

2. Dan Phelan, senior program editor for the CBC radio program *World Reports,* has said: "I was a reporter a long time so I know basically what I want. It's like a parade, and each story is a float and you have to put it together so that there's a beginning and an ending." How do you think Phelan defines the news and what does his role as journalist appear to be? Comment on the pros and cons of this type of journalistic approach to news.

3. "The ideals of journalism play an important role in structuring our media environment." Discuss.

CHAPTER

9

New Communications Technologies in a Canadian Context

INTRODUCTION

TECHNOLOGY IN GENERAL, and electronic communications technology in particular, is a significant force in modern society. As Jacques Ellul, a French philosopher, has claimed:

> All technical progress exacts a price; that is, while it adds something on the one hand, it subtracts something on the other.

> All technical progress raises more problems than it solves, tempts us to see the consequent problems as technical in nature, and prods us to seek technical solutions to them.

> The negative effects of technological innovation are inseparable from the positive. It is naive to say that technology is neutral, that it may be used for good or bad ends; the good and bad effects are, in fact, simultaneous and inseparable.

> All technological innovations have unforeseen effects. (Dizard, 1985, p. 11)

The Canadian philosopher George Grant makes the case in *Technology and Empire* that the foundation of all modern liberal industrial and post-industrial societies, including Canada, is to be found in technique and technology:

> the belief that human excellence is promoted by the homogenizing and universalizing power of technology is the dominant doctrine of modern liberalism, and . . . that doctrine must undermine all particularisms. . . . English-speaking Canada as a particular is wide open to that doctrine.

Somewhat in elaboration of the above views are those of the Englishman Raymond Williams (1975), who has argued that television technology is an extension of the industrial revolution and feeds the mass society that industrialization created. As social institutions were created and cultural content generated, television, as a technological tool, came to realize both positive and negative potentialities.

Mainstream American scholars have been inclined to see technology as benevolent and technological change as progressive. This is the view of which Grant was speaking. American optimism appears to stem from an economic history in which the development and use of machines to create wealth has been regarded as of widespread benefit to American society over the past two hundred years.

In contrast to the mainstream scholars are Marxist American scholars such as Herbert Schiller (1984), who maintains that pressure to develop and apply communications technologies comes from political and economic forces steered by multinational corporations and military research and development in communications hardware. Working in Canada, Vincent Mosco's (1989) views also emphasize political and economic considerations.

Canadian Robert Babe (1988, 1990) has introduced another orientation to technology partic-ularly relevant to this book. He has argued that Canadian policy-makers have been dazzled by technological developments and that public policy in broadcasting and telecommunications has been seriously distorted by at least five myths about communications technology. The two most prominent of those myths are what Babe calls technological nationalism and technological dependence. The first claims that Canadian nationhood depends on the use of communications technologies to tie the nation together. The second myth examined by Babe is that technological change is inevitable and that, when Canada employs all available techniques, our society will be transformed in undefined but presumably beneficial ways.

The perspective developed in this chapter attempts to take into account the opinion of all the above authors. We also attempt to encompass Winner's notion, discussed in Chapter 6, that technology consists of (a) pieces of apparatus, (b) techniques of operation to make the apparatus work, and (c) social institutions within which technical activities take place.

The past few decades have seen an enormous explosion in our capacity to communicate. This has been brought about largely through the amalgamation of communication with computers. The basis of that amalgamation has been the silicon chip, a device that, as it becomes smaller and smaller, against all initial expectations, becomes more and more sophisticated and efficient as well as inexpensive.

The changes brought about through this tremendous expansion of communicative capacity are legion. A selection of newspaper headlines from the mid-1980s gives us a sense of the changing environment.

- "New firm cashes in on TV's news boom"
- "Sidewalk summit launched ethnic pay TV pioneers"

- "Pay TV licensees secure top deals as on-air launching draws closer"
- "Telidon adds market zap to Dominion Directory"
- "Cable TV tunes into high-tech wizardry"
- "Satellites: Impinging on North American copyright laws"
- "International copyright agreements and the need for a new legal framework"
- "Electronics revolutionize publishing industry"
- "Computers enable printer to increase flow of black ink"
- "Privacy and the computer state"
- "Terminal man"
- "Videotex net for farmers to be launched by Sasktel"
- "Rogers-Belzberg group granted cellular licence"
- "Home computer David takes aim at Goliaths"

By the turn of the decade, slightly different preoccupations with technology were in evidence.

- "Satellite, fibre optics team to direct telecom traffic"
- "High-definition TV at theatre near you"
- "Video Jukebox puts tape library a phone call away"
- "Industry races to tune in as HDTV looms"
- "O&Y opens first Canadian studio in its video conferencing network"
- "NAC joins with Telesat Canada in high-definition TV experiment"
- "Long-distance new telecom battle ground"
- "You can be two places at once with telecom"
- "Tax mailboxes are coming"
- "Bell battles French service for videotex market"

- "Final buys being worked out to create global switchboard"
- "Voice mail booming"
- "E-mail the fastest word around"
- "Nintendo and IT&T discuss telephone link"

As the headlines indicate, the changes in the communications environment are of a number of different types. The major changes are in:

1. the technology used to process and shape information;
2. market dynamics, such as economies of scale, or, in other words, national and international dynamics as a result of technological form;
3. the patterns in the content of information that are and will become available (and hence consumed by audiences);
4. the patterns of participation by various types of cultural institutions, for example, large corporations, small entrepreneurial groups, Crown corporations, etc.;
5. the investment patterns in the information sector and, as a result, the emergence of new information services and ownership dynamics;
6. the legal framework appropriate to an enhanced information sector in which more information is packaged many times over but slightly differently for various, narrowly targeted audiences.

In this chapter we will review some of these quite fundamental changes to the global communications infrastructure, discuss their implications for Canada and Canadians, and suggest a strategy for proceeding in this new communications environment. In the first edition our major focus was on broadcasting. The major issues we discussed were providing signals to all regions and designing content for a multiplicity of regions and cultures, rural and urban.

In this edition we summarize the evolved state of technology and issues in broadcasting and introduce a new discussion, that of telecommunications and information systems, an area that has vastly increased in importance since the publication of the first edition.

A TECHNO-INDUSTRIAL EXPLOSION IN COMMUNICATIONS

As Peter Lyman points out in *Canada's Video Revolution,* we can now direct minute amounts of electricity that carry in their patterns all sorts of information. The basic device that has given us this power is the semiconductor, a silicon chip on which is printed more and more complex integrated circuits capable of such functions as information sorting, calculations, and storage.

To digital semiconductor technology is added optical technology, or fibre optics. Whereas electrical pulses have been and still are being used, fibre optics use light pulses. Their major advantage is a 10,000-fold increase in transmission capability over a copper wire of the same bulk. This vast increase in capacity is complemented by other developments, such as a set of international standards to ensure system compatibility and ever more sophisticated signal and transmission manipulation, including compression and multiplexing (using one path for more than one set of signals) to produce Integrated Services Digital Networks (ISDNs, combining voice, data, facsimile, and video in the same channels). The increased transmission capability is substantial, to say the least.

The third element of technological development in communications is the satellite. Satellite technology in conjunction with communications technology has led to the communications satellite. Such satellites serve a simple function. They are points to which signals can be sent and from which signals can be received. Being so high in the sky, they can receive and transmit signals from places widely separated by geography. Interlinked with other satellites, they can form a global network for signals to be beamed around the world.

A final technological development is the spread of the personal computer. Five years ago the significance of this device and its widespread use were not apparent. By the early 1990s, it was already apparent that no government, no office, no professional, no researcher, no business, and no organization that had anything to do with information could fully do so without such a device. Whether it is used for word-processing, doing budgets or mailing lists, filling out forms, communicating with others, recording or printing information, accessing distant data bases or purchasable data bases on compact discs, or any other task, the personal computer has become a necessary piece of equipment in the modern information society. Moreover, its diffusion throughout society has allowed for a speedy transformation of information services out of print-on-paper to computer-accessible digital signals.

As with practically any technological explosion, there is an associated industrial explosion. And as with any recent major industrial explosion or expansion, the large corporations are best positioned not only to benefit from new market possibilities but also to direct technological development in ways that favour their activities. As noted in previous chapters, this comes about not only because of the borrowing power of these businesses but also through economies of scale that allow the expense of new technologies to be paid for by their vast markets. As well, large companies control the market to such an extent they can create markets for the technologies they wish to introduce. We will bypass this techno-industrial dynamic and concentrate on the evolving forms of communications technology and how they restructure the communications environment of Canada.

THE TECHNOLOGICAL FOUNDATIONS OF TELEVISION BROADCASTING

Television broadcasting has always been closely connected to its technological form. Historically, networks were formed on the basis of terrestrial technology, that is, microwave towers that beamed programs across the country. This ability to distribute nationally via a series of microwave-linked stations was basic to the economics of program production as well as the form of programming. For example, the national evening news was made possible because of microwave technology. Until 1958, videotapes were flown out to the regions from the production centre(s) for broadcast.

The commitment to national distribution through microwave-to-local-station technology created the network structure that exists today in many countries. In Canada it was the basis for the creation of both the CBC and CTV/TVA, and is influencing the evolution of the Global Network.

The advent of satellites, coupled with both satellite dish reception and cable redistribution of signals, has added new possibilities for signal distribution. For example, satellites (with cable) have created the possibility of superstations, that is, individual stations whose signal is delivered nationally. While some of these have evolved – particularly specialty services such as Much-Music, Cable News Network (CNN), and the pay TV channels – satellites (with cable) have been used more as a technological alternative for the delivery of signals and the continuation of the already established network structure. Satellites (with cable) have greatly expanded the choice of

channels available. Figures 9.1 and 9.2 describe the coverage of the two satellite series in use in Canada. (Each satellite within a letter series has the same footprint.) Table 9.2 lists the services that use each satellite.

With the expansion of the number of available channels has come the need to find funding to ensure their existence. Traditional formulae for funding, such as subscriber revenues, public subsidy, and/or advertising, are being or will be used for these new services. But new relationships are also evolving. Two examples point out some elements of these new funding relationships.

MuchMusic is a vehicle for the promotion and advertisement of products, specifically sound recordings. It keeps interest in sound recording high and continuously follows market trends, serving as a guide to consumers. To facilitate this role, record companies make both videos and performers available to participate in this promotional activity. The cost of programming is minimal; indeed, it is in the interest of the record companies to ensure cheap and easy distribution of the signal to consumers. Given this perspective, one can understand what an industry coup it was when MuchMusic persuaded the CRTC to allow it to offer its service on basic cable for a very small additional ($0.08), non-discretionary fee.

Religious television, and specifically Vision TV, is a second example of new economic relationships evolving in the provision of television services. The evangelical role of most religions puts them in much the same position as the sound recording industry. They have a vested interest in subsidizing the distribution of their programming.

With these players in the game of providing signals, the principle of using communication services, in this case a television channel, for the promotion of an industry or activity opens

TABLE 9.1 Telecommunications and Broadcasting Downlink Channel Assignment from Canadian Communications Satellites (April 1, 1990)

Anik D1 104.5°W, 6/4 GHz

Horizontal Polarization
1A	RadioNet 1
2A	Telecommunications
3A	CBC
4A	CBC
5A	CANCOM – NBC
6A	CBC
7A	Occasional Use
8A	CBC
9A	CBC
10A	CBC
11A	CANCOM – PBS
12A	CANCOM – CBS

Vertical Polarization
1B	TSN
2B	Global
3B	MuchMusic
4B	CANCOM – CHCH
5B	CANCOM – ABC
6B	
7B	CANCOM – TCTV
8B	CBC – House of Commons
9B	CANCOM – CITV
10B	CBC
11B	CANCOM – CHAN
12B	CBC – House of Commons

Anik C1 107.3°W, 14/12 GHs

Vertical Polarization West Beam
T1	
T2	
T3	
T4	
T5	Occasional Use
T6	
T7	
T8	
T9	ACCESS Network
T10	YTV
T11	The Family Channel
T12	Super Channel
T13	
T14	
T15	The Knowledge Network
T16	

Horizontal Polarization East Beam
T17	Musique Plus
T18	ASN
T19	Super Ecran
T20	
T21	Radio Québec
T22	Quatre Saisons
T23	Le Canal Famille
T24	RDS – Le Réseau des Sports
T25	TVOntario La Chaine
T26	TVOntario
T27	
T28	Ontario Legislature
T29	YTV
T30	The Family Channel
T31	
T32	

Anik D2 110.5°W, 6/4 GHz

Horizontal Polarization
1A	Telecommunications
2A	Telecommunications
3A	Telecommunications
4A	
5A	
6A	MéteoMédia
7A	
8A	Vision/TV
9A	TV5
10A	Occasional Use
11A	Telecommunications
12A	CBC – Newsworld

Vertical Polarization
1B	
2B	
3B	
4B	Telecommunications
5B	NOVANET
6B	CTV
7B	Occasional Use
8B	CTV
9B	Occasional Use
10B	CHSN
11B	First Choice
12B	CTV

FIGURE 9.1
Anik C Footprint

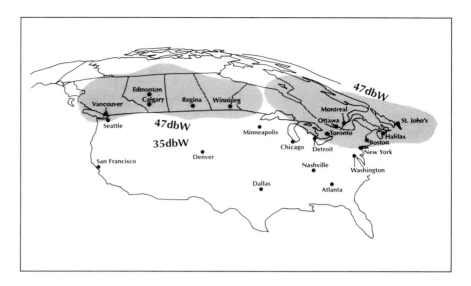

NOTE: This is the area covered by Anik C's half-Canada spotbeams with full-power (47 dbW) radiation. Beyond the footprint, larger-than-standard dish antennas are needed for reception.
SOURCE: Telesat Canada.

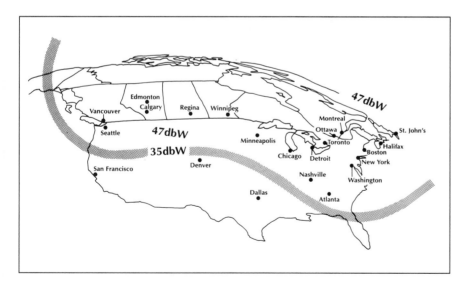

FIGURE 9.2
Anik D Footprint

NOTE: This is the area covered by Anik D with full-power (35 dbW) radiation, including all of Canada and part of the U.S.
SOURCE: Telesat Canada.

TABLE 9.2

Current and Alternative Cable Tiering Structure

Current Structure*	*Alternative Structure*
Basic Tier (including augmented channel service)	**Alternative Basic Tier**
- Canadian channels, public and private, which qualify for priority carriage under CRTC regulations	- Canadian channels, public and private, which qualify for priority carriage under CRTC regulations
- Community channel where required	- Community channel
- The proposed TVCanada services	- Proposed Canadian all-news channel
- Parliamentary channel	- Optional conventional Canadian channels, as permitted by CRTC
- Optional channels as permitted by the CRTC, including the American 3 + 1 and, in some cases, independent U.S. stations	**Second Tier**
- "Barker" channel, which promotes discretionary tier	- Canadian specialty channels (subject to higher Canadian content requirements than at present)
Discretionary Services	- Optional conventional American signals including 3 + 1 and any additional American signals now carried on basic
- Canadian movie channel (First Choice/Superchannel/Super Ecran)	**Premium Tier**
- Canadian specialty channels (The Sports Network, MuchMusic, Life Channel)	- Canadian movie channels
- American specialty channels approved for carriage by CRTC requirements for carriage on second tier)	- Canadian specialty channels (i.e., those that choose not to meet
- American specialty channels that are complementary to licensed Canadian services	

SOURCE: *Report of the Task Force on Broadcasting Policy.* Ottawa: Supply and Services, 1986.

the door to further expansion in the kinds of organizations that might become television producer/distributors. Over the long term, expansion of producers to other groups that have a vested interest in subsidizing distribution of the programming challenges the journalistic role of television. What would the CRTC do if the Canadian Chamber of Commerce today applied for a broadcast licence to provide general educational programming on the contribution of business to society? What might the CRTC do in 10 years?

For the time being, an expansion of educational and other social service information is more likely, partly because the programming is already available, produced inside and outside Canada. Health information programming both for the average person as well as for professional development, skills upgrading, or retraining is quite possible. Similarly, business information can be created, packaged, and transmitted easily and quickly to highly specific target audiences. Cultural programming, formerly available in one location, can be transmitted across the country into almost any location where a satellite receiving dish can be erected, or where a cable company has set up a dish receiver and offers the programming on its cable system. Premium television (television for which one pays a premium above the basic cable rate) and foreign television services (in addition to American services) are also possible as advertiser-supported systems.

Other services, which require some adaptation of the technology, are also feasible. For example, point-to-point distribution in which signals are sent only to certain addresses is not difficult. The scrambling of signals allows for universal distribution but (theoretically) non-universal reception. Scrambling also provides for security as well as economic return through the control and sale of descramblers.

With the vast increase in channel capability that a combination of all available technology makes possible, none of these services theoretically need interfere with any other. The challenge in responding to these myriad technological developments is to design and market all services for the cultural and economic benefit of Canadians as a whole. Cable companies facilitate rising to that challenge by the tiering of services. Tiering is really an application of the marketer's old standby, packaging. It amounts to including one package of offerings for basic cable service and alternative premium packages at other levels of service. Table 9.2 describes in general terms the current method of tiering of cable companies alongside a proposal for an alternative put forward by the Broadcasting Task Force (1986).

The socio-cultural implications of tiering are considerable. Certain services of cultural, political, or economic benefit could be linked to popular services so that, in effect, the latter carried the former. To take an obvious example, if all educational services were available as an add-on to a basic tier plus a full package of entertainment services for which the consumer had to pay a premium, the system designer would, no doubt, become a national villain. However, without local cable control, the potential organizing influence of tiering disappears.

PROGRAMMING IMPLICATIONS OF SATELLITE-BASED TECHNOLOGY

The clearest implication of satellite-based technology and an enabling regulatory framework is an increase in the number of domestic and international buyers of television programming. These new buyers will be the new networks or specialty services, i.e., the superstations, such as Murdoch's Sky Channel. In contrast to the networks, which have acted as vertically integrated packagers and programmers, many of the new players will not be in a position to produce programming. Rather, following the trend of already operating broadcasters, they will purchase programs. This change is increasing opportunities for Canadian independent producers.

A second implication is that programs are being made to appeal to more than one market. In Canada, the inability of the CBC or any other broadcaster to pay the full cost of programming requires independent producers to come up with at least half of their funding in other mar-

TABLE 9.3 The Canadian Broadcast Program Development Fund: English and French Projects Contracted

	Number of Projects	Total Budget* $	Telefilm Canada $
French			
Production	49	68,537,058	22,744,243
Script and Development	28	2,344,254	909,172
Amendments to previous year contracts	—	—	(456,154)
Sub-total	77	70,881,312	23,197,261
English			
Production	64	114,654,424	37,392,645
Script and Development	50	2,808,015	1,162,598
Amendments to previous year contracts	—	—	2,358,522
Sub-total	114	117,462,439	40,913,765
Total	191	188,343,751	64,111,026

* Includes total production and co-production budgets.
SOURCE: Telefilm Canada Annual Report, 1988-89.

kets. The implementation of Telefilm Canada's broadcast fund, wherein one-third of the funding is available for assured prime-time broadcast programs, makes independent productions feasible. In certain circumstances the Telefilm contribution may be raised to 49 per cent. Until 1984, the response of the private broadcasters and other elements of the private sector had not been overwhelming (see Tables 9.3 and 9.4), but predictions were that they would make greater use of the fund. This has occurred. In 1984 the CBC received 72 per cent and the private sector 28 per cent of Telefilm funding, but by 1989 the CBC was receiving only 42 per cent while the private sector had increased to 44 per cent and educational television had entered the picture with 13 per cent.

A third implication of satellite-based technology is the challenge the technology presents to regulation. Regulation has an historical basis in the scarcity of distribution facilities, i.e., the airwaves. With channel scarcity no longer a limiting factor, there are bound to be both domestic and international pressures to allow easy access to all manner of programming. These pressures have already been felt, and a general loosening of the regulatory framework occurred in 1985. If the Mulroney government or subsequent federal governments continue to integrate the economy of Canada with the U.S., no doubt we will see further replacement of regulation with so-called market forces.

A fourth implication derives from the simple mathematics of increasing the number of ser-

TABLE 9.4 The Canadian Broadcast Program Development Fund: Total Canadian Broadcaster Participation

Broadcasters	Drama $	Variety $	Children $	Documentary $	Total $
Private Sector and Educational Television					
Conventional Television					
CTV	4,915,000	—	165,000	—	5,080,000
CTV Affiliates	1,061,000	70,000	100,000	—	1,231,000
Global	1,725,000	—	—	236,000	1,961,000
Independents	1,690,454	1,107,065	40,000	429,300	3,266,819
Télé-Métropole	1,963,136	2,155,000	544,419	200,000	4,862,555
Quatre Saisons	3,515,529	329,400	130,000	—	3,974,929
Educational Television					
Radio-Québec	525,000	—	3,678,575	1,829,251	6,032,826
TVOntario/ La Chaîne française	40,000	122,000	15,500	126,500	304,000
Access	—	—	—	19,510	19,510
Knowledge	—	—	—	—	—
Pay Television					
First Choice	—	—	—	—	—
Super Channel	131,000	—	—	—	131,000
Super Écran	224,000	25,000	—	—	249,000
Specialty Services					
Canal Famille	—	—	343,415	—	343,415
TV5	—	188,000	—	22,500	210,500
Vision TV	—	—	—	65,000	65,000
Sub-total	15,790,119	3,996,465	5,016,909	2,928,061	27,731,554
Public Sector					
CBC	4,772,244	1,359,253	4,447,000	1,552,415	12,130,912
CBC-Regional	878,825	1,130,000	—	175,000	2,183,825
Société Radio-Canada	3,169,500	2,375,000	—	603,000	6,147,500
Société Radio-Canada – Regional	—	—	—	—	—
Sub-total	8,820,569	4,864,253	4,447,000	2,330,415	20,462,237
Total	24,610,688	8,860,718	9,463,909	5,258,476	48,193,791

SOURCE: Telefilm Canada Annual Report, 1988-89.

vices. The audience fragments further with the addition of each additional service. The returns to producers are thus fractionalized by the addition of each service. Audience fragmentation increases pressure to operate in the largest possible market. It also forces costs, and therefore quality of production, down as far the audience is willing to tolerate in defence of the bottom line. A familiar illustration of this pressure is in animation. While Disney worked with 24 frames per second and drawings complete with full backgrounds, shading, and shadows, modern companies work with as few as 12 frames per second and emphasis on foreground.

The corollary to audience fragmentation is that although there will be more program buyers in the market, as the Canadian experience with pay TV has demonstrated, there may be little net increase in the size of the audience. In other words, the money available for programming may not expand appreciably. In fact, if we open the skies to all programmers it may very easily turn out that foreign programmers end up the beneficiaries, as an increased number of foreign program packagers find themselves in a position to exploit Canada as a spillover market.

A fifth implication of satellite-based technology involves the sequencing of releases to various markets. At the present time, feature films are released to theatres, followed closely by release to videocassette distribution, then pay TV, and then broadcast television. Made-for-TV movies are shown first on pay TV and may be followed by other forms of distribution. In the mid-eighties this sequencing seemed up for grabs. By the early 1990s it appeared to be carved in stone. For example, pay TV has not managed to act as a distributor for home-video recording, perhaps because recording of any kind is anathema to the industry.

POSITIONING CANADIAN PROGRAMMING

With the inevitable continuation of the integration of the Canadian and American economies, fast or slow depending on what party is in power, Canadian programming must position itself in a North American context. It can do so, and expect some level of success, in a number of ways. The first way is by feel – not by feeling one's way into the market but by the feel of programming. If we refer to Brian Stewart's comments about how the American networks function in contrast to the CBC (Frum, 1990), we can understand how the point of view of the CBC might be appreciated by both Canadians and Americans. If, as part of its all-news operation, the CBC actually set out to package an "objective" North American news service, it might be able to carve a market niche for itself. A parallel initiative might be taken in other kinds of programming, especially drama. In the same way that British dramas have a distinctive "feel," so do Canadian productions, especially CBC specials. Packaged and promoted properly, such programs might find acceptance in the U.S. and other countries around the world.

The alternative strategy is to approach the matter in cold economic terms. In *Canada's Video Revolution*, Peter Lyman, an economist, claims that the basic variable in becoming competitive is a level of investment more or less equivalent to that spent by others in the marketplace. If the Americans spend $1 million, then Canadians must spend an equal amount to compete in the same market. (The position of the Canadian dollar with respect to the U.S. is not insignificant in this regard.) This and the market-niche approach are detailed in two articles by Strick (1988) and Edwards (1988).

A third mechanism currently being used in Canadian production involves a changing role for the CBC as well as for the private broadcasters. In addition to (or to replace) their in-house spending on production, the broadcasters can provide pre-sale funding for productions that, together with Telefilm funding, can bring productions some distance toward full funding.

Another mechanism, curiously unused by the Canadian networks, is the exploitation of their purchasing power to gain access for Canadian productions to the American market. The neglect of this mechanism suggests that it is not of benefit (or not feasible for) broadcasters to "play hardball" in this manner for the benefit of their confrères, the producers.

The decision to Canadianize the CBC by bringing Canadian content up to 90 per cent removes the CBC from actively competing with other Canadian program buyers and driving up the price. Theoretically, this should bring the price of programming down for other buyers. Even if the remaining Canadian program importers will not save money, the CBC will be redirecting funds into Canadian production.

Co-productions between Canada and various European countries, especially with France and, ironically, more between Anglophone than Francophone Canadian production units and French production units, are also being used to gain access for Canadian work to the European markets.

The CRTC has considered on a number of occasions changing the rules for the production of Canadian content. The industry has argued that if dollars invested were considered instead of number of hours of programming, there would be a greater chance for Canadian programming to be made that would find an export market. The counter-argument is that there would also be a chance that such a change in regulation would allow the private broadcasters

yet another way to backslide on production of Canadian content.

In educational program development, potential opportunities for co-operation are appearing on the horizon and fading into the distance. The constitutionally allocated responsibility for education to the provinces encourages needless duplication in the production of educational programming, even in the face of severe budgetary restraint. And there are other impediments to co-operation, such as the lack of parallel operations. Already programming produced in one province is rarely used by another. For instance, the Knowledge Network in British Columbia uses such a high level of imported programming that it cannot obtain a broadcasting licence and must distribute its programming by satellite and cable. With co-operation between provinces, not only could Canadian content be enhanced but program budgets could be built up to levels that might encourage export.

A possible role for the federal government has also emerged in recent years. The following analogy helps introduce that role. Relations between Japan and the United States have been somewhat strained of late because of a continuing trade surplus on the Japanese side. In response to U.S. pressure, the Japanese promised some years ago to try to make it easier for American goods to enter the Japanese market. But statistics show no substantial change. The Americans have taken a different tack. They are saying to the Japanese: "Your low level of imports of U.S. goods is your problem. We have tried to increase our exports to you but have been rebuffed. We want you to show an increased level of importation of U.S. products. If you do not, we will take retaliatory action to restrict our imports from your country."

The Canadian government could take an analogous stand. In face of the continuing inability of

Canadians to find U.S. markets for Canadian cultural products, including books, records, television programs, and movies, Canada could put the burden of stimulating changes on the shoulders of the U.S. We could negotiate with the U.S. to set a reasonable level of market participation and then request the assistance of the U.S. in breaking through the rigidities of the U.S. market to build toward that level. In return, we could offer a continued purchase of U.S. cultural products in Canada.

A combination of some or all of the above mechanisms may succeed in maintaining a presence of Canadian cultural products in Canada and help to create new export opportunities. On the other hand, with other countries trying to do the same, and especially with the 1992 co-ordination of the European economies, the going will not be easy. It would certainly be a boost to the economy for Canada to balance trade in cultural products. At present, film and television alone represent a $2-$3 billion drain on our economy. Also, we are not significant participants in the hardware market, a market said to be worth $10,000 million annually in the U.S. as of 1990. Nearly all of our purchases of television and associated equipment come from foreign sources.

HOME COMMUNICATION COMPONENTS: THE CULTURAL JOKER

If desired, the power of a satellite can be increased to the point where the costs of individual receiving dishes are lower than cable redistribution on the ground. At this point the satellite is referred to as a Direct Broadcast Satellite (DBS) and the possibility for regulation weakens, especially in southern Canada where spillover signals from American satellites are certain to be present. However, it is much less costly to the public purse and to business to have a lower-powered satellite that requires a fairly expensive receiving dish and therefore encourages distribution in dense areas by cable. In this case, the increased costs of receiving signals are passed on to the consumer.

The cultural significance of a satellite-to-cable system is that it can be licensed and therefore regulated. The licensing and regulatory processes acquire their cultural power by being in a position to demand certain conditions of the licensee, whether the licensee is a broadcaster, cable operator, or pay TV company. These conditions, if enforced, can aid major program purchasers to negotiate entry of Canadian programming into foreign markets. Obviously, the stronger the licensee, given the proper regulatory structure, the more power that licensee has in working to benefit Canadian programming.

The potential cultural power, which can be a part of a regulated system, is lost when purchasing power is spread out among many individual buyers. This is exactly what happens with videocassettes, videodiscs, software for personal computers, interactive video games, videotex and teletext, digital audio, and all other home communications components. Take, for example, videocassettes. Videocassettes are now rented or bought through a myriad of video shops equivalent to record and book stores. These stores stock what costs little and sells most. And what sells most are the highly promoted U.S.-produced movies that have already proven to be box office successes. Nothing can be done to interfere with the choice of the individual consumer. To single out video shops for regulation and not book stores, for example, would be discriminatory. To attempt to control book stores would be censorship. The conundrum is obvious.

Based on the market penetration of VCRs and the choice offered to the consumer by even a poorly stocked store, video rental shops have clearly beaten out pay TV as a distribution mechanism for home consumption of movies. In so doing they have blocked one more avenue for regulation that might have, through regulated consumption patterns, encouraged Canadian production.

NEW TECHNOLOGIES AROUND THE WORLD: SATELLITES AS A CASE STUDY

To this point we have explored the significance of new communications technologies from a rather narrow angle. First, we have concentrated our attention on Canada. Second, we have examined new technologies from a cultural-industrial context with emphasis on television-based services. In the present section we will look at one central technology, satellite systems as they are being advanced around the world, in an overview largely based on a special issue of *Communication Research Trends* (1983).

Satellite systems are now being used extensively throughout the developed world and in some parts of the developing world. There are private business satellite systems and national satellite systems sometimes owned by the state, at other times owned jointly by business and the state. Other satellite systems are owned by global consortia and are designed to be used by member nations who pay a fee on the basis of use.

To take some examples, INTELSAT is a global satellite commercial telecommunications network that operates 16 satellites in geostationary orbit above the Atlantic, Pacific, and Indian oceans. These satellites link 375 earth stations in 140 countries. The major investors of the

106 member nations are the U.S., Britain, France, West Germany, Japan, and Canada. Together they hold just over 50 per cent of the shares. The technical success and efficiency of INTELSAT have been based on sticking strictly to its commercial function (Snow, 1980). In spite of this success, Luyken (1984) argues that INTELSAT serves the interest of the developed countries in the design of the pathways while countries in outlying regions are rarely linked to one another. Consistent with the history of the design of international communications systems that we will outline in Chapter 10, INTELSAT serves the dominant economic interests. In addition, costs of using the system, although intended to be equitable, are still a major barrier to participation by Third World countries.

The second type of satellite system or network is the national, and in some cases regional, satellite. The U.S. has a bevy of them, Canada has its Aniks, Indonesia has its own (Palapa), and a number of other countries, including Brazil, Australia, and India, are working toward or have recently put in place national satellite systems. In addition, nations in geographic proximity, such as Scandinavia and various European countries, are active in the development of satellite systems. In the case of Europe, at least three are now launched, based on the differing ambitions and interests of the various European nations.

There are two major international issues in the development and use of satellite systems. Both arise, to some degree, out of the technology. The first is the problem of *signal penetration* into countries without their permission, a broader problem than spillover. Spillover consists of signals not really intended for the receiving country. Following a 1971 resolution of the World Administrative Radio Conference for Space Technology (WARC-ST), in 1982 the UN adopted a resolution requiring a nation's prior consent before signals could be aimed toward it. Prior to this resolution, the U.S. had argued that there should be no barriers to the "free flow of information." The Third World and the Communist countries had argued for prior consent. Sweden and Canada had put forward a compromise suggesting that countries of a region agree among themselves (Queeney, 1978).

Reflective of this concept of regional agreement, in October, 1989, the European Directive on Broadcasting adopted a policy, "Television Without Frontiers." This policy is a major step toward the guarantee of a free market in programming among the countries of the European Community. Countries are free to have stricter rules, but other members' signals may not be blocked if they comply with the Directive's minimal conditions. These include a ceiling on advertising time, exclusion of tobacco advertising, and controls on sponsorship operations (*Cable and Satellite Europe,* November, 1989, pp. 17-25).

According to Jeremy Kinsman, former assistant deputy minister in the federal Department of Communications, "The Americans hate the directive. They think it's horrible. We think it's necessary." (*Canadian Communication Reports,* 16, 24, December 31, 1989, p. 2). Jack Valenti, president of the Motion Picture Association of America, the man who has, on more than one occasion, undermined the resolve of Canadian governments to take dramatic action in the distribution of films in Canada as a means of building our film industry, used less emotive but more threatening words.

The principal issue that is absorbing me right now is the European Community's broadcast directive which aims to impose a majority quota on all non-EC material that comes into the European Community television marketplace – which, of course, means an impedi-ment and a barrier to a free marketplace insofar as American programs are concerned. The President of the United States, the Secretary of State, the Secretary of Commerce and the United States Trade Representative have all been supportive. They have made it clear to the chancellories of Europe that the imposition of this quota is an intolerable thing to the U.S. (*Ibid.,* pp. 2-3)

The second major technological issue involves *orbit-* and *spectrum-sharing.* The problem here is that, while suitable access to geostationary orbits and the radio spectrum should be granted, especially in the case of the latter, many nations are not in a position to use what they might be allotted. Anthony Smith (1980) reports that, at the 1977 meeting of WARC on spectrum allocation, the United States had a contingent of engineers able to evaluate each decision on the basis of engineering studies already conducted. Clearly, these engineers were in an excellent position to take care of U.S. interests, while many other countries lacked the necessary resources to look out for their own interests.

Rothblatt (1981) argues that an engineering approach ought to be taken to orbit/spectrum resource-sharing. This would allow countries such as the U.S. to use the allotments of other countries until they are in a position to use them. At that time, the U.S. would be obligated to come to an agreement on use. It is difficult to see how such a proposal benefits any country other than the developed countries, especially the U.S. Part of Rothblatt's argument is based on the notion that, in due course, orbit-sharing will be less of a problem. What may diminish the scarcity of orbital sites is the presence of geostationary platforms composed of large computer/communications systems capable of providing a multitude of communications and information services simultaneously to a great number of users.

How Is the Development of Satellite Systems Justified?

As mentioned in a previous chapter, communications services are customarily justified in humanitarian terms. In fact, the rhetoric usually expresses a long-rejected view of communications as a strategy for development. That view is the general and vague assumption that modernization on a Western industrialized mode will promote economic and social development. As a major element of the modern world, the mass media are seen to be strategic in such a modernization program. One example of such assumptions was in the Satellite Instructional Television Experiment (SITE) undertaken by India, using an American satellite. Some 2,338 rural villages scattered across India received four hours of programming daily. The objectives of SITE were:

- to contribute to family planning;
- to improve agricultural practice;
- to contribute to national integration;
- to contribute to school and adult education and to teacher training;
- to improve occupational skills, health, and hygiene.

As might have been predicted, some success was obtained in achieving the goals that involve the transmission of information. However, little restructuring of social relations or behaviour was observed.

Another example of development rhetoric is found in deliberations over the development of AUSSAT, the Australian national satellite launched in 1985. The major feature of the satellite was to be a "Homestead and Community Broadcast Satellite Service." While that was certainly the justification for persuading the taxpayers of the value of the satellite, as launch date approached the benefit to remote homesteads and communities, such as interactive services, seemed to become increasingly remote because they would be such costly ventures.

A recent study (Paltridge, 1989) indicates that making use of the first generation of satellites proved prohibitively expensive for distance educators and it was only through rather massive state subsidy that any public entity could afford to use the satellite. Even the private sector found the charges prohibitive in comparison with what was available through state-owned Telecom Australia's optical fibre and coaxial land lines. As Paltridge points out, AUSSAT is heading into its second generation (i.e., the launch of replacement satellites) without the first set of satellites having been able to come close to paying for itself.

Paltridge's study suggests that satellite-based communications is prohibitively expensive for Australia and could never expect to be cost effective. However, the economics of the matter are apolitical – the politics are that AUSSAT has been restricted in the services it can offer and the areas in which it can compete in order not to undermine existing infrastructure, specifically the land lines of Telecom Australia. Also, Telecom Australia has proceeded with the development of land lines after studies indicated that these would provide much cheaper telecommunications over the long run.

Paltridge lists a great number of changes that would be required for AUSSAT ever to pay for itself. The length of the list suggests that a satellite system might never pay. In contrast to this scenario, in Canada a greater number of clients use the Anik satellites (see Table 9.2) and the commitment to satellites is partly justified by Canada's attempt to remain competitive in the space communications business. Also in contrast to Paltridge's assessment of the cost effectiveness of satellites in Australia, the tiny island of Tonga (which has been allotted 16 orbital slots in geostationary orbit) has been persuaded by two American entrepreneurs to consider forming a consortium of businesses and governments in the region to launch its own satellite.

However things emerge in Australia and elsewhere, it would appear that the original rationales of health and education get nudged out of place by launch, equipment, and operating costs. As the situation evolved in Scandinavia, once Nordic electronic and aerospace firms realized that the satellite might become a vehicle for their participation in the space equipment market, their lack of interest disappeared and they fully supported the development and launch of NORDSAT. Once that happened, the cultural intent of the satellite was eclipsed.

Social Implications

As noted with SITE, satellites are used in relaying information to communities in a position to receive them. The general assumption is that democratic equality and geographic mobility, especially for young children, are universal desiderata. Therefore, information delivered by satellite is universally beneficial. The truth of the matter is that remote people and remote land are transformed by the information of the centre rather than having initial need of it. Whether that transformation occurs in response to employment or trading opportunities, through education, or through exposure to a televisual presentation of a sumptuous lifestyle and situation, these people and their society become a hinterland community rather than a centre unto themselves. In becoming a hinterland, certain opportunities open in their home community

while others close. More significantly, a far vaster array of opportunities open for them at the centre. The remote, now hinterland, community, like all others similarly transformed, begins to provide physical and human resources for the centre. Thereby the centre builds its strength.

Legal Implications

Not only satellite systems but all new communications technologies present a set of legal problems for the global community. Those problems are centred on the issue and law of *copyright*. They are further enmeshed by such issues as what constitutes sovereignty, and what right nations have to license and regulate communication signals of all types coming into their country.

On the matter of copyright, the state of affairs is rather messy. Although there are international copyright conventions to which most nations are signatories (specifically the Berne Convention and the Universal Copyright Convention), there are different levels of these conventions, and the levels agreed to by the U.S. and Canada do not deal at all well with technologies that had yet to be invented at the time of their signing. In Canada, specifically, radio communication has been given the fairly narrow interpretation in the courts as needing to involve electromagnetic waves. This excludes cable and satellite transmission. Similarly, delivery of signals to a multiplicity of private homes has been interpreted not to be "public display" and is therefore not subject to the copyright owners' permission. In the U.S., although there is a broader definition of public display, cable carriers become exempt if they are passive carriers of signals engaged in secondary transmission (the movement of a signal from point A to point B). Much the same principle holds for satellites.

Copyright becomes a consideration only when the satellite is a DBS intended to be used by an audience. If the satellite signals are to be redistributed by a cable company, the satellite owner becomes exempt, but the cable company pays copyright fees.

As Hylton and Mann (1983) point out, this is hardly satisfactory. They propose a set of general principles that should be used in updating copyright law.

1. As a general rule copyright owners should be entitled to remuneration for any electronic dissemination of their works according to the actual reach of the audience receiving such works. How the public views the material should not matter, nor should the directness of the transmission, the nature of the signal (i.e., broadcast versus cable or satellite signal), or from what source payment is made.

2. Copyright owners should not be entitled to receive duplicate remuneration in respect of the communication of their works to a single audience.

3. The need to avoid duplication liability to copyright owners, and the interest of the public in obtaining access to a wide range of programming, may make it necessary to provide limited exceptions to the right of copyright owners to control satellite communication of their works.

4. The principle relating to copyright liability must be considered in the context of other regulatory issues relating to satellite communications.

Sovereignty, which includes the right of nations to control their own information environment, is also facing a major challenge by new communications technologies. For example, in Europe where there is an extensive spillover of satellite signals, major efforts are being made to conform to the regulations of the various countries. Different countries have different regulations, especially with regard to advertising. Without some kind of accord, "border stations" (i.e., stations set up in one country to take advantage of immunity to the laws of the country in which its target market is located) would abound and introduce international friction. Similarly, difficulties are arising over the flow of data across borders because that flow is transmitted on privately owned satellite networks such as Satellite Business Systems. At both the national and international levels, problems are also being created. With geostationary platforms on the horizon, distinctions often the basis of regulation and spectrum allocation – such as between fixed, broadcasting, maritime, common carrier, domestic, international – are becoming next to impossible to make. Such challenges are being addressed daily by the International Telecommunications Union. Canada has a special role to play in these issues because it is a close neighbour to the nation that is most aggressive in pursuing its rights to distribute information broadly and charge for the privilege of receiving it.

A Changed Canadian Television Environment

Communications satellites have always had the potential to change fundamentally the distribution of television signals in Canada. They were doing so gradually as many Canadians outside areas serviced by cable companies bought satellite receiving dishes. However, the licensing of Cancom was a major fillip to this transformation.

Cancom, more or less, is cable in the sky, and is licensed to carry eight conventional channels and ten radio superstation services to remote and underserved communities. It is funded by a basic fee per month. These services are delivered by satellite (Anik D) to local communities. From there they are redistributed

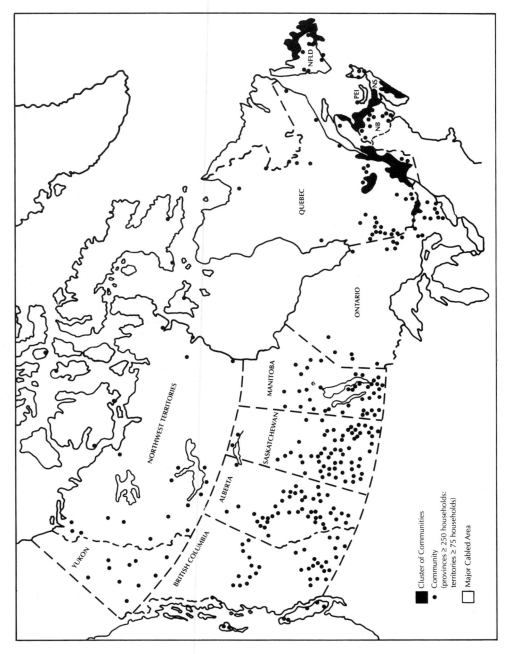

SOURCE: CRTC application by Orbitel Communications Company of Canada Inc. (Cancom).

to individual households by cable or rebroadcast transmitter. To some degree Cancom was licensed to counteract the illegal reception and redistribution of U.S. television services. More recently the CRTC has changed its regulations, thus allowing Cancom to participate in some major urban markets in Canada.

The original market for Cancom consisted of approximately 450,000 households scattered across Canada (see Figure 9.3). The Cancom package has a selection of American network programming found on three English-language Canadian stations plus the Canadian programming of these three stations. Cancom drew away households already receiving programs by American satellite because the American satellite services only include American pay TV services and none of the networks, and because of an increasing tendency by the Americans to scramble their signals. Cancom's licence puts it in a good position to take advantage of new television service directions in Canada, including:

- developing Canadian superstations;
- becoming a major carrier for the U.S. networks;
- gaining access to the U.S. market by packaging Canadian programming for U.S. audiences;
- developing new Canadian cable-to-satellite services for urban areas.

In recent years Cancom has created five regional cable companies that pair economically viable communities with those that cannot support a cable system alone. Cancom is also using VSAT (Very Small Aperture Technology), which permits two-way data as well as visual communications to virtually anywhere the 1.8 metre dishes can be placed, to bring automated banking services to remote communities. Big business is also interested in the technology; Canadian Tire has linked up its 370 dealers and distributors, and IBM, Ford, General Motors, and Federal Express use the service between cities for annual meetings, training seminars, and investment presentations. Finally, Cancom also provides Direct-To-Home (DTH) broadcasting of ten channels for 6,000 subscribers beyond the reach of even the regional cable companies: 18,000 more potential subscribers may be enlisted (*Broadcaster*, September, 1988, pp.10-11).

Lyman looks forward to a rosier future for Canadians as a result of Cancom. It has become even rosier for Cancom because of the opening to Cancom of the major urban markets. But in terms of its home viewing packages it is a rosy *economic* picture, not a rosy *cultural* picture. Cancom bombards rural, semi-rural, and small-town Canada with a plethora of American and Canadian urban-generated programs and advertising that will portray the lives, concerns, dreams, hopes, fears, products, and squalour of the city. True, Cancom subscribers will be in touch with "the world" as it is portrayed in the sports, drama, sitcoms, etc., of nightly television fare. But how will that fare actually improve their quality of life? As noted earlier, it will transform them from a small centre into a hinterland. It may provide greater equality of opportunity with urban dwellers, but it will decrease the diversity of life and culture in the nation. (Laba, 1988, has addressed this issue in a more general context.)

The issue becomes slightly more disturbing when we consider native communities. There, as we point out in Chapter 11, and as Valaskakis (1988) has documented, the most significant element of enhanced communications services is the transformation of a way of life in conflict with urban, white cultural values. If we consider that small-town and native Canada comprise cultures distinct from urban Canada, and if we value those differences, we must slide past the economic question and ask the more profound cultural question: what will Cancom do for Canada?

FRONTIERS OF TECHNOLOGY

The various technologies discussed so far are relatively recent but they are all in place in Canada or elsewhere. Other technologies are finding their way into business markets and, in some cases, the home market. Before we look at these new frontiers, a few words about technology itself are necessary.

Technology is capable of structuring markets on the basis of its power as a tool and also because of its design and its allure. The design aspect can be illustrated with satellites. An investment by the Canadian government in DBS satellites of the same power and capacity as the Americans' would keep Canadian communications in an add-on relationship to the American system. The use of a different technological type or power of satellite would separate our services from theirs. Presumably that would give us more power to direct our own future. But it might also backfire by encouraging Canadians to purchase equipment to receive only American signals directly.

The allure of technology captures both regulators and individual citizens (McNulty, 1988). We are often in danger of spending more on the delivery system than on the content to make the delivery system justifiable, just in order to have the latest and best technology. For example, the per student (note, not per viewer) costs of the Knowledge Network delivery system in British Columbia are astronomical. Costs of such a magnitude would be unthinkable in the province's three universities. Yet the allure of satellite distribution of educational services not even available on basic cable in the Vancouver area is there.

New electronic communications technology also has an anti-democratic element to it. In addition to its centralizing tendency, the emplacement of technology has the potential for creating information have-nots. For example, Lyman proposes that the CBC abandon its microwave broadcast system in favour of a satellite-to-cable or satellite-to-local rebroadcast system (STV or Subscription Television). If basic cable does not come free and if it is not universally available, this is untenable. Certainly for the CBC to abandon its broadcast signal without universal free cable or its equivalent in services everywhere in Canada would be socially regressive.

But on to the frontiers. The digitalization of information of all kinds is proceeding apace. Monthly, if not weekly, we are faced with yet another development, large or small. Sitting in the wings, as it was four years ago, but apparently closer to crashing into the consumer market is high-definition television (HDTV), which provides a clearer picture by employing 1,125 as opposed to 525 scanning lines. The picture is sufficiently improved to allow projection on an 8.5 x 11-foot screen. High-definition television may completely alter the delivery system of movies to theatres as well as change the viability of the theatre itself. Movies may be delivered by satellite for projection after descrambling or decoding.

The difficulties with HDTV are twofold. First, there has not been an agreement on world standards. The Americans and the Japanese are each vying for their system. Second, HDTV is, in a technical sense, very information-rich. Transmitted by satellite, it requires a great amount of transponder space. Similarly, each station would take up a good chunk of the radio spectrum. However, if space platforms with vast expansion numbers of transponders come into being, or if a vast expansion of optical fibres is laid, or if further means can be found for signal compression, HDTV may become the standard for home reception. Home reception, in response, will undoubtedly include much larger screens. Think of it, a theatre in every home!

Digital audio broadcasting or DAB is also on the horizon and will likely take over within the next ten years. Why is this likely? Because, like the production of compact discs in comparison with LPs, it is a cheaper way to go. According to the Canadian Association of Broadcasters, the new technology offers the same quality of sound as other digital technologies like the compact disc, it is cheaper to transmit, and all signals can fit on one radio band. Tests are currently being conducted and standards, as well as spectrum allocation, are being discussed by the World Administrative Radio Conference (WARC).

The area filled with opportunity, mainly because of the widespread acceptance of personal computers, is *interactive services.* Canadian consumers were first introduced to interactive services through Telidon, Canada's version of videotex, an encoding-decoding device that can stand alone or be hooked up to the home television set and from there, via cable, to a computer with a central database. The idea of Telidon (see Lorimer, 1990) was that Canadians would have immediate electronic access to vast storehouses of information with up-to-the-minute accuracy. It didn't quite work out.

We have, however, come a long way since the days of Telidon. Few children do not have contact with video games. Like Telidon, video games are a form of interactive service. But perhaps more significantly, few offices are without interactive capability, whether it be a local area network (LAN) of computers, access to a larger mainframe at company headquarters or at a database company, or to such services as are provided via INet 2000. The whole of the academic community works not only through a worldwide system of electronic mail but also in interaction with mainframe computers generally resident at their home institutions. Similarly, professionals such as doctors, lawyers, and engineers are computerizing and availing themselves of on-line (which is to say, interactive) services.

These developments, considered as a whole, are resulting in fundamental changes in the way society can work and is working. Some sense of how powerful these changes are comes from visionary predictions of a few years back. Back then communications gurus were predicting the end of the book, the end of the office, the end of work patterns as we knew them. The predicted dramatic change has not happened, although certain pockets of change can be found in work patterns. On the whole, however, change has been incremental, but it has been more substantial than it might at first seem. In the remaining part of this chapter, we will provide an account of some current thinking on the impact of communications technology on modern society. Two books are key to this account, *The Pay-Per Society* by Vincent Mosco and Mark Hepworth's *The Geography of the Information Economy.*

A MATTER OF INVENTION

Everyone understands that we invent technology. Technology is the application of science, the translation of scientific principles into mechanisms, from steam engines to microchips. What fewer people realize is that we also invent society. (The closest we come to a discussion of this phenomenon is in Chapter 5.) Technological invention and social invention come together in the following manner. As we develop whole new areas of technology in response to perceived social needs, for instance motorized transportation and print or electronic-based communications, we create the necessity to invent social institutions to ensure that society as a whole benefits. For example, printing presses and books were marvelous inventions of communication that made knowledge much more accessible to a wider group in society. But in the early days of the industrial revolution, books were unaffordable to many wage labourers. Thus a social invention in the form of ownership collectives was formed from which individuals could borrow books. Eventually this idea was taken up by the state to form the modern public library. (This is the beginning concept for an exploration of these issues in the Simon Fraser University-produced video, *Information, Technology and Democracy: Breakdown on the Electronic Highway.*

Western society is distinguished by its embrace of technology, a wholehearted embrace ever since the days of Sir Francis Bacon (1561-1626). Even though some theorists, such as Ellul, have misgivings about the technologization of modern society, technology is absolutely central to its operation. The most we could do would be to slow it down or to insist on making informed choices. In this regard, the approach proposed by Julie James Bailey, to require cultural impact statements for new technological proposals, may be a wise move (Bailey, 1990). But as biotechnology continues to be seen to "hold such promise" and the place of nations in the world economy is profoundly affected by who is first to develop new technology, such a slow-down is unlikely. A turn-around is probably absolutely impossible.

Given that we are firmly in the clutches of this technological imperative, we must strive to understand the most fundamental elements of an area of technology and what inherent tendencies there are in its application. Then we must invent such laws and institutions to develop technology so that it is as universally benefi-

cial as possible. In communications, patent and copyright laws and acts covering information, education, libraries, the arts, broadcasting and telecommunications are key. All the institutions that derive from those laws and acts are also crucial.

The two fundamental aspects of communications enhanced by communications technology are: (1) the separation of information about an entity or phenomenon from the entity itself, and (2) the reorganization of space and power that results from that separation.

The separation function can be explained as follows. A farmer who has grown up and has years of experience in a particular locale has access to a vast storehouse of knowledge expressed in behaviour, feelings, superstitions, and articulated understandings that can retrieve the past, explain the present, and foretell the future of that locale. Such is the wisdom of elders and locals, and thus have many observant farmers succeeded over the past hundred years. As opposed to even ten years ago, however, agricultural researchers with access to a fairly powerful computer, sophisticated mathematical models, years of old records, and several years of detailed data gathered by communications satellite through infrared monitoring can likewise retrieve some of the past, explain the present, and foretell the future. Such is the power of formal knowledge, communications, and information-processing.

The separation between a phenomenon and information descriptive of it allows a reorganization of the spatial relation connected with the phenomenon concerned. Most significantly, it allows a shift in control from a multiplicity of scattered points, each proximate to a phenomenon, to a central location that controls activities in a far-flung hinterland. As the information gathered increases – and it has increased enormously with digitalization, computers, information-gathering satellites, transmission capability, and information-processing capacity – the degree to which effective control can be exercised also increases.

Once the central processing centre has gained appropriate levels of information, it can begin to replace the on-location decision-maker. But the central processing centre can also introduce a further level of sophistication. It can bring in information about other locations, e.g., the state of world production of a certain crop, the state of markets, or even the state of government subsidies in other countries. It may even be able to predict more accurately events based on distant but related events.

This wider variety of information at the centre places greater power at the centre and tends to lessen the influence of the on-location expert. In fact, it may transform that person from a decision-maker into a person who responds to centralized analyses, a process sometimes called *deskilling*. Thus the potato farmer in P.E.I. who grows for McCain no longer choose what variety, how much to plant, what fertilizers to use, and so forth. He or she grows in a prescribed way under contract a predetermined tonnage of a particular variety. This is a relatively beneficial example of centralized decision-making that guarantees a predictable income. However, when the prairie wheat farmer cannot hope to break even because two central information-processing giants, the United States and Europe, are having a war over agricultural subsidies, the beneficial aspects of centralized information and decision-making power disappear. The benefits of centralized information-gathering and analysis also disappear rather dramatically when the central information source is wrong, as it has been often in managing the Atlantic and Pacific fisheries. Also, in spite of their imperfections, centralized information centres have a tendency to increase the exploitation of a resource. Thus, when mistakes are made, hundreds of hinterland producers may lose their livelihood.

The social and economic impacts of separation of information and entity are even more crucial. First, information itself becomes a separate product that can be bought and sold. Second, increased power accrues to the information centre.

A third implication deriving from this separation and centralization is an extension of the market into activities previously outside market forces. When rubber trees were discovered in Brazil and the properties of rubber were made known to Europeans, parts of the Amazon were transformed from untamed jungle into hinterland rubber farms and an integral part of the market system of Europe. When saplings were spirited out of the region and transplanted to a more human-hospitable climate, the jungle took over once again, as did the bats in the opera house in Manaus. Today, armed with the knowledge of Oriental tastes for mushrooms and antlers, some Canadians take to the woods in certain seasons and transform the countryside into an Oriental hinterland, at least for a short period.

An example of the extension of the market into a new area that involves only information and communication is illustrated in Tables 9.5 and 9.6. These tables record the behaviour of the consumer magazine industry in Canada over the past year. Think of what this new information product tells about not only the magazine industry but also the preoccupations of Canadian society. These tables create an information commodity that can be sold to a wide variety of organizations and individuals for whom it is valuable. Obviously such data are only one piece of the puzzle, but certainly they comprise a very interesting piece.

TABLE 9.5 Per Cent Change of Ad Pages Sold by Canadian Consumer Magazines, December, 1988, to November, 1990

	Months monitored during 12-month period ending		Total ad pages during 12-month period ending		
	Nov.'89	Nov.'90	Nov.'89	Nov.'90	% Change
Women's Service					
Canadian Living*	12	12	1,080	1,130	+4.6%
Chatelaine*	12	12	1,233	1,067	-13.5%
Homemaker's*	7	8	244	318	+30.3%
Recipes Only*	7	8	181	166	-8.3%
Images	6	6	212	221	+4.2%
You/Verve	4	4	114	95	-16.7%
Madame au Foyer	7	8	194	223	+14.9%
Bien Manager*	7	8	163	150	-8.0%
Châtelaine*	12	12	1,080	921	-14.7%
Coup de Pouce	12	12	944	908	-3.8%
Coup de Pouce Extra	4	3	63	36	-42.9%
L'Essentiel	12	12	252	290	+15.1%
Femme Plus	12	12	292	234	-19.9%
Women's Fashion					
Domino	4	4	270	185	-31.4%
Flare*	12	12	1,068	965	-9.6%
Toronto Life Fashion	9	7	644	537	-16.6%
Clin D'Oeil	12	12	1,532	1,082	-29.4%
Elle Québec[1]	3	12	253	850	-
Business					
Canadian Business	12	12	866	782	-9.7%
Financial Post Magazine[2]	12	11	428	370	-13.6%
Report On Business	12	12	804	804	-
Profit[3]	11	11	519	380	-26.8%
Enroute	12	12	798	754	-5.5%
A+	10	10	545	494	-9.4%
Commerce	12	12	912	764	-16.2%
General Interest					
Maclean's*	12	12	1,828	1,623	-11.2%
Reader's Digest*	12	12	781	737	-5.6%
Saturday Night*	12	10	394	243	-38.3%
Time*	12	12	2,119	1,940	-8.4%
TV Guide*	12	12	1,876	1,608	-14.3%
L'Actualité*[4]	12	12	1,083	1,307	+20.7%
Selection Du Reader's Digest*	12	12	619	585	-5.5%
TV Hebdo*	12	12	1,533	1,474	-3.8%

Shelter/Special Interest/Lifestyle

Cdn. House & Home	6	8	448	529	+18.1%
City & Country Home*	10	10	525	580	+10.5%
Homes	8	8	364	312	-14.3%
Select Homes & Foods[5]	8	8	332	258	-22.3%
Décoration Chez Soi	10	10	722	688	-4.7%
Decormag	10	10	561	482	-13.3%
Les Idées De Ma Maison	11	10	964	764	-20.7%
Renovation Bricolage	11	10	411	344	-16.3%
Angler & Hunter	10	10	160	191	+19.4%
Ont. Out Of Doors	10	10	320	348	+8.8%
Outdoor Canada	8	9	363	316	-12.9%
Harrowsmith	6	6	374	352	-5.9%
Equinox	6	6	351	354	+0.9%
Canadian Geographic	6	6	128	163	+27.3%
Destinations	6	8	230	333	+44.8%

NOTE: The figures refer to twelve-month monitoring periods ending in November, 1989, and November, 1990. The numbers beside each title indicate the number of months (not issues) the title was monitored. These numbers vary depending on the magazine's publishing schedule, whether it was a new launch during the monitoring period, or whether it folded during the monitoring period.

*Publication has provided data to accommodate regional ads.
1. Launched September, 1989. 2. Formerly *Moneywise;* renamed May, 1990. 3. Formerly *Small Business;* renamed November, 1990. 4. Increased frequency from monthly to fortnightly in March, 1990. 5. *Canadian Living Food* merged with *Select Homes* in October, 1989.

SOURCE: *Masthead, The Magazine about Magazines,* January, 1991. Used with permission of The Auditor and Masthead magazine.

TABLE 9.6 Per Cent Change in Circulation by Canadian Magazines, September, 1989, to September, 1990

Publication	Total Paid	Total Nonpaid	% change vs. Sept. ' 89
Canadian	-	141,155	+18.3%
EnRoute	-	133,342	-5.2%
Pets	325	58,523	-3.2%
Cycle Canada	30,222	927	-11.1%
Moto Journal[1]	15,398	428	+39.6%
World of Wheels	35,857	92,211	-30.3%
Best Wishes*	2,600	141,330	+0.2%
C'est Pour Quand?*	-	50,372	+3.8%

Mère Nouvelle	-	43,275	+0.4%
New Mother*	-	164,775	+5.3%
Great Expectations	1,221	151,187	+2.9%
Mon Bébé*	-	49,201	+3.7%
The Port Hole	-	26,098	+19.8%
Today's Bride[2]*	26,820	77,773	+4.2%
Wedding Bells	29,259	70,884	-0.4%
A+	96,863	293	+0.6%
Hamilton	669	37,509	-0.5%
Highlights	-	38,536	+8.9%
Lethbridge[3]	222	17,252	-5.0%
London	-	45,215	+1.8%
MTL (English)[4]	-	56,479	+12.6%
MTL (French)[5]	548	71,299	+9.9%
Moving To (Toronto)*	-	41,500	-1.3%
Okanagan Life[6]	78	16,267	-12.7%
Ottawa	1,233	43,448	-2.1%
Vancouver	2,005	74,205	+3.4%
Network	-	150,000	-
Tribute	-	300,800	-0.6%
Wine Tidings	23,336	1,851	+1.3%
Cottage Life	39,489	36,507	+3.5%
Going Places	81,190	26	+2.0%
Goodlife	-	270,256	-0.1%
Legion	528,639	836	-0.3%
Leisure Ways	576,203	37	+12.5
Ontario Living	-	52,047	+2.0%
Touring	390,207	-	+10.5%
Western Living	1,804	254,739	+2.7%
Westworld Alta.	284,395	65	-
Westworld B.C.	406,996	34	-
Westworld Sask.	103,497	71	-
Today's Health	10,174	396,410	+706.9%
Country Estate	1,417	69,030	+6.3%
Decormag[7]	18,383	42,275	-4.8%
Habitabec Montreal	-	108,350	-36.5%
Homes	-	96,809	+3.5%
Real Estate News[8]	-	90,378	+0.4%
Age d'Or/V.N.	11,169	30,962	-1.2%
Snow Goer's Guide	18,625	122,918	-3.6%
Primetime[9]	-	204,745	-72.3%

Super Ecran	-	130,800	-6.0%
TV Week	77,332	5,026	+2.6%
Homemaker's	-	1,300,127	+0.7%
Madame au Foyer	-	304,959	-2.3%
Today's Parent	37,489	98,818	+32.3%
Woman to Woman	44,584	1,024	-1.3%
You/Verve	84,011	119,899	+1.1%
TG	1,610	95,349	-40.4%
Campus Canada	-	95,800	-1.2%

NOTE: Figures from the Canadian Circulation Audit Board, September, 1990, period. Only magazines with comparative data are listed.

*Publisher produces statement annually in March. Figures shown are for March, 1990, period.

NOTES 1-9: Average circulation for the six-month period exceeds +/-5 per cent of issue analysed. 1. Average circulation for the six-month period is 12,800. 2. 97,712. 3. 16,469. 4. 51,415. 5. 61,161. 6. 15,306. 7. 56,407. 8. 85,516. 9. 394,885.

SOURCE: *Masthead, The Magazine about Magazines,* January, 1991. Used with permission of The Auditor and Masthead magazine.

THE GEOGRAPHY OF THE INFORMATION ECONOMY

Mark Hepworth has explored some of the geographical manifestations of communications technology in *The Geography of the Information Economy.* Now working in England, Hepworth did much of his initial research in Canada. He described the evolution of the physical location of modern businesses in the context of developments in information technology.

One example Hepworth discusses is that of the individual firm. He uses *The Globe and Mail* as a case in point. *The Globe* has always attempted to appeal to the elite of Toronto, a city that sees itself as and to some extent is the industrial centre of Canada. In appealing to this upscale market, it is continuously vulnerable to forays by other Toronto papers, especially the *Toronto Star,* a much higher circulation mid-market broadsheet that regularly produces Saturday editions of over 100 pages.

Much of the content carried by *The Globe* has always been of interest outside Toronto; however, the difficulty has been cheap and timely delivery of that information. So, in 1978 *The Globe* set up a research and development collaboration with the *Los Angeles Times* and in October of 1980 began beaming up from Toronto an electronic facsimile to a communications satellite, which was beamed down again to Vancouver, Calgary, Brandon, Ottawa, and Moncton. Hepworth's diagrams (Figures 9.4 and 9.5) show how the operation works. The result in circulation figures is that sales outside Ontario have risen from 20,000 to about 150,000. Were the paper, which now calls itself "Canada's National Newspaper," to increase its non-Toronto content and actually to identify the location of stories for readers, its sales would doubtless

FIGURE 9.4 The Organization of Computer Network-Based Newspaper Production

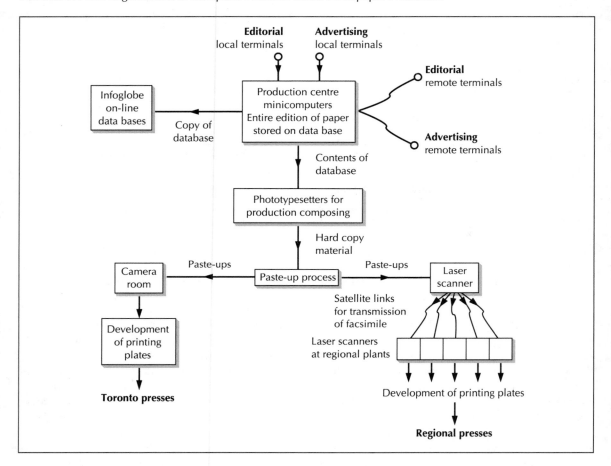

increase further. Hepworth reports also that the costs of the out-of-Toronto edition have been cut and the size of the paper increased.

The Globe and Mail is not the only paper to be operating in this manner. To name just a few, the *Wall Street Journal* and *USA Today* not only distribute copies within North America by satellite, they do the same for Europe. Similarly, the London-based *Financial Times* and the *China Daily News* are imported to the U.S. by satellite. When Robert Maxwell and Conrad Black were each trying to buy the *Jerusalem Post,* the purchase price appeared to indicate that both contemplated satellite delivery to centres around the world that might be interested in news from Israel.

FIGURE 9.5 The Globe and Mail Network

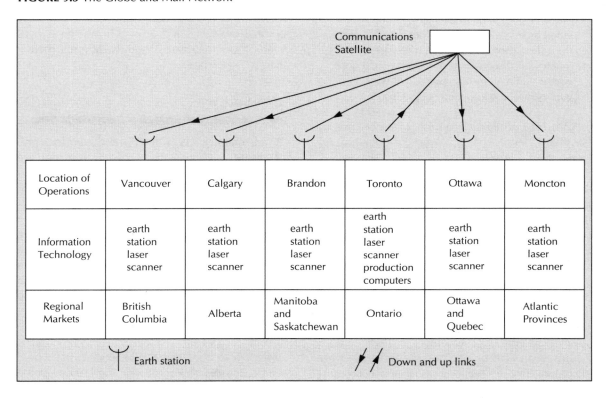

Location of Operations	Vancouver	Calgary	Brandon	Toronto	Ottawa	Moncton
Information Technology	earth station laser scanner	earth station laser scanner	earth station laser scanner	earth station laser scanner production computers	earth station laser scanner	earth station laser scanner
Regional Markets	British Columbia	Alberta	Manitoba and Saskatchewan	Ontario	Ottawa and Quebec	Atlantic Provinces

Earth station   Down and up links

A second, much changing area that Hepworth discusses is financial markets. Traditionally, firms have offered shares and other investment opportunities on a particular stock market in the country of their head office. Since the major stock exchanges of the world have become electronic and can be monitored from any location, not only does it become possible for traders to participate in markets far from where they are located, but also trading can take place during the working hours of many different stock exchanges. Putting together the trading hours of a variety of exchanges, for example, London, New York, and Tokyo, allows for a 24-hour trading day. Combined with more flexible rules about trading, this encourages wider participation and makes possible worldwide trading services for those who care to make the investment in communications technology. In short, parallel to our example of the farmer, Knight (1984, p. 15) notes:

In the days of domestic trading and before the technological era, [stock trading] information was best provided by people meeting in one place at particular times using facilities provided by a stock exchange floor. . . . It is clear the international capital markets lie not so much with those who provide a physical floor where trading can take place, but with those who control the information systems.

Which companies benefit? According to Stonham (1987, p. 13), so far 24-hour trading goes on in a few large companies. "The names involved [in Europe] are predictable so far: large companies like ICI, BAT and Glaxo from the U.K.; Honda, Hitachi, and Matsushita from Japan, Royal Dutch Shell and Phillips from the Netherlands." On the other hand, the market for on-line financial information is growing by 30 per cent per year (Hepworth, 1989, p. 174).

Other developments follow scenarios parallel to what we have outlined for *The Globe* and for financial markets. For example, information services have been seized by some municipal governments as the basis for inner-city regeneration. Multinational firms are beginning to plan for flexibility between national locations in production to respond to labour costs, labour unrest, exchange rates, and so forth. Hepworth argues that the delivery of components "just in time" for them to be used, as opposed to accepting deliveries well ahead of time and stockpiling to ensure supply when needed, represents a trade of information for material capital.

Perhaps the most controversial claim Hepworth makes is that information centres need not be located next to manufacturing centres. While true, it is also the case that all the services – financial, labour, and transportation – are in place for control in traditional centres of manufacture. While new industries may choose deliberately to locate elsewhere, and some clearly have, the pace of change is not excessively rapid. However, if municipal governments in favoured

climatic locations are aggressive in selling themselves, and office rents continue to rise in old control centres, the banks willing, growth of head offices may take a slightly different pattern than it has to date.

SUMMARY

This chapter has outlined the dimensions and some of the specifics of change that are being brought about through the development of new communications technologies. New technologies are changing the structure of the communications environment. As that structure changes, old industries and regulations are being placed in jeopardy while new opportunities are emerging. It is important that we understand the nature of these changes so that Canada and Canadians participate as fully as possible in the new communications environment.

On the basis of what we have reviewed here and what has been written more broadly on the subject, a strategy can be developed that would seem capable of working for the benefit of the Canadian industry and Canadians as a whole. The practicality of the matter is another issue. As we mentioned, not only are certain interests within the industry in conflict with such a national strategy, but foreign producers will be sure to act vigorously to protect their share of the Canadian market.

A parallel exploration of these issues has been created in a set of three papers by Edwards (1988), Strick (1988), and Overduin (1988). Edwards focuses on a national policy for development in telematics or computer communications. Strick analyses the opportunities that a free market will present for Canadians in the development of satellites and associated telecommunications technologies. Overduin discusses the interaction between professional roles and technological opportunities. As a group, they are a useful supplement to this chapter.

With respect to the material presented in this chapter, in spite of domestic and foreign competition, it would appear that as a result of a number of different developments, there is a very positive outlook for Canadian independent television producers. The emergence of new buyers with limited capital for program production, CBC cutbacks, and expansion of public funding to independent production through Telefilm Canada are all part of that outlook. In the face of estimates of what Canadians spend on entertainment, the federal government seems to have a steady resolve not to allow such consumption to be a continuing drain on the economy. Ultimately, increased production cannot fail to have some positive cultural benefit for Canadians. However, realizing that benefit will be difficult in an environment that requires that foreign sales always be calculated into the profitability formula.

From a cultural and political perspective, the international picture is fraught with difficulties. Foreign cultural products from industrial countries threaten to inundate the globe, whether via satellite signals, legitimate distribution, or pirate operations. While international agreements may be signed to stem the tide to some degree, the general movement in trade is in the opposite direction. That movement will continually work against national cultural interests and in favour of the economic interests of producers. In balance, given Canada's capacity for production, we may neither suffer nor gain culturally from such a situation. Economically, we have a better chance to gain. Larger producers have more to gain while smaller producers have much to lose, both economically and culturally.

Domestically, as illustrated by Cancom, the changes now happening are working toward the increased distribution of centre-produced materials to rural hinterlands. The effects of such increases remain to be seen.

REFERENCES

Babe, R. "Emergence and development of Canadian communication: dispelling the myths," in R. Lorimer and D.C. Wilson, *Communication Canada.* Toronto: Kagan and Woo, 1988.

Babe, R. *Telecommunications in Canada.* Toronto: University of Toronto Press, 1990.

Beale, A. "The question of space: transportation in relation to communication with some implications for broadcasting," in Lorimer and Wilson, eds., *Communication Canada.*

Bruce, Robert R., J.P. Cunard, and M.D. Director. *From Telecommunications to Electronic Services: A Global Spectrum of Definitions, Boundary Lines and Structures.* Report of the Study of Telecommunications Structures: International Institute of Communications, London. Toronto: Butterworths.

Canada. *Report of the Task Force on Broadcasting Policy.* Ottawa: Ministry of Supply and Services, 1986.

Communication Research Trends, 4, 2 (1983).

Dizard, Wilson P. *The Coming Information Age: An Overview of Technology, Economics and Politics.* New York: Longman, 1985.

Edwards, L. "Telematics in Canada: The Vanishing Opportunity," in Lorimer and Wilson, eds., *Communication Canada.*

Ellul, Jacques. "The Technological Order," *Technology and Culture,* 3 (Fall, 1962).

Frum, Linda, ed. *The Newsmakers.* Toronto: Key Porter, 1990.

Grant, George. *Technology and Empire.* Toronto: Anansi, 1969.

Hepworth, Mark. *The Geography of the Information Economy.* London: Belhaven Press, 1989.

Hylton, John, and J. Fraser Mann. "International Copyright Agreements and the Need for a New Legal Framework," *Broadcaster* (August, 1983).

Knight, J. "The interconnection of European stock exchanges," *The Stock Exchange Quarterly* (December, 1984), pp. 14-16.

Laba, M. "Popular Culture as Local Culture: Regions, Limits, and Canadianism," in Lorimer and Wilson, eds., *Communication Canada*.

Lorimer, R., ed. *Creating Information and Ideas.* Calgary: Detselig, 1991.

Luyken, Georg-Michael. "New Communications Technology and Global Information Handling," in J. Sack and F. Frejes, eds., *The Ideology of the Information Age.* Norwood, N.J.: Ablex Publishing, 1984.

Lyman, Peter. *Canada's Video Revolution.* Toronto: James Lorimer, 1983.

Machlup, Fritz. *The Production and Distribution of Knowledge in the United States.* Princeton, N.J.: Princeton University Press, 1962.

McNulty, Jean. "Ideas about Technology and Nation-Building in Canadian Broadcasting," in Lorimer and Wilson, eds., *Communication Canada*.

Mosco, Vincent. *The Pay-Per Society: Computers and Communication in the Information Age.* Toronto: Garamond, 1989.

Overduin, H. "Westex News: A Case Study of an Experiment into Journalism of the Future," in Lorimer and Wilson, eds., *Communication Canada*.

Paltridge, Sam. *Australian Satellites: Promises, Performance and the Next Generation.* Mel-bourne: Centre for International Research on Communication and Information Technologies, Policy Research Paper No. 1, 1989.

Plant, Christopher. "PEACECAT and Development in the Pacific Islands," M.A. thesis, Simon Fraser University, 1980.

Queeney, Kathryn M. *Direct Broadcast Satellites and the United Nations.* Alphen aan den Rijn: Sijthoff and Noordhoff, 1978.

Rothblatt, Martin A. "International Orbit Spectrum/ Spectrum Development Policy and the Growth of Geostationary Satellite Communications," *Journal of Media Law and Practice,* 12, 2 (September, 1981).

Sauvé, J. "Notes for a Speech to the Canadian Cable Association," Toronto, June 2, 1976.

Schiller, H.I. *Information and the Crisis Economy.* Norwood, N.J.: Ablex Publishing, 1984.

Smith, Anthony. *The Geopolitics of Information.* London: Faber and Faber, 1980.

Snow, Marcellus S. "INTELSAT: An International Example," *Journal of Communications,* 30, 2 (Spring, 1980).

Stonham, P. *Global Stock Market Reports.* Alder-shot: Gower, 1987.

Strick, J.C. "Socio-Economic Influence of Satellite Communications Technology," in Lorimer and Wilson, eds., *Communication Canada*.

Valaskakis, G. "Television and Cultural Integration," in Lorimer and Wilson, eds., *Communication Canada*.

Williams, R. *Television: Technology and Cultural Form.* New York: Schocken Books, 1975.

STUDY QUESTIONS

1. New communications technologies are continually being developed and introduced. What factors tend to influence their introduction in Canada? Refer to specific technologies in your answer.

2. "Underpinning all the media and communications systems in general is the technological base. The creation of new technology, its management, and its distribution are the ultimate tests of modern power and the ability to dominate." (H. Schiller) Discuss this statement.

3. Does Canada need communications satellites?

CHAPTER

10

The Global Geopolitics of Information

INTRODUCTION: JOURNALISM IN HISTORICAL PERSPECTIVE

I N THE OPENING chapter of *The Geopolitics of Information,* Anthony Smith quotes a speech given to the Manchester Chamber of Commerce by the famous explorer-journalist, H.M. Stanley, the man who found Livingstone in "deepest Africa."

> There are 50 millions of people beyond the gateway to the Congo, and the cotton spinners of Manchester are waiting to clothe them. Birmingham foundries are glowing with the red metal that will presently be made into iron-work for them and the trinkets that shall adorn those dusky bosoms, and the ministers of Christ are zealous to bring them, the poor benighted heathen, into the Christian fold.

Smith notes that, far from being a servant of some set of business interests, Stanley was first and foremost a newsman.

> His professional integrity was unassailable. But his information was collected under the

inspiration of a socially accepted doctrine of colonialism, in which the pursuit of loot, markets and the Christian faith were subsumed into a single quest, which was undoubtedly emotionally uplifting for his audience in imperial England. (Smith, 1980, p. 25)

Smith's example is not atypical of the attitude to the gathering of information and its transformation into news at the height of the British Empire. Nor is it atypical of all the information-gathering services the British had at their disposal. A review of nineteenth-century studies of "exotic" societies reveals a rendering of whole cultures through the eyes of colonialists. Indeed, Smith makes the claim that the Stanley example is simply a reading of the world view of the dominant culture.

Contemporary Equivalents

The penetration of the interests of the information-gathering culture into the information-gathering process has not abated in modern times. While those interests may be expressed less blatantly, they are nevertheless as present now as they were in Stanley's days. Consider CBC foreign correspondent Brian Stewart's discussion and examples.

> The American networks have a clear mindset. What does it mean for Washington? How will the president handle this? How will it affect our relations abroad? It is a kind of imperial outlook, easy to develop if you're a superpower. In a sense it's easier to write for the Amnets because the focus is always so sharp. In international relations, if it doesn't affect the U.S. it scarcely exists.
>
> As a Canadian reporter you're much more anxious to paint the broad picture; you usually are not much concerned with Ottawa's reaction, as Canada is often peripherally involved.

> You can go to town on the intricacies of the power relationships – and your editors back home have a greater patience for the soft shadings of the story.
>
> For example: covering Lebanon for the Canadians you can delve into interfactional rivalries and cultural differences; the Amnets will fret about whether U.S. forces will be dragged in, or how Israel will cope. When I went to the Southern Sudan for NBC and came back with clear evidence that a massive famine was starting, NBC stuck it on a shelf for two weeks before slipping it on as a closing item on a weak news night. It wasn't part of their focus. The CBC would have led with it. (Frum, 1990)

Third World nations have claimed for some time that the manner in which the developed world collects information continually puts the developing nations at risk by portraying them according to Western, developed-world news values instead of evaluating them in their own context. Thus, in the eyes of those affected by the news, things have not changed. World views are still very much the foundation of the structuring of information in the news, as they are in all forms of knowledge.

Knowledge Is Organized To Serve the Interests of Those Who Collect It

The news is neither disinterested nor objective; nor is social science; nor, in fact, is science. *Knowledge is organized to serve the interests of those who collect it.* Reporters conceive of what information is to be sought, what elements of it are important, and how it should be discussed. For those who are written about and who have no access to telling their own story, the consequences are rather drastic. As Smith (p. 27) says: "To be imprisoned inside the misinterpretation and misunderstanding of others can be a withering form of incarceration. It is a fate which can afflict whole nations and cultures as painfully as individuals."

To understand the problems inherent in the dissemination of information we must know who the global collectors and distributors are. Also, we must know how their interests are reflected in the structure and content of global information.

The Free Press in an Open Society

As we have outlined in previous chapters, the doctrine of a free press and a free and open information system is entrenched in Western societies and is crucial to their continued existence as free and open societies.

As it is understood in Western countries, democratic rule requires that political parties be able to put their opinions before the electorate in order to gain the opportunity to govern a nation or region. Once one party has gained power, other parties still need to put their views forward, either as criticism or as alternative policies. In other words, in keeping with democratic principles, the ruling party is required to act in a way that is apparently not in its own interest but is in the interest of a democratic society. It must maintain a free press: it must maintain open access to the lines of communication in society so that the general population can inform itself about competing alternatives to the policies of the government in power.

Another important element of the notion of free and open information, as we have come to know it, is **the freedom of access to information, the right to know**. A free press requires open access to information governments collect and create so that informed comment can be made on their policies. It is not difficult to understand why access to information and the

freedom to publish are fragile freedoms when so much is at stake for those who have the power to restrict information access and flows.

The principle of a free press gives competing elites the right of access and allows comment on anything they might so choose, especially government policy. It provides the general public with a range of alternatives that can provide the basis for electing a government, taking broader political action, or, more generally, considering options and understanding society.

The freedom to inquire and to know and freedom of expression, however, are only part of the story. A further freedom has come to be associated with a free press – the freedom to make information and ideas known as widely as possible, that is, **the freedom to distribute information**. Essentially this is a freedom to pursue markets for information unencumbered by restrictive regulations. For a free press in the hands of private owners to operate in a capitalistic society, those gathering the information must be free to exploit their markets. They must be free to sell the fruit of their labours in information-gathering and interpreting to whomever might want it. This extension of the principles of a free press is known as **free flow of information.** It means that the press believes it must be free not only to gather information from anywhere but also to circulate it to anywhere a potential customer of the information might be found.

The whole sector of information industries is founded on the principle of access to information, freedom to publish, and freedom to exploit markets. The press and media empires of the Western world depend for their existence on these principles and are certainly not interested in any reformation for dealing with information that would undermine their operations. They are most vociferous in protecting these freedoms with respect to information-gathering and distribution. The principle of free flow also very conveniently protects their entertainment arms. While protecting information against restrictive policies, they can rather easily extend the principle to any cultural or information product, i.e., movies, books, television programming, etc.

As Smith points out, this leads us, increasingly quickly, into a conundrum. International agreements that create consistent policies worldwide for seeking and exploiting of information provide the foundation for the emergence of immense information and entertainment corporations. While these corporations serve the needs of equally immense countries, their size and power dwarf that of many small countries. The bargaining power of small countries to have their information needs attended to or even respected is slight.

So what does the global news and information system look like?

THE GLOBAL NEWS AGENCIES AS EMBODIMENTS OF A FREE PRESS

On any single day there is a high degree of similarity in the media in the coverage and treatment of stories. This is especially true with the international stories. The reason is that most papers and other news media subscribe to common sources for their foreign material, one or more of several global news agencies.

A Portrait of the Globals

Approximately 1,200 news agencies operate in the world; the four large Western agencies are Reuters, Agence France Presse (AFP), Associated Press (AP), and United Press International (UPI). Together these four agencies put out 34 million words per day and claim to provide nine-tenths of the entire foreign news output of the world's newspapers and radio and television stations

(Smith, 1980, p. 72). Other international agencies worth noting are the German agency, Tanjug of Yugoslovia, EFE of Spain, and Kyodo of Japan. There are also several regional or ideologically alternative agencies for the non-developed, non-capitalist world, such as ASIN, a Latin American and Caribbean news exchange pool, and NANAP, the Non-Aligned News Agency Pool (Boyd-Barrett, 1980). Table 10.1 provides information on the operations of these agencies as well as others of some influence, including TASS, the news agency of the Soviet Union.

Dominance by the Large and Non-Profitable

The Western agencies maintain dominance over the market by being large and non-profitable. AFP operates with indirect subsidies through the purchase of the service by offices within the French government. The other three agencies, Reuters, AP, and UPI, depend on a vast subscribership to support their operations, yet they make little profit. This low profit discourages other entrepreneurs and alliances of nations from setting up rival services that are able to break even. In other words, the agencies provide news so cheaply that no one else can compete. UPI itself seems continually on the verge of bankruptcy. Consequently, for its global coverage, much of the Western world has come to rely on one French, one British, and two American organizations to collect and wholesale international news. Beyond these agencies there are, of course, the television networks, the BBC, and the foreign correspondents of individual media outlets. But the global agencies are the dominant players and set the context for other information-gathering. A review of the dynamics and history of the news agencies and their relations to national govern-

TABLE 10.1

Some Internationally Active Agencies

Press Agency	Number of countries served	Number of subscribers	Number of countries covered by correspondents and stringers	Number of words issued daily	Number of regular staff	Number of correspondents in foreign countries
AP (U.S.A.)	108	1,320 newspapers 3,400 broadcasters in U.S. 1,000 private subscribers	62 foreign bureaus	17 million		559
UPI (U.S.A.)	92	7,079 newspapers 2,246 clients outside U.S.A. +36 national news agencies	81 foreign bureaus	11 million 200 news pictures	1,823	578
AFP (France)	152	12,000 newspapers 69 national agencies	167 countries 108 foreign bureaus	3,350,000 +50 news pictures	1,990 incl.	171 full-time corres. 1,200 stringers
Reuters (U.K.)	147	6,500 newspapers 400 radio and TV stations	153 countries	1,500,000	2,000 incl.	350 full-time corres. 800 stringers
TASS (U.S.S.R.)	80	13,000 subscribers 200 subscribers to TASS photo 325 foreign subscribers	110 countries 40 bureaus		professional staff 560	61 corres.
DPA (FRG)	78	144 foreign subscribers 55 film services	80 countries 37 film services	115,000	800 incl.	105 full-time corres.
ANSA (Italy)	69	1,600 (approx.)	69 bureaus	300,000	568 incl.	47 full-time corres. 295 stringers

Agency						
EFE (Spain)	32	1,734	52	500,000	545	123
Kyodo (Japan)	37	33 national agencies 40 foreign news agencies 64 Japanese newspapers 59 commercial radio and TV stations 14 non-members newspapers	37 bureaus	220,000 characters in Japanese 35,000 words in English	1,900	
Tanjug (Yugoslavia)	103		46	75,000 to 120,000 +40-50 news pictures	896 incl.	46 full-time corres.
IPS Inter Press Service (Latin America)	36	19 national agencies 400 newspapers, weeklies, and institutions	50	100,000	390	44
MENA (Middle East)	25	13 national agencies for exchange of news 21 national agencies for exchange of photos	35	185,000 200 documentary films 200 news pictures	500 incl. corres.	35 full-time

SOURCE: The World of News Agencies Working Paper No. 11 of the UNESCO Commission for the Study of Communication Problems, 1978.

ments points out why the identity of the agencies is so important.

The Colonial Roots of the Globals

Anthony Smith maintains it is impossible to examine the global news agencies without considering their relation to capitalism. He maintains that capitalism is as much an information system as a system of finance and productions, as we are beginning to see more clearly as we enter the "information age." The imperial nations of the nineteenth century accomplished the integration of the world's resources into the markets of Europe. Such an accomplishment depended as much on an information network as it did on physical resources and transportation. In fighting for privileged trading positions over a period of several hundred years, the various European nations became masters at seeing economic potential in the appetites of their compatriots and in the resources, human or physical, of newly "discovered" nations. So keen was their appetite that they were able to cast aside fraternal connections with human beings of different races, question whether they had souls, and, as if to decide the matter in advance, create slaves of them.

These same nations and nationals acquired a position as purveyors of information, whether of the mundane sort to the newspapers of the land or of the more esoteric variety, as, for example, Darwin's several works inspired by his travels on the ship *Beagle*.

These systems of transportation and information were the foundation of contact between Europe and other world civilizations. However, they were structured in such a way to benefit Europe. Europe defined itself not as a civilization that had created untenable living conditions for its population, thus forcing emigration onto the underprivileged, but as the colonizer, the spreader of the one true civilization and religion to a heathen and more or less empty world. For a time, the communication of information depended on its physical carriage along with goods and people from Europe to the colonies and back. Eventually, submarine cables, laid along sea routes, and cables across land outpaced the speed of physical carriage. The British especially were eager to put the latest and best communications technology in place to span their empire.

The news agencies built their routes on the backs of the colonial information system and transformed the whole scope of news dissemination. Founded by a Frenchman, Charles Havas, in 1835, the first news agency grew out of a translation agency that then sold its translations to newspapers. With the coming of the telegraph, the number of newspapers the agency could sell to increased enormously. With the primacy of national interests in the nineteenth century and the division of the world into various European "empires," other nationally based agencies soon emerged. The first two were begun by two of Havas's employees, Bernard Wolff (Germany) and Paul Julius Reuter (England).

Havas, Reuter, and Wolff were all expansionist entrepreneurs working at the edges and propelled by the energy of three European empires. The world was split three ways among them with Havas gaining monopoly control of Latin America, which he held from 1870 to 1920 when his monopoly was broken by the U.S.-based United Press Association. From his base in Britain, Reuter took over the Low Countries and moved into Austria, Greece, and the area surrounding the Black Sea. Thwarted by the refusal of *The Times* to use his service, he provided information for other, mostly provincial, British newspapers. His service was so creditable that he was allowed to use British government telegrams as a source of news from India.

Reuters was seen as an independent news service operating at arm's length from the British government; however, during the First World War, the managing director of Reuters doubled as director of propaganda.

The Entry of the Americans

The First World War brought the United States and the American news agencies onto the world stage. The obvious connections between the European agencies and their national governments and the virtual news blockade of Latin America provided the Americans with the opportunity to move out of their domestic confines. So successful have the Americans been in their operations that Smith claims that the whole of Latin America operates on the same news values as the U.S. The territorial monopolies have disappeared and been replaced with a scale of operations that ensures market dominance. As we noted earlier, the big four claim 90 per cent of the world's foreign news.

Since the entry of the American agencies during and following World War One, a variety of other agencies have attempted to gain a foothold in the international market. Some, such as the Chinese agency, Xinhua, have been national efforts, while others, representing numbers of developing countries, have been aided by UNESCO. Many of these latter agencies have exchange or service relations with parallel organizations in other regions and also with the larger agencies to give them access to world news in exchange for what they provide on the local scene.

Inevitable problems arise in the use that other countries and regions make of the material the regional agencies create. Smith cites the coverage of Surinam independence: not a single Latin American paper carried the story on its front page on Surinam's first day of independence,

November 26, 1975 (Smith, 1980, p. 71), despite Surinam being in South America. Apparently the absence of coverage was simply the result of the U.S. agencies not feeding the story. At times there are also problems of access to news sources for Third World agencies, which do not exist for the larger agencies. Such access problems are typical. When Canada's first astronaut was being interviewed shortly before he was launched into space, individual interviews were scheduled for Voice of America, AP, and UPI. Twenty minutes were set aside for all Canadian journalists (*Saturday Night,* March, 1985, p. 27).

The Performance of the News Agencies: The Bias of News Values

The most publicized shortcoming associated with the global agencies is the type of coverage given to Third World countries. The general view has been that there is an overemphasis on tragedy and disaster. Table 10.2 summarizes the actual pattern of coverage. A separate study carried out for UNESCO by Phil Harris of Leicester University found that the weakest aspect of the agency-created news story was the presentation of the Third World in a rather sketchy and ethnocentric form (Smith, 1980, p. 91). According to Western news values, only the unusual or exceptional is newsworthy. Such a definition favours the status quo and entrenched interests and provides a basis whereby society can continually restate its dominant ideology to the perpetual disadvantage of disenfranchised groups.

GLOBAL NEWS FLOWS

Hester (1974) identifies another major contributing factor to the distortion of the news from the Third World. While the defini-

TABLE 10.2

Subjects of AP Latin American News

Subject Categories	From Latin American Bureaus %	On U.S. AP Trunk Wire %
Accidents	5.01	2.34
Agriculture	0.86	1.36
Art, culture, and entertainment	1.16	0.00
Crime and criminal violence	13.81	47.66
Disasters	3.61	11.72
Domestic government and politics	15.65	14.06
Economics and business	7.58	2.34*
Education	1.04	0.00
Foreign relations	19.19	6.25
Human interest features	2.81	5.47
Labour	2.20	0.00
Military and defence	1.16	0.00
Miscellaneous	1.04	0.78
Prominent people	1.47	3.91
Religion	0.79	1.56
Science and medicine	1.34	2.34
Sports	23.23	0.00*
Totals (per cent)†	101.95	99.79
Number of items	1,636	128

* A few sports items were retransmitted on AP sports wires in the United States. A few business items were used on the AP-Dow Economic Wire.
† Totals do not equal 100 per cent because of rounding.
SOURCE: Al Hester, "International News Flows," in Alan Wells, ed., *Mass Communications: A World View* (Palo Alto: Mayfield Publishing, 1974). Reproduced with permission of the author.

tion of news causes journalists to select a certain minority of events out of the possible universe of events, several filtering or gatekeeping processes further select the material that ends up in the newspaper. What we see in our papers is the result of news values being applied several times over. They are applied by the global agencies, but are also applied by the reporters for the national bureaus, the national bureaus themselves, the media who subscribe to the agency services, and the individual users of the media. As they are successively applied by people who have a very limited knowledge of the country being discussed, it is easy to understand why certain subjects of AP Latin America News – such events as coups, floods, and debt defaults – are overrepresented. Hester points out the amplification of distortions at one site, between what arrives from the Latin American bureaus and what Associated Press puts on its trunk wire (Table 10.2).

Attempts to Compensate

Whoever shoulders the heaviest burden of guilt, the problem is recognized but the solution has yet to present itself. Few newspeople would deny the existence of a systematic distortion of what we in the developed world receive as news about the developing world. That distortion does indeed appear to come about through the definition of news. But the majority of newspeople would claim it is precisely that definition of news that sells papers and captures audiences for television. Soft news on development, for example, is not read. It is not even picked up by countries and regions in the Third World when it is provided. The relative lack of success the Soviets have had in their short-wave radio services compared to the BBC points to the crux of the problem in assessing how far one can go in using the media for the direct presentation of ideologically based issues. Smith discusses this problem in some depth and points out the efforts made by Tanjug, the Yugoslavian agency, to ensure a worldwide circulation of Third World news (see also Robinson, 1981).

There are two central issues with regard to the agencies. The first is the dominance the French, British, and Americans have over foreign news. The second is the perspective presented along with "the facts of the matter." If the U.S. government relies on ABC television news for information on foreign events, as a spokesperson for ABC claims in the television documentary *Inside TV News,* might we not assume that an American viewpoint pervades the operation? And if the BBC can be berated in the British House of Commons for failing to provide a sufficiently British perspective on the Falklands War, can we not assume there is a certain pressure on all journalists to maintain a national perspective? The answer seems to lie in Brian Stewart's comments quoted at the beginning of this chapter about his work

for NBC as opposed to the CBC. They are absolutely unambiguous in supporting the notion that any news organization reflects a set of values, often those of the primary audience for which it is providing news. Another indication can be found in a fairly widespread rumour that circulated in Canada during the Dubin inquiry into drug use in sports: that American television royalties to the Olympics would dry up if a major U.S. runner were exposed for testing positive for steroid use. The truth of the rumour did not matter as much as the fact that it seemed to be generally believed.

Smith uses the example of the overthrow of the shah of Iran to clinch the argument that the news agencies provide an ethnocentric perspective on foreign news. He points out that prior to the collapse of the Pahlavi dynasty, there was no inkling in the Western press that the "reforms brought in by the shah were progressively unacceptable to the people of the country. The Ayatollah Khomeini was portrayed, if at all, as a religious zealot and not given any credibility as a spokesperson of a firmly entrenched set of values. The British press reported on the jobs lost to British and American firms, ignoring the plight of the Iranians themselves. The land reforms that consolidated the shah's power did less than nothing for putting land in the hands of a greater number of people, and these reforms obliged the country to import 50 per cent of its food, where previously it had been self-supporting. In the American press, they were presented as positive modernizations. After thousands had been killed in riots during the shah's regime, it was still presented as having a broad base of popular support.

In general, a viewpoint emphasizing modernization versus reactionary religious zealotry was put forward. As AP put it late in 1978, "modernization has collided with ancient social and religious traditions whose proponents have refused to budge" (Smith, 1980, p. 99). Suppose a Canadian newspaper had reported at the end of the Trudeau era and after John Turner's failure to be elected Prime Minister that "liberalization and social development have collided with the traditional vested interests of business whose proponents have yet to come to grips with the 1980s." While no doubt some Canadians are of that opinion, it certainly distorts, as does the AP statement on Iran, the vibrancy of and popular support for the ideologies voiced by the governments both in Canada and in Iran.

A more recent example that has yet to be exposed is that of Romania and the Ceausescus. How a Stalinist dictator with a human rights record far worse than the majority of the Communist bloc could be so warmly embraced by the West prior to the collapse of communism in Eastern Europe points to the follies and tragedies that ideological rivalry can create. When the story is finally written detailing how the West propped up the Ceausescu regime and suppressed information about conditions within the country, there ought to be demands for safeguards against the repetition of such a sorry situation, a situation that has emerged once again, in the dealings of the West with Islam and, specifically, the arming of Iraq.

THE PRODUCERS AND CONSUMERS OF WORLD CULTURAL PRODUCTS

In the same way that world news is dominated by a few very large players, so are the entertainment industries, especially television and movie production. The difference is that the Americans play an even larger role than they do in the news agency business.

As Figure 10.1 shows, Canada is not alone in being an avid importer of the imagination industries of the U.S. and other countries. Many nations and virtually all of the Third World find themselves in exactly the same position. A close examination of Figure 10.1 also reveals an interesting pattern of importing and exporting reflective of the economic size and political alignments. It illustrates the difficulties for small and developing nations, both of which are net importers, when they trade in information and entertainment products. The pre-eminence of the United States in Western markets, followed by Western Europe, is notable. Equally notable is the pre-eminence of the Soviet Union with respect to Eastern Europe. Whether both these patterns will change substantially after 1992 with a more closely integrated Europe and sooner, with the falling away of communism in Eastern Europe, is yet to be seen. It would be surprising if they did not.

Consuming Exported Cultural Products

As with news, both the quantity and the quality of imported cultural products must be examined. In work done over the past few years, a number of students and Lorimer have pointed out the kind of content that finds its way into school learning materials not imported directly but adapted for use in Canada or created from "scratch" by branch plants of multinational companies.

- In certain elementary readers a preponderance of American authors tell American stories about American events in American settings.
- In others, only the non-fiction was written by Canadians. The fiction was written by Americans and a few Britons.
- In social studies, an emphasis on the process of inquiry pushed out a systematic treatment of concerted information that would be necessarily Canadian.

FIGURE 10.1

Domestic and Imported Television Programs

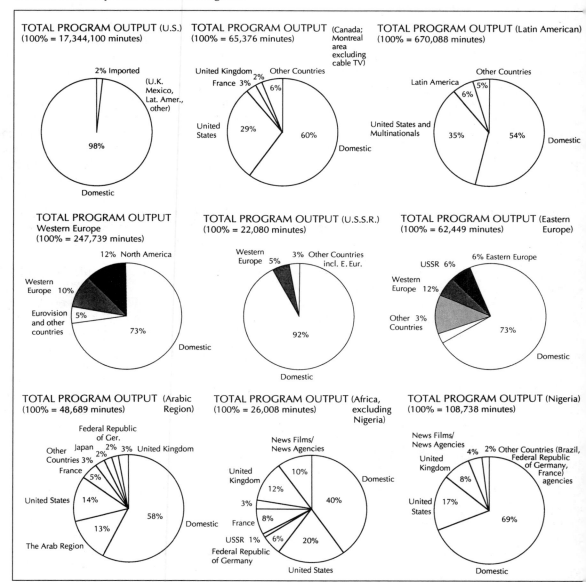

SOURCE: UNESCO, Reports and Papers on Mass Communication: Tapio Varis, No. 100 International Flow of Television Programs UNESCO, 1985.

- In a dictionary, American words such as the names of all the states of the U.S. were deleted in favour of an odd collection of substitutes such as "deke" and "micmac," the latter being described as a canoe rather than the indigenous people of the Atlantic region of Canada (Lorimer, 1984). Subsequent work showed that science books put forward a view of scientific investigation that eclipses the relevance of the subject matter to the student's life in favour of understanding the position of the scientific investigator (Carscallen, 1984).

More recent inquiry into the absence of Canadian content in school learning materials has focused beyond the identities of educational publishers and beyond the American-oriented traditions of Canadian education. The inadequacy of market demand mechanisms in comparison with the continental organization of production contributes to the lack of cultural character in Canadian school texts. Another contributing factor is the anti-cultural interpretation that has been given to the writings of the father of modern education, John Dewey, an interpretation that reflects the general social ideology of America (Lorimer and Keeney, 1988).

How To Read Donald Duck

Other investigators have examined entertainment products for their ideological content. One of the better-known studies of the introduction of ideology, in this case into comic books, is Dorfman and Mattelart's *How to Read Donald Duck: Imperialist Ideology in the Disney Comic*. The authors make a strong case for a high level of ideological intrusion into material assumed by most to be free of "political" content.

On the basis of an extensive review of some 200 Disney comics available in Latin America, Dorfman and Mattelart claim that the Disney world denies the political realm, yet simultaneously it has a clear politics, and that politics is profoundly personal, centring on personality characteristics and family interactions. Donald Duck leads the life of the idle rich, yet he has the consciousness of the dominated. He blames his constant unemployment on his personality, just as he sees the rich as "lucky" in that they seem to "attract wealth." Moreover, the rich are made morally legitimate by being unhappy victims of their own wealth. These politics are profoundly personal and highly adventuristic, but they lack the crucial nurturing elements of childhood, especially the guidance of child-parent relations. For Huey, Louie, and Dewey, it is not unlike a prettified Dickensian orphanage.

Other countries are presented in caricatures based on the very symbols those countries use to attract tourists. Such names as "Unsteadystan" (Vietnam), "Aztecland" (Mexico), "Inca Blinka" (Peru), and "Sphinxia" (Egypt) even mock Third World countries. More significantly, they provide a basis for a distorted self-knowledge, a device that divides Third World people among themselves in negative stereotypical understandings of one another. People who object to oppression are dismissed as eccentrics and egomaniacs with charisma, and are trivialized (e.g., Soy Bhien and Char Ming). Protest movements are portrayed as completely lacking in seriousness. The people can be totally diverted from their causes by a lemonade stand.

The exploitation of the Third World is legitimized from within a comparative context. The ducks, working with the unknowing participation of the natives, are contrasted to the up-front criminality of the Beagle Boys. The ducks, implicit citizens of the U.S., are put forward as representatives of "civilization, wealth and industrialization." As such, they lay claim to the treasures and resources of Third World backwaters that would merely be corrupted if they knew the value of their own wealth.

The politics of exploitation and, at times, of outright robbery and injustice are cleansed in the waters of innocence we normally attribute to the imaginative world of the child. It is justified implicitly as a process of civilizing and modernizing.

THE WORLD INFORMATION ORDER: A FREE PRESS IN A GLOBAL CONTEXT

In our examination of information generation and international information flows, several points have been made. The first is that information is gathered, organized, and distributed within a doctrine that applauds free access to information, freedom of expression, and the free flow or the freedom to distribute information. These notions are rooted in the liberal democracies of the industrialized world.

The major characteristic of these democracies is a sufficient political consensus to allow for the coexistence of a number of sets of confluent or overlapping interests. This coexistence is enshrined in information policy by the respect paid to press freedoms, a respect that allows for private ownership of the press and free inquiry, expression, and distribution. It is a stable society indeed that can hand over to the marketplace the generation and responsibility for distribution of ideas!

These freedoms have contributed to the political, social, and economic health of the developed world. However, their entrenchment has led to a lack of thorough understanding of the value and dynamics of other systems at both the practical and theoretical levels. For example,

the *potential* of a "free" press is often compared to the *realities* of a state press.

The global news agencies are a major element in the international operations of a "free" press. The agencies were built to serve the colonizing activities and the industrial development of Europe. Just as the New World was divided for its resources among the European powers, so it was similarly divided among the early European news agencies. World War One, as noted earlier, heralded an end to these territorial monopolies and the arrival of major American players.

The present overwhelming dominance of AP, UPI, Reuters, and AFP over the world's foreign news continues that colonization and has had unfortunate consequences for the developing world. Third World countries are represented to the developed world within news values that emphasize the exception over the rule. The citizens of Third World countries often know of each other through the unusual, or exception-oriented, information-gathering and editing processes of the developed world. Stories about them are written and edited by people who have sketchy and simplified notions of their countries and peoples. Myths are held to be true, as in the case of Iran and Romania, despite obviously contradictory social phenomena. Yet, to counteract such distortions and maintain readership is not a simple matter.

A similar problem exists in regard to education and entertainment. A massive, highly capitalized industrial production of movies and television programs based in the U.S. distorts our knowledge of other cultures and swamps attempts at national expression and distribution for all but a few countries in the developed world, let alone the developing world.

The press traditions that have protected and are protecting the liberal democracies of the developed world are ill-suited to serve the developing world. While developed nations gain the information they need for the exploitation of the developing world, the developing world receives little it can use to begin to redress the gross inequalities between North and South. In more political terms, having gained political independence and having expected to gain from that formal move overall sovereignty, the nations of the Third World are discovering to what degree they are dependent for their often very low standard of living on the information institutions and markets of the developed world. Trade and information routes still run to the old imperial centres rather than between points of the periphery. Moreover, participation in international markets demands the acceptance of certain business practices and ultimately the evolution of a certain class of people whose manner of thinking and overall ideology must be consonant with those of the business world in which they live.

The pattern of global information creation and flow, who owns and controls it, along with its characteristic content, we can term the **world information order**. The systematic jeopardy it introduces to some nations, especially those of the Third World, and the systematic advantage it creates for others, especially the U.S. as well as other developed countries, are the reasons why there has emerged a call for a **new world information order**.

THE NEW WORLD INFORMATION ORDER

Conceptually, the call for a new world information order arises out of an attempt to redress the imbalance in how the various nations of the world are served by the evolved international system of communication. Politically, it arises from a shift in the balance of power in the United Nations and specifically within UNESCO. With the achievement of formal political independence, Third World nations, the vast majority of which were former colonies of Europe, have obtained an independent voice in the United Nations and considerable influence over such agencies as UNESCO.

The Exploitation of Dominance

The international debate focuses on three points. (1) Historically, communication services together with evolved information technologies have allowed dominant states to exploit their dominance. Through historical patterns and enabling technology, such as communication satellites, they have assumed a presence in the cultures and ideologies of less dominant states, i.e., other nations throughout the world. Whether that presence comes through being the only source of foreign news or from beaming satellite signals into another country, such a presence is strongly felt by nations of the Third World. In this equation Canada plays both sides of the fence. On the one hand we complain about the invasion of American programs and put in place Canadian content regulations on television and radio. On the other hand we have a foreign short-wave service called Radio Canada International and we endeavour to sell Canadian communications technology – telephone systems and communication satellites – and Canadian programs through the CBC and through private production companies to other nations, including Third World nations.

Economies of Scale and Dominance

(2) The second central point of the international debate is that economies of scale in information production and distribution threaten to give increased dominance to those already dominant. However, any attempt to counteract a worsening

situation must avoid feeding into the hands of repressive governments that would curtail freedom of expression and information circulation.

Who Controls the Technology?

(3) The mobilization of technology has been accomplished by a few transnationals as a vehicle for the exploitation of markets rather than to serve the cultural, social, and political needs of nations. In other words, the large corporations have seized the opportunity to develop and use communication technologies, but they have employed these technologies primarily to exploit the value of these audiences to advertisers, as opposed to providing information, education, and entertainment to these audiences for their benefit or for the benefit of the larger cultural whole.

The MacBride Report

International debate over the design of a world information order has been focused on the MacBride Report, a 312-page report by a UNESCO commission that studied communication problems on a global scale. The theoretical underpinnings of this report are found in two principles that were accepted by two intergovernmental conferences, the first held in San Jose de Costa Rica in 1976 and the second in Kuala Lumpur in 1979. They are:

1. Communication policies should be conceived in the context of national realities, free expression of thought, and respect for individual and social rights. (UNESCO, 1980, p. 40)
2. Communication, considered both as a means of affirming a nation's collective identity and as an instrument of social integration, has a decisive role to play in the

democratization of social relations in so far as it permits a multidirectional flow of . . . messages, both from the media to their public and from this public to the media. (UNESCO, 1980, p. 41)

To conceive of communication policies as national realities rather than as the right of any individual to communicate with any other individual in any place in the world is a fundamental delimitation of free flows of information. Because corporations are conceived legally to be persons with some accompanying rights, large multinational or transnational corporations have been able to translate the right of the individual to communicate freely into a right for them to broadcast their programs or sell their papers in any market in the world.

When communications are seen as "national realities," then, the individualistic claims of corporations are defused without being directly attacked. This approach puts in its place a respect for a collectivity, the nation. It also recognizes the contribution that information can make to that collectivity. It is easy to understand how respect for national realities could cause a nation to be wary of importing the standard fare of American or Canadian television with its sumptuous surroundings and, especially in game shows, easy access to wealth.

Respect for collectivities, however, can be abused and become unnecessarily restrictive of individual freedoms. Hence, communications policies must also be conceived "in the context of free expression of thought," which curtails the ability of the state to infringe on individual freedom and insists on an acceptance of plurality. In other words, ideas should be freely considered in order that the collectivity can enrich itself.

A third element in this first accepted principle further limits the freedom of the national collectivity: communication policies should be conceived in the context of "individual and social rights." While such a phrase may appear open to interpretation, and indeed there is a wide difference among nations as to how it is and might be interpreted, the concept is not totally lacking in anchorage. Individual and social rights are dealt with in the Universal Declaration of Human Rights to which all nations are signatories. In addition, there are various "accords," including the Helsinki accords that address individual and social rights. These documents provide a foundation for the interpretation of this phrase by speaking of the rights of individuals and social groups to think and act in a manner they see as best within the necessary confines of a social order; the rights of individuals and groups are not to be subordinated to narrow state-defined interests. Western nations, especially, are concerned for individual and sub-national group rights, which are indeed abused in both the developed and developing world.

The second principle, accepted by the intergovernmental meeting in Kuala Lumpur, manages to restate the first principle in terms likely to be slightly more satisfactory to those concerned with bringing about a new world information order. It puts forward the integrity of a culture or nation, "its collective identity and social integration," while maintaining that communication has a key role to play in enhancing that identity through its power to democratize information flows. It might be claimed that such a statement respects core freedoms of individuals and groups and that such a respect is the necessary foundation for any collectivity to thrive. Note that while it is difficult to object to such a principle, it is a potential threat to the vast economic interests of the producers of information and cultural products in the developed world. Not only is it threatening to the standard content of entertainment programs, but also it challenges technologies that only serve to increase the flow of information from the top down, or from the centre to the periphery.

THE CONTINUING DEBATE ON THE NEW WORLD INFORMATiON ORDER

The call for a new world information order and principles such as the ones passed in San Jose de Costa Rica and Kuala Lumpur have not been universally heralded as a foundation for a new, just world society. Objection has been especially strong in the Western world and specifically within the Western press. It is not difficult to see why they might object. From the point of view of the owners, the possibility of collapse of foreign markets is alarming. From the point of view of journalists, while the report comes up short of recommending the licensing of journalists (indeed, it states that "we share the anxiety aroused by the prospect of licensing and consider that it contains dangers to freedom of information" [p. 236]), many journalists see the report as chipping away at the freedom they need to do their job properly. Whether they are misinformed about the report or whether there is a solid basis for a real fear remains to be seen.

Following the writing of the MacBride Report, the aftermath of debate, and the disenchantment and withdrawal of the U.K. and the U.S. from UNESCO, the debate on the world information order has been both muted and at a stalemate. In *International Image Markets* Mattelart, Delcourt, and Mattelart (1984) sought to inject heterogeneity in information generation and flows by proposing the development of close working relationships between countries in Europe and the Americas that have Latin-based languages. Such relationships were intended to help break the dichotomy of the developed and developing world, between the existing information order and calls for almost the opposite in a new information order. While the book is a must for students serious about such issues, it seems inspired by an attempt to increase the stature of France. It also has had little effect.

As the 1980s were ending, voices calling for a respect of the cultural integrity of developing countries were surprisingly absent. By the early 1990s, cultural politics were being replaced with the politics of economies. Many developing countries saw their future in economic integration within large trading blocs, reasoning that participation in global trade would necessarily bring the information systems required to assist in economic, and perhaps cultural, development. On the communications front itself, the first item on the agenda was the creation of a new level of digital information systems using large computers and data bases, smart terminals in the form of personal computers, and much expanded capacity of data communications by both fibre and satellite.

As was pointed out in Chapter 9, there are some who would argue that this, most recent, technological upgrading holds increased promise for Third World nations. It may, if only the developed world has the will to work toward that goal.

CBC Foreign Correspondents at Ryerson

The typical responses of Western journalists to the new world information order were audible in an annual symposium held in 1983 by the School of Journalism at Ryerson Polytechnical Institute in Toronto. Each year the CBC brings its foreign correspondents home for a short debriefing session to discuss the past year and make decisions for the following year. At this time they make themselves available to an audience composed primarily of journalism students at Ryerson. In the 1983 session a question was asked about the new world information order.

Jan Lazowski: You're talking about something that is going on at UNESCO and that is being sponsored by the Soviet Union, the Eastern Bloc and a lot of the Third World countries. The Western countries are absolutely opposed to it because, among other things, it makes provisions for the licensing of journalists.

Knowlton Nash: The idea is that the licensing is supposed to be a safeguard for journalists but it seems to most of us, or many of us certainly, and certainly I think it seems to the spokesmen for the government of Canada, and certainly the United States, that it's a first step toward the controlling of journalists and controlling what they report and how they report it. I think the essential motivation for those who want the New World Information Order in UNESCO is really to make the media an instrument of the state so that it reflects what the government of the day happens to think is the best thing for the people of that state. And that's a concept of journalism, or a concept of the media that Western nations . . .

David Halton: If I could just come in here I think there is a danger in seeing this issue in too starkly black and white terms. Understandably we've all been upset by the idea of licensing foreign correspondents and an attack on press liberties and so on. At the same time, the notion that the Western media are doing a good job of reporting on Third World problems is, I think, at best, a debatable one. I think there is a tendency for Western coverage of Third World countries to be crisis-oriented, to concentrate on wars, on coups. This gentleman's question, when are we going to have ongoing coverage of Grenada now that the troops are coming out, certainly is a legitimate one. I think a perfectly understandable complaint of some Third World countries is that the Western media, the wire services in particular, do not focus on the kinds of developmental problems that are absolutely essential for many of these countries, when your first priority is to feed your people and so on. This is the kind of reportage we're not getting in the Western wire services.

Knowlton Nash: Yes, there is a journalistic problem there, of course, but how you resolve it, whether you resolve it by making, in effect, the news media an instrument of government is really the question.

Don Murray: I'd like to take a little issue with you here because at UNESCO, this whole issue has just been debated in . . . Paris. . . . As Jan was saying there were resolutions put forward by the Soviet Union which would tend toward the licensing of journalists and the U.S. stood up and said very clearly, "Anybody votes for that and we pull out." The resolution was dumped. UNESCO pulled back considerably knowing full well that the U.S. was very angry. The U.S. still pulled out or announced that it was going to pull out and, in my opinion, having looked at the conference and watched it, I suspect that the Reagan administration really wasn't too concerned . . . [speaker trails off] . . . Last week when it made this decision to pull out of UNESCO it simply used the New World Information Order, which has become extremely diluted in the hands of UNESCO authorities. The U.S. was looking for a cheap foreign policy victory and they decided to give a shock to UNESCO, which doesn't have a lot of backers in the United States, but I think on pretty flimsy grounds.

Joe Schlesinger: What is journalism for? Is it to put out stuff that pleases the people that

you write about, the countries that you write about? Or is it to put out information that others may be interested in, and that's put in a way that interests other people? It's all right to say that you should have more news about development in the Third World countries [but people] aren't going to read it – we find it hard, for instance, to put even Canadian news into American papers.

David Halton: . . . There's really a certain hypocrisy in this debate. We, in Canada, have been debating and passing legislation on Canadian content on the Canadian airwaves for years. . . . Here we are, a lot of people in Canada, a lot of editorialists saying "Why should the Third World be concerned about their intake? Let them take the American movies and the Dallases along with Nestlé's milk and so on." Surely there's an element of hypocrisy there when in Canada we're concerned about our identity and protecting it to some degree from things like American programming and we say the Third World countries shouldn't bother about this.

Two Other Perspectives

Two other commentaries on the new world information order are worth noting. The first is Tom McPhail's *Electronic Colonialism*. McPhail takes much the same stance as David Halton, claiming, in essence, that developed nations practise a kind of journalism designed to augment their own national interests. He takes Canada as an example. A "free press," he argues, is a "development" press supportive of capitalism. The purpose of the Western press is to "confer a rightness on the social order." Canada has developed a series of cultural and regulatory agencies such as the National Film Board, Telefilm Canada, the CRTC, even the CBC, which are designed to interfere with the "free flow of information." Further, legislation seeks to enhance the national media, such as Section 19 of the Income Tax Act, whereby advertising is deductible only when Canadian media are the advertising vehicle. Finally, he argues, we show every sign of continuing in the same vein with the advent of new technologies.

The thrust of McPhail's argument is that developing nations should be allowed to do the same not only for the electronic media but also for the press. They should be allowed to develop print and electronic communication systems that foster their national development and integrity as separate and distinct cultures. It would follow that our responsibility would be to aid as much as we can in that process.

Anthony Smith takes quite a different perspective in *The Geopolitics of Information,* maintaining there is little doubt that the developing nations have a legitimate complaint. However, it appears to him that the Western media cannot accept the articulation of the solutions such as were emerging, at the time he was writing, in the activities of UNESCO and the MacBride Commission.

What bothered Smith most was that the statements of the strongest proponents of the new world information order did not capture how humankind might be improved through a different use of information, communications, knowledge, and entertainment. Rather, Smith saw in these writings the very limited imagination of a bureaucrat whose aim it was to control information generation and distribution so well that the result would be more equitable for all. If Smith's perspective can be summarized in a sentence, it would be that although the cause is just and changes need to be made, we have yet to find a manner of thinking about the issue that will cause us all to seize the matter and work toward a resolution.

SUMMARY

In this chapter we have outlined perhaps the most fundamental issue facing global communications today. That issue is, How can the world community design global communications for equal benefit to all?

The chapter began with an illustration of how the press and the mass media have served the interests of their own countries and civilization. In contrast, the prevailing ideology of the role of the media within developed Western countries is that they must be free of government control and have a freedom of access to information, and that, as an extension of free speech, they should be free to distribute information into all markets (the free flow of information doctrine). However apt the free flow doctrine might be within a country, between countries it pits the market-seeking forces of media conglomerates against the responsibilities of national politicians to assist their country and its culture to develop. At times national politics and international media penetration of markets may not be in conflict. At other times they are.

The global news agencies are vivid historical and contemporary illustrations of a free press (also media) in action. While providing inexpensive information around the world, certain biases are introduced into that information by the way it is collected, by whom, and for what dominant set of users. Generally speaking, the greatest benefit derives to the economies of the organizers of the agencies. Patterns of production, import, and export in news are parallel to those in the entertainment industry.

These patterns of information flow have been called a world information order. The inequitable treatment of all nations has produced a call for a new world information order. How that might be brought about has not been resolved. The MacBride Report has put forward principles that should be respected, principles that have received majority but not full endorsement by every country. In addition, the means of ensuring respect for those principles are not agreed on. Within Canada and Britain there is already a considerable range of opinion on how such principles might be enshrined.

Media owners and some journalists dismiss the whole matter as something that fundamentally interferes with the process of gathering and distributing news. Other journalists (and one commentator) are sympathetic but do not see anything that has emerged as a real solution to an admitted problem. And another commentator would have us extend aid to empower others to do more than follow the Canadian example. He would have them extend the principles Canada has evidenced in its electronic communications to all forms of communications systems of the Third World.

What we have not represented here is the diehard capitalist position, supporting the free market, which is to say a position espousing the free flow of information and damn the consequences. But it would not be unreasonable to assume that such a position is at least part of the motive behind the withdrawal of the United States from UNESCO.

REFERENCES

Boyd-Barrett, J.O. "Cultural Dependency and the Mass Media," in Gurevitch et al., eds., Culture, Society and the Media. Toronto: Methuen, 1982.

Carscallen, Anne. Untitled Master's thesis draft, Simon Fraser University, 1984.

Dorfman, A., and A. Mattelart. How to Read Donald Duck: Imperialist Ideology in the Disney Comic. New York: International General Editions, 1975.

Frum, L. The Newsmakers. Toronto: Key Porter, 1990.

Hester, Al. "International News Agencies," in Alan Wells, ed., Mass Communications: A World View. Palo Alto: Mayfield Publishing, 1974.

Jensen, Arthur R. Bias in Mental Testing. New York: Free Press, 1980.

Lorimer, Rowland. The Nation in the Schools. Toronto: OISE Press, 1984.

Lorimer, R., and P. Keeney. "Defining the curriculum: The role of the multinational textbook in Canada," in S. De Castell, A. Luke, and C. Luke, eds., Language, Authority and Criticism: Readings on the School Textbook. London/Philadelphia: Falmer Press. 1988.

Mattelart, A., X. Delcourt, and M. Mattelart. International Image Markets: In Search of an Alternative Perspective. London: Comedia, 1984.

McPhail, Thomas. Electronic Colonialism: The Future of International Broadcasting and Communication. Beverly Hills: Sage Publications, 1981.

Robinson, G.J. News Agencies and World News: in Canada, the United States and Yugoslavia. Fribourg, Switzerland: University of Fribourg Press, 1981.

Ryerson, School of Journalism. Round Table discussion of CBC journalists, 1983.

Siebert, F., T. Peterson, and W. Schramm. Four Theories of the Press. Urbana: University of Illinois Press, 1956.

Saturday Night (March, 1985), p. 27.

Smith, Anthony. The Geopolitics of Information: How Western Culture Dominates the World. London: Faber and Faber, 1980.

UNESCO, Commission for the Study of Communication Problems (MacBride Commission). The World of News Agencies, Working Paper #11, 1978.

UNESCO. Many Voices, One World: Communication and Society, Today and Tomorrow (MacBride Report). Paris: Unipub, 1980.

Wells, Alan, ed. Mass Communications: A World View. Palo Alto: Mayfield Publishing, 1974.

STUDY QUESTIONS

1. Media managers sort out important news from the trivial. As a result we get a good selection of all the important news of the world. Is this a simplistic statement? Using examples, argue your case.
2. Walt Disney was once nominated for the Nobel Peace Prize. Did he deserve it?
3. Define the new world information order and discuss the reasons why a call for such an order exists.
4. Complex communications technologies have been developed (and are continually being developed) in the leading industrialized countries; these technologies have come to be used also in the Third World. What are the challenges facing various people in Third World countries (e.g., government officials, politicians, businessmen, teachers, consumers) in their use and adaptation of the technologies for their own needs?

CHAPTER

11

The Domestic Geopolitics of Information

INTRODUCTION

A S WE HAVE seen in the previous chapter, certain patterns have emerged in considering how information is generated and distributed throughout the world. These patterns are connected to history, the relative power of nations, and political ideology. The global wire services serve the long-established, powerful, capitalist, industrialized nations. In serving such nations, the global information systems do not merely fail to serve business, government, and cultural interests of less powerful, less industrialized, and politically different nations, but, more significantly, they interfere with the industrial development and the ability to develop and sustain distinct national cultures in such nations.

THE POLITICS OF INFORMATION

T he disparities in opportunity that are introduced by the way information is organized do not result from a planned malevolence on the part of powerful capitalist nations. Rather, the pursuit of their own self-interest conflicts with the independently articulated and pursued self-interest of the less developed nations. Only when the less developed co-ordinate their interests exactly with the developed nations can both exist in "beneficial" coexistence.

Metropolis-Hinterland Theory

The view that an inevitable difference of interest exists between developed and developing nations is not merely a political perspective. It can also be derived from a well-accepted theory most often used by geographers but that has also been applied in economics, sociology, and communication. That theory is variously called metropolis-hinterland, centre-periphery, centre-margin, empire-colony, and several other combinations of the above. Its major proponent was the Canadian economic historian, Harold Innis. The centre-periphery theory can be applied equally to global and to national or, for that matter, regional or local affairs.

The writings of Innis on the fur trade, the cod fishery, the bias of communication, and relations of empire and communication contain various statements of his metropolis-hinterland theory. The theory can be summarized in the following manner. A metropolis or centre or empire is to be regarded as a seat of power. The most fundamental aspect of that power is its organizing dimension. Thus, North America was "explored" by various European powers for what it could contribute to European economies. The European economies were the centres or metropolises reaching out into the hinterlands to gather materials to enhance themselves as powers. What we learn of the history of the period was how well those colonies functioned as hinterlands, that is, how well the fisheries or the fur trade served the Europeans. These were the significant aspects of North America as opposed to, for example, what Indian confeder-

ations had to offer for enlightened government in Europe. It was not a relationship between equals.

Centre-Hinterland Dynamics in Canadian History

The power of the metropolis was not only expressed in what became historically significant. The activities or dominant patterns of life of the hinterland directly flowed from their relation to the centre. For example, for a great number of years, the British attempted to enforce a ban on settlement in Newfoundland because this would give an unfair advantage to those who wintered-over to bring their goods to market in the spring. No self-respecting member of the bourgeoisie would want to winter-over, so all were forbidden to do so. Similarly, after the conquest of New France, the British survey system was introduced into Quebec and effectively disrupted the French system of long and narrow river lots with a "common" up behind those lots *("rangs")*. It also diminished the ability of the French Canadians to continue to form tightly knit village communities (Rioux, 1978). The same survey system played a major role in the Red River Rebellion of 1869 and was imposed upon the region after the rebellion was quashed in 1870.

More fundamentally, the activities of explorers, traders, and settlers were governed by the centre. If the centre needed fish, fish were caught, not so much to eat in the colonies but to make money to fish more or better or to bring the fisherman's life closer to the style of living at the centre. If the centre needed fur for fashionable beaver hats, then fur was gathered. If the taste for furs radically declined with changes in fashion, as indeed it did, then the whole of the economic and therefore social and political activity of the periphery was altered. Not only did various traders become bankrupt, but the primary producer, or at least gatherer, the Indian, often starved. The Indian had been brought into an economy that depended on the whims of European fashion and had come to depend on the money and goods supplied by the trader. Like all single-commodity producers, he was extremely vulnerable to market fluctuations.

Things are no different today. Thanks to the efforts of certain interest groups in the urban centres of North America and Europe, the hunt for seal pups off the coast of Newfoundland has been brought virtually to a halt. Numerous Newfoundland families have lost not only their income but part of their sense of self-worth as a result of the instability of these markets.

Other manifestations of centre-periphery relations could be seen in the political arrangements of the day. When the British conquered the French at the Plains of Abraham, the consequence was the replacement of one bourgeoisie, the French, with another, the English. In those days, there was no question of each business having equal right to do business. Licences were granted only to those the governor saw fit to license.

Similarly, the Family Compact was the group in Upper Canada given political and effective business control over the affairs of the colony. As Canadian history shows, even William Lyon Mackenzie's popular uprising was not enough to dislodge them from the empire-anointed position of power. Likewise, until well into the twentieth century, the Canadian Prairies were touted as the "breadbasket of the empire." And more than one British farmer, inspired or not by Kipling, saw himself as manning the "outpost of empire" on the Canadian frontier. If he faltered in his vision, he could rely on his children, who were encouraged in their school books to see themselves accordingly.

Social and cultural relations also derived from the relation of the hinterland to the metropolis. The defeat of the North West Company at the hands of the Hudson's Bay Company is a story that cannot be told without due attention to the privileges granted to the latter by the (British) court of the empire. Similarly, one can only understand ethnic relations and the defeat of the Métis led by Louis Riel and Gabriel Dumont by reference to Anglophone power of the English over the French in Canada. (Beale, 1988, provides a particularly interesting discussion on the organization of Canadian geography into a social space. Her paper develops the ideas outlined here.)

Hinterland Relations

The relations of the hinterland, not just to the centre but also to other points on the periphery, are centre-dominated. Two neighbouring farmers, like two towns, are more liable to be producing goods in competition for the market of the centre than to be producing goods that complement each other. Also, it may be easier to travel to another town twenty miles down the track than to one three miles distant because the former is on the route to the centre whereas the latter is on a separate route to the centre. The history of land speculation and personal wealth in Canada is tied closely to the choices made by the railroad builders. Whole towns – and their inhabitants – were destined to oblivion because they bet on the wrong route for the iron horse.

Transportation routes became communication routes with the development of wire services. Just as the patterns of trade and settlement were derived from the needs of the centre, so information of significance to the centre was both gathered from and distributed to the hinterlands. The running of telegraph lines along the routes of the railroad is the most obvious physical manifestation of the parallel relation of communications to transportation, trade, and settlement. Letters and newspapers also travelled the same routes. Just as important to Sir John A. Macdonald's dream of binding the nation together with a railroad was a notion that encompassed the transmission of information as well as the transportation of people and goods.

The emplacement of the telegraph, quickly followed by radio, the telephone, and television, and the emphasis on the availability of Canadian radio and television signals to all Canadians (which Parliament has insisted to be a major part of the mandate of the CBC) demonstrate how important to our politicians is the job of organizing the nation around the eastern centres of Montreal and Toronto. As spokespersons for western Canadian resource-based economies are so fond of pointing out, trade relations are governed by the interests of the manufacturing centres, not the interests of the hinterland resource provinces. Were Alberta, Saskatchewan, and British Columbia allowed to sell their resources without interference from Ottawa in terms of export limits and prices, there is little doubt that these provinces would be better off financially, at least in the short term. However, perhaps a more fundamental question is, would there have been and would there be a Canada had the various settlements in British North America not been integrated with the eastern manufacturing centres?

COMMUNICATIONS IN A CULTURAL, CENTRE-HINTERLAND PERSPECTIVE

While communications can be studied as a separate entity with its own separate dynamics, communications is a part of a social system. Structurally, it both complements and reinforces the way society is organized. In this section, we will examine one perspective on the role of communications in northern Canada.

The Berger Report and the Position of Northern Native People

In a landmark report resulting from an inquiry into the advisability of building a gigantic oil and gas pipeline down the Mackenzie River Valley, Mr. Justice Thomas Berger outlined the issues he saw as background to the interaction between southern Canadians and the Inuit and Dene in the North. The perspective we summarize here is taken from "Cultural Impact," a chapter in Volume 1 of the Berger Report, *Northern Frontier: Northern Homeland.*

Two elements predominated in white-native interactions in the early days of contact, now over two centuries ago. They were trade (in furs) and religion. Both were powerful devices of transformation of native life. Religion represented a broad challenge to traditional patterns of life. To Europeans, the hunting and gathering of food and material goods as a way of providing the necessities of life seemed not only lazy but somehow also extravagant and irreligious. The Christian practice of the cultivation and maximal exploitation of resources was seen, by Europeans, as a necessary condition for the emergence and development of civilization. The land needed to be put to use by the native people under the guidance of whites in order that the native people themselves could be integrated into Christian civilization. In the context of the North, that meant a systematic gathering of furs for European markets in exchange for the "products of civilization." Such a trade represented a systematic exploitation of the only retrievable resource (for the time) in an otherwise "barren" land. In the context of the North, Christian ideology stopped short of forcing land into a system of private ownership, as had been the case in the Canadian Prairies. Essentially, this was because whites were unable to see a benefit in their ownership of the land.

This fur-based interaction, if we ignore for a moment the ethnocentric bias inherent in it and the power relations emanating from that bias, provided mutual benefit for native and white. The native people participated in the fur trade with comparatively little disruption in their patterns of living. They continued as semi-nomads, living in small groups off the land, and merely modified their yearly cycle to include visits to the Hudson's Bay Company outpost to trade furs for food, guns, and, in the neighbouring church, prayer. So satisfactorily did this interaction work out that when northern natives talk of a traditional life, what they are referring to is not pre-white, pre-fur trade days but rather the days of the fur trade.

Stable and beneficial as this situation was, it did not change the reality of the growing dependence of the native people on the markets, the technology, and the food and other staples of the south. The instability of the markets would eventually reveal that dependency in a rather cruel manner and envelop native people in the web of Western civilization.

Communications and the Spiral of Dependency

After World War Two, the northern fur economy collapsed. Its collapse brought the welfare state into Canada's northern communities. The elements of the welfare state included family allowances, old age pensions, welfare payments, government housing, nursing stations, schools, and wage labour. While each aspect of the welfare state was benign in intent and was intended to meet a particular set of needs, it was nevertheless designed on the assumption that the traditional way of life was no longer tenable. And it was to transform every aspect of northern native life.

The welfare measures set up a spiral of growing dependency that has undermined northern native culture to the extent that in some communities, up to 90 per cent of adults will have received social assistance at some time during the year. Let us run through that spiral of dependency in the general case to illustrate some of the dynamics. We will start at the point where a hunter finds that he does not have enough money to pay off the debts he has incurred from the previous season, essentially because the bottom has dropped out of the fur market.

Faced with this situation, he can turn either to wage labour or to welfare. If he engages in wage labour he must stay near the settlement to be near his job. This prevents him from hunting so that he becomes almost fully dependent on wages. If he goes hunting and misses any more than a few days on the job, he is fired. If he goes on welfare, the welfare officer becomes interested in the whole family, especially the children and their education. The welfare officer points out that his application for assistance will be given more favourable consideration if he shows that he is "responsible" by sending his children to school.

Then, once he is on welfare, looking for wage labour becomes a desirable thing in the eyes of the welfare agency; hunting is seen to be neglect of his responsibility to earn a living. In fact, "regulations will not permit welfare money to be spent on hunting clothing, bullets or gasoline for boats and snowmobiles" (*Globe and Mail*, September 2, 1989, p. D8). Similarly, if chances present themselves to return to the traditional way of life, in abandoning the settlement the man and his family are seen as irresponsible, or at best as romantics who do not have the discipline to live in a civilized setting.

If ever the man is forced to return for assistance, such interpretations of his behaviour are presented to him. Behaviour not patterned after the white way of doing thing is denigrated, while things that are white, even though they may be less self-sustaining, are praised. If the man complains further, when confronted with these interpretations, for example by complaining that the school teaches little that his son can use to learn to fish, trap, and hunt, he is seen to be simple, refusing to accept the inevitable decline of the old ways.

Each move he makes in accepting further assistance from white civilization draws him further away from his ability to sustain himself and his family independently. Not only do work and welfare encourage him to stay near the settlement, which usually is distant from any hunting grounds, but other forms of assistance have the same effect. If he has taken up housing in the settlement, his subsequent departure with family can be seen as abandonment. Certainly it is a queer idea to continue to pay for a house while he and his family are absent. Likewise, if his children enter school, taking them out of school is a sign of lack of value for education. Medical services also require remaining near the settlement. Often, they require extended care in southern cities such as Edmonton, Toronto, or Montreal.

As the children reach high school age, if they have not been in a residential school already, they usually must leave their family to attend school in one of the larger settlements. The longer the children attend school, the more their abilities are limited and focused on survival only in the wage economy. They do not learn how to hunt, trap, and fish or to find their way through the frozen and apparently featureless snow and ice. Instead, they learn how to operate heavy equipment so that they can be employed as wage-earners for southern development companies. Or, in an apparently better scenario and against all odds, they gain credentials, such as a law degree, to work on behalf of their people. Liberating as this may sound, they then enter the undefined territory between their traditional culture and contemporary white culture, a territory that requires both substantial peer support and a tremendous strength of will. Should they fall prey to the shock of this transformation of their lives, of course, they can always seek solace in the church, whose values are fundamental to southern, white civilization.

Well-meaning as each of these support programs may be, each further envelops the family in a dependency relation to southern white culture. Each program is intended to provide a more satisfactory level of service, schooling, welfare, health, job training, etc. Each program, in its turn, cannot help but exacerbate dependency problems.

The only ways out seem impossible. Full integration, even if it were deemed desirable, is not viable because the economy is not sufficiently developed to turn all native northerners into wage-earners or business entrepreneurs. Complete rejection is also impossible because many have lost survival skills, and animal stocks for food and fur have been depleted.

Dependency and Development

There are many negative elements of bringing white society and services to native people in the North. White society did not begin, nor does it continue, to pursue development and to offer and enhance social services with the purpose of wreaking havoc among native northern culture. The point in raising these issues is to argue that while each of trade, wage labour, education, welfare, and communications does provide benefits, the manner in which they have been introduced and are managed fails to maximize opportunities for northern native people. In general, it fails to allow them to integrate traditional lifestyles and values with the opportunities of southern white society. Perhaps if native northerners were to play a greater role in defining the basis of their interaction with white society there might be greater benefit all round. Even if things were not to work out better, respect for democratic values suggests that southern Canada owes them that opportunity. It might also help avoid a hinterland dependency.

Magic in the Sky

Communications is essentially an add-on component intended to enhance the level of "service" in information to northern communities, but it directly envelops northern native peoples in the culture of the south. The NFB's *Magic in the Sky* explores some of the dynamics of how that envelopment takes place. Some of the history of Canadian developments in communications provides a fuller background.

Canada began experimenting with communications in the North because of the irregularity in radio signals. The problem was that the same electrical disturbances that produced the northern lights also interfered with radio signals. At times radio was perfectly adequate; at other times it was impossible. The quality of the signals was improved, but various experiments showed that the interaction of radio signals and this electrical activity in the atmosphere was inevitable and that there were firm limitations on the use of radio signals as a means of communication in the North. Reliable communications in the North could not depend on the airwaves. Since land lines were impossible, the answer was satellites.

Early satellites were designed to enable individuals and communities to communicate with each other. Because the satellites were relatively low-powered, powerful ground stations were required to send and receive signals. Once this was discovered to be a satisfactory means of communicating, development moved quickly. Satellite power was increased, as was their capability to transmit numbers of signals until, with a four-foot stationary receiving dish, it was possible to receive good-quality signals of any kind, including television.

Suddenly, communication between individuals and communities was replaced with the possibility of receiving as many or more channels as any southern Canadian could. By means of satellites and dishes, people in isolated northern communities had travelled through history almost from the days of Fessenden's rudimentary experiments with voice transmission to the present day.

The significance of these developments for Inuit and other northern native communities, as *Magic in the Sky* points out, was considerable. In place of traditional values of sharing, young people were introduced to individualism and greed. Social status was linked not to an ability to provide for more than one's own family, but to the ability to collect and hold material goods for oneself. The personal politics we have discussed as endemic to popular culture items, where status is conferred upon those of particular body types, with particular ethnic backgrounds, and with particular personality traits, suddenly became the way the outside world worked. Most of all, consumerism, the necessity to have all manner of consumer products, as well as the necessity of a culture to produce all manner of consumer products, became a guiding force. All these things were made doubly attractive by the sumptuousness of the settings in which both

advertised products and entertainment programs were presented.

Imagine having lived in an environment
where a crackling radio brought sporadic items
of world news on an erratic basis. The qualities
of the technology itself suggest distance.
Contrast that with sitting down one day and
seeing the crowded, bustling street of Toronto
or New York, the luxurious shoreline of Howe
Sound where *The Beachcombers* was shot,
and so forth. Suddenly it is all there in full living colour right in the living room, 400 miles
from the North Pole and a $1,000 plane fare
from Montreal. In the same way that a whining
and crackling radio would lead a listener to
perceive world events as distant, the daily fare
of murders, assassinations, coups, wars, plane
crashes, social unrest, and the like has also
crept into the daily life of northern native people much in the same way that DDT has found
its way into the egg shells of the gyrfalcon. A
fine welcome to the modern world.

In spite of the news, satellite communications have served to draw northern communities
further into the ideology of the industrialized
world. They are given values and viewpoints
that make them aliens in their own culture.
Thereby, their culture is made vulnerable to
eclipse by the industrialized south. This especially affects the children. Communications is
the latest of the services southern Canadians
have provided to northern native communities
that, while offering them relief from immediate
discomforts, lock them into a dependency relationship to our culture.

The preceding description is intended to be
an overview of the process of acculturation.
Numerous studies have explored this process in
detail. One particularly useful compilation is a
publication by the Department of Communication Studies of Concordia University: *Communication and the Canadian North* (1983).

An even more recent discussion can be found
in Valaskakis (1988).

Reinforcement of the Prevailing Order

As Chapter 10 has shown and as this section of
this chapter also demonstrates, communications services are part of the social order. One
Marxist commentator calls them an ideological
state apparatus (Althusser, 1971). Just like economic arrangements (the fur trade), education,
health, and welfare, in their structure these services re-express the power relations of the state.
In drawing people into them, as producers or
consumers, they force such people to participate in relationships consistent with the dominant relations and ideology of the state (McNulty,
1987). As we have argued here, communications forms one more level of social activity
that further reinforces the relation of particular
groups to the prevailing order.

CANADA AS A CULTURAL HINTERLAND

One of the strengths of Innis's concepts of
centre and hinterland is that there is no
one centre, nor does a country or region have
solely a hinterland relationship to a variety of
other industrialized countries, such as West
Germany and Japan.

In various ways Canada can be seen as a
cultural hinterland of the United States. What
effect does this have on Canadian cultural
expression? How might the metropolis-hinterland perspective allow us to understand our
cultural relations with the U.S. and plan policy
accordingly? We will concentrate here on two
areas of cultural expression, the writing contained in school learning materials and television broadcasting.

Textbooks and the Structure of Knowledge

In the previous chapter, several examples were introduced illustrating the kind of content to be found in learning materials in Canadian schools. We noted that the content was not Canadian when it might have been and that some of the Canadian content inserted into materials adapted from foreign sources was either trivial or wrong. To add two other examples in that vein from one reading series published by Ginn (Clymer, 1972), in the American edition 60 milk trucks deliver 50,000 quarts of milk whereas in the Canadian edition 60 milk trucks deliver 2,000 quarts of milk. In another place in the series, in the American edition 2,500 postal workers sort 5 million letters while in Canada hundreds of workers sort thousands of letters and packages.

The importance of these and other examples is multilayered. In the first place, Canadian school children seem to know more about the U.S. than they do about Canada. Second, the structure of the subject matter as it is developed in the centre actually persuades educators of the hinterlands that information about the hinterlands is relatively unimportant compared to information oriented to the centre. In the previous chapter we used the example of science: by emphasizing scientific inquiry over scientific knowledge about the environment in which one lives, examples become secondary and therefore less appropriate to the lives of the students.

Science is just like nearly every other subject inasmuch as the structure of inquiry has been developed to play down knowledge of direct relevance to students in their immediate cultural and physical milieu. In the study of language arts and literature, the structure of language is first stressed, followed by examples of "quality" prose. This allows learning materials to be devel-oped that neglect to introduce students to the literature of their own country. In a third subject area, social studies, a similar structural change has held sway for some time but now seems to be on the wane. This perspective emphasizes inquiry (just as in science) and decision-making over the study of the social fabric itself. One publisher, McGraw-Hill Ryerson, has designed a series for grades 1 to 6 called Social and Environmental Studies that devotes one grade to the study of Canada and all other grades to the abstract study of neighbourhood, community, region, nation, and so on. This approach, which emphasizes universals over particulars, is to be found in many other subjects. The study of "great" artists over contemporary art of the nation and region similarly neglects that which is familiar to the child. The study of "world-renowned" musicians also isolates students from serious consideration of music produced in Canada.

The point of these examples is that the structure of knowledge is defined at the centre. It serves the centre not so much by infiltrating the materials with information about the centre but by putting forward a perspective that emphasizes the development of knowledge that will be of greatest use to the centre. For example, the acquisition of scientific knowledge is of primary benefit to industries based at the centre. It allows them to expand their power to produce products for any environment. It may benefit the regions. It may allow them to control some local conditions. Similarly, the acquisition of social scientific information enables us to understand the dynamics of new, evolving social situations that heretofore we have not experienced. It is rare for those new social relations to emerge in the more stable environment of the periphery.

If we delve further into metropolis-hinterland relations, we can see how this redefinition of knowledge to the detriment of the hinterlands comes about. *The Nation in the Schools* (Lorimer, 1984) examines two areas that shed light on this process. The first is the education of teachers; the second, the business of educational publishing

The Politics of Teacher Education

The major findings of the work on teacher training indicated the presence of an extremely strong centre-margin process. In the first place, many of the professors appointed to teach teachers in Canadian universities are foreign-born and -trained. In recent years this problem has decreased somewhat as a result of Department of Immigration rulings favouring the hiring of Canadians. But throughout the 1970s, only 60 to 70 per cent of professors hired to teach in the universities were Canadian, 55 to 60 per cent of whom received first degrees in Canada (von Zur Muehlen, 1981). (Data were not reported in the above study on final degrees.) Other studies have reported that up to 90 per cent of books sold in university bookstores are foreign-authored and -produced. These statistics are not introduced to be anti-foreign. Canada has benefited greatly both from foreign-born academics and from foreign-produced information. The point is that in training Canadian university students in general, and Canadian education students in particular, we rely on *imported* personnel and *imported* materials. As a result we cannot avoid an imported perspective.

Nor can it be claimed that once these foreign academics come to Canada they are immersed in a Canadian environment and leave behind that of the country in which they were trained. A survey (Lorimer, 1984) found that nearly 50 per cent of conference attendance and academic publishing involved American conferences and publishers. The other 50 per cent

was accounted for by both local and national Canadian conferences and journals.

Centre-margin processes could be seen further in the hiring practices of school boards. Only approximately 15 per cent indicated definitely that they gave preference to teachers with a knowledge of Canadian phenomena over non-Canadian phenomena, for example, Canadian history over world, European, or American history. Even when the job involved Canadian geography or history, preference was rarely given to Canadians. Nor were teachers, once hired, encouraged by very many school boards to upgrade themselves with Canadian subject matter.

The courses teachers take in their training reflect the same centre-biased viewpoint. Not a single university offering an education degree in Canada requires more than one course introducing the Canadian educational system in its social, legal, cultural, or historical context. Many do not require even one course. Further, in educational foundations in general, there are approximately double the number of psychologically oriented courses as there are social, cultural, historical, and legal courses combined.

The Politics of Educational Publishing

Educational publishing presents essentially parallel phenomena. The Canadian elementary/high school market is dominated by large multinational publishers, some of which are Canadian-owned although most are not. Data collected in the seventies indicate that two-thirds of the market was accounted for by eight multinational firms. Eighty-six per cent of the market was controlled by these plus a further ten firms, only three of which could be said to be nationally oriented, Canadian-owned companies. These statistics, when combined with our findings on the patterns of the content and design of textbooks and the structure of knowledge they advance, suggest that these companies are oriented not to a Canadian market but to a global mass market. They attempt to produce materials that are easily transferable between markets by dealing in generalities and emphasizing knowledge of benefit to the centre, to which every province and state is a hinterland.

Beyond content that favours mass market-oriented materials, a number of other practices were identified. Multinational publishers, sometimes in concert with educators, seek to ensure their continued, centre-oriented dominance of the market by using expensive "cosmetics," such as four-colour printing that can only be afforded in a very large market. Also, massive pre-publishing investments prepare the market to receive the learning materials. This preparation consists of a continual presence of sales reps in the school system for at least one year prior to a major adoption, plus contracting with numbers of opinion-leading educators as consultants in a variety of regions. Their consultancies naturally lead them to promote the product as well as to pilot test the materials. Most importantly, this massive investment prepares the market by means of publication of the materials prior to a decision being taken by the province to purchase: it is nothing less than a very high stakes poker game.

It has been found, also, that the publishers are not actively engaged in trying to promote interprovincial co-operation in the acquisition of materials. Their reluctance to push this rationalization very hard appears to originate in the fear that it would give more power to the province-consumers once they pooled their purchasing power. In a situation where the materials are not developed under contract, the publishers have sufficient bargaining power to publish materials that are potentially saleable in a wide variety of markets.

The Nation in the Schools also discusses the long-term interactions between publishers and the education profession. As both Lorimer and Keeney (1988) and Lorimer (1984) argue, educational philosophy has become married to the interests of centre or mass market producers.

The conclusion to be drawn is that while the content of learning materials reflects metropolis-hinterland relations, the processes involved in the production of both learning materials and teachers indicate a profound infusion of metropolis-hinterland dynamics in the education system as a whole, an infusion that will increase as computers play a larger role in the classroom. Under the Free Trade Agreement Canada is committed to an open competitive market in computer services, including software and courseware. The implication from this conclusion is that the Canadian educational system is not serving Canada or Canadians particularly well and is likely to prolong our hinterland status.

The Domestic Politics of Canadian Television Services

The structure and content of educational materials are not as often debated as are television services. But the dynamics, although played out differently, are much the same. Television began in Canada with the importation of signals from the U.S. Before any Canadian station was on the air, Canadians had purchased television sets and were receiving U.S. signals.

Television production itself began in Canada as a public enterprise. In the face of a vigorous American entertainment industry spilling over into the new medium of television, this initial conception was intended to help hinterland Canada survive the onslaught of the entertainment centres in New York and Los Angeles. As

Judy LaMarsh reiterated in a 1967 White Paper, broadcasting is "a means of preserving and strengthening the cultural, social and political fabric of Canada." In the early days of television a great number of productions were mounted, and many live broadcasts of plays and programs were produced in television studios in Toronto. At the same time, a certain amount of material was also purchased for rebroadcast.

The CBC and Its Complement

Not long after the first public television broadcasts, private entrepreneurs were allowed to inaugurate services to "complement" the offerings of public television. However, because the motivations of private television were so different from the public service, the nature of the "complement" was different from what many expected. Whereas the public service was conceived from a cultural perspective, private stations were conceived by their owners as vehicles for making money. That is, they saw themselves as capable of delivering sufficiently large audiences to advertisers to attract their advertising. They reasoned that they would be able to ask enough for the access to these audiences that they would have sufficient funds not only for the acquisition of programs but also for a healthy profit besides.

As the Special Senate Committee on Mass Media (the Davey Report) showed, they were right. The basis of this belief was the assumption that all sorts of American-produced materials could be acquired for a fraction of the cost of production. As the first Lord Thomson said, "A television broadcasting licence is a licence to print money." To the private broadcaster, content is only important for its ability to attract audiences. It is obvious how a great emphasis on gratuitous sex and violence can emerge from such an orientation.

The Pursuit of Profit

The notion the private broadcasters had of "complement" was any programming the public broadcaster was not providing. More importantly, this notion included a fundamentally different, profit-seeking operation. The private broadcasters thus were happy enough to let the CBC go its own cultural way. While the CBC pursued the good of the nation, they would pursue the maximization of audiences for sale to advertisers. Only when the CBC stumbled on something that garnered large audiences, such as *Hockey Night in Canada,* were the private stations concerned about competition with the public broadcaster. As competition heated up between the two services in the bidding for foreign programming, complaints about subsidized competition could be heard.

The Dance of the Entrepreneurs

In addition to the private contingent came another set of players, the border stations. American businesspeople soon realized that from a position just inside the American border, television signals could assemble audiences and sell them to advertisers in competition with the Canadian stations. Since Canadians had built the majority of their major cities within broadcast distance of the border, why not make a profit in providing them with American television?

The Canadians were not far behind. If Americans were going to provide technically mediocre television signals that required a jungle of roof aerials in every Canadian city near the U.S. border, and if these signals were unlicensed in Canada, why not put up one first-class aerial and run wires from that aerial to everyone in the neighbourhood. Thus was born yet another set of television entrepreneurs, the cable companies.

There was a brief lull after the cable companies were licensed to bring in a maximum of four U.S. signals in exchange for providing access to members of the community to create programming. But recently yet another set of entrepreneurs has entered the field, the specialty services and pay television companies. They were allowed to enter the market for two reasons. The first was technological development. One of original reasons for regulating the airwaves was the finite amount of space available for stations, but technology that vastly increases the number of signals that can be fitted on to various parts of the radio spectrum is now in place. The second reason was that pay TV companies promised to divert a certain amount of their profits to the development of Canadian production. This promise has so far proved to be as much a dream as the large profits that were to be the basis of funding.

Profits and Hinterland Dynamics

The centre-hinterland relations that this account of television services illustrates arise both from the expansionist activities of the American entertainment centres and their outpost messengers just south of the border, and from the assimilative activities of our private sector to import entertainment products from the U.S.

Living as we do in the shadow of the American empire, we are continually aware, partly because of centre-hinterland processes, of the production of the United States. As the Americans capitalize on each new technology, we spend a certain amount of time worrying over the consequences for us of their exploitation and exportation of that technology and its products. But before long it becomes apparent to the private sector that money is to be made in importing those products. In combination with the profits to be made by American exporting,

Canadian importers have good reason to want to bring in such products, as they have proven to be popular with Canadians. The incentive structure, i.e., the ease and reliability of profit-making, favours the importer. Thus, rather than set up in competition with the Americans, we merely transport to our country (and their hinterland) their products.

While this activity creates profits for the private sector that allow it to grow and provides services for us to attain a certain "quality of life," it diminishes our ability to create cultural products for ourselves. It creates growth but not development. With minimal production on the periphery, creative artists must make the pilgrimage to the centre. Once arrived, no matter how great their talent, they must produce within the dominant genres. At the same time, as they move and begin to participate in the industry, they confirm the possibilities of export back to Canada (and elsewhere) by their ability to understand how the genres must be adapted to that end. A CBC documentary, *Solid Gold,* reviews the various Canadian groups that have been internationally successful in popular music over the years. One of the surprising aspects of this presentation is the number of Canadian groups, from the Crewcuts and the Diamonds to the Band. It is doubtful that many Canadians realize how extensive our participation has been. Certainly, no claim was advanced that the music produced by Canadians was distinguishable from that produced by the Americans.

The matter is not confined to production dynamics. It is not hard to understand how the force of four U.S. channels, together with CTV, Global (an Ontario network), the other private stations, and the CBC's own importing activity, has developed in Canadians a taste for American entertainment programs. When Canadians produce something distinctive, it must run counter to centre-hinterland forces and fight an uphill battle to attract a Canadian audience away from its accustomed diet. The power and expansiveness of the American centre is evident in the tiers of both American and Canadian entrepreneurs that it supports, from the border stations to the private networks and stations, to the cable companies and pay TV operators.

Against such odds work Canadian television producers. The viewing habits of Canadians show an appreciation of and interest in Canadian programs. A CBC study (1990) provides the following information. First, as shown in Figures 11.1 and 11.2, whether throughout the broadcast day or in prime time, between 1984-85 and 1988-89 there has been a steady increase in the viewing of Canadian programs as a proportion of all viewing. These trends are consistent through both English and French television. When gains are divided up into those made by the CBC versus those made by cable stations and broadcasters other than the CBC, including the educational and other specialty channels, if measured throughout the broadcast day the non-CBC sector accounts for all gains. But if measured during prime time, the CBC accounts for one-third of the gains while non-CBC programmers account for two-thirds. (In interpreting these and other figures it is important to remember that throughout this period the CBC was subject to continuous cutbacks in funding from the federal government.)

Figures 11.3 and 11.4 show the differing patterns of viewing of the types of foreign and Canadian programs on English television during prime time. The major categories of foreign programs watched are movies/drama (between 55 and 63 per cent) and variety (between 10 and 11 per cent). Viewing of Canadian programs is more evenly spread among program types.

The situation for French television is a little different. Besides fewer foreign programs, as Figures 11.5 and 11.6 show, during prime time on Francophone TV movies/drama and variety are dominant but not as much so as for English foreign programs. Other categories have a healthy percentage share of viewing hours. With regard to foreign programs the sole significant category is movies/drama. All other viewing accounts for about 1.5 per cent of time.

Other figures in the same study demonstrate a close correspondence between per cent of Canadian-produced programs broadcast and the per cent of Canadian-produced programs viewed. In other words, to achieve their market share Canadian producers have not flooded the market with programs, many of which are not watched.

THE CANADIAN NEWS AND CENTRE-HINTERLAND RELATIONS

A basic question for our purposes in studying centre-hinterland dynamics is whether news programming contributes to these dynamics or works to counteract them. Two studies, one of CBC English radio news (Lorimer, 1984), the other of English- and French-language television news (Siegel, 1983), will help to answer this important question.

CBC National Radio News (in English)

The first thing to note about CBC radio news is that it is Canadian in focus.* As Tables 11.1 and 11.2 show, more than half of the stories are Canadian. The frequency then drops to 14.1 per cent. These are stories about the U.S., our closest neighbour and a "newsworthy" nation. Then

* Kate Cockerill, Laine Lunde, and Bill Richards helped to collect and analyse the data for this study, which was directed by Rowland Lorimer.

FIGURE 11.1

Viewing of Canadian/Foreign Programs on TV, 6:00 a.m. to 2:00 a.m.,
All TV Stations

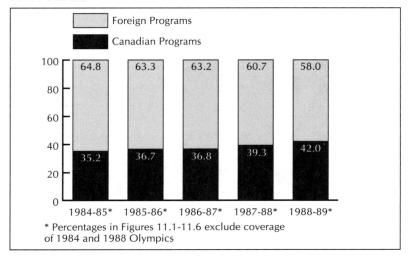

SOURCE: CBC Research (A.C. Nielsen, September-March).

FIGURE 11.2

Viewing of Canadian/Foreign Programs on TV, 7:00 p.m. - 11:00 p.m.,
All TV Stations

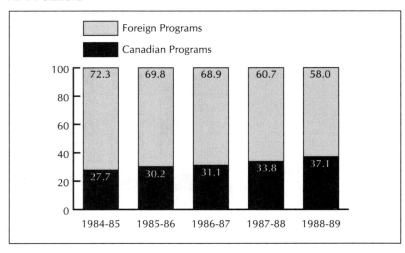

SOURCE: CBC Research (A.C. Nielsen, September-March).

FIGURE 11.3

Viewing of Various Types of Foreign Programs, English TV, 7:00 p.m. - 11:00 p.m.

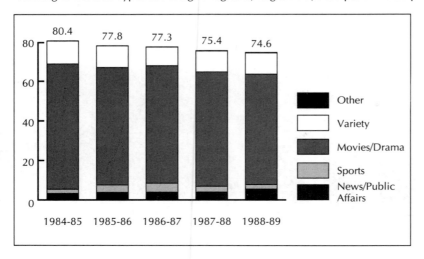

SOURCE: CBC Research (A.C. Nielsen, September-March).

FIGURE 11.4

Viewing of Various Types of Canadian Programs, English TV, 7:00 p.m. - 11:00 p.m.

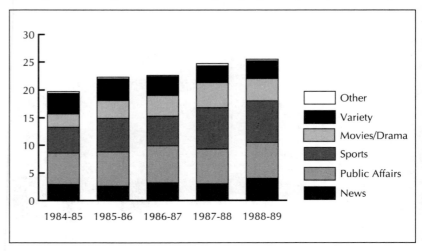

SOURCE: CBC Research (A.C. Nielsen, September-March).

FIGURE 11.5

Viewing of Various Types of Canadian Programs, French TV, 7:00 p.m. - 11:00 p.m.

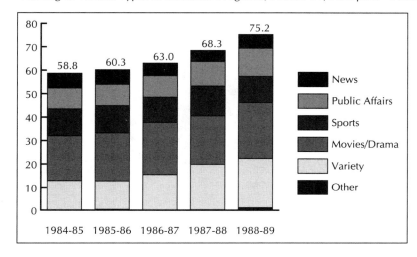

SOURCE: CBC Research (A.C. Nielsen, September-March).

FIGURE 11.6

Viewing of Various Types of Foreign Programs, French TV, 7:00 p.m. -11:00 p.m.

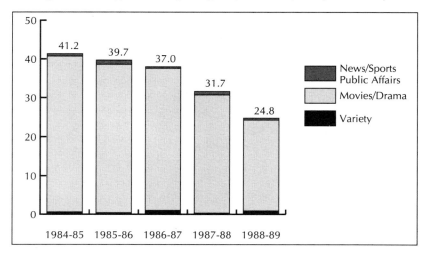

SOURCE: CBC Research (A.C. Nielsen, September-March).

follow European countries and the Middle East. The Middle East was a particular hot spot in 1982, the year these data were collected.

The second noteworthy point is the dominant categories of content covered in the news stories. As Table 11.3 shows, political stories stood out as the most frequent (43.9 per cent). (Table 11.4 breaks down the political stories into subcategories.) Following politics is economics, at 15.9 per cent, and then come a cluster of categories led by labour and followed by crime, law, disaster, human interest, and energy.

The third point is the shift in frequencies of categories of stories as a function of their location: the national capital, provincial capitals, major cities, rural settings. As Table 11.5 illustrates, some categories – business, the environment, labour, religion, science, and human interest – increase in frequency as the setting shifts from the Canadian centre to the periphery. The most dramatic increases are to be found in the categories of crime and disaster. Others – political and economic stories – decrease. The remaining themes do not change significantly.

The final significant point is the frequency of stories as a function of the province in which they occurred. As Table 11.6 demonstrates, the frequencies almost exactly follow the relative populations of the provinces. Only Newfoundland is out of place. However, one other, less visible anomaly must be mentioned, the correct ranking of Quebec but the extreme drop in frequency between Ontario and Quebec. While the study did not attempt to calculate what percentage of the Ontario stories were accounted for by the presence of the nation's capital in Ontario (and Table 11.5 suggests that they were considerable), the overall effect appears to downplay the place of Quebec in Canada.

Taken together these four points appear to indicate that the CBC radio news is a counterforce to metropolis-hinterland dynamics as they

TABLE 11.1

Distribution of Stories by Region

Region	Percentage
North America	68.3
Europe	13.2
Middle East	5.8
Eastern Bloc	4.3
South America	2.9
Asia	2.7
Africa	2.2
International	.6

TABLE 11.2

Distribution of Stories by Country

Country	Percentage
Canada	54.2
United States	14.1
Britain	4.7
Russia	2.9
Israel	2.5
France	2.0
Others (each)	<2.0

TABLE 11.3

Distribution of Stories by Major Theme

Theme	Percentage
Politics	43.8
Economics	15.9
Labour	6.5
Crime	4.3
Law	4.0
Disaster	3.9
Human interest	3.8
Energy	3.6
Environment	2.9
Science	2.6
Business	2.5
Religion	1.7
Culture	1.5
Medicine	1.3
Sports	0.8
Education	0.5
Communications	0.4

TABLE 11.4

Distribution of Stories by Minor Theme

Theme	Percentage
Elections/parties	19.4
Foreign relations	13.5
Nuclear arms	12.4
Conflict	8.8
Economic policy	7.8
Legislation	6.3
Human rights	5.7
Scandal	5.1
Domestic policy	4.9
Terrorism	4.7
Military	3.1
Trade	2.9
Defence	2.5
Parliament	2.4
Off-shore policy	0.2
Civil service	0.2

apply to Canada as a nation. Concentration on Canadian stories in conjunction with an emphasis on politics and economics indicates that the CBC puts forward information about the day-to-day events that keep Canada a stable, economically functional nation. The CBC does not emphasize the kinds of stories, such as crime and disaster, that the wire services tend to emphasize in their coverage of hinterland countries. Nor, more significantly, does it fall prey to accepting stories about the U.S. as superseding Canadian stories in their newsworthiness. Not even in other data collected on length and placement of story did a secondary rank for Canadian stories occur.

The latter two of the four points, on shifts in frequency of content and on provincial coverage, relate to centre-hinterland dynamics within Canada. In Canadian stories, as we move away from the national capital, political stories become less dominant; in percentage frequency, they halve. The percentage frequencies of every other

category except communication, the media, and culture increase. The predominant categories at the two levels of major cities and provincial capitals become politics, economics, labour, and to a lesser extent crime, and in major cities but not provincial capitals, human interest. In the rural category, we have a further levelling effect with the top five categories in order of frequency being political, a three-way tie with economic, disaster, and crime, and then business. The environment and labour follow not too far behind.

The most dramatic frequency shifts that pay into centre-margin dynamics are the increases in the reporting of crime and disaster in rural stories. Other frequency differentials that might have had the same influence – e.g., a great number of science, medicine, and technology stories based in the major cities; a great number of religion and human interest stories with rural settings – do not appear. The only other category to move in the direction that a centre-over-margin bias would suggest was law, a category that appeared constant in all settings except the rural, where it disappeared. To some extent, the number of business stories with rural settings could be seen as countervalent to centre-margin pressures.

Overall, it would be difficult to claim that CBC national radio news exacerbated centre-margin forces. In fact, the most reasonable interpretation of these data appears to be that they work as a credible contrary force. That contrary force is enhanced by a frequency of stories by province that matches the relative size of provincial populations.

English and French Television News Services: The CRTC Study

As Siegel (1983) reports it, the findings of the Boyle Committee of the CRTC into media bias are a "devastating indictment of the state of French-

TABLE 11.5

Distribution of Canadian Stories by Theme and Locality

Major Theme	National Capital	Provincial Capital	Major City	Rural
Business	2.0%	2.2%	4.6%	12.9%
Communication	.5			
Crime	1.0	7.6	7.3	14.5
Culture	3.0	2.7		
Disaster	.5	1.3	1.8	14.5
Economic	19.0	22.3	20.2	14.5
Energy	2.5	5.4	2.8	3.2
Environment	.5	1.8	4.6	8.1
Labour	4.5	10.3	11.9	8.1
Law	5.0	5.4	6.4	
Media	.5			
Medicine	.5	3.6	1.8	
Political	59.0	27.7	22.0	19.4
Religion	.5	1.3		1.6
Science	.5	3.1	2.8	
Sports	.5	1.3	2.8	
Human Interest	1.0	2.7	10.1	3.2

English interaction in the broadcast media: it was almost non-existent" (p. 222). The major findings of Siegel's content analyses, which appear to have been a major part of the research base for the Boyle Committee, are as follows:

1. The differences between French-language and English-language broadcasts far outweighed similarities.

2. Of the 1,785 stories examined, only 259 appeared in both French and English and more than half of those 259 dealt with international issues. Siegel estimates the common ground between French-language and English-language newscasts was about 15 per cent.

3. Differences in viewpoint emerged in the analyses of Canadian events, the international scene, perceptions of newsworthiness, emphasis on personalities, and geographic sources.

4. Half of the French-language television newscasts were devoted to Quebec.

5. English-language services were broader in their coverage of the national scene although the Maritimes and B.C. received little attention. Seventeen per cent of the stories were Quebec-oriented.

6. Greater emphasis was placed on political personalities by French-language news.

7. English-language news gave more coverage to the U.S. than did French-language news, which gave increased emphasis to Western Europe.

8. French-language newscasts had three times as many stories on constitutional issues as did English-language newscasts.

9. Seventy-three per cent of news stories on television and radio together come from four cities: Ottawa, Toronto, Quebec City, and Montreal.

TABLE 11.6

Distribution of Canadian Stories by Province

Province	Percentage
Ontario	50.9
Quebec	11.7
British Columbia	10.5
Alberta	7.3
Manitoba	4.9
Saskatchewan	4.5
Newfoundland	3.6
Nova Scotia	2.6
New Brunswick	1.9
Prince Edward Island	1.5
Yukon and Northwest Territories	0.5

10. In one four-month period, only 3 per cent of the French-language news stories in the major national evening newscast dealt with any part of Canada other than Quebec. In the English-language newscasts, only 9 per cent originated in Quebec at a time when a general election was bringing the Parti Québécois to power for the first time.

11. In one three-day analysis of 252 stories, only three appeared on all five networks.

Siegel attributes these differences to the structure of the broadcasting system and journalistic norms, an interpretation that seems reasonable enough. But what is relevant to our discussion is the apparent cultural vibrancy evidenced in these findings. Unfortunately, it was a vibrancy centred on a particular point in history when the Quebec French and the Ontario English were having a falling out.

Consider the findings and the political situation at the centre of the study this way. Was not the social movement that brought the Parti Québécois to power newsworthy for Quebecers? Did not the personalities of the political players have a major effect on carrying that social movement? Is there not a great deal of differ-

ence even between various French- and English-language stations in newscasts, not comparing across languages? Is there not a profound cultural difference between the Quebec French and the Ontario English and, for that matter, between the West and the Maritimes in perspectives on Canada?

The answer to all of these questions may well be "yes." If so, perhaps the claim can be made that we should pride ourselves in media so responsive to social movements and viewpoints rather than those that faun government policy, in the case of the situation reported, the centralized federalism of the day. We might even claim that we have a rather progressive press that plays to the interests of these movements and not to a more conservative national interest. As Cliff Lonsdale, CBC's head of Radio and TV productions (Europe), has noted:

> It is sometimes suggested that we could have a majority of programs common to both our television channels. I'm not at all sure, personally, that would be as they say, a "Good Thing." It strikes me as being the sort of situation that might appeal rather more to a committee of civil servants than it would to the public. (Lonsdale, 1983, p. 11)

On the other hand, there is no denying that the average Anglophone has little sense of what is going on in any part of Francophone Canada except as it relates to politics in general and specifically whether Quebec will remain in Canada. The opposite (for Francophones) is almost equally true.

One thing the data do make clear: no single metropolitan centre holds sway over the Canadian media and therefore probably the popular "Canadian mind." While 73 per cent of stories at this time period may have emanated from four central Canadian cities (and perhaps that is overplaying their centrality for the rest of

Canadians), our radio data show that over the longer term, at least with CBC English-language radio, such findings are not so pernicious. If anything is alarming it is the degree to which the Maritimes and B.C. are underrepresented. But again, the radio data do not support this as a long-term trend.

Avoiding Hinterland Dependency: A Short Course on Resource-Led Development

In *Prairie Capitalism,* Larry Pratt and John Richards argue against the notion that being a resource hinterland to a manufacturing centre necessarily entails a permanent dependency status. They claim that if the owners of the resource act as passive rentiers, and if the raw materials are exported directly to central markets, then a dependency status is sure to become entrenched. A dependency status is also likely to become built into the system if the resource owners allow the price of a commodity to rise less quickly than prices rise on the various finished products that the centre manufactures using the resource base.

These two conditions, however, may not be inevitable. As Pratt and Richards suggest, resource hinterlands can have considerable bargaining power in dealing with large resource-extraction companies. They examine two provinces, Saskatchewan and Alberta, and identify two different strategies for combatting a growing dependency in a resource-based economy. Saskatchewan has made greatest use of the public-sector strategy while Alberta has made greatest use of the public sector for creating manoeuvring room for the private sector.

The general strategy they outline is what they term **resource- or staple-led development**. The first aspect of a successful staple-led economy is the appropriate collection of economic rents.

They define economic rent as an excess in income arising in any industry above that necessary to generate a normal return to the man-made capital and labour employed. The power to collect rents, just like the power to command profit margins or wage levels, depends on the relative power of the group in society. In an optimistic society where it is assumed that technological progress will overcome any resource scarcities, the power of the resource owner is small. In a pessimistic scenario, for instance, when we believe that we may run out of oil or that there may not be enough food to feed the world, the power of the resource owner to command high prices (collect higher rents) is greater. But whether in optimistic or pessimistic times, the possession of an abundance of a resource provides significant cost advantages in certain staple industries. For Alberta these are in petrochemicals and certain types of agriculture. For Saskatchewan they are in petrochemicals, potash, and agriculture.

The key to collecting an appropriate level of economic rents is public entrepreneurship. Especially in pessimistic times, there are considerable opportunities for public entrepreneurship. Such entrepreneurship involves the exercise of the bureaucratic imagination. How might provincial governments step in to accrue maximum rents without facing an uncontrollable backlash or a withdrawal of the companies involved in extracting the resource? What kinds of royalties, taxes, licences can be devised to keep production going while bringing to the owners, the people, a maximum return for their property? In addition, what kinds of tax measures or transportation regulations could be enacted to maximize the development of related or "linked" industries to the resource?

This last consideration leads us to Pratt and Richards' second major point. Forward and backward linkages must be exploited. They define forward linkages as industries that use the region's staples to transform them further, for example, potash into fertilizer. Backward linkages are industries that provide inputs to the staple sector, for example, agricultural machinery manufacture or pipeline manufacture.

Leakages must be counteracted to the maximum degree possible. To explain, any economic activity puts money into the economy in the form of wages, profits, and rents. As this money is spent, it sets off another round of spending in the wages, profits, and rents of businesses that depend on the resource-extraction industry for their existence. Leakage occurs in terms of savings, taxes that leave the region, and the purchase of imported goods. The more of these there are, the less is the amplifying effect on the economy.

AVOIDING HINTERLAND DEPENDENCY: POSSIBILITIES FOR COMMUNICATIONS

An analogy can be drawn between natural resource riches and the resource base for the development of entertainment and information programming. Its basis is the fact, confirmed by the Broadcasting Task Force (1986), that whenever Canadians are given a choice of watching Canadian programming over foreign programming, many choose the Canadian. The second basis upon which Canadians have a comparative advantage in communications is that only Canadians can produce Canadian cultural artifacts.

Cultural Production as a Unique Resource

If we think of Canadian cultural artifacts as the staples to lead linked development we may have a good strategy for Canada's cultural future. Our present cultural policy is to give enormous advantage to imported cultural products and grant to them an even greater competitive advantage than they already have over Canadian cultural producers. We do this in a number of ways. First, because of their large home markets, foreign producers (especially the U.S.) have a competitive edge. What the U.S. producers gain from sales in Canada is gravy on the basic profit they make in their enormous home market. With all development costs recovered in the home market, sales in Canada represent extra profits on a base of only production costs. But that is just the beginning of the competitive edge.

Slitting Our Own Throats

We also provide an expensive infrastructure, which in effect subsidizes the distribution of foreign products. To take a first example, Canada, for example, has spent millions of dollars to put up communications satellites, yet foreign content producers have equal access (with domestic producers) to this infrastructure.

In the recording industry, when master tapes are imported, the tax assessed on them is based on the value of the raw materials upon which the recording is made. Besides the competitive advantage resulting from home market sales, we do not even tax on the value of the imported material.

Canada allows foreign owners to participate also in many businesses oriented to the distribution of cultural products, such as movie theatres. With no base in Canada, little moral suasion can be used to persuade them to insert Canadian cultural products among the mass cultural products that predominate in their distribution system.

Canada has very lax competition laws, too. In the U.S. the movie production houses were forced to divest themselves of their interests in movie theatres on the grounds that such a vertical integration did not allow sufficient competition. In Canada no such requirement has ever come into effect. Periodically distributors agree to give all movie theatres a fair chance to bid on the right to first showings of movies. However, as attention shifts away from them they return to their preferential dealings with the large chains.

In terms of Pratt and Richards' model, we have not collected the appropriate economic rents on the sale of Canadian audiences and the sale of the Canadian communications infrastructure to foreign producers and distributors. At the most extreme, the public entrepreneurs could legitimately devise schemes where the costs of Canadian production could provide the basis for pricing (i.e., taxing) imported cultural goods to bring imported material in line with those costs. Also, we have not built up forward and backward linkages nearly enough. (Taking the movie industry as one example, the backward linkages would be to books while the forward linkages would be to broadcast and rebroadcast rights, video shop sales and rentals, and so forth.) Finally, the leakage of money out of the economy in the cultural area through the purchase of foreign cultural materials is astronomical, as Audley's (1983) figures in Chapter 2 show.

Support Programs

The federal government and most provincial governments have begun to realize that the state of cultural production in Canada is counterproductive from both a cultural and a business perspective. A variety of programs have been put in place, some aimed at increasing the opportunities for artists and other cultural workers (e.g., the Canada Council), and other programs are oriented to putting in place stable production houses and facilities to form the foundations of a vibrant cultural industry.

Perhaps the best-known example is the effort made by the federal government to establish a healthy film production industry. When we realize that in 1980 the estimated wholesale revenue from the sale of films to the Canadian market for both theatre and television was $219 million and that 98.2 per cent and 92.7 per cent respectively of that spending went to foreign producers (Audley, 1983, p. 317), it is easy to understand why the federal government is willing to make a massive investment to try to help Canadians acquire a decent share of that market. It makes eminent sense if only because we cannot afford to lose all of these Canadian dollars to foreign producers.

The federal and various provincial governments have taken steps to help Canadian publishers participate in the Canadian book and magazine market. In that industry, the schemes have been many and varied, from learning material development plans through outright grants, half-back schemes on lottery tickets, subsidies on sales, subsidies to sell international rights, the development of a copyright act that would favour domestic rather than foreign producers, etc. Each of these plans has had some success, as have many of the plans in other areas, but a striking breakthrough has yet to be achieved.

One of the visible success stories has been the Canadian content regulation on AM radio. Beginning in 1971, all AM stations licensed in Canada were required to devote 30 per cent of their air time to Canadian content. As a result of this single regulation, there has sprung up a lively rock music production industry in Canada's major cities. So successful is it that not only is Canada producing international stars but foreign performers of stature are coming to Canada to record. While producer David Foster's attempt to base himself in West Vancouver was short-lived, André Perry's Le Studio in Morin Heights, Quebec, is a mecca for rock-and-roll artists.

Once room is created in the distribution system within Canada for Canadian cultural products, then Canadian audiences apparently will jump at the chance to consume them and secondary linked activities will also grow from that basic market presence. As Pratt and Richards note, the real opportunities will be created by the efforts of politicians and governments. From the early signs of the effects that emerged from a variety of tentative steps, there is little doubt that Canadian artists and entrepreneurs will use the opportunities created by governments to benefit all Canadians.

SUMMARY

The domestic geopolitics of information are not unlike the global geopolitics. Canada suffers, as do non-dominant groups within Canada, from the historical, economic, social, and communications structures that have been built up to serve empire, empire U.S.A., and empire Canada. As a result, in learning materials, broadcasting, the recording industry, writing, theatre, dance, and other modes of cultural expression, one can find the guiding finger of that cultural industry in the content produced. With respect to cultural dominance from outside, Canada worsens her own position with laws and infrastructure and subsidy programs that actually help foreign producers attain a level that exceeds that of domestic producers. In addition, importers are given free rein to bring foreign cultural products into the country to compete with those indigenously produced.

All, however, is not lost, either in the practical world of program production or in a theoretical way of seeing things. As we illustrated, news programming can be designed to counter metropolis-hinterland dynamics, and as Pratt and Richards have demonstrated, a theoretical position can also be introduced to demonstrate the nature of hinterland power. That model can as easily guide cultural industries as it does resource industries.

With regard to policy, four levels of concern must be addressed to improve our domestic status in the cultural industries. (1) Opportunities must be created for Canadians to participate in articulating their own culture. (2) For participation to be significant, steps must be taken to ensure that the incentive structure to produce content does not grossly favour only mass market materials to the neglect of the Canadian cultural market. (3) The various cultural professions must be nurtured from within a national framework so that they develop and maintain a coherence. Out of that coherence will emerge a distinctive Canadian voice. (4) Issues of ownership are also significant. It appears that the various levels of government have realized that importers are not the ones to take on the development of Canadian cultural production. Far more suitable to take on this task for both domestic and international consumption are the small Canadian producers who abound with entrepreneurial energy. The issue of ownership cannot be underestimated. Foreign owners do not have (indeed, cannot have) Canadian interests at heart. Importers are compromised. Programs for the development of Canadian cultural expression need to be directed at Canadian owners whose production is already centred on Canadian cultural expression.

REFERENCES

Althusser, Louis. *Lenin and His Philosophy*. London: New Left Books, 1971.

Audley, Paul. *Canada's Cultural Industries: Broadcasting, Publishing, Records, and Film*. Toronto: James Lorimer, 1983.

Beale, Alison. "The Question of Space," in R. Lorimer and D.C. Wilson, eds., *Communication Canada*. Toronto: Kagan and Woo, 1988.

Berger, Thomas. *Northern Frontier, Northern Homeland: Report of the Mackenzie Valley Pipeline Enquiry.* Ottawa: Queen's Printer, 1977.

Canada. *The Uncertain Mirror: Report of the Special Senate Committee on Mass Media,* Volume I, 1970.

Canada. *Report of the Task Force on Broadcasting Policy.* Ottawa: Ministry of Supply and Services, 1986.

Canadian Broadcasting Corporation. *Annual Report,* 1981, 1985.

Canadian Broadcasting Corporation. *Canadian-Produced Programming for Canadian TV Audiences: How Are We Doing?* Ottawa: CBC, 1990.

Clymer, T., ed. *Reading 360.* Toronto: Ginn, 1972.

Concordia University, Communication Studies. *Communication and the Canadian North.* Montreal, 1983.

Innis, H.A. *Essays in Canadian Economic History.* Edited by Mary Q. Innis. Toronto: University of Toronto Press, 1956.

Lonsdale, C. "The Canadian Media and National Unity," in *Bilingualism and the Media: Canada and Wales.* Aberystwyth: Canadian Studies in Wales Group, 1983.

Lorimer, Rowland. *The Nation in the Schools.* Toronto: OISE Press, 1984.

Lorimer, Rowland. "An Analysis of CBC Radio News in English," unpublished paper, Simon Fraser University, 1984.

Lorimer, R., and P. Keeney. "Defining the curriculum: The role of the multinational textbook in Canada," in S. De Castell, A. Luke, and C. Luke, eds., *Language, Authority and Criticism: Readings on the School Textbook.* London/Philadelphia: Falmer Press, 1988.

Lyman, P. *Canada's Video Revolution.* Toronto: James Lorimer, 1983.

McNulty, Jean. "The Political Economy of Canadian Satellite Broadcasting," paper presented at Canadian Communication Association meeting, Montreal, May, 1987.

National Film Board. *Magic in the Sky,* directed by Peter Raymont, produced by Peter Raymont, Arthur Hammond. Ottawa, 1981.

Pratt, Larry, and John Richards. *Prairie Capitalism: Power and Influence in the New West.* Toronto: McClelland and Stewart, 1979.

Rioux, Marcel. *Quebec in Question.* Trans. James Boake. Toronto: James Lorimer, 1973.

Siegel, Arthur. *Politics and the Media in Canada.* Toronto: McGraw-Hill Ryerson, 1973.

Valaskakis, G. "Television and Cultural Integration," in Lorimer and Wilson, eds., *Communications Canada.*

von Zur Muehen, Max. "Foreign Academics at Canadian Universities: A Statistical Perspective on New Appointments during the Seventies," mimeo, December, 1981.

STUDY QUESTIONS

1. Thomas Berger, in *Northern Frontier, Northern Homeland,* discusses the successive intrusions of white civilization upon Inuit culture. Discuss the role of communications technologies in this vein.

2. Your village on Ellesmere Island has just been offered the opportunity to have a satellite dish and distribution system installed free by a multinational oil company. Until now there has been no television reception in your village. What matters do you think should be considered in deciding whether to accept the company's offer?

3. In the Siegel study of CBC television news, it was found that the French and English services provided different versions of "reality." Discuss the possible benefits and dangers of these differences for Canadians.

4. "A staple-led economy, being necessarily continentalist, is a continual threat not only to Canada's economic and political but also to its cultural sovereignty." Discuss.

CHAPTER

12

Canada in an Information Age

INTRODUCTION

T HROUGHOUT THIS BOOK we have explored the role of communication and the media in contemporary society. The purpose of this final chapter is to review those explorations, integrate and extend the discussion of the various chapters, and consider the ongoing cultural significance of communication and media, especially for Canada and Canadians, as we move toward the twenty-first century.

COMMUNICATION, MASS COMMUNICATION, THE MASS MEDIA, SOCIETY, AND POLITICS

T he first area, which we explored in Chapters 1 to 3, encompassed the five terms listed in the above heading. We noted, first of all, that communication is infused in every aspect of our lives, acting along two axes of influence. The first axis, one of breadth, encompasses society, politics, economics, education, culture, technology, the family, and the individual. The second axis, one of depth, encompasses the nature of the coding of meaning into a dominant form of communication in society – oral, literate, electronic – and the implications, for the basic dynamics of society, of the structuring tendencies inherent in each form. In discussing the "breadth" axis our intent was to demonstrate that communication is intrinsic to all human endeavour. With the "depth" axis we touched on such variables as social cohesion, legal and institutional form, the nature and dynamics of social stability over time, the sphere or expanse of a society, and interaction between the social process and communication form.

In Chapter 2, we considered the relation between the mass media, mass communication, and the broader area of communication as a whole, noting that each (as listed in the above order) was a subset of the other. The mass media are the dominant form of communication in modern society. In describing mass communication we drew attention to both historical precedents to the mass media and the general dynamics of large centralized institutions creating content for large and unknown heterogeneous audiences.

Finally, still within this first area, in Chapter 3 we explored the national organization of mass communication systems, the interaction of such systems with the society, and the politics of the nations of which they are a part.

The first three chapters lay the groundwork for subsequent chapters. However, the implications, as discussed in Chapter 1 and extended somewhat here, are not to be neglected. Consider for a final time the ideas advanced in Chapter 1. First, communicational forms consist of both a medium (that might also, sometimes, be labelled a technology) and a social organization that makes it possible for the medium to operate. That is to say, whereas book-publishing companies contract out their printing and may

be single-owner, self-financed operations requiring relatively little capital and technical expertise, television stations are fairly large, complex, differentiated organizations requiring, among other things, financial, managerial, journalistic, and technological contributions. Second, if we accept that very general communicational forms – oral, literate, and electronic – influence the social order, it is reasonable to assume that the mass media, which are composed of a mixture of these general communicational forms, also act as a structuring influence on society. It then follows that the spread of common mass communicational forms throughout all societies of the world may have a homogenizing influence. (This theme is picked up with specific reference to technology in Chapter 9.) Third, because communication spans all human endeavour, its influence on social life is widespread, including, one might postulate, on our world view, i.e., our social philosophy or belief system.

What are some of the implications of these three points? Consider Table 12.1. Column 1 describes the communicational forms we discussed in Chapter 1 with a slight expansion. For the purposes of this final discussion we have split electronic into three parts, oral, audio-visual, and textual-numeric. Column 2 describes the communicational context and/or the dominant technology of the form; column 3 outlines the analytical framework that derives most directly from the communicational form; column 4 describes the social philosophy/belief system complementary to the derivative analytical framework.

As Table 12.1 illustrates, each communicational form develops in a different context and encourages quite a distinctive manner of thinking and social belief system. In overview, oral communication takes place through face-to-face interaction. It is fundamentally social. As investigations have shown in a variety of areas, including anthropology (Goody, 1977), communications (McLuhan,

TABLE 12.1

The Social Structure of Communication

Communicational Form	Communicational Context/ Dominant Technology	Analytical Framework	Social Philosophy/ Belief System

Oral	– face-to-face
	– multifaceted
	  e.g., voice
	  modulation,
	  gesture
		– interpretation
		  of intent
		– consistency
		  of actions
		  with character
			– focused on
			  personalized
			  environmental
			  constants
			– pluralistic

Literate	– indirectly
	  social
	– individual
	  interacts
	  with text
	– text can
	  stand alone
		– logical
		– linear
		– conceptual
		– structuralist
		– scientific
		  method
			– hierarchical
			– development of
			  conceptual constants
			– single concept
			  supremacy
			– scientific

Electronic Oral	– mediated by
	  radio and
	  telephone
		– memory-based
		– impressionist
			– capture of the
			  Zeitgeist

Electronic Audio-visual	– television
	– iconic
	– dramatic
	– socially
	  produced
		– impressionist
		– multi-
		  interpretative
		– post-modernist
			– pluralistic
			– celebratory of
			  variety, particu-
			  larity, novelty

Electronic Textual-numeric	– computers/
	  telecommunications
	– text- and machine-
	  oriented
		– trends analysis
		– inferential
		  statistics
			– extensivity
			  possibly leading
			  to elitism

1962, 1964; Innis, 1950, 1951; Ong, 1982), history (Eisenstein, 1983), and classics (Havelock, 1976), it is associated with an analytical framework focused on interpretation of intent of actors whether those actors are human beings or a pantheon of gods. This leads to a personalized or anthropocentric world in which environmental constants such as the sun, moon, stars, signs of the zodiac, earth, air, seas, rivers, trees, rocks, animals, and so forth are made into a set of basic influences on life. Social interaction takes place and is interpreted within the framework of this set of forces and each person is a member – by virtue of time and date of birth or family membership or sex – of one or more groups, i.e., aquarians, moon worshippers, the bear clan. The pluralism inherent in this system provides a variety of interpretative structures that vie for allegiance and are not necessarily consistent one with another.

Literate communication, on the other hand, is only indirectly social. Both writer and reader engage a text, one creating, the other interpreting. The text must have internal consistency and comprehensiveness. It must be capable of standing apart from its author as a meaningful statement in and by itself. Literate analysis is linear – moving from point to point (not contextualized as is oral communication by body language and tone of voice or audio-visual communication by pictures and sound). It leads to the development of general and specific explanatory concepts that form into a system or general theory. The concepts have a hierarchical relation one to another and, over the course of time, form an explanatory framework – in specific instances, a scientific theory. For example, the behaviour of objects relative to other objects was defined by a number of specific laws until Newton suggested the notion of gravity to explain such behaviour. Later, Einstein proposed his general theory of relativity and Newton's notions were recast as specific instances within Einstein's more encompassing framework.

Out of the literate analytical process have developed structuralist theories typical of the physical and biological sciences and now found in a variety of social science and humanities disciplines, including literature (Frye), anthropology (Lévi-Strauss), language (Jakobsen, Chomsky), psychology (Piaget). The hierarchical nature of the conceptual frameworks developed in literate society focuses the development of ideas on the production and testing of conceptual constants leading toward the supremacy of general concepts that seem to explain all related phenomena, as in relativity theory.

Electronic oral communication, exemplified by radio and the telephone, is socially mediated by technology and focused on the human voice and the rhetorical structure of the message. Like oral communication it relies on the memory of the listener, but, at least on radio, it is often created first in written form and then delivered orally. Electronic oral communication is affected by how the speaker contextualizes his/her message by (a) voice modulation, (b) the manner in which ideas are expressed, e.g., choice of words and whether the ideas are expressed within a narrative form, and (c) the overall interrelationship of ideas in the message as a whole, e.g., the sequencing of ideas or placing opposing ideas in the mouths of different actors.

The analytical framework associated with electronic oral communication is memory-based and impressionistic of both message and messenger. The accompanying social philosophy is oriented to the ability of certain speakers to capture in words the information, attitudes, and understandings the audience already has, sometimes called the *Zeitgeist*. The phrase "does it ring true" is often operative. This can lead to reliance on certain speakers as believable, independent of whether their content stands up to detailed scrutiny.

Electronic audio-visual communication is most obviously exemplified by television. It is also only indirectly social and mediated by technology. It recreates or re-presents the social through its pictures and spoken words. Based on its orientation to visual images it can be said to be an iconic medium. It is also a dramatic medium. Together these properties allow it to attempt to recreate the sound and sight of persons completely focused on significant events. In real life, few have the luxury of complete focus on any event or person: diapers have to be changed, boring jobs must be done, phone calls unrelated to the plot must be answered, etc.

The production of audio-visual images is a social process involving a large and diverse team, with each member attempting to contribute to a complementarity of images – whether by lighting, framing, dialogue, ambience, or editing style – to create the intended impression (see Chapter 4). In some sense, electronic audio-visual communication is the re-creation of face-to-face communication in a full visualized context conceived by the literate mind.

Because an infinite number of images and impressions can be created by even slight variations in the produced piece of communication, the analytical framework most appropriate to this form of communication is a post-structuralist, multi-interpretive analysis pointing to the organizing attributes of the produced message. Foucault, Derrida, and post-modernism, though different from one another, can be understood as complementary to this communicational form. The complementary social philosophy to this iconic form is pluralism, an acceptance of variety, particularity, and novelty (within the limits of a prevailing school of thought or expression) that celebrates the human condition.

Electronic textual-numeric communication exemplified by computers and telecommunication is the least social communicative form of the five discussed here. At best it may involve an individual creating input; however, computers may suffice for all aspects – inputting, reception, and analysis. The information typical to this form of communication is monitored (the number of items sold at a particular cash register) or sampled (a market or political poll). The communicators involved – both information creators and audience – have the capacity to analyse and benefit from vast quantities of detailed information. Examples are banks, insurance companies, central governments, or any other institution dealing with a large mass of information.

The analytic framework most suited to this form of communication is descriptive and inferential statistics. The complementary social philosophy is based on the extensiveness of information at the command of the analyst. This emphasis has the potential to lead to elitism, derived from an identification of those who have the technical and analytical capacity to work with extensive data. Business feudalism reminiscent of governing courts, seigneurs, war lords, or, in more contemporary forms, global conglomerates, oligarchies, monopolies, and Japanese-style business (involving both lifetime employment and state/business co-ordination) would be consistent with this form of communication.

Mass communication is a hybrid communicational form, combining elements of literate, electronic oral, electronic audio-visual, and electronic textual-numeric communication. As such, it sets up a dynamic tension between the tendencies inherent in each analytical framework, social philosophy/belief system, and communicational form of which it contains parts. If, in their operations, the mass media can play into the biases of each existing communicational form, they can enhance their influence on and centrality to society.

The future, even with an expanding mass communications sector in place, promises a rich social dynamic. Even as they succeed, the dominance of the mass media giants – the global press and media lords of business – will be undermined by others: the small book publishers, specialized periodical publishers, filmmakers, and rural radio stations. To borrow and adapt a phrase from monarchists, "The media are dead, long live the media!"

Chapter 2 was primarily definitional of the mass media. We have already touched on the implications beyond those outlined in Chapter 2 in our discussion of the bias of communicational forms and their inherent relation to the mass media. To summarize: the social production of images within largish, technologically oriented institutions by groups of professionals, each with their own practices and ideals, for largely unknown audiences places certain constraints on the production of meaning that the mass media are able to undertake. From one perspective, while ensuring a high-quality product, it also interferes with monolithic rule by one group, such as owners, journalists, or politicians.

At the conclusion of Chapter 2 we discussed media boundaries, that is, where social behaviour and image production interact, anticipating the discussion of plugging and identity production in Chapter 4. As commercial images increasingly infuse themselves into entertainment, it will be interesting to note the boundaries of tolerance of the audience.

Chapter 3 outlined a completely separate set of constraints on the operation of the media – the interaction between national political processes and the dynamics of political communication in the mass media. We sought to establish some basic variables in the interaction between media and government to reveal the extent to which modern communications are part of the operation of complex industrial and post-industrial society. It is perhaps in longitudinal and comparative contexts that this area becomes most stimulating. In such explorations, how media systems can be profoundly affected by such specific elements as annual budgets or government scandal and, at the same time, by such general elements as political traditions is of particular interest. With expanding use of polling and the tendency for media to release their findings while political parties and governments often do not, the understanding of and responsiveness to the political preferences of the public no doubt will continue to be a site for contests of power and legitimacy.

THE PRODUCTION AND CONSUMPTION OF MASS COMMUNICATION

For some readers, the content of Chapter 4, which documents the production of images and the tendency to become resigned to or, alternatively, to marvel at the exercise of creative communicational power by those currently holding the strings, may be both suggestive and fascinating. Nonetheless, after several millennia following the achievement of literacy, if the dominant means of communication are used primarily to produce enticing and alluring images whose primary aim is to amuse and maintain consumption, it is dubious that our inheritors will look upon our time as a golden age of human achievement.

The attempt on the part of social analysts to capture the richness and variety of human creativity, while not neglecting established social fabrics and fundamentals out of which meaning is constructed, is encouraging. This is being accomplished by combining structuralist and post-structuralist analytical frameworks (Curran, 1990; McQuail, 1990). These more sophisticated analytical frameworks provide the basis for the realization that the media can affect perception and behaviour quite fundamentally. Perhaps with that realization and the inevitable boredom of peeping in on the lives of the rich and famous, we may look to an emergent media-based enhancement through the spread of information, education, and aesthetic creativity. However, those may only be the dreams of educators.

In detailing the creative process and its potential allure, Chapter 4 underscores the importance of the attitudes and professional ideals of image-makers, that is journalists, designers, camera operators, editors, and so forth. They determine whether the public good will be considered or turned aside for whatever reason, be it libertarianism, the inability to achieve objectivity, or the primacy of legal structures over human values and agency (if the law doesn't direct me, who am I to decide not to pursue audiences with any form of sensationalist program they will watch?). Thankfully, at the present time, the Canadian journalistic community has a fully working conscience, as *The Newsmakers* points out.

Chapter 5 deals with media consumption and harkens back to the end of Chapter 2 and our discussion of the boundaries of media and audience. The notion that the audience participates in the meaning-generation process of the mass media is fairly recent. As we noted, it arose in reaction to the pessimism of European intellectuals seeing the cultural richness of rural peasant life replaced by the life of the urban wage-earner, who, on the whole, led a freer life but, from the point of view of the intellectuals, an exhausting, confined, and culturally barren one. Industrialization did indeed produce an urban working class for whom life has never been a bowl of cherries. However, it also produced opportunity

for individuals to seek control over some small means of production of some market good. With that control came the potential for economic advancement and material wealth. The concept of the audience-as-participants in media and meaning production also derives from the clear interaction between lived cultural patterns and media representations.

The notion that the mass audience participates in the production of media products by providing content and being sought out as an audience is empowering. And it certainly has some veracity. However, it tends to underplay the boundary between player and audience. In a rich, expanding, and expansive social system that places a positive value on social, cultural, and political diversity, the notion that the general public is empowered by being media participants offers a great deal in terms of social cohesion. But when those who control the means of production, that is, either private owners or the state, feel that they must exercise the full extent of their control, the audience-as-participant perspective is a convenient distortion. It allows for

1. the presentation of elite culture in the name of edifying values that are "of universal benefit"; or

2. extensive political control to facilitate the presentation of analysis designed to assist "everyone to understand his or her true communal and individual interests"; or

3. the deprivation of a national community from its ability to reflect its own distinctive concerns and therefore of the cultural value of these "cultural" industries in the name of industrial development and the economic well-being of the country, specifically, the desirability of "world-class" cultural industries able to participate in global markets.

The potential restrictiveness of mass media audiences-as-participants reveals the necessity for an open media system that encourages wide participation of all members of society. It also provides a rationale for an exploration of our third area, the various loci of control over mass communication.

THE LOCI OF CONTROL OVER MASS COMMUNICATION

The state, industry owners, professional content producers, and technology: each of these four has a critical influence on the form and role of the mass media on society. Surrounding each are key issues resulting from the continual changes and developments in each sector.

State Involvement

The key issues surrounding state involvement are (1) the nature and degree of state involvement; (2) the guiding philosophy of state involvement: elite art, popular culture, or industry; (3) the degree to which the media should be used for education.

For a very long time, information has had a special status in society. That status has taken material form in the library. Public libraries, as Basil Stuart-Stubbs (1981) has pointed out, are ownership collectives. They are ancient institutions that have been in existence ever since information has been recorded, whether on clay tablets, papyrus, paper, or film. Their collective nature arises from their function: to acquire information that they then lend to others. Public libraries are based on the dual notion that an individual cannot own all the information to which he or she may want or need access and that one's access to wealth should not determine one's access to information.

Industrial society established this approach to information in the name of the public good. Works that explained technology and industry of the industrial period were written and published. Many found their homes in libraries of workers' organizations. The value of information and of the collective organization necessary for a reasonable level of access by a social group was established.

While these ownership collectives were originally established by groups themselves (for example, the libraries of Mechanics' Institutes) and later promoted in the name of the general public good by private philanthropists such as Carnegie, eventually the state took them over, just as it did education in the name of the general public good.

The state was also involved in other media developments. Governments were and continue to be both major publishers and major contractors for publishing services. After arduous struggle, the state finally allowed free comment from those who also provided printing services. As a result, the press of the Western world was able to grow to its present stature without competition from instruments of the government. Had such competition existed, not only would the press have been smaller but it probably would have been a much more politically destabilizing influence.

In short, from the beginning and in a variety of ways, the state has been involved in media development that has continued through to the electronic information age. The public element of information access was carried through to the electronic age, although with some difficulty. Marconi, through patent law, attempted to control the development of radio communication. He leased his radio sets, along with his employees as operators, and refused to let his employees communicate with those using non-Marconi equipment. Only by governments declaring the airwaves to be a public resource was Marconi's grip on radio communication broken. Once this attempted monopoly was broken, and as Fessenden's invention for carrying voice communication was taken up, governments found themselves getting into the business of broadcasting. Only a very few countries, including the United States, decided to let private enterprises rule the airwaves. State-owned radio and television are much more common around the world, even in Western capitalist countries.

Today, Western society appears determined to impose a monetary value on information, especially when it is in electronic form. Thus, we are placing information dissemination much more fully into the hands of private entrepreneurs. The development and employment of electronic communications technology have required vast research and development funds. The hardware and software, for the most part, are now controlled by private corporations whose reason for existence is profit. Because of these material realities, we are seeing a shift away from the maintenance of public and collective participation in dealing with information. Primarily, this is because producers and their representatives are gaining control over information access (through the creation of databases) rather than users and their representatives (libraries and other social governmental agencies).

It is not that information corporations are pushing their interests on an objecting society. As both Audley's *Canada's Cultural Industries* and Lyman's *Canada's Video Revolution* point out, economists have discovered their oversight of information and culture as economic activities. Governments, too, have initially encouraged this whole sector to expand through their willingness to fund technological research and development.

To the list of those who are promoting the economic recognition of information, i.e., information corporations, economists, and governments, we must also add information workers, especially owners of intellectual property. Such workers include those on the creative side – artists, singers, composers, writers – and those on the manipulation or recording side – secretaries, librarians, computer programmers, database managers. These information workers are emerging as a powerful group with a stake in the full economic recognition of information products.

As the full economic value of information is recognized, a public presence becomes increasingly difficult to maintain. This is not just on account of the cries of the private sector to be left to accrue their profits. It arises as well from the desire and need to exhaust every market to cover the costs of information production. In addition, private control is related to a change in the dominant technology used for the transmission of information.

A Guiding Philosophy for State Involvement

Three bases may be considered for guiding state involvement in communications and cultural industries. They are art, culture, and industry. If we can accept that the constant of communications and cultural industries is artistic, then, at least according to Woodcock (1985), there is a case to be made against any state intervention. Art is both universal and particular. It develops out of the particular situation of a particular artist. It gains its universal quality from the ability of the artist to capture the universal condition in particular material. To allow the state to intervene is to introduce an illegitimate guiding hand that compromises both art and artists.

Woodcock names Prime Minister Trudeau and his early culture minister, Gérard Pelletier, as leaders of state intervention. He characterizes Trudeau's view as stemming from the notion that the arts add "an essential grace in the life of civilized people" (p. 108) and that the role of government should be as follows:

> I do not think that modern society, or the artist as a member of that society, need fear a generous policy of subsidy to the arts by governments as long as those governments have the courage to permit free expression and experimentation – and, for that matter, to take it in good part if the mirror held up to their faces is not a flattering one.

Woodcock disagrees, claiming that no matter how liberal the state, government aid inevitably sets a general course for development for the arts, which compromises the necessary distance between artist and political power.

We are more inclined to the view that the development of the electronic media and cultural industries are a late twentieth-century method of enhancing community identity. We see mass communication and cultural industries as involving much more than artistic expression, and therefore requiring much more than policies oriented purely to artistic expression. There are two approaches that deserve consideration. We will discuss them together.

A cultural approach to the involvement of the state in communications assesses expression within any medium for its ability to generate social, cultural, or even spiritual value within the context of the community. The difference between an artistic and a cultural approach is the element of community. In making a judgement of an item of culture, artistic values come together with the nature and values of the community in which they are created. On the other hand, an industrial approach assesses the contribution cultural products can make to the economy.

An overview of policies supporting book publishing can be used to illustrate. As of 1990 there were, at the federal level, two major programs of support for Canada's book publishers. The more generous of the two, the industrial program, was run by the Department of Communications (DOC). The less well-endowed cultural program was run by the Canada Council.

The industrial program of the DOC provides assistance to companies through its Book Publishing Industry Development Program. Its aim is to increase sales and their position in the marketplace. Commercially successful firms are rewarded with support that is intended to allow them to grow further. The program particularly supports firms that wish to undertake projects aimed at the profitable educational market. The final goal of the program, as the Minister of Communications has often noted, is to create a domestically owned industry that has a significant share of the domestic market.

Note that there is no reference to the cultural value of the type of book publishing undertaken. Rather, support is given on the basis that book publishing is, by definition, a cultural industry. The mechanisms and criteria used by the government to allocate support are similar to those that might be used with any business. The manner in which special support is justified for cultural industries has been discussed by Rotstein (1988). As he points out, economists, when considering the need for specific support for culture, speak of **merit goods, market failure,** and **infant industries**.

The aim of the Canada Council program, as the application forms point out, is to "offset publication deficits on books which make an original contribution to Canadian literature or identify and address public concerns in Canada." Areas of writing that are supported by this program include poetry, drama, fiction, non-fiction, and children's literature.

Here, culture is central and the contribution must be "original" and "to Canadian literature"

– therefore it must be judged as literature – or "identify and address public concerns in Canada." To make decisions on whether individual works or publishing programs qualify, the Canada Council creates panels made up of persons who are publishers, booksellers, librarians, or generally involved in the artistic and cultural community. Through the creation of these committees, politics enter the picture. The Council is therefore careful to be seen to select from persons who are knowledgeable about the culture of the country and who also represent all regions, ethnic groups, genders, political orientation, and so forth.

Parallel considerations enter into justifying and designing support programs in other areas of communications and cultural industries. Programs now exist in Canada for filmmaking, sound recording, and periodical publishing, as well as book publishing. In broadcasting, the cultural value of broadcasting and special responsibilities of the CBC are laid out clearly in the Broadcasting Act. These objectives provide the means to justify public subsidy.

The important issue is not whether we should have industrially based (and necessarily technologically oriented) or culturally based communications and cultural industries policies. In an era of cultural industries, in the fact of the aggressiveness of U.S. entertainment industries, and in recognition of the technological juggernaut that makes it ever easier for producers to market their products worldwide, we have little choice. The important issue is to understand the consequences of an industrially based policy in order to plan a complementary culturally based policy. Four of those consequences follow.

1. Participation in the wide variety of technological formats for cultural products will take money away from new production.

2. Industrial development compels us to encourage the development of large, interna-

tionally active corporations oriented to world markets and concerned only to a degree with domestic culture.

3. Focusing on large international players introduces a homogenizing influence and increases the distance between Canadians and the cultural products produced by Canadians.

4. We must re-assess the role of public corporations. This does not mean that the public sector should be slashed back. Public companies can be used for a variety of purposes, including: to provide a window on the industry; as chosen vehicles to bring products to market; to undertake long-term development; to provide services to outlying communities; to foster infant industries (see Hardin, 1974).

Education and the Media

Education, according to the Canadian constitution, is a provincial responsibility. The provinces have been very protective of their responsibility for education and this protectionism has led to thirteen different educational systems in Canada, one for each province except New Brunswick, which has one for Anglophones and one for Francophones, plus two for the territories. This protectionism has also provided the base for a rampant professionalism neglectful of national culture and has led to a severe restriction of the market power of educators in the learning materials marketplace. The producers, operating in a transnational market, have greater power than the consumers, who are limited in their bargaining power at best to the size of their provincial population of students.

With broadcasting satellites in place, educational programming will be created for purchase by anyone who cares to receive it. The CRTC decision to allow cable companies to offer a U.S.-based service, The Learning Channel, despite the objections of a consortium of provincial education television producers, demonstrates that the educational market is as open as the home entertainment audience.

Given these technological developments, the provinces must consider their insistence on autonomy, which has led to each making its own bargain on how to homogenize its interests with those in the U.S. The foundation of that reconsideration needs to be the development of production consortia, the materials of which must be as widely used as possible in Canada.

The implication of such a development is a reconsideration of curricula, but without a view to homogeneity across the land. A culturally based heterogeneity must be preserved alongside an appropriate homogeneity in those areas of the curriculum where it is warranted. To do otherwise will severely jeopardize the future of the country.

Ownership

The key issues surrounding the role of industry owners are: (1) variety in the types of media owners; (2) foreign versus domestic ownership; (3) concentration of and transnational ownership.

Variety in Ownership

In times (such as the early 1990s) when the influence of large, privately owned, global corporations is increasing worldwide, when Western governments are curtailing their support for public-sector corporations, and when Communist societies are allowing their media to Westernize, it is easy to drop discussions of the need for variety in types of media owners. To provide an example, in early 1990, Southam took over more than a dozen weekly newspapers in and around the Vancouver area. It already owned the two dailies in Vancouver itself. Concern was

voiced in many quarters about concentration of ownership. Officials responsible for the administration of the Competition Act were sent out to investigate, and a local opposition MP persuaded the government to hold hearings of the (Parliamentary) Standing Committee on Communications and Culture. Subsequently, the hearings were cancelled when the MP in question became party critic of a different portfolio. The cancellation was probably not a great loss. The hearings appeared destined to be confined to whether Southam or some other large corporation should control the weeklies.

The larger issue is this. At present, no law or understanding works to preserve independent, single-enterprise media outlets. If one large Canadian media conglomerate cannot, by law, acquire them because it already owns too many in the same geographical area, then another can. There is no legal equivalent in the media to an "agricultural land reserve," which would preserve certain media for certain purposes by maintaining a particular ownership form. The best we have in dealing with the private media are hearings before various committees and agencies such as the CRTC and the Standing Committee on Communications and Culture. One other mechanism actually does exist within the CRTC: it is category of licence. So far, this mechanism has not been used extensively to encourage a balance in the variety in forms of ownership so that, for instance, as many educational as commercial licences were granted. But the possibility of issuing more educational and community licences does exist.

Meanwhile, however, at all times, any independent is vulnerable to takeover by a larger corporation that can increase profits by making it part of a larger chain. When considering the public interest, one large corporate owner is hardly different from any other. On the other hand, as Herschel Hardin never ceases to point out, if one is considering variety in ownership, that is to say, single-enterprise ownership, public owners such as Crown corporations, direct government ownership, other forms of non-commercial owners such as co-operatives, public-sector institutions such as universities, or coalitions of interest groups active in an area of human endeavour such as churches, then there is something worth talking about. But without a legal infrastructure to restrain large companies from takeover and small companies from selling, that discussion is academic.

Foreign versus Domestic Ownership and Control

In a world where every possible ounce of profit is wrung out of every piece of information, the issues of foreign versus domestic *control* of information and foreign versus domestic *production* of information are pressing economic concerns. They are even more pressing economic concerns because, in the competitive struggle of the marketplace, the images and symbols available for consumption, e.g., the golden arches of McDonald's, or the moral superiority of this or that empire, are those that have won out in a mighty economic battle for domination. They are not dominant for political or cultural reasons.

In such a world, for the most part, considerations of the public good disappear. Gone with them, for instance, is the gentlemanly patronage of the publisher, the willingness to undertake a project destined to lose money but somehow seen to be a major contribution to culture and civilization. In its place are innumerable devices, formulae, and vast amounts of money whose primary purpose is to capture large audiences so that, in the case of television, for example, they can be sold to advertisers.

Opting for domestic ownership is a way of introducing the interests of the community into the boardrooms of large corporations. Just think, for instance, of how powerless the Royal Commission on Newspapers would have seemed if it were dealing with the two U.S.-based Gannett and Hearst organizations as the two corporate giants in Canada. In the arena of domestic ownership there appears to be some reason for optimism. In 1990, for instance, the U.S. Congress was looking for ways to restrict foreign ownership of cable television. Were such a measure to be put in place, it would assist in maintaining domestic ownership laws and practices in Canada.

The full acceptance of foreign ownership leads to and is complemented by the notion of free flows of information. In earlier chapters, we mentioned the notion of free flows of information. As we pointed out, the rhetoric behind the notion sounds noble and fine. All individuals should be free to communicate with all other individuals the world over. It is implicitly or explicitly claimed that in such a way we can achieve a universal brother and sisterhood and, thereby, world peace. The actualities of free flows are quite different. As we illustrated in Chapter 10, free flows of information mean the right of those who dominate the world information system to continue to dominate that system. This certainly does not mean that information flows freely among all who may want to use it for whatever purpose.

The issues of foreign control over domestic information are focused, between Canada and the U.S., on Section 19 of the Income Tax Act, which disallows tax deductions of Canadian companies for advertising carried on U.S. border stations. Similarly, it disallows deductions for advertising in U.S. magazines sold in Canada.

Put this way, Canada appears to be acting unfairly. We seem to be not allowing the

American border stations to carry on with their business. But the other side of the coin is this: Canada has the right, as does every sovereign nation, to control broadcasting within its boundaries; all Canadian stations require licences to operate; yet the border stations can operate in complete disregard of Canadian law and regulatory procedure. These border stations are absolutely free to ignore the Canadian Broadcasting Act. Yet this Act is the basis for the operation of our broadcasting system.

One of the few actions open to Canada in the case of the border stations is to take retaliatory measures by disallowing advertising deductions and retaining the right to interfere with the signals as we so choose once they have been beamed into Canada. The present practice is called **simultaneous program deletion and substitution.** When two identical programs are being broadcast at the same time and retransmitted on the same cable system, one originating from a Canadian station and one from a border station, the Canadian station can request that its signal with its advertising be substituted for that of the border station. Beyond the matter of national sovereignty, the penetration of Canada by foreign television signals and programs is taking away the opportunities for Canadian broadcasters to maximize the profit they can make from the programs they have purchased.

Now we have both sides of the story. But the matter does not end there. As a May 6, 1985, story in *The Globe and Mail* pointed out, the border stations in the Association of American Broadcasters are continuously lobbying their government and threatening ours with retaliation so that they might be allowed to carry on their businesses unencumbered by Canadian legal restraints.

With Direct Broadcast Satellites, broadcasters need be nowhere near the border to beam their signals into Canada, as we discussed in Chapter 9. Trans-border flows have become more, rather than less, problematic to Canadian cultural sovereignty. The Free Trade Agreement and recent changes to Canadian copyright law provide the legal basis for domestic and foreign (mostly) American copyright holders to collect revenue from Canadian cable companies that bring in "distant signals" from U.S. stations. The implementation of royalty fees means nothing less than an increased flow of revenues to the U.S. from Canada, in the order of $50 million per annum (*Globe and Mail,* October 3, 1990, p. B1).

A slightly different but equally perplexing problem is arising in computer communications. When we purchase foreign computer equipment or, especially, when we store our own information in databases outside our country, we export jobs and move into a position where the survival of foreign companies that maintain the equipment and those databases becomes part of our interest. With databases, once we have such interests in the survival of foreign companies, supporting a realignment of information management along national lines becomes quite problematic.

Such considerations are based in economics. The political ramifications, however, are more crucial. In a time when economic sanctions are frequently used to bring pressure to bear on other countries and when access to information is an integral part of economics, one must be very careful in putting one's own data in the hands of foreign-based companies. American companies may be and often are prevented from trading with certain other nations. Canada may wish and often has wished to remain a trading partner with both the U.S. and a third nation that is out of favour with the American government (Nicaragua was a good case in point). Had there been a greater consensus in American opinion on Nicaragua, there possibly would have been some harassment of Canadian companies using American databases, even if it were done on the basis of a misunderstanding.

Just as there are both economic and cultural issues involved in control, so both types of issues are involved in considerations of foreign versus domestic production. The economic issues are simpler and more straightforward and we have discussed them to some degree in previous chapters.

All predictions suggest that the information economy will expand considerably over the next years. Further, it appears that there will be as large an expansion in business information flows as in flows of entertainment products. Business information will include hardware, software, and database markets while the entertainment side will include hardware and content. The expected Canadian market for hardware alone in 1990 is predicted to be $1 billion. In 1980, Canadian consumers, producers, advertisers, and governments spent $5.4 billion in the publishing, broadcasting, recording, and film markets (Audley, 1983).

With domestic production having a domestic market share in books of 20 per cent, records, 6.8 per cent, theatrical films, 1.8 per cent, and television drama, 4 per cent, obviously such large expenditures on foreign-produced materials are a considerable drain on the economy. With a very minuscule participation in computer hardware and a limited participation in software and databases, the situation cannot get much better. The dramatic possibilities for profit and expansion, the other side of the coin, can be seen in the success of such companies as Northern Telecom and Maclean Hunter, both large and successful international companies.

The cultural implications are considerably more subtle and complex. The debate over Canadian content in learning materials, radio and television programming, films, books, libraries, and so on, has been raging ever since the advent of these technologies and institutions. As the media come to play a greater social and cultural role in our lives, the degree to which Canadian realities are reflected in those media will become ever more important. The matter is simple: the more we consume media images, the greater is the importance of those images.

The emerging issue is where culture and business intersect, in business communication. If Canadian businesses, unions, professionals, in fact, if Canadians in all walks of life become members of North American (which is to say American) and global (which is, as often as not, to say American) information networks, three problems will arise.

First, it will be difficult to maintain any distinctiveness at a national cultural level. Information networks will be established that encourage businesses and individuals to distinguish themselves, specialize, and operate successfully in a North American or global business environment. Second, as these information networks produce opportunities for businesses and individuals, an increasing momentum will occur to encourage their users to see themselves in terms of the organization of information basic to the network.

A third problem will be an increasing governmental difficulty in serving the interests of Canadians. Because of a government's geographically constrained concerns, if it must deal with a majority of companies whose operations are only fractionally oriented to Canada, then its power is that much lessened. Attempts to preserve some national integrity, such as setting up nationally organized databases, will be seen as uneconomic rearguard actions intended to save the politicians' own skins at the ballot box.

Concentration and Transnational Ownership

We have discussed concentration of and transnational ownership within the headings of variety in ownership and foreign versus domestic ownership and control. We need only add a few words. As Chapter 7 illustrates, the momentum toward concentration and globalization cannot be denied, nor can the ability of such corporations to bring the news of the world to our doorsteps. However, such an ownership form is not necessary for such access to news. The international news agencies are perfectly capable of supplying international feeds that are no more or less high in quality than what global news corporations can do on their own. In fact, in needing to serve a variety of masters, the international agencies are arguably less vulnerable to bias. The major issue in increasing concentration of ownership and globalization is the degree of potential control that lies in the hands of a very few, untouchable mega-corporations.

The Production of Content

The key issues surrounding the role of professional content producers are: (1) the degree of autonomy these professionals should have from their employers; and (2) professionalism versus participation.

Professional Autonomy

The mass media are, for the most part, owned by large corporations whose interests are business interests. In being, for the most part, large business institutions, they require financial, technical, and professional expertise. The question is, given that the interest of owners is in creating profit, how much control should the owner be able to exercise over the content of the media outlet he or she owns? Are the ideals of the profession and the traditional relationships between publisher and editor, station owner and producer, enough? Or should there be more formal mechanisms to protect professional autonomy?

Different countries have different traditions. In Australia, for example, journalists have walked out under terms negotiated in their union contracts in response to the presence of the owner in the newsroom. In most other English-speaking countries without such strong unionization, such an event is quite unusual.

There is probably no correct answer to the requirements and need to protect professional autonomy. It is most likely an issue best left to the journalistic community. It would be surprising if, around the world, journalists were to jump into bed with owners, although with much better salaries than they have had historically, the attractions of middle-class life are tempting. However, if journalists do abandon the public interest, then we are surely in for a period of social unrest and political destabilization as the voice of the public is silenced.

Professionalization versus Participation

A few years ago, one of the rallying cries against the mass media was that they were one-way rather than two-way flows of information. They are no less so today although, as illustrated in various chapters, we are beginning to understand the nature of the very muted return flow of information from the media consumer to the media producer. This issue has been taken up both domestically, by the Kent Royal Commission on Newspapers, and internationally, in the MacBride Report. Thelma McCormack (1983) has compared the approaches of these two reports, and we have used her ideas as a starting place for this discussion.

Tom Kent sees the major problem of newspapers in Canada to be the increasing concentration of ownership. His notion is that ownership concentration has led to what he terms a "rationalization," which also might be termed a centralization of expenditures. In turn, this has led to a centralization of content and development, budgetary procedures that ensure profit to the neglect of news, and generally a denigration of the historical function of newspapers, which is to inform readers of important events and to provide a range of interpretation of those events.

Kent introduces a modernization paradigm by arguing for the development of professional qualifications and ethos. He believes that by increasing their professionalism through training, continuing education, self-policing, and the like, journalists can increase their power essentially by exercising their professional autonomy in a manner similar to doctors.

McCormack's analysis is that, on the one hand, owners seek economies of scale in expanding their production. On the other hand, journalists seek protection from the increased power of the owners through professionalism. This counter-move is designed to make journalists responsible not to the owners but rather to their own ethics and their interpretation of "social responsibility."

The major drawback of this scenario is that it increases the isolation of both the owners and the journalists from the audience. McCormack considers that, if the journalists were to participate in owning newspapers, they would be accountable economically for their ideals and might, via this accountability, tailor their ideals to meet the needs, as expressed though subscriptions, of their readers. (The troubled record of *Le Monde*, a French newspaper owned by journalists, suggests otherwise. Opportunities for stock ownership by employees provided for by the Maclean Hunter-owned Sun newspaper chain is a less radical model of journalistic participation in and resultant accountability through ownership. As much as anything, it probably demonstrates the lack of control that journalists have over the content of the newspaper for which they work.)

In contrast to Kent, the MacBride Report focuses on inequality, power, and technology. Following the reasoning of the MacBride Report, professionalism contributes to inequality and the dependency of the audience on elites. Professionalism increases the sophistication of a one-way flow. It confirms the right of the audience to receive information. At the same time, it eclipses the goal of access and participation. It denies the public a role in agenda-building.

In McCormack's and MacBride's view, media power derives from the media being part of the social process, not part of a semi-autonomous elite. Yet, unless media are part of the social process, as Desbarats (1985) points out, they will be distrusted as much as big government and big business. Professionalism cuts off active consultation. Without that consultation, what the media produce may be true but it may not be authentic. Truth is derived from a logical, literate analysis. Authenticity is derived from the nature of community.

Within the Canadian context, both Kent's concern for professionalism and MacBride's concern for participation have their place. The increased power of owners must be matched by a power over content. As we discussed in the previous section, there must be a balance between industrial and economic concerns on the one hand and cultural concerns on the other, here represented by owners and journalists respectively. In broadcasting, that balance is attempted by regulation. In the book-publishing industry, it is done by means of variously designed support programs. With newspapers, the acceptance by both owners and journalists of state interference as infringing on the freedom (and power) of the press makes it difficult to combine cultural and business interests. Liberal government inaction on the Kent Report and the rescinding by the Conservative government of an order-in-council preventing greater cross-ownership in the media of any particular place have made it abundantly clear that the power to enforce business priorities rests firmly in the hands of the present contingent of large owners.

Professionalism, however, may be more appropriate to Canada than McCormack believes. In the Third World, where the professional class is very small in comparison with the peasant class, increased professionalism would indeed lead to the inequalities and lack of participation that MacBride suggests. But in Canada, where the professional class is extremely large in comparison to Third World nations, where there is no peasant class, where the poor are a much smaller percentage of the population, and where journalists produce both the tabloids and the broadsheets that typify our newspaper environment, it is dubious whether newspapers isolate the audience from participation in agenda-building.

Technology

The key issue surrounding the role of technology is the nature of the control that should be exercised over technology. In the same way that technology is invented, so social structures, institutions, and practices must be invented to ensure that technology is used for the benefit of the many rather than the few. As noted, given international economic competition, technological development will continue as quickly as funds are found somewhere in the world to promote it. The interests of the public are to ensure that sufficient funding is found to monitor technological development thoroughly and to create the means, in some cases enact laws, to take into account all members of society. Without such means we are confronted with significant inequities. We are, after all, talking about access to information, a foundation of democracy.

The difference between working with an older industrial and technological system, i.e., print, and a newer one, film and video, can be illustrated by referring to the development of this book and other material associated with it. In drawing out this contrast, we should point out that it would seem that the technologies and the practices surrounding film and video are more attuned to capturing returns in the form of fees and royalties from original productions than are the technologies and practices associated with print. Two chapters of this book were developed primarily from other books on the subjects of those chapters. Chapter 9 was based on Peter Lyman's *Canada's Video Revolution,* Mark Hepworth's *The Geography of the Information Economy,* and Vince Mosco's *The Pay-Per Society.* Chapter 11 was developed from *The Geopolitics of Information* by Anthony Smith. In both those chapters, the original authors' words were changed, but to a great extent the meaning was, and was intended to be, the same. In certain instances new information was added; in other instances ideas were reformulated and changed intentionally.

The work became ours essentially because, as authors, we put the matter in our own words. It became ours as a result of the foundation of copyright law wherein the expression of an idea can be protected but the idea itself cannot. (Copyright law differs from patent law, in which the exact composition of, say, a chemical compound can be protected.) Consequently, had we summarized their work by using the topic sentence of every paragraph, we would have been guilty of plagiarism. We would have infringed on their copyright. On a related point, we need not have made our debt to these authors so obvious. We could have neglected the notes in each chapter acknowledging our debt and only cited them when directly quoting. However, because part of the job of this book is to open the field of communications to those unfamiliar with it, we emphasized the contributions of those authors.

Quite a different situation presents itself in the video materials available to complement this book. There is no way we could have reconstructed programs such as *The Press and the Prime Minister, Inside TV News,* and *Magic in the Sky.* First, there are the economic and creative realities of video production. To match the production values and the treatment provided in these programs was beyond our budget and certainly would have taxed our every creative ability. Second, each of these programs has captured footage now impossible to obtain for which we would have had to purchase rights, presuming that those rights would have been purchasable. Consequently, we purchased the rights to broadcast these whole programs in British Columbia, the first province in which the book and video materials were used together. The original "authors," that is, the copyright holders, maintained the copyright and collected the royalties.

We, in turn, made several programs, mostly composed of original footage, but also containing clips from other sources, for which we acquired rights. In some cases, our requests were denied or the fees were too high and we found ourselves having to overlook certain examples that were historically salient. Such a situation is anathema to print scholarship but is a market reality in electronic communications. One can only compensate by inserting verbal descriptions to replace graphic examples. But that is rather like trying to appreciate the Mona Lisa without ever having seen it or any reproduction of it.

One other problem arose both with the programs we attempted to acquire and with the clips we acquired for use in our programs. This problem would not have arisen had we been dealing with print materials. In asking for permission to broadcast some of the above-mentioned whole programs, we were at first stymied by the inability of the producers to grant us those rights. In each case, this difficulty arose from the fact that they had used footage from other sources to construct their programs. In obtaining that footage, they had not made clear their intent to sell the program to other broadcasters for use. Thus, they were forced to go back to the contributors and get permissions. In our own case, in numerous instances involving commercial material, we were granted permission for use only if we restricted our distribution to the educational sector in Canada. Therefore, we ended up in a position where we could not sell the programs to the CBC or PBS unless we were to return to the source of the materials and to the original artists, unions, etc., to pay them in order to gain a higher level of clearance. The contract on the following page (Figure 12.1) illustrates the nature of the agreement we entered into to gain access to certain material.

Very easily, the usefulness of the programs others had made and the feasibility of our program could have been spoiled by the inability to gain permissions or to pay the requisite fees, not to mention lawyers' charges for tracking down the people involved. As it was, we had to delete one sequence in *Magic in the Sky* that contained the standard introductory segment to the Sunday night Disney television program, because someone did not or could not obtain permission for it to be used. (The segment has Tinkerbell flitting around the Disney castle lighting it up with glints. See how print works in contrast to video!)

One of the major advantages of participating in an ever-changing communications environment is that there is always considerable demand for content for evolving technological

FIGURE 12.1

```
                          FILM FOOTAGE/CLIP AGREEMENT


Date:                 May 3, 1985
Licensor:             The Collection Administrators C/o Eagle/Cine-Circle Prods.
                      2230 Hillsboro Avenue, Los Angeles, CA 90034


Licensee:             Simon Fraser University C/o Dr. Martin Laba + Dr. R. Lorimer
                      Dept. of Communications, Burnaby, Brit. Col. V5A1S6
                      Western Video Co. 30 E 6th Ave, Vancouver, B.C. V5T164(David)
Footage/Clip Description:                                                  Baker
                          One clip of Chuck Berry singing "Maybellene"
Name of Production:       from Hollywood A Go Go #16.

                      SFU ROCKS
Permitted Use of Footage/Clip:  To be used only in the academic video course
                      of study which will be carried by The Knowledge Network,
                      a non-profit, gov't and/or public funded cable TV station.

Permitted Term of Use:    10 years

License Fee:              Twenty-Five Dollars ($25.00) U.S.
(All reproduction, handling and shipping charges will be paid by Licensee.)
```

Subject to the provisions hereof, Licensor hereby grants to Licensee, without warranty, a non-exclusive and non-transferable license to use said footage/clip in the production described above, but only for the purposes hereinabove set forth. This license is granted on the following terms and conditions:

1. Licensee will not make any reproduction of or from the footage/clip whatsoever, in whole or in part, except for the use in connection with the production herein described.

2. Licensee represents, warrants and agrees that it will obtain all required authorizations, consents and releases and pay all re-use fees necessary for the use of the footage/ clip hereunder, including, but not limited to, consents from any copyright owners and from all guilds and unions to the extent required under applicable collective bargaining agreements; and that if any music is included in the footage/clip, as used hereunder, Licensee will obtain all necessary music synchronization, mechanical and performing rights from the copyright proprietors of such music and such other persons, firms, associations, societies, corporations and/or record companies as may own or control any rights and/or recordings hereto.

3. Licensee will indemnify Licensor, and its agents, employees and representatives, and save and hold them harmless of and from any and all loss, cost, damage, liability and expense including attorneys' fees, arising out of any claim whatsoever which may be brought based upon Licensee's use of said footage/clip hereunder. Licensee further acknowladges that a breach by Licensee of any of its representations, warranties or undertakings hereunder will cause Licensor irreparable damage, which cannot be readily remedied in damages in an action at law, and may, in addition thereto, entitle Licensor to equitable remedies, costs and attorney's fees.

```
                                        The Collection Administrators

                                        By
```

```
Agreed to and Accepted

By
```

forms. In other words, new technologies usually provide new opportunities. Once a technology has been introduced – e.g., videocassette recorders, videogame machines, videodiscs, compact discs, multiple television channels, communications satellites – opportunities quickly arise as the machine takes hold in the marketplace. At first these opportunities are seized by producers for other technologies. Thus movies are now distributed on videocassette just as they were and are on television. Books have been made into movies since the early days of film. Music was made over into music videos. Films are placed on videodiscs. And so forth.

But each new technology has the capacity to encourage production for itself. Numbers of movies are now being distributed through videocassettes and never shown in theatres. Television programming took its place alongside movies re-shown on television. In a kind of reverse action, some successful movies have created books rather than the other way around. Videos are now almost a necessity in launching new music, and packages of music videos are being created and marketed.

The cultural advantage of all this activity is that it can create increased opportunities for cultural production. As long as restrictive practices are not allowed to interfere with opportunities for Canadians, this environment of opportunities can create a culture out of which exciting creative expression will grow.

THE NATURE AND IMPACT OF GLOBAL AND DOMESTIC MASS COMMUNICATION SYSTEMS

In examining the geopolitics of both global and domestic communications systems, we applied a metropolis/hinterland model to describe the dynamics of both systems. That framework brought out how the centres dominate production and how, thereby, they create content to reflect values and issues salient to them. In the case of domestic systems, knowing that they are responsible to produce, or to allow to be produced, content of interest to the hinterlands, they allow mechanisms to ensure that hinterland issues are never entirely absent, at least from the perspective of the centres. However, close inspection shows that hinterland issues are quite secondary and that the facilitation of content exchange between hinterlands (e.g., between Saskatchewan and New Brunswick) is quite lacking.

In the case of global communications, in the Western world, essentially because the Americans have been so insistent on operating in a "free market," international safeguards do not exist to ensure that the voices of all nations are heard – even in their own lands. (As Chapter 10 shows, things have not been that different in Eastern Europe vis-à-vis the Soviet Union.) As a result, countries with developing economies have brought this balanced flow agenda forward and it has been embraced by UNESCO.

Chapter 9 outlined the extensive contribution communications technology and communications satellites make to this centre-over-hinterland bias. Modern technology makes it possible for people living in very impecunious circumstances to be informed about events taking place around the world. It also makes it possible for them to be amused at the antics of the players in modern sitcoms, or to watch investigative journalism expose fraud and deceit. But even though it is perfectly capable of doing so, this technology rarely provides any viewer with the skills and understandings necessary for him or herself to advance his/her own interests or those of his/her community. Nor is much information provided of other countries at the same stage of economic development, which might show perspectives and problems.

The creation of educational programming and of programming available from countries that are not major exporters is purely a matter of organization and political will. Whether at the domestic level, between educational broadcasters in the various provinces, or at the international level, through the exchange of programs between countries who might benefit most, it is not a matter of a massive investment in program production. Rather, it is a matter of exchange or purchase of already produced content and then a certain cost in translation. There is some cost, but the expense is not exorbitant. What makes it so easy for countries of the developed world to produce their own programs is that they are rich enough to do so. Having created such programs, it can then export them, at far below the cost of producing even a cheap imitation, to all buyers. No co-ordination or exchange is required. And there are enough sales to keep a sales force active and to keep the profits flowing.

Counter-initiatives do exist. Led by Canada, an Anglophone agency called the Commonwealth of Learning has been set up among Commonwealth countries to help developing countries benefit from production capability elsewhere. The 1990s should demonstrate the success of this agency. A parallel Francophone agency is also in the works and may be capable of assisting developing Francophone countries. Perhaps with the linkages formed by these initiatives, trade in entertainment programs will increase between hinterland countries and regions.

There is no doubt that the centre/hinterland model emphasizes the unequal relations between the two types of communities. It does not, for instance, encourage a comparison between outlying regions that are hinterlands and others that are self-sufficient. There is no doubt that hinterland contact with a centre encourages economic and sometimes cultural development. The point is to find the mechanisms necessary for that development not to eclipse indigenous expression.

COMMUNICATION, CANADA, AND THE WORLD

Finding an appropriate role for Canada in the context of the issues we have raised throughout this book is certainly a challenge, and open to a range of opinion. We would suggest that our position as

1. a rich nation;
2. with a large geographical area;
3. with a tradition for the development and adoption of advanced communication technology;
4. with an immediate neighbour who is the largest producer and an aggressive exporter of entertainment and knowledge products with whom we have entered into a free trade agreement;

uniquely suits us to play a leadership role in global communications. This does not mean that we should become a leading exporter of communications hardware and software. But we can lead the way in proposing the means by which the greatest benefit can be had from modern mass communications by all nations, communities, and individuals.

SUMMARY

This final chapter highlights some of the major points of the preceding chapters within the context of their implications for society in general and Canada in particular. It reviews the five areas identified in Chapter 1 that we have explored on a chapter-by-chapter basis.

Here we have extended our previous analysis of oral, literate, and electronic communication based on the information and concepts contained in previous chapters. This extension carries the discussion slightly ahead of current theory and prepares the reader for possible future developments in the field. We also discuss further implications of the definition of mass communication outlined in Chapter 2 and of the interaction between government and the media explored in Chapter 3.

Our discussion of the production and consumption of mass communication synthesizes Chapters 4 and 5, pointing to empowerment of the audience brought about by current conceptions of media/audience interaction but also to the potentiality of those conceptions to induce audience passivity because of the large government/big business organization of production.

Our discussion of the various points of control and influence of the mass media focused on the implications of the nature and significance of some level of control being vested in each of government, business, the profession, and technology. Within each of these categories we identified major issues demanding the attention of policy-makers and the general public. Addressing such issues is key to the communications systems and the nature of the culture Canada will create for itself.

Our review of the nature and impact of global and domestic communication systems returned to the dominator/dominated dynamics inherent in current systems and brought out by the centre/hinterland model we employed to discuss them. We noted the vulnerability of the present dominant players, arguing that political will would be sufficient to turn the mass media into instruments much more facilitative of social goals.

Finally, our overview of Canada's place in the world suggested a specific role for this country – in a communications context – consistent with our global position and our political values.

REFERENCES

Canada. "The Federal Cultural Review Committee" (Applebaum-Hébert Report). Ottawa: Minister of Supply and Services, 1982.

Canada. *Royal Commission on National Development in the Arts, Letters and Sciences* (Massey Report). Ottawa: Queen's Printer, 1952.

Canada. *Royal Commission on Newspapers* (Kent Report). Hull: Canadian Government Publishing Centre, 1981.

Canadian Broadcasting Corporation. *Inside TV News*. Montreal, 1982.

Canadian Broadcasting Corporation. *The Press and the Prime Minister*. Toronto, 1977.

Curran, James. "The New Revision in Mass Communication Research: a Reappraisal," *European Journal of Communication*, 5, Nos. 2-3 (June, 1990), pp. 135-64.

Desbarats, Peter. "Watchdog of Others Shrinks from its Own Accountability" (and other articles in "Eye on the Media" column), *The Financial Post*, 1985.

Eisenstein, E.L. *The Printing Revolution in Early Modern Europe*. Cambridge: Cambridge University Press, 1983.

Frum, Linda, *The Newsmakers: Behind the Cameras with Canada's Top TV Journalists*. Toronto: Key Porter, 1990.

Globe and Mail, May 6, 1985.

Goody, Jack. *The Domestication of the Savage Mind*. Cambridge: Cambridge University Press, 1977.

Hardin, Herschel. *A Nation Unaware*. Vancouver: J.J. Douglas Ltd., 1974.

Havelock, E. *Origins of Western Literacy*. Toronto: OISE, 1976.

Innis, H. *The Bias of Communication*. Toronto: University of Toronto Press, 1951.

Innis, H. *Empire and Communications*. Toronto: Oxford University Press, 1950.

Lorimer, Rowland. "Implications of New Technologies of Information," *Scholarly Publishing* (April, 1985).

McCormack, Thelma. "The Political Culture and the Press in Canada," *Canadian Journal of Political Science* (September, 1983).

McLuhan, M. *The Gutenberg Galaxy.* Toronto: University of Toronto Press, 1962.

McLuhan, M. *Understanding Media.* Toronto: McGraw Hill, 1964.

McQuail, Denis. "Caging the beast: constructing a framework for the analysis of media change in Western Europe," *European Journal of Communication,* 5, Nos. 2-3 (June, 1990), pp. 313-32.

National Film Board. *Magic in the Sky,* directed by P. Raymont, produced by P. Raymont and A. Hammond. January, 1981.

Ong, W. *Orality and Literacy: The Technologizing of the Word.* New York: Methuen, 1982.

Rotstein, A. "The Use and Misuse of Economics in Cultural Policy," in Lorimer and Wilson, eds., *Communications Canada.*

Simon Fraser University. *Media Information Canada,* Part 1 of a 5-part series, *Mass Communication in Canada.* Burnaby, B.C., 1985.

Simon Fraser University. T*he Fashionable Image,* Part 2 of a 5-part series, *Mass Communication in Canada.* Burnaby, B.C., 1985.

Simon Fraser University.*Video, Vinyl and Culture,* Part 3 of a 5-part series, *Mass Communication in Canada.* Burnaby, B.C., 1985.

Stuart-Stubbs, Basil. "Scholarly Communication and the New Information Order," *Canadian Journal of Information Science* (1981).

UNESCO, International Commission on Communications Problems (MacBride Commission). *Many Voices, One World.* Paris: Unipub, 1980.

Woodcock, George. *Strange Bedfellows: The State and the Arts in Canada.* Vancouver: Douglas & McIntyre, 1985.

STUDY QUESTIONS

1. Contrast the perspective of the Kent Commission to that of the MacBride Report. Is each appropriate to its venue, or does the MacBride Report have some relevance to Canada?
2. Do you think Canada is in a position to play any unique role in the international communications order, given our status as a rich but underdeveloped country?
3. What is the future of public-sector broadcasting?
4. What is the future of Canada in an information age?

Index